Criminal Law in Turkey

Criminal Law in Turkey

Second Edition

Feridun Yenisey

This book was originally published as a monograph in the International Encyclopaedia of Laws/Criminal Law.

Founding Editor: Roger Blanpain
General Editor: Frank Hendrickx
Volume Editors: Frank Verbruggen & Vanessa Franssen

Wolters Kluwer

Published by:
Kluwer Law International B.V.
PO Box 316
2400 AH Alphen aan den Rijn
The Netherlands
E-mail: international-sales@wolterskluwer.com
Website: lrus.wolterskluwer.com

Sold and distributed by:
Wolters Kluwer Legal & Regulatory U.S.
7201 McKinney Circle
Frederick, MD 21704
United States of America
E-mail: customer.service@wolterskluwer.com

ISBN 978-94-035-3442-8

e-Book: ISBN 978-94-035-3443-5
web-PDF: ISBN 978-94-035-3444-2

The Author

Prof. Dr. Feridun Yenisey (born September 17, 1944) studied Law at the University of Istanbul (1965–1970), where he worked from 1971 to 1990. He received his Ph.D., with a thesis on *Appeals in Criminal Law*, in 1978. In 1983, he was appointed Associate Professor. In 1989, he was appointed Professor at the Faculty of Law at Istanbul University. In 1990, Professor Yenisey became Professor at Marmara University in the Faculty of Law and stayed there until September 2001. In May 2002, he received a call from Bahçeşehir University School of Law, where he is serving as Professor of Criminal Law and Criminal Procedure.

Professor Yenisey was the founder (1991) and head of the Research and Learning Centre for Criminal Law and Criminology at Marmara University and is the Director of Institute for Global Understanding of the Rule of Law at Bahçeşehir University since 2002. He was a member of the Istanbul University's Institute of Legal Medicine and of the Legal Medicine Branch of the Ministry of Justice. He was the Dean of the Faculty of Mass Media of Marmara University (1991–1993) and Dean of Bahçeşehir University School of Law (2009). He has established the Max Planck Institute for Foreign and International Criminal Law and Bahçeşehir University Joint Research Group on European Criminal Law at Bahçeşehir University. He is the Director of this Research Group.

He conducted research in Austria (Institut für Strafrecht und Kriminologie der Universität Wien), in Germany (Max-Planck-Institut für ausländisches und Internationales Strafrecht, Freiburg i.Br.), and has taught courses on comparative criminal law in the USA (Syracuse University, College of Law; South Texas College of Law; William Mitchell College of Law; Kansas University School of Law; Atlanta's John Marshall Law School; Georgia State University School of Law). Professor Yenisey is a member of the Association Internationale de Droit Pénal. He is the author of several books and articles on criminal law.

The Author

Table of Contents

List of Abbreviations

ABD	*Ankara Barosu Dergisi* (Periodical)
AdD	*Adalet Dergisi* (Periodical)
ADR	Alternative Dispute Resolution
ANAP	*Anavatan Partisi* (Motherland Party)
AsCK	Military Penal Code
AY	*Türkiye Cumhuriyeti Anayasası* (the Constitution of the Republic of Turkey)
b.	*Band* (cilt)
BasK	*Basın Kanunu* (Press Act)
BK	*Borçlar Kanunu* (Code of Obligations)
BMTDY	*Birleşmiş Milletler Tarih Yıllığı* (Periodical)
Cass.	*Court of Cassation* (Yargıtay)
CD	*Ceza Dairesi* (Chamber of the Court of Cassation)
CGIK	*Ceza ve Güvenlik Tedbirlerinin İnfazı Hakkında Kanun* (Act on Execution of Punishments and Security Measures)
CGK	*Ceza Genel Kurulu* (General Assembly of the Court of Cassation)
CHP	*Cumhuriyet Halk Partisi* (The Republican People's Party)
CIK	*Cezaların İnfazı Hakkında Kanun* (Code of Enforcement of Punishments)
CMK	*Ceza Muhakemesi Kanunu* (The current Turkish Penal Procedure Code)
CMUK	*Ceza Muhakemeleri Usulü Kanunu* (The Repealed Turkish Penal Procedure Code)
ÇASÖMK	*Çıkar Amaçlı Suç Örgütleri ile Mücadele Kanunu* (The *Repealed* Act on Combating Profit Oriented Organized Crime)
ÇKK	*Çocuk Koruma Kanunu* (Child Protection Act)
ÇMK	*Çocuk Mahkemeleri Kanunu* (The Repealed Juvenile Courts Act)

List of Abbreviations

DP	*Demokrat Parti* (Democratic Party)
E	*Esas* (Main Case)
EU	European Union
ECHR	European Convention on Human Rights
ECtHR	European Court of Human Rights
HSK	*Hakimler ve Savcılar Kurulu* (Council of Judges and Prosecutors; Former HSYK: High Council)
IBD	*İstanbul Barosu Dergisi* (Periodical)
IBM	*İstanbul Barosu Mecmuası* (Periodical)
IçBK	*İçtihadı Birleştirme Kararı* (United Decision of the Court of Cassation)
IHFM	*İstanbul Üniversitesi Hukuk Fakultesi Mecmuası* (Periodical)
IKID	*İlmi ve Kazai İçtihatlar Dergisi* (Journal of Scientific and Judicial Interpretation)
K.	*Karar* (Decision)
KaçK	*Kaçakçılıkla Mücadele Kanunu* (Act on Combating Smuggling)
KHK	*Kanun Hükmünde Kararname* (Decree in Power or Act)
KK	*Kabahatler Kanunu* (Law on Misdemeanors)
KTK	*Karayolları Trafik Kanunu* (Road Traffic Act)
MHP	Nationalist Movement Party
MK	*Medeni Kanun* (Civil Code)
MKYK	*Memurlar ve Diğer Kamu Görevlilerinin Yargılanması Usulü Hakkında Kanun* (Act on Adjudication of Civil Servants)
n.	Paragraph Number
OHAL	State of Emergency
PVSK	*Polis Vazife ve Salahiyet Kanunu* (Police Act)
RG	*Resmi Gazete* (Official Gazette)
TBMM	*Türkiye Büyük Millet Meclisi* (Turkish Grand National Assembly)
TCK	*Türk Ceza Kanunu* (The Turkish Penal Code)
TCKT	*Türk Ceza Kanunu Tasarısı* (Penal Code Bill)
TL/TRY	Turkish Lira
TMK	*Terörle Mücadele Kanunu* (Anti-terrorism Act)
TRY	Turkish Lira
YD	*Yargıtay Dergisi* (Periodical)
YKD	*Yargıtay Kararları Dergisi* (Journal of the Decisions of the Court of Cassation)

Acknowledgments

I humbly dedicate this book to the Syracuse University College of Law. I have benefited from the generous institutional support of the Syracuse University Law School, under Dean Michael Hoeflich, and from the support of Louise Lantzy, Director of the H. Douglas Barclay Law Library, who provided generous and ready help on numerous occasions, especially as I tried to learn the complexities of Westlaw, Lexis, and the Internet while I was completing the first edition of this book in 1992. I am forever grateful for the support of my sister, Ayşe Tezel, and her husband, Hasan Tezel M.D when I was visiting Syracuse University College of Law. I am deeply thankful for the assistance of Thaddeus J. Holynski in editing the first edition of this manuscript.

Juris Doctor Ayşe Özge Atalay supported me in revising the manuscript in 2016. Her help reshaped this publication. There have been essential changes in Turkish Criminal Law between 2016 and 2018. Ayşe Tezel, a professionally qualified contract interpreter at the US Federal Courts, worked with me on inserting the changes contained in complex legal texts into this updated version. I am also thankful to Phyllis Cox for her reading the entire text with me in 2014 and later in 2020 when she visited Bahçeşehir University for giving lectures on comparative legal issues. Her input will be very helpful for foreign readers for a better understanding of complex legal concepts of Turkish Law. Additionally, she edited the third edition of the English translation of the Criminal Procedure Code done by me.

I also appreciate the valuable assistance of Hasan Can Bekci, my administrative assistant at the Institute for Global Understanding of the Rule of Law. He solved all technical problems that occurred during this last edition of this monograph.

I hope that this book will provide its readers with a useful introduction to Turkish Criminal Law.

Acknowledgments

General Introduction

§1. The General Background of the Country

I. Geography and Population

1. Turkey is a country situated between Europe and Asia. It covers an area of 780,043 km^2: 755,688 km^2 in Asia and 23,764 km^2 in Europe.[1] Turkey's neighbors are: Greece, Bulgaria, Georgia, Armenia, Azerbaijan, the Islamic Republic of Iran, Iraq, and the Syrian Arab Republic. Its capital is Ankara, and, for administrative purposes, Turkey comprises 81 provinces.

2. The climate in Turkey varies widely. From east to west, Turkey is approximately 1,565 km wide. It has a continental climate in Middle Anatolia, while the climate on the southern and western coasts of Turkey is subtropical and Mediterranean.[2] The coast of the northern part of the Black Sea is always rainy. It is mountainous in the east, and while the high northeastern plateaus have warm summers and severe winters, the central plateau has hot, dry summers and cold, wet winters. The average mean temperatures of summer and winter for Istanbul are 23.8°C and 5.9°C, Ankara 23.3°C and 0.1°C, Izmir 27.8°C and 8.7°C, and Adana 28.2°C and 9.4°C.

3. The population of Turkey has been characterized by rapid growth. In 1927, the population was 13,648,000, with a density of 18 people per km^2. In 1985, the population was 44,737,000, with a density of 56 people per km^2. In 1990 the population of Turkey had grown to 56,969,000. According to official estimates, at mid-year 1991, the population was 57,326,000, and the population density was 73.5 per km^2. According to the 1990 census, the populations of the principal cities were: Ankara 2,559,471, Istanbul 6,620,241, and Izmir 1,757,414. Urban population was 70% of the total population in 2010. According to the 1995 census, the national population had risen to 63,405,326. Population in 2007 was estimated at 71,158,647; in 2009 estimation was at 74,815,707,[3] in July 2012 at 79,749,461 and in 2019 at 83,154,997.[4]

---

1. https://www.harita.gov.tr/images/urun/il_ilce_alanlari.pdf.
2. Türkiye İstatistik Yıllığı.
3. www.nvi.gov.tr.
4. https://data.tuik.gov.tr/Bulten/Index?p=Adrese-Dayal%C4%B1-N%C3%BCfus-Kay%C4%B1t-Sistemi-Sonu%C3%A7lar%C4%B1-2019-33705&dil=1.

Although the principal language is Turkish, spoken by 90% of the population, there has been and remains no restriction on the rest of the population to speak their *different language* in their daily life. In 1928, Latin characters of the written Turkish language were introduced to replace the Arabic characters.

Islam is the religion of 99% of the population. However, Turkey is a secular state. Islam was entrenched in the 1924 Constitution as Turkey's official religion, but an amendment in 1928 removed this provision.

In 1986, an estimated 100,000 Christians were living in Turkey. There is also a small Jewish community in Turkey living chiefly in İstanbul and İzmir.

II. Economic Orientations

4. In 1927, during the period of the new Turkish Republic, there was no industry in Turkey. Beginning in 1927, the state provided for new factories. Five-year plans were introduced under Soviet influence. Between 1950 and 1960, there was a growth of 7.7% per year, but at the same time, there was a high rate of inflation.

5. The political strife and labor strike of the 1970s caused inflation to rise by more than 100%. At the request of the International Monetary Fund (IMF), reforms relating to the Market Economy were made by the Demirel Government in January 1980, and these were continued by the military regime after September 12, 1980. The program had positive effects on the Turkish economy.

With the introduction of the Customs Union with the European Union (EU) and stabilization in political life after the 1995 Elections, the Turkish economy grew in 1996. By the end of 2002, significant progress had been made toward achieving the goals of the program.

Economic summary of 2019: GDP/PPP: (Turkish Lira) TRY 4,320,191 million; per capita USD 9,213; real growth rate: 0.9%;[5] inflation: 11.84%[6] (compared to 8.4 in 2007); unemployment: 13.7%; labor force: 28 million.[7]

According to OECD report, the economic forecast summary for Turkey (December 2020)[8] reads as follows:

> The recovery started during the summer, driven by vigorous quasi-fiscal stimulus and external demand, now faces significant headwinds. The number of COVID-19 cases surged again in autumn. Policy support has been scaled down to contain the current account deficit, inflation and exchange rate depreciation. GDP is set to contract by 1.3% in 2020, and—absent renewed macroeconomic tensions—it is projected to grow by 2.9% in 2021 and 3.2% in 2022. Unemployment is expected to increase. Contingent liabilities and the current account

5. https://data.tuik.gov.tr/Bulten/Index?p=Yillik-Gayrisafi-Yurt-Ici-Hasila-2019-33671.
6. https://data.tuik.gov.tr/Bulten/Index?p=T%C3%BCketici-Fiyat-Endeksi-Aral%C4%B1k%202019-33861.
7. https://data.tuik.gov.tr/Bulten/Index?p=%C4%B0%C5%9Fg%C3%BCc%C3%BC-%C4%B0statistikleri-2019-33784.
8. http://www.oecd.org/economy/turkey-economic-snapshot/.

deficit remain very large, and high-risk premia and the exchange rate depreciation have hampered the outlook. Recent stability-oriented policy measures can enhance domestic and international sentiment and support the recovery. Physical distancing measures need to be fully enforced, and additional confinement measures may be needed. Confidence in the quality of official communication on the spread of the pandemic should be restored. Improving the transparency and the coherence of monetary, fiscal, quasi-fiscal and financial policies would help improve domestic and international confidence. Reducing employment costs and promoting more flexible formal employment forms would boost job creation in the formal sector.

III. Political System

6. Turkey is a Republic (Article 1, AY). It is described in Article 2 of the Turkish Constitution[9] as a democratic, secular and social state governed by the rule of law.[10] According to Article 3, the Turkish State is an indivisible whole with its territory and nation. The provision establishing the form of the state as a republic cannot be amended, nor can such amendments be proposed.

Sovereignty is vested in the nation unconditionally and without reservation, and the nation exercises its sovereignty through the authorized organs as prescribed by the principles laid down in the Constitution. The right to exercise sovereignty cannot be delegated to an individual, group or class. No person or agency may exercise a state power that does not emanate from the Constitution (Article 6, AY).

Everyone possesses inherent fundamental rights and freedoms that are inviolable and inalienable.

The fundamental objectives and duties of the state are to safeguard the independence and integrity of the Turkish Nation, the indivisibility of the country, the republic and democracy; to ensure the welfare, peace and happiness of the individual and society; and to strive to depoliticize them (Article 2, AY).

7. The Turkish Grand National Assembly (*Türkiye Büyük Millet Meclisi,* TBMM) has legislative authority. There is no longer a second assembly, like the Senate, which existed under the 1924 Constitution. The deputies (600 in total) are elected directly in accordance with the Electoral Act (No. 2839). Every Turkish citizen over the age of 18 is eligible to be appointed deputy.

The term of office in the Assembly is five years. Parliamentary elections and the election of the president shall be conducted on the same date (Article 77, AY).

9. E. Özbudun, *Constitutional Law*, in Introduction to Turkish Law, ed. *Tuğrul Ansay, Don Wallance Jr., Işık Önay,* Seventh Edition, Ch. 2, Deventer: Kluwer, 2020, p. 21; V. Bıçak & Z. Arslan, *Constitutional Law: Turkey*, Holland: Kluwer Law International, 2004.

10. C. Rumpf, *Das Rechtsstaatsprinzip in der türkischen Rechtsordnung*, Bonn, Berlin: Bouvier, 1992, p. 373.

The TBMM has control over the Executive Body through acquiring information and supervision by means of parliamentary inquiry,[11] general debate,[12] censure, parliamentary investigation,[13] and written question[14] (Article 98, AY).

IV. Form of Government

8. Since the transformation of the structure of the state in 2018 (*infra*, paragraph 51), the executive body is composed of a President of the Republic (Article 104, AY), vice-presidents and ministers appointed by the president (Article 106, AY). The Council of Ministers has been abolished. The president now has criminal responsibility (*infra*, paragraph 98).

The presidential governmental system is regulated in Articles 104 and 106 of the Constitution. He is the head of the state and has the executive power of the republic (Article 104/1, AY); he represents the Republic of Turkey and ensures the implementation of the Constitution (Article 104/2, AY). Statutes enacted by the National Assembly and international treaties (Article 104/11, AY) shall be made public by the president (Article 104/5, AY). But if the president has some concerns about an enacted law, he is empowered to return the law for reconsideration (Article 104/6, AY) or may decide to hold a referendum if he deems it necessary for laws regarding the amendment to the Constitution (Article 104/12, AY). In cases where the president is of the opinion that a statute is unconstitutional, he is entitled to bring a case to the Constitutional Court for annulment of that statute (Article 104/7, AY).

The president is empowered to issue "presidential decrees" (Article 104/17, AY) and "presidential by-laws" (Article 104/18, AY), which shall not be submitted[15] to the Grand National Assembly. In order to compensate for this large power given to the president, the Constitution regulates that presidential decrees are limited to matters related to the executive power: Fundamental rights, individual rights and duties of the individuals shall not be regulated by presidential decrees. A second limitation in this matter is the wording of the Constitution: If a provision in the Constitution requires a regulation explicitly by a law, the president is not entitled to issue a presidential decree on that matter. Furthermore, if the Grand National Assembly introduces a law on the same matter after the presidential decree, the presidential decree shall be null and void (Article 104/17, AY). Presidential decrees and by-laws shall be published in the Official Gazette (*Resmi Gazete,* RG) (Article 104/19, AY).

The president, as the head of the executive, appoints and dismisses the vice-president and ministers (Article 104/8, AY), high-level state officers and regulates

11. A "parliamentary inquiry" is an examination conducted to acquire information on a specific subject (Art. 98/2, AY).
12. A "general debate" is the consideration of a specific subject relating to the community and the activities of the state at the Plenary of the Grand National Assembly of Turkey (Art. 98/3, AY).
13. A "parliamentary investigation" is an investigation about the vice-presidents and the ministers conducted according to the fifth, sixth, and seventh paragraphs of Art. 106 (Art. 98/4, AY).
14. A "written question" is a request for information addressed to the vice-presidents or ministers by deputies to be answered in writing within fifteen days at the latest (Art. 98/5, AY).
15. Previously, "decrees in power of act" (KHK) prepared by the government had to be sent to the Grand National Assembly for approval. This requirement no longer exists.

the procedures and principles regarding this appointment by a presidential decree (Article 104/9, AY). Article 106 of the Constitution regulates this procedure as follows:

> After the president has been elected, he appoints one or more vice-presidents (Article 106/1, AY). The vice-president shall represent the president if the office of the president is vacant (Article 106/2, AY).

9. Local governments are: (a) the special provincial administration under the leadership of the governor, appointed by the central government, (b) municipalities under the leadership of elected mayors (in cases where the population is over 750.000, there is a metropolitan municipality), and (c) villages under the village headman. The Law on Metropolitan Municipalities, adopted in November 2013, extended the scope of the municipalities' competences. As a consequence, some small municipalities' weak capacity to deliver public services has been strengthened. Nevertheless, despite this legislative change Turkey entered a few reservations to the Council of Europe's Charter of Local Self-Government.[16]

10. The Act on Establishing a Civilian Oversight Commission of Law Enforcement Officers (Act No. 2016-6713) has been published on May 20, 2016 in the Official Gazette. The aim of this Act is to establish a commission that is going to work at ensuring a more effective and faster complaint system dealing with complaints against law enforcement officers. The Act further aims to enhance transparency and credibility, and also to provide a central system for keeping records of crimes allegedly committed by law enforcement officers and tracking them. The Commission is established permanently within the Ministry of Interior.

V. The Constitution

11. The current Constitution was put into force by the Act No. 2709, after the approval by the Turkish Nation of a referendum on November 7, 1982. In 2010, the Constitution was amended substantially, as will be discussed below. These amendments were followed by attempts to draft a completely new Constitution, which have failed, and further amendments; the last amendment to the Constitution was made on July 7, 2018.

16. REF to be added.

A. 2010 Amendments

12. The 2010 amendment package consisted of twenty-six Articles, most of them related to the future, but one essential provision related to lift the impunity of the leaders of the 1980 military coup:[17]

(a) *Equality before the law (Article 10, AY):* The second paragraph of Article 10, which was amended in 2004, read as follows: *"Men and women shall have equal rights. The state has the duty that this equality is put into practice."* With the reform of 2010, this paragraph was complemented with the following sentence: *"Measures taken for this purpose shall not be interpreted as contrary to the principle of equality."* Furthermore, another paragraph was added to this Article: *"Measures taken for the children, the elderly and the disabled persons, widow spouses and orphans of persons who died in war or on duty and incapacitated persons and veterans cannot be considered as contrary to the principle of equality."* Thus, this paragraph offers a constitutional basis for affirmative action for women, children, elderly and disabled persons and for widows of soldiers killed at war and for veterans.

(b) *Protection of personal data (Article 20, AY):* The reform of 2010 introduced a new constitutional right to request the protection of personal data: *"Everyone shall have the right to obtain information about data concerning him, to access to or request the rectification and erasure of these data and to be informed about whether these data are used in conformity with envisaged purposes. Personal data processing shall be achieved on the grounds provided by law or by the consent of the data subject."* Thus access, alteration, erasure and processing of personal data[18] shall be aim oriented and regulated by law.

(c) *Freedom of movement (Article 23, AY):* The right to leave the country shall only be limited by the decision of a judge on account of a criminal investigation or prosecution only. Citizens of the Turkish Republic cannot be prevented from leaving the country on the ground that they have not fulfilled their civic obligations. This amendment thus restricts the grounds for limitations to the freedom of movement of the Turkish citizens. For instance, persons accused of not having fulfilled their tax obligations can go to a foreign country without being stopped at the borders, unless there is a court order prohibiting them from leaving the country.

---

17. Article 24 repealed the Provisional Art. 15, which provided judicial immunity for the leaders and for civil or military bureaucrats serving under the military regime of the Sep. 12, 1980, military intervention.

18. S. Atak, *Kişisel Verilerin Korunmasına İlişkin Avrupa Birliği Yönergesinin Temel Özellikleri*, Bahçeşehir Üniversitesi Hukuk Fakültesi Kazancı Hakemli Hukuk Dergisi, Temmuz Ağustos 2009, pp. 59–60, 200; A. Döner, *Şeffaf Devlette Bilgi Edinme Hakkı ve Sınırları*, İstanbul: Vedat Kitapçılık, 2010; S. Kili, *Turkish Constitutional Developments and Assembly Debates on the Constitutions of 1924 and 1961*, İstanbul: Robert College Research Centre, 1971; N. Yüzbaşıoğlu, *Anayasa Hukuku El Kitabı*, İstanbul, Beta, 2008.

(d) *Rights of children (Article 41, AY):* There is an enlargement in children's rights: Every child has the right to adequate protection and care and the right to have and maintain a personal and direct relation with his/her parents unless it is contrary to his/her high interests.
(e) *Amendments related to the fundamental rights and duties in connection with labor relations and conditions:* The first paragraph of Article 51, AY was deleted and simultaneous membership in more than one labor union in the same sector has become possible (Article 51, AY). *Article 53, AY:* Civil servants and public officials gained the right of collective bargaining. However, in the case of raising a dispute between the civil servants and the government, the parties may apply to the *Public Officials Arbitration Board* whose decisions shall be final and have the force of a binding collective agreement. *Article 54, AY:* The right to strike has been extended and the possibility of a lockout limited. The labor union shall no longer be liable for any material damage in a workplace, ensuing from deliberately negligent behavior of the workers and the labor union during a strike. Politically motivated strikes and lockouts, solidarity strikes and lockouts, occupation of work premises, labor go-slows and other forms of obstructions are no longer prohibited. *Article 69, AY:* A proposed amendment on making it difficult to dissolve a political party did not pass.
(f) *The creation of an Ombudsman*: In 2010, the title of Article 74, AY was changed into *Right to petition, right to information and appeal to the Ombudsman.* The Ombudsman shall act as a mediator between state and citizens, and assess complaints about the functioning of the administration. The function of Ombudsman shall be created under the TBMM Presidency. The Chief Ombudsman shall be elected by the parliament for four years. The Constitution also regulates the required votes during the election.

    The parliament elected Turkey's first Head Ombudsman in November 2013, in conformity with the Constitution (Article 74, AY). The objective of the *Act on the Ombudsman* (2013–6328) is to establish the Ombudsman, an independent institution that will examine, investigate and submit recommendations concerning all sorts of acts and actions. Another objective of this Act is to establish fairness with respect to attitudes and behaviors of the administration within the framework of an understanding of human rights-based justice and legality. By creating the Ombudsman, the act provides for an effective mechanism of complaint concerning the public services. Applications in languages other than Turkish are also admissible. The Ombudsman had received 3502 complaints by September 2014, and addressed 2170 including complaints related to *Gezi Park* demonstrations. The latter were found eligible, without requiring prior exhaustion of administrative remedies.
(g) *Loss of membership of Parliament:* Article 84 of the Constitution, entitled Loss of Membership had a fifth paragraph with the following wording, which was removed by 2010 amendment: *"The membership of a deputy whose statements and acts are cited in a final judgment by the Constitutional Court as having caused the permanent dissolution of this party shall terminate on the date when the decision in question and its justification are published in the Official*

Gazette. The speaker of the Turkish Grand National Assembly shall immediately take the necessary action concerning such decision and shall inform the plenary of the Turkish Grand National Assembly accordingly."

If a political party is banned from the parliament, the members of this party can remain in parliament as independent members; only the individuals who caused the dissolution of their party shall lose their membership.

(h) *Structure of the Constitutional Court:* The constitutional amendment of 2010 also changed the composition of the Constitutional Court (Article 146, AY) (*infra*, paragraph 363).

(i) *The Council of Judges and Prosecutors:* The composition of the *Council of Judges and Prosecutors* has been amended in 2010 and 2014 (Article 159, AY) (*infra*, paragraph 22).

B. Attempts to Make a New Constitution and Subsequent 2017 Amendments

13. In July 2011, efforts to frame a completely new Constitution for the Republic of Turkey were initiated. The current Constitution is based on the military coup in 1980 and is in force since 1982. The Constitution provides for the possibility of amendments (Article 175, AY) but prohibits changes to the first three articles which are about the form of the state, the characteristics of the Republic, the integrity, the official language, the flag, the national anthem and the capital of the state, as well as issues related to the powers of local governments and decentralization. A Parliamentary Conciliation Committee was established in 2013, where all political parties (four in total) were represented equally to prepare a new constitution for Turkey. While a consensus was reached about sixty articles (including a number of provisions regarding the protection of fundamental rights and freedoms), there was no consensus on key issues such as the separation of powers, a new definition of citizenship without ethnic references, mother tongue education, issues related to the link between state and religion and the possible amendment of the first three irrevocable articles of the current Constitution. As there was no further progress, the ruling party withdrew from the Parliamentary Conciliation Committee in December 2013, in the course of discussions about the first three articles, and the committee was dissolved. Thus, this reform effort was interrupted. There was another attempt in 2016, in order to continue the work from where it has stopped, but it was not successful.

The developments went in a different direction after 2016. The changes to the Constitution aimed to abolishing the parliamentary governmental system and instituting the presidential government. This transformation was accomplished in August 2018 (*infra*, paragraph 51).

§2. Criminal Law, Criminal Justice and Criminal Science

I. Definitions and Forms of Criminal Law

A. General Criminal Law

14. Criminal law consists of substantive criminal law, criminal procedure and the law on the execution of sanctions. All these branches of general criminal law interact with each other and constitute a whole system.

15. Substantive criminal law regulates the general principles of crime. The related principles are contained mainly in the First Book of the Turkish Penal Code (Articles 1–75, TCK). The crimes are defined in Book Two (Articles 76–345, TCK) (*infra*, paragraphs 192–251).

16. Until 2005, criminal offenses were divided into two categories: felonies *(cürüm)* and misdemeanors *(kabahat)*. Since 2005, the Penal Code regulates only crimes *(suç)*. According to the principle of legality, offenses (and their penalties) must be provided and clearly defined by law. There is a general Penal Code and many special regulations in other laws. The TCK applies to all penal legislation (Article 5, TCK).[19]

B. Criminal Procedure Law

17. Criminal procedure law deals with the rights of the accused and the duties of the state to combat crime. It tries to reach a balance between these two requirements. The old Turkish Code of Penal Procedure (CMUK) was a translation of the German Code of Penal Procedure as it was in 1929. This Code was repealed in 2005 and replaced by another Penal Procedure Code (CMK), which entered into force on June 1, 2005.

C. Code on the Execution of Punishments and Security Measures

18. The enforcement of criminal judgments is not a separate branch of criminal law. There were some provisions on the enforcement of criminal judgments in the repealed Code of Penal Procedure. There was a Code on Enforcement of Punishments (CIK), which originated in 1965 and regulated the sanctioning system. However, the execution of prison penalties was not regulated in detail in this code. This field of law was subject to government ordinances.

In 2005, the old Code on Enforcement of Punishments and the existing government ordinances were replaced by the Bill on Corrections, prepared by the Dönmezer Commission in 2002 (*infra*, paragraph 561). This law regulates inmates'

19. F. Yenisey, *Il nouvo dritto penale turco: an bilanco dopo sette anni*, in *Criminal Law of the Republic of Turkey*, Padova University Press, S. Riondato & R. Alagna (eds.), 2012, p. 25.

rights and obligations, and has been in force since June 1, 2005, under the name Code on Execution of Punishments and Security Measures (CGIK).

II. Overview of the Criminal Justice System

A. Prosecution Service

19. The public prosecutor (*infra*, paragraph 368) is obliged to prosecute or bring a case whenever there is sufficient evidence indicating that the accused individual (Article 160/1, CMK) has committed a crime.

20. In Turkey, internal security and judicial duties are performed by the police, the gendarmerie and the coast guard (*infra*, paragraph 369). With respect to the investigation of criminal offenses, all law enforcement officers act under the supervision of the public prosecutor.

21. There was a second procedure under the name of "private claim" (*şahsi dava*, Article 344, repealed CMUK) (*infra*, paragraph 428), whereby the injured party was entitled to bring both a civil and a criminal complaint against the offending party. This provision is, however, no longer included in the new Code. Instead of covering injuries by a claim submitted to the criminal court, if the accused is convicted, there is now a procedure of victim-offender mediation (*infra*, paragraph 393) applicable to a restricted number of offenses.

B. Courts, Prosecutors and Justices

1. Council of Judges and Public Prosecutors

22. The Council of Judges and Public Prosecutors (HSK) is a constitutional council, which decides all personnel matters relating to judges and prosecutors (Article 159, AY).

The Council of Judges and Prosecutions, which consists of two chambers and thirteen members, shall function according to the principle that the courts shall be independent and the tenure of judges shall be secure (Article 159/1, AY). Members shall serve for four years and may be re-elected. Except for the Minister of Justice and the Vice Minister of Justice, the members of the Council shall only assume duties prescribed by law and shall not be appointed or elected to another office by the Council.

The Minister of Justice is the president of the Council, and his vice minister shall be an ex-officer member of the Council. The president of the Republic selects four members from ordinary judges or public prosecution, one member from administrative judges or public prosecutors. The Grand National Assembly of Turkey selects three members from the members of the Court of Cassation, one member from the members of the Council of State and three members from academic members in the field of law. At least one of these three must be an academic member of a law school and one must be a lawyer. The applications shall be made to the office of the speaker of the Assembly, which conveys them to the joint committee composed of members of the committees on constitution and justice. This joint committee shall elect three candidates for each vacancy with a two-third majority of all the members; if this cannot be accomplished in the first round, then in the second round a three-fifth majority of the total number of members shall be required. If this cannot be accomplished in the second round, also, the Grand National Assembly of Turkey shall elect a candidate holding a secret ballet for each candidate and choosing the one who has received the highest number of votes (Article 159/3, AY).

The Council shall exercise the functions of appointing, transferring, imposing of disciplinary penalties, removing from office and promoting the judges and public prosecutors of civil and administrative courts, making final decisions concerning the changes in the territorial jurisdiction or abolition of a court upon the recommendation of the Ministry of Justice.

Inquiries and investigations regarding job performances, conducts and alleged offenses of judges and public prosecutors shall be carried out (upon the proposal of the related chambers and with the permission of the President of the Council of Judges and Prosecutors) by the councils, inspectors or by senior judges or senior public prosecutors.

Except for dismissal from the profession, decisions of the Council will not be subject to judicial review.

The Council shall establish a secretary general, who shall be appointed by the Council's president from their first category judges and public prosecutors recommended by the Council. The Council shall appoint the Council's inspectors, judges and prosecutors, with their consent to temporary or permanent functions in the Council. The judges, public prosecutors and internal auditors shall be appointed by the Minister of Justice, with their consent, to temporary or permanent functions in relevant, centrally affiliated institutions of the Ministry of Justice.

2. Offices of the Criminal Peace Judgeship and Enforcement Judgeship

23. The office of the criminal peace judgeship (*infra,* paragraph 372) has jurisdiction during the preparatory inquiry to render decisions such as pre-trial arrest or search and seizure, as well as other decisions as required by law. The office of the enforcement judgeship (*infra,* paragraph 615) deals with issues of disputes between inmates and correction authority.

3. Trial Courts and Courts of Legal Remedies

24. Turkish structure of court organization has three layers: (1) Courts of the first instance, (2) regional courts of appeal, and (3) the Court of Cassation.

The court of general jurisdiction (*infra*, paragraph 351) and the court of assizes (*infra*, paragraph 352) have trial jurisdiction over criminal matters in the first instance. Peace court was repealed in June 2014 by Act No. 6545 (*infra*, paragraph 350). There are no lay judges in the Turkish court system.

Since February 2014, there has been no specialized court for organized crime and terrorism; but such courts have been introduced again (*infra*, paragraph 355).

Military courts have been abolished by the constitutional amendment in 2016; thus, only military disciplinary courts remained (*infra*, paragraph 357).

As of July 2016, the regional appeal courts, dealing with fact and law issues have been put into force (*infra,* paragraph 360). The Court of Cassation (*infra*, paragraph 361) deals with the legal aspects of a judgment. It does not examine the facts found by the trial judge. However, there are many extraordinary post-trial remedies available in Turkish law (*infra*, paragraph 557).

The state council (*Danıştay*) deals with the revision of administrative claims. This high court therefore plays an important role in criminal cases having a link with administrative law. The Military High Administrative Court has also been repealed by constitutional amendment in 2016.

The Constitutional Court (*infra* paragraph 363) was established in 1961. It exercises a posteriori control of the consistency of the laws with the Constitution. The 2010 constitutional amendment changed the composition of the Constitutional Court (Article 146, AY), and the 2012 amendment introduced the individual petition to the Constitutional Court claiming the breach of constitutional rights, if they are also covered by the ECHR.

C. *The Defense*

25. The profession of attorneys is regulated by Act No. 1136 of 1969. In Turkey there was one bar association in each province as well as a National Bar Association. The Law on Lawyers was amended in July 2020, by the Act No. 7242: In provinces where there are over 5000 lawyers, a group of at least 2000 lawyers may set up a second bar association. This amendment aimed to create more than one bar association in some provinces, for the sake of a pluralistic system. The "Second Bar Association of Istanbul" has been established according to the recent legislation on September 28, 2020.

In addition to providing free legal assistance to the poor, the Bar has become a very important institution since the amendment of the Code of Penal Procedure in 1992.[20] Today, the Bar appoints a lawyer for the accused in the preliminary investigation before the police hearing should the accused request one.

26. The independence of attorneys from the government has been assured. The attorney for an accused has a special defender status in criminal cases. His/her status is not just the representation of the accused; he/she has also rights, which are regulated in the Penal Procedure Code (*infra*, paragraph 418).

20. Article 56, KHK 700, dated Jul. 7, 2018, related prohibiting the National Bar Association from submitting suggestions for improvements to the legislator for the administration of justice, which was originally regulated in Art. 115/3, of Lawyers' Act No 1136.

D. Assisting Institutions to the Criminal Justice

27. The Ministry of Justice is responsible for the enforcement of the Penal Codes and supervises the public prosecution service. According to the law, the Minister of Justice is entitled to give orders to the public prosecutor at the Court of Cassation to bring a case to the Court of Cassation as a legal remedy (Article 309, CMK), but it may not give an order not to prosecute at the level of the courts of the first instance. The presidential governmental system introduced since July 7, 2018 resulted in change of structure of all governmental bodies, including the Ministry of Justice. The Ministry of Justice is now attached to the elected president, and there are offices under the Ministry of Justice. Articles 38–64, of the Presidential Decree[21] No. 1 about the Organization of the Office of the President, dated July 10, 2018 regulates the new infrastructure of the Ministry of Justice.

28. Justice Academy. Gives training to future judges and prosecutors and continuing legal education to lawyers, is an independent body.[22]

29. Institute of Legal Medicine. A centralized Institute of Legal Medicine, supervised by the Ministry of Justice, gives scientific reports about evidence when a court asks for it.[23]

30. Supervision of inmates. The Turkish prison system includes closed, half-closed, open and special penal institutions (*infra*, paragraph 567). After an inmate is classified as such, he is held under the supervision of the prison's staff (*infra*, paragraph 575).

III. Directions Within Criminal Science

31. There has been a sharp rise in urbanization since the 1950s. The migration from rural areas to the cities still continues today. The unplanned growth of cities has created new problems.[24] The existing number of police officers is insufficient to meet these new problems; moreover, not all of them are deployed with maximum efficiency.

21. There is a distinction between "presidential decree" (cumhurbaşkanlığı kararnamesi) and "executive order" (cumhurbaşkanı kararı) (Ş. İba & Y. Söyler, Yeni Hükümet Sisteminde Cumhurbaşkanlığı Kararnamesi ile Cumhurbaşkanı Kararının Nitelik Farkı ve Hukuki Sonuçları, Anayasa Yargısı, Cilt: 36, Sayı: 1 (2019), 195–223.

22. The Justice Academy was created by Act No. 4954 in 2003. Article 2 of KHK 703, dated Jul. 9, 2018, however, closed it down and transferred its duties, as well as its properties to the Ministry of Justice until the Academy was re-opened.

23. N. Alkan, 5237 *Sayılı Türk Ceza Kanunu'nun Adli Tıp Yönünden Değerlendirilmesi*, Sayı: Türkiye Barolar Birliği Dergisi, Mayıs/Haziran, 2005, pp. 58, 149; M. Gönlübol & T. Ataöv, *Turkey in the United Nations, a Legal and Political Appraisal*, Ankara: Ajans Turk Press, 1960; O. Polat, *Klinik Adli Tıp-Adli Tıp Uygulamaları*, Ankara, Seçkin Yayınları, 2014.

24. S. Dönmezer, *Criminality in a Small Community of Rapid Urbanization and Industrialization,* in Annales de la Faculté de Droit d'Istanbul XXII, No. 38 (1972–1974): 55; N. Gürelli, *Urbanization and Crime,* in Annales De la Faculté De Droit D'Istanbul XXII, No. 38 (1972–1974), p. 357.

Turkish criminal science currently focuses greatly on adjusting Turkish law to European standards. Many Turkish legal scholars study at European universities. Whereas at the beginning of the century, the French influence was dominant, today, in the field of criminal law, scholarly exchanges with German universities and institutions are prominent.[25] Books published in the Turkish language expose Turkish lawyers to recent developments in the field of criminal law in Western Europe.[26] Since the Criminal Law Reform of 2005, there are plenty of new publications about the principles of the new criminal law. The new statutes have not been effectively applied since then; the difference between the previous law, its jurisprudence and the current principles of criminal law are in contradiction in the mindset of lawyers who have been educated in law schools according to the previous law. Moreover, the expectation of a new Constitution after the election in June 2015 made the application of law uncertain.

Furthermore, the decisions of the European Court of Human Rights (ECtHR) and rulings of the Turkish Constitutional Court rendered upon individual petition have been affecting the development of Turkish law. In addition, US law also has some influence, as Turkey has adopted direct and cross-examination.

32. Legal Education. One of Atatürk's most significant reforms was university reform. In addition to the Law Faculty of Istanbul, a second law faculty was set up in Ankara. Many German scholars of Jewish origin taught at Turkish Universities during the 1930s.[27] After 1980 the number of law faculties increased. As of 2020, the total number of law faculties is 82 in Turkey.[28]

Since 2001, there has also been training for judges and public prosecutors, provided by the Ministry of Justice, and after 2003, by the Justice Academy, in conjunction with universities focusing on human rights. The number of judges and prosecutors who speak a foreign language is increasing.

Legal education is one of the major discussions within the Turkish law reform in general. The theory-oriented legal education, which does not put any emphasis on practical skills, has been criticized by many scholars. Legal education in the twenty-first century has been the topic of an international conference organized by the Union of Turkish Bar Associations[29] and Council of Higher Education, which recommended increasing the points for entrance required for application to law schools.

---

25. S. Dönmezer, *Turkey*, in International Handbook of Contemporary Developments in Criminology, ed. E.H. Johnson, Westport, Connecticut: Greenwood Press, 1983, p. 594.
26. H.H. Jescheck, *Almanya Federal Cumhuriyeti Ceza Hukukuna Giriş*, İstanbul: Beta, 2007; A. Eser, *Son Yüzyıl İçinde Almanya'daki Ceza Düzenlemeleri, Geçmişe Bir Bakış ve Gelecekteki Eğilimler* (1989) Nos 1–2, p. 12; T. Demirbaş, *Kriminoloji:* Gözden Geçirilmiş 5. Baskı, Ankara, Seçkin, 2014, p. 29; D. Soyaslan, Kriminoloji (Suç ve Ceza Bilimleri), 3. Baskı, Yetkin, Ankara 2018, p. 44.
27. A. Önder, *Der Einfluss des deutschen Rechts auf das türkische Strafprozessrecht, Annales* XXII, No. 38, İstanbul, 1974, 365; O. Oehring, *Bibliographie zum türkischen Recht*, Berlin, 1982.
28. https://yokatlas.yok.gov.tr/lisans-bolum.php?b=10094.
29. *21. Yüzyılda Hukuk Eğitimi* (Legal Education in the Twenty-First Century), the book of the international conference, Bahçeşehir University/The Union of Turkish Bar Associations/ Atlanta's John Marshall School of Law; J.E. Moliterno, *Exporting American Legal Education*, in: Prof. Dr. Feridun Yenisey'e Armağan, Beta, İstanbul 2015, p. 1949.

Another approach for improving the quality of legal education is the introduction of a bar exam in Turkey. An examination to obtain the right to exercise the profession was introduced. However, the examination was postponed until the first-year students in 2001 were to graduate (Act No. 4765 dated 2002), and it was abolished by the Constitutional Court in 2006 because of the uncertainty raised by bar associations that the law did not foresee how the questions for this examination ought to be prepared. Efforts to make a new act resulted with the enactment of the Law No. 7188 in 2019: an exam for all law-related professions has been introduced. The details of the exam are regulated in the Act for Higher Education, additional Article 41.

§3. Historical Background

I. The Period of Islamic Law and Secularization

33. There is no evidence of the Islamic Law in the modern Turkey's laws today. However, during the Ottoman Empire (which lasted from 1300 until 1920), Islamic Law was the source of criminal law.[30] Rules were stipulated in a casuistic manner.[31] There was no complete and systematic penal code. Islamic law classified crimes into two groups.[32] Crimes listed in the first group (crimes against God) were defined and their punishments determined by the written sources of Islamic law. The second group comprised those crimes for which definitions and punishments were left to the discretion of the sovereign. Judges or high-ranking officials were entitled to define and punish crimes in this category in their own names.[33]

During the later stage of the Ottoman Empire there were legislative efforts such as *Mecelle* (Civil Code) and the adoption of Western codes. Reception was the main method of legislation at the time of the foundation of the new Turkish Republic in 1920.[34]

During the period of Islamic Law, before 1839, the criminal justice system depended on courts with one judge (*Kadı*), and in principle no legal remedies existed. Only political pardon was possible. Even after the principles of Western European criminal law were introduced in the Ottoman Empire, secular law and Islamic law were applied side by side until Atatürk's legal reforms began in 1920. The court structure was based on the French model.

---

30. F. Selle, *Prozessrecht des 16. Jahrhunderts im Osmanischen Reich*, Wiesbaden: Otto Harrossowitz, 1962, p. 9; F. Yenisey, *Ceza Yargılamalarında ve Adli Teşkilatta Cumhuriyet Öncesi Durum ve Cumhuriyetten Sonraki Gelişmeler,* in Atatürk Sempozyumu, İstanbul Üniversitesi, 1981, p. 39; Atar, *İslam Adliye Teşkilatı, Ortaya çıkışı ve İşleyişi*, Ankara: Diyanet İşleri Başkanlığı, 1982, 4; J. Krcmarik, *Beitraege zur Beleuchtung des islamischen Strafrechts*, Leipzig, 1904.
31. J. Starr, *Law as Metaphor: From Islamic Courts to the Palace of Justice*, Albany, US: State University of New York Press, 1992.
32. U. Heyd, *Studies in Old Ottoman Criminal Law*, Clarendon: Oxford, 1973, p. 18.
33. F. Yenisey, *Die Entwicklung im türkischen Strafrecht von 1960 bis 1983*, Zeitschrift für die gesamte Strafrechtswissenschaft, 96, Berlin/Boston: Walter de Gruyter GmbH, 1984, Heft 1, p. 212.
34. G. Plagemann, *Von Allahs Gesetz zur Modernisierung per Gesezt, Gesetz und Gesetzgebungen im Osmanischen Reich und der Republik Türkei*, Berlin: Lit Verlag, 2009, p. 35.

34. The Decree of Reorganization *(Tanzimat-i Hayriye Fermanı)*, known as the Noble Edict of Gülhane *(Gülhane Hattı)*, of November 3, 1839, brought fundamental changes in the political structure of the Ottoman Empire. The first modern TCK was the Imperial Penal Code *(Ceza Kanunname-i Hümayunu)*, published in 1858. It was the Turkish translation of the French Penal Code of 1810 and it remained in force until 1926. This Code was the first systematic Western-styled code, and it contained a general theory of crime.[35]

35. After the First World War, Turkey was occupied by several nations. The resistance against occupation evolved into a struggle for independence. Kemal Atatürk called for an organized, armed resistance. On January 20, 1921, a Constitution was ratified and the TBMM declared that it had the right to make laws and declare war. During the political development from Ottoman Empire into a nation state, Islam served as a source of national unity.

II. The Period of the Turkish Republic (Parliamentary Democracy)

A. *Turkish Republic: 1923–2007*

36. The Republic was founded in 1923 and the Constitution amended in 1924. Until 1946, Turkey was governed by a one-party parliamentary system. During the period of National Liberation two elections were held. After the second election, in 1920, Mustafa Kemal Atatürk formed a majority group without opposition. The 1924 Constitution made the transition from a one-party system to a multi-party system possible. With a few changes, the 1924 Constitution laid down the guidelines for the organization of the whole Turkish state until 1960.

37. The secular Constitution of 1924, the passage of new legislation and the creation of a new Faculty of Law in Ankara were important changes for Turkey.[36]

The first TCK of the Turkish Republic, based almost entirely on the Italian Penal Code of 1889, was enacted on March 13, 1926 and put into effect on July 1, 1926 (Act No. 765). The TCK has been amended many times, and more than half of its articles have been changed. After the last amendment was made on January 3, 2003, the new TCK repealed it in 2005.[37]

35. A. Gökçen, *Tanzimat Dönemi Osmanlı Ceza Kanunları ve Bu Kanunlardaki Ceza Mueyyideleri*, İstanbul, 1989.
36. V. Versan, *The Kemalist Reform of Turkish Law and Its Impact*, in: *Atatürk and the Modernization of Turkey*, ed. J.M. Landau, Ch. 16, Boulder, CO: Westview, 1984, p. 249.
37. An English translation of the Turkish Penal Code may be found in Seçkin (publisher), V. Bıçak & E. Grieves, *Türkçe-İngilizce Türk Ceza Kanunu*, Ankara, 2007, and the translation of the repealed Penal Code in the American Series of Foreign Penal Codes, No. 9, *The Turkish Criminal Code*, ed. Ansay, Yücel & Friedman, London: Sweet and Maxwell, 1965.

38. Until 1943, elections took place under a single party, the Republican Populist Party (Cumhuriyet Halk Partisi, CHP). After 1945, the multi-party system developed, and the Democratic Party (*Demokrat Parti*, DP) was founded. In 1950, the DP obtained 53.3% of the vote, and the CHP received 14.2%. In the period from 1950–1960, the DP lost its popularity.

39. The military National Unity Committee (Milli Birlik Komitesi), which took power[38] on May 27, 1960, appointed a commission to prepare the draft of a new Constitution.[39] After the military intervention in 1960,[40] a new Electoral Law was adopted. In the elections of 1965, the newly formed Justice Party (Adalet Partisi, AP) won an absolute majority of the votes. From 1961 to 1980, eight parties were represented in the TBMM. The Constitution was approved by national referendum and adopted on July 20, 1961.[41]

40. On September 12, 1980, the armed forces, led by General Kenan Evren, took over the government in a bloodless intervention.

During the period of the military regime and the *Anavatan Partisi* – Motherland Party (ANAP) Government, many essential laws were changed and new laws adopted. In April 1991, the Anti-Terrorism Act (Act No. 3713) was enacted.[42]

41. ANAP lost the elections in October 1991, and a coalition was formed with DYP and SHP.[43] On June 18, 1999, by Act No. 4388, AY Article 143, was amended: Military judge and prosecutor were removed from the panel of state security courts. Parallel to the amendment to the Constitution, the Act on State Security courts was amended (1999–4390) accordingly. The Act dated June 16, 2004, No. 5190 has abolished the state security courts (*infra*, paragraph 355).[44]

42. On August 2, 2002, the Grand National Assembly decided that early elections were to be held on November 3, 2002.

---

38. W.F. Walter, *The Turkish Revolution 1960–1961*, Greenwood, The Brookings Institution, 1963.
39. F. Yenisey & S. Tellenbach, *Zur strafrechtlichen Entwicklung in der Türkei*, Juristenzeitung, 1985, p. 378.
40. W.F. Weiker, *The Turkish Revolution 1960–1961*, Westport, CT: Greenwood, 1980, 1 et seq.
41. E. Hirsch, *Die Verfassung der Türkischen Republik*, Berlin: Frankfurt A.M., 1966.
42. Although (before the amendment in 2001) the Constitution prohibited amnesty for political crimes, the 1991 Anti-Terrorism Act tacitly granted amnesty for all crimes by means of a *conditional release from prison* (*infra*, para. 617), provided that the individual had served one-fifth of his prison term. As a result of the new bill, some 5,000 political prisoners have been released. There is a similar bill enacted by the parliament in July 2020, with the aim of reducing the overcrowding of prison population (*infra*, para. 562).
43. J. Bennet, *The Europa World Year Book 1993*, vol. II, London: Europa Publications Limited, 1993, p. 2836.
44. In 2001, the Constitution was amended to include: the *right to a fair trial* (Art. 36/1, AY); a regulation on excluding factual findings obtained in violation of existing written Acts; a ban on the death penalty (except for war crimes, for crimes committed under circumstances of close threat of war and for acts of terrorism, which was later abolished in 2004); and a prohibition of deprivation of liberty for not being able to fulfill a contractual obligation (Art. 38, AY). The same provision already contained the principle of non-retroactivity of criminal acts.

Provisional Article 15, AY placed an obstacle to bringing a lawsuit with respect to any decision or measure taken by the National Security Council, or any legislative activity from September 12, 1980, to the date of the formation of the Bureau of the TBMM. Act No. 4709 of 2001 abolished this exception. Article 25 of the Act on the Constitutional Court had previously brought in another obstacle prohibiting applications on the basis of unconstitutionality of Acts enacted during the September 12 Regime. The Constitutional Court abolished this provision on July 9, 2002.[45] Thus, the requirement of the ECHR that regulates free access to court is fulfilled.[46]

43. In 1985, a panel of legal experts worked out the first version of the Draft TCK. However, the government was changed and it did not become law. Still, many articles with new ideas taken from the Draft Code were later incorporated into the penal law. Therefore, it can be argued that this Draft Code was the core for further reform. It was expanded to a systematic restructuring of the administration of criminal justice. It was also a source of inspiration for the 2005 reform.

44. The 2002 Reform Package included a new draft law on Court Organization, Draft Penal Code, Draft Penal Procedure Code and a Draft Code for Corrections. It puts forward, for instance, the idea of out-of-court dispute resolution for minor crimes (mediation). The reform package of 2002 was the main source for the new legislation of 2004, which entered into force in 2005.

45. The 2005 TCK respects the principle of humanity and takes into account previous decisions of the ECtHR. For instance, the code observes the principle of guilt, even with respect to unintentional crimes. But when the guilt is minor and the damage suffered by the suspect is insignificant, there will be no prosecution. Furthermore, the code respects the principle of legality (*infra*, paragraph 165).

46. The 2005 Penal Procedure Code introduced general fair trial principles in Turkish criminal procedure. For instance, the functions of investigation, prosecution and adjudication are strictly separated. Individuals prosecuted for similar facts will be treated equally under the same rules and principles (principle of equality). Investigators and judicial authorities should observe the rights of victims at all stages of the proceedings. Furthermore, individuals who are under suspicion of having committed a crime or who are prosecuted are presumed innocent until their guilt has been proven. Any action against the presumption of innocence should be prevented and damages suffered should be repaired.

45. E. 2002/121, K. 2002/121, RG. Aug. 31, 2002.
46. Impunity is one of the major problems in the area of crimes committed in unrest situations. The government tries not to punish some crimes committed by law enforcement officers committed under extraordinary circumstances. The above-mentioned two examples of impunity were repeated very recently: intelligence agents, acting illegally, shall not be held responsible criminally, administratively or civilly (Art. 26/2, MİTK). The same applies to civilians who committed crimes in the night of Jul. 15, 2016, in order to prevent revolting soldiers' overthrow of the existing regime.

B. AK Party Regime: 2007–2015

47. In April 2007, Prime Minister Erdoğan nominated Foreign Minister Abdullah Gül as the ruling party's candidate for president. Gül, however, failed to win the necessary two-thirds majority in the Parliament. A Constitutional Court decision later nullified the vote, citing a lack of a quorum. The opposition boycotted the vote. Gül withdrew from the race in May and was victorious in the third round of elections in August 2007. Recep Tayyip Erdoğan was nominated by the President of the Republic, Abdullah Gül to form the cabinet.

48. Military coups and alleged deep state networks have been the focus of political discussion in Turkey and are exemplified by trials relating to the 1980 coup and the Post-modern Coup of February 28, 1997. Later, a number of high-profile cases, individual criminal proceedings and investigations were launched under anti-terrorism legislation against former members of the Army.

In June 2013, protests started against the urban development project in Istanbul *Taksim* square recreation park (*Gezi Park*) and spread to other cities. With the involvement of some violent demonstrators, police used force, six people including one policeman died, thousands were injured, over 3500 were taken into police custody and some of them were detained on suspicion of being members of a terror organization. Following allegations of excessive use of force by the police, administrative investigations were launched against 150 law enforcement officers. One of the wounded protesters died in March 2014, and a new wave of protests started.

As a consequence of the *Gezi Park* demonstration, regulations related to the freedom of assembly were changed in March 2015, by the amendments related to internal security acts.

The 4th Judicial Reform Package supported the *social unification* and some mayors, accused of aiding terrorist organizations, were released from pre-trial detention. Consequently, rules about pre-trial detention have been amended in 2015 (*infra*, paragraph 466).

49. In light of the growing problem of Syrian refugees, the Act on Foreigners and International Protection was adopted in January 2013. This law was needed since there are a large number of refugees and smuggled migrants passing through Turkey to find asylum in European Countries. This legislation provides for judicial remedies and legal aid for migrants.

50. Since their enactment, the 2005 codes have been amended several times. The amendments consisted in numbered reform packages. For instance, the 3rd Judicial Reform Package was adopted in July 2012, and was of particular importance for pre-trial detention (*infra*, paragraph 465). The 4th Judicial Reform Package, adopted in April 2013, provided judicial remedies for a number of issues on which the ECtHR had condemned Turkey. It introduced a distinction between freedom of expression, on the one hand, and incitement to violence or to committing acts of terrorism, on the other. The aim was to reduce the pressure on the media by state officials, the firing of critical journalists and website bans. The 5th Judicial Reform

Package was announced in September 2013, by the government, submitted to the Parliament in February 2014, was signed by the President and published on March 13, 2014.

III. Presidential Government

51. Two general elections were held in Turkey in 2015. The first one was on June 7, 2015. AK Party, which had governed Turkey since 2002, lost its parliamentary majority and won 258 seats with 40.9% of the vote. The main opposition CHP also lost some seats. The Nationalist Movement Party (MHP) saw an increase in their vote share. The Peoples' Democratic Party (HDP) achieved votes over the 10% election threshold. Since after the first election the appointed Prime Minister was not able to form a government, five months later another election was held.

According to the outcome of the second election AK Party achieved 49.4% of the vote, CHP achieved 25.4% of the votes. MHP won just under 12% of the vote, while HDP won 10.7% of the vote, coming fourth in terms of votes but third in terms of seats.[47]

There was a failed state coup on July 15, 2016. Some revolting members of the military blocked the Bosporus Bridge on the night of July 15, 2016. Right after that, in many cities in Turkey, similar actions against the government started. The national television, occupied by the revolting soldiers, announced that the military regime (*sıkı yönetim*) had been launched in all Turkey. Right after this announcement, however, the president made a call to the public from his mobile phone broadcasted by a private television channel to resist this illegal movement by going out of their houses and assembling in squares or airports. A large majority of citizens responded to this call. Thus, a clash started between revolting soldiers and citizens.

At the end, the attempt was not successful and the prime minister and the president took over the control in the country. This attempted coup has been charged to a religious group led by a leader who lives in Pennsylvania, USA. It has been argued that this religious group has formed a parallel government in Turkey (FETO PYD), inserted officials, judges, governors into the legitimate elected government and now has attempted to overthrow the legal government by means of force. Whoever was in connection with the parallel state was under prosecution.

A state of emergency (OHAL) was announced a few days later after the coup, which lasted until July 18, 2018. Under the emergency regime, the government was entitled to issue decrees in power in the Law of Emergencies, which are not controllable by the Constitutional Court.

In January 2017, Law No. 6771 amending eighteen Articles of the Constitution was enacted by the parliament and has been approved in a referendum on April 16, 2017. This amendment package changed the governmental system in Turkey from parliamentary to a presidential system with a strong executive power.

The amendments entered in force at different times. After the first set of amendments,

---

47. The decision of the Supreme Electoral Council dated Nov. 11, 2015, 2310 (RG Nov. 12, 2015, 29530).

related to the election of the president and the members of the parliament entered in force, the presidential election and general elections were held together on June 24, 2018. Recep Tayyip Erdoğan was elected as the President of Turkey. The elected president took the presidential oath on July 9, and the new presidential system began officially.

The presidential system abolished the prime ministership and the cabinet. The president has the power to appoint and dismiss the ministers and high rank officers. Duties and powers of the ministries are regulated in the presidential decree no.1.

The OHAL was lifted in July 2018. The two-year long emergency ruling made significant impacts on democracy and fundamental rights. Several restrictive elements of the emergency administration have been integrated into the Criminal Procedure Code. The Judicial Reform Strategy package was adopted and the first legislative package has been enacted. The presidential system introduced in 2018 resulted in centralized power to the presidency; the democratic accountability of the executive branch is very limited in the new presidential system and there are problems in respect of the separation of powers between executive, legislative and judiciary. As the COVID-19 crisis unfolded, the executive took a number of measures. In the light of the COVID-19 pandemic, no OHAL was declared and the necessary measures to be taken against the pandemic need to be legalized by the parliament.

The president announced the judicial reform strategy for 2019–2023 in May 2019, which includes aims such as protection of rights and freedoms, improving judicial independence and impartiality, enhancing the efficiency of the criminal justice system and simplification of criminal procedure. There shall be a guarantee of geographical tenure which prevents judges being transferred from one province to another province in an interval of two years. The first legislative package implementing the judicial reform strategy was adopted in October 2019, and introduced many legislative changes. Amongst them, the amendment in Anti-terrorism Act Article 7/2, according to which speech made within the limit of freedom of press or made with the purpose of criticism shall not be a crime, is certainly worthy of mention. Additionally, in July 2020, the second legislative package was adopted. It introduced speedy adjudication (*infra,* paragraph 397) and simplified procedures (*infra,* paragraph 400), where the public prosecutor or the court is empowered to render a judgment *in camera* without holding a hearing, but if the accused proposes, there shall be a regular main trial hearing.

The presidential system in Turkey is in its early stages and it is too early for an overall evaluation. The parliament is currently trying to adapt itself to this new system which empowers the members to submit proposals of laws to the parliament.

§4. Sources and Classifications of Criminal Law

I. International Sources of Criminal Law

52. International Treaties and Acts passed by the TBMM are sources of criminal law and will be applied directly by the Turkish criminal courts. Turkey has signed many international treaties.

These include:

UN CONVENTIONS

- Statute of the International Court of Justice (June 26, 1945)—RG August 24, 1945.
- Convention on the Prevention and Punishment of the Crime of Genocide (December 9, 1948)—RG March 29, 1950.
- Convention on the Privileges and Immunities of the United Nations (February 13, 1946)—RG March 21, 1950.
- Convention (IV) relative to the Protection of Civilian Persons in Time of War (August 12, 1949)—RG January 30, 1953.
- Convention on the Political Rights of Women (December 20, 1952)—RG June 2, 1959.
- Convention relating to the Status of Refugees (July 28, 1951)—RG September 5, 1961.
- Convention on the Abolition of Slavery, the Slave Trade, and Institutions and Practices Similar to Slavery (September 7, 1956)—RG January 6, 1964.
- Single Convention on Narcotic Drugs (March 30, 1961), as amended by the Protocol amending the Single Convention on Narcotic Drugs, 1961, RG January 5, 1967.
- Convention for the Suppression of Unlawful Seizure of Aircraft (December 16, 1970)—RG March 31, 1973.
- Convention on the Reduction of Statelessness (September 13, 1973)—RG August 15, 1975.
- Convention Relating to the Status of Stateless Persons (September 28, 1954)—RG October 25, 2014.
- Vienna Convention on Consular Relations (April 24, 1963)—RG September 27, 1975.
- The Convention on Crimes Committed in Airplanes (September 14, 1963)—RG May 4, 1975.
- Convention on the Means of Prohibiting and Preventing the Illicit Import, Export and Transfer of Ownership of Cultural Property (November 14, 1970)—RG January 26, 1981.
- Convention on the Prevention and Punishment of Crimes against Internationally Protected Persons, Including Diplomatic Agents (December 14, 1973)—RG May 1, 1981.
- UN Convention on Psychotropic Substances (February 22, 1971)—RG March 7, 1981.
- Vienna Convention on Diplomatic Relations (April 18, 1961)—RG December 24, 1984.
- The Convention on the Elimination of All Forms of Discrimination against Women (CEDAW) (September 3, 1981)—RG October 14, 1985.
- Convention Against Torture and Other Cruel, Inhuman or Degrading Treatment or Punishment (December 9, 1975)—RG August 10, 1988.
- Convention for the Suppression of Unlawful Acts against the Safety of Civil Aviation (September 23, 1971)—RG May 17, 1989.
- International Convention Against the Taking of Hostages (June 3, 1983)—RG April 29, 1988.

- Convention on the Rights of the Child (September 2, 1990)—RG December 11, 1994.[48]
- United Nations Convention against Illicit Traffic in Narcotic Drugs and Psychotropic Substances (December 19, 1988)—RG November 25, 1995.
- Convention on the Prohibition of the Development, Production, Stockpiling and Use of Chemical Weapons and on their Destruction (August 31, 1994)—RG May 3, 1997.
- International Convention for the Suppression of Terrorist Bombings (December 15, 1997)—RG April 17, 2002.
- International Convention for the Suppression of the Financing of Terrorism (January 10, 2000)—RG April 17, 2002.
- International Convention on the Elimination of All Forms of Racial Discrimination (October 13, 1972)—RG June 16, 2002.
- Optional Protocol to the Convention on the Elimination of All Forms of Discrimination against Women. New York (October 6, 1999)—RG September 18, 2002.
- Optional Protocol to the Convention on the Rights of the Child on the Sale of Children, Child Prostitution and Child Pornography (September 8, 2000)—RG June 28, 2002.
- International Covenant on Civil and Political Rights (December 16, 1966)—RG July 21, 2003.
- International Covenant on Economic Social and Cultural Rights (December 16, 1966)—RG August 11, 2003.
- United Nations Convention against Transnational Organized Crime (December 12, 2000)—RG March 18, 2003.
- United Nations Convention against Transnational Organized Crime Additional Protocol to Prevent, Suppress and Punish Trafficking in Persons, Especially Women and Children (December 12, 2000)—RG March 18, 2003.
- United Nations Convention against Transnational Organized Crime Additional Protocol against the Smuggling of Migrants by Land, Sea and Air (November 5, 2000)—RG March 18, 2003.
- Optional Protocol to the Convention on the Rights of the Child on the Involvement of Children in Armed Conflict (March 25, 2000)—RG March 18, 2004.
- International Convention for the Suppression of Acts of Nuclear Terrorism (September 14, 2005)—RG May 8, 2012.
- Second Optional Protocol to the International Covenant on Civil and Political Rights, Aiming at the Abolition of the Death Penalty (December 15, 1989)—RG December 27, 2005.
- Optional Protocol to the International Covenant on Civil and Political Rights (December 16, 1966)—RG August 5, 2006.
- Convention on Cybercrime (November 23, 2001)—RG May 2, 2014.

---

48. Turkey also signed the Optional Protocol to the Convention on the Rights of the Child. This Protocol grants authorization to the UN Committee on the Rights of the Child to examine individual applications.

COUNCIL OF EUROPE CONVENTIONS

- The ECHR (November 4, 1950)—RG March 19, 1954.
- Protocol No. 6 to the Convention for the Protection of Human Rights and Fundamental Freedoms Concerning the Abolition of the Death Penalty (April 28, 1983)—RG July 1, 2003.
- Protocol No. 8 to the Convention for the Protection of Human Rights and Fundamental Freedoms (March 19, 1985).
- European Agreement Relating to Persons Participating in Proceedings of the ECtHR (March 5, 1996)—RG May 12, 2004.
- Convention for the Protection of Human Rights and Dignity of the Human Being with Regard to the Application of Biology and Medicine: Convention on Human Rights and Biomedicine (April 4, 1997)—RG April 20, 2004.
- European Convention for the Prevention of Torture and Inhuman or Degrading Treatment or Punishment (November 26, 1987)—RG March 2, 1988.
- Protocol No. 1 to the European Convention for the Prevention of Torture and Inhuman or Degrading Treatment or Punishment (November 4, 1993)—RG April 10, 1997.
- Protocol No. 2 to the European Convention for the Prevention of Torture and Inhuman or Degrading Treatment or Punishment (November 4, 1993)—RG April 10, 1997.
- Criminal Law Convention on Corruption (January 27, 1999)—RG January 20, 2004.
- Civil Law Convention on Corruption (November 4, 1999)—RG April 24, 2003.
- Convention on Laundering, Search, Seizure and Confiscation of the Proceeds from Crime (November 8, 1990)—RG June 22, 2004.
- The European Convention on Extradition (December 13, 1957)—RG November 26, 1959.
- Second Additional Protocol to the European Convention on Extradition (March 17, 1978)—RG May 21, 1991.
- The European Convention on Mutual Assistance in Criminal Matters (April 20, 1959)—RG October 16, 1968.
- Additional Protocol to the European Convention on Mutual Assistance in Criminal Matters (March 17, 1978)—RG May 26, 1987.
- Convention on the Transfer of Sentenced Persons (March 21, 1983)—RG April 7, 1987.
- European Convention on the International Validity of Criminal Judgments (May 28, 1970)—RG March 13, 1977.
- European Convention on the Transfer of Proceedings in Criminal Matters (May 15, 1972)—RG March 13, 1977.
- The European Convention on the Suppression of Terrorism (January 27, 1977)—RG March 26, 1981.
- Council of Europe Convention on the Prevention of Terrorism (May 16, 2005)—RG January 13, 2012.
- European Social Charter (October 18, 1961)—RG July 14, 1989.
- European Convention on the Exercise of Children's Rights (January 25, 1996)—RG February 1, 2001.

- Convention for the Protection of the Architectural Heritage of Europe (October 3, 1985)—RG April 20, 1989.
- Convention on the Conservation of European Wildlife and Natural Habitats (September 19, 1979)—RG February 20, 1984.
- European Convention on the Protection of the Archaeological Heritage (Revised) (January 16, 1992)—RG August 8, 1999.
- Anti-Doping Convention (November 16, 1989)—RG October 12, 1993.
- European Convention on Spectator Violence and Misbehavior at Sports Events and in Particular at Football Matches (August 19, 1985)—RG January 26, 1990.[49]
- Protocol No. 7 to the Convention for the Protection of Human Rights and Fundamental Freedoms, as Amended by Protocol No. 11 (November 22, 1984)—RG March 25, 2016.
- Additional Protocol to the European Convention on Extradition (October 15, 1985)—RG May 5, 2016.
- Second Additional Protocol to the European Convention on Mutual Assistance in Criminal Matters (November 8, 2001)—RG May 5, 2016.
- Third Additional Protocol to the European Convention on Extradition (October 11, 2010)—RG May 5, 2016.
- Fourth Additional Protocol to the European Convention on Extradition (September 20, 2012)—RG May 5, 2016.
- Council of Europe Convention on Preventing and Combating Violence Against Women and Domestic Violence RG-(March 8, 2012) (*infra,* paragraph 319).

II. National Sources

53. Turkish criminal law is based on social values. These values are called substantive sources. The principle of natural law influences the positive rules of law, which are valid for the political interest groups and for the government. Criminal law restricts the fundamental rights of individuals. Therefore, this restriction should be defined as clearly as possible. This principle is called, the certainty of the sources or *lex certa.*

54. Direct Sources of Criminal Law. In Turkish criminal law, the Constitution, international treaties and acts passed by the TBMM are direct sources of criminal law. Presidential decrees are issued on matters related to the executive power shall not be source for criminal law (Article 104/17, AY). Repealed governmental decrees (Decree in Power or Act (*Kanun Hükmünde Kararname,* KHK)) that were later ratified by the parliament and thus had the force of law, as well as administrative decisions were not considered sources of criminal law (repealed Article 91, AY).

The Constitution governs the general principles of criminal law and defines the boundaries of personal freedoms. No act can be contrary to the Constitution.

49. Three additional Protocols to the European Convention on Human Rights have not yet been ratified. Protocols 4, 7 and 12.

Because criminal statutes can limit personal freedom, the principles of criminal law should be contained in the Constitution. Many principles of criminal law are laid down in the Constitution of 1982 as an effort to bring the Republic of Turkey to the level of Western European standards.

Acts are objective and non-personal statutes made by the Grand National Assembly and put into force after publication in the Official Gazette. However, some acts enacted between May 27, 1960, and September 12, 1982 were not voted in by the Grand National Assembly due to a temporary exception to making laws which existed at that time.

The most important direct source of the Turkish Penal Law is the new TCK. The special criminal laws are direct sources as well (Article 5, TCK). Presidential Decrees (previously named Decrees in Power of Act) are not a source of criminal law (*infra*, paragraph 65).

The criminal statutes of foreign countries are not applied directly, but if the TCK makes reference to a foreign criminal statute, it becomes a direct source for the Turkish judge pursuant to Article 19, of the TCK.[50]

55. The Act of 1928, No. 1322 contains the principles applicable to the enforcement of Acts.[51] An Act is in force within the whole of Turkey forty-five days after its publication in the Official Gazette, so long as there is no provision in the act itself providing otherwise. Some criminal acts are in effect for certain periods of time only. If there is no designated time period, the act is in force for an unlimited period of time.

56. Indirect Sources of Criminal Law. In Turkish Law, customary law, morality, the judgments of the courts and doctrine are indirect sources of law; these cannot create criminal penalties and sanctions.[52] However, these indirect sources can be regarded as a (ground of) justification: for example, if custom allows taking some apples from a tree, it is not considered theft.[53] However, if there is a clear reference to a customary law in a criminal statute, then the customary law is considered a source of criminal law (*infra* paragraph 145).

57. In Turkish criminal law, Judgments of Unification of Opinions from the Different Court of Cassation Decisions (*içtihadı birleştirme kararı,* in other words, the

---

50. If the crime is committed in a foreign country, the law of the place where the crime was committed is considered a source for the Turkish court (Art. 10a, repealed TCK). According to this 1991 rule, the punishment imposed by the Turkish court cannot be more severe than the punishment allowed by the law of the foreign country in question. Article 10a of the repealed code has been taken to the new code as Art. 19 (*infra*, para. 92).
51. This statute is repealed by Art. 231 of KHK 703, dated Jul. 2, 2018, but shall be applied until a new regulation by a presidential decree is issued (Provisional Art. 15 of KHK 703).
52. M. Kaban et al., *Yargıtay Ceza Genel Kurulu Kararları*, Ankara: Adalet Yayınevi, 2001. O. Şirin (ed.), *Yargıtay Ceza Genel Kurulu Kararları Kapsamında Yeni Ceza Mevzuatının Yorumu*, 2008.
53. Cass. CGK Oct. 26, 1987, E. 6-406, K. 499; B. Öztürk & M.R. Erdem, *Uygulamalı Ceza Hukuku ve Güvenlik Tedbirleri Hukuku*, TCK Değişikliklerine Göre Yenilenmiş 20. Baskı, Ankara 2020, Seçkin Yayınları, p. 70.

united decisions of the Court of Cassation) have the effect of a binding act. According to Article 45, of the Act of the Court of Cassation, No. 2797, courts must apply the united decision of the Court of Cassation to cases with similar facts.

Since July 2016 the regional courts of appeal are rendering decisions related to legal problems in their regions. There are some differences between these courts concerning the application of the same legal provision. Therefore, a chamber of the High Court of Cassation has been appointed to check such differences and rule about the unification of deviances (Statute about Courts, Act No. 5235, Article 35/2, as amended by KHK 696, approved by Act No. 7079, dated February 1, 2018) (*infra*, paragraph 558).

In order to be able to be promoted to a higher position in their profession, judges must earn points from decisions that are approved by the High Court (*kanun yolu değerlendirme notu;* Article 28, Judges and Public Prosecutors Act, No. 2802, as amended by Act No. 6723, dated July 1, 2016). Because of this regulation, the decisions of the regional appeal courts and the Court of Cassation are very important for Turkish judges.

58. General Criminal Law. The TCK and Code of Penal Procedure govern General Criminal Law.

59. Specific Criminal Law. Specific criminal law (*infra*, paragraph 252) is composed for instance of the Criminal Law for State Officials (*infra*, paragraph 187), Juvenile Criminal Law (*infra*, paragraph 358), Economic Criminal Law (*infra*, paragraph 257) and Environmental Criminal Law (*infra*, paragraph 255), the Military Penal Code (AsCK) (Act No. 1632, dated May 22, 1930), the Act on Turkish Armed Forces Discipline (Act No. 2013-6413) and the Code for Military Discipline Jurisdiction (for war-time) (Act No. 477, dated June 16, 1964; *infra*, paragraph 357). Although military courts were abolished in 2017, the aforementioned military statutes are still in force.[54]

---

54. F. Demirağ, *Türk Ceza Kanununun Genel Hükümleri Işığında Askeri Ceza Kanunu,* Seçkin, Ankara 2016; İ. Ergutekin, *Askeri Ceza Hukukunda Emre İtaatsizlik Fiilleri,* Seçkin, Ankara 2016.

Part I. Substantive Criminal Law

Chapter 1. General Principles of the Turkish Criminal Law

§1. The Principle of a State Governed by the Rule of Law

60. According to the Constitution, the Republic of Turkey is a democratic, secular and social state governed by the rule of law (Article 2, AY). This principle has two meanings in the application of criminal law. As a formal principle, the principle of a state governed by the rule of law prevents the misuse of criminal law. The principle of legality is derived from this principle.

As a substantive principle, the principle of a state governed by the rule of law determines the structure of the criminal statutes. Article 38, of the Constitution governs the formal side, and Article 17, AY regulates the substantive side of this principle; to wit: *No one shall be subjected to penalty or treatment incompatible with human dignity.*

61. Another important duty of the state governed by the rule of law is to secure domestic order. The state has *ius puniendi* over acts that have been committed in its territory. Without security and peace neither the single individual nor the society of free culture can flourish. Therefore, the state uses its power of punishing to maintain the rule of law.

§2. The Principle of Humanity

62. Under the principle of humanity, the human being is accepted as the main value in all legal affairs.[55] Human dignity and pride are sacred. The idea of equality also corresponds to the above concept (Article 10, AY). The free will of human beings should be protected. Torture is banned in accordance with this view (*infra*, paragraph 199).

---

55. K. İçel & K. Bayraktar, *Türk Ceza Hukukuna İlişkin Açıklamalar,* in Almanya Federal Cumhuriyeti Ceza Hukukuna Giriş, ed. H.H. Jescheck, İstanbul: Beta, 1989, p. 135; A. Gündüz, *Security and Human Rights in Europe, European Community Institute,* Istanbul: University of Marmara, 1994.

§3. The Principle of Legality

63. No one can be punished for an act that is not expressly defined by law as a crime. No one can be subject to punishment or measures of security (detained or committed to an institution or asylum) when not prescribed by law in force at the time that the alleged criminal act was committed. Also, no one shall be given a harsher penalty for an action than the penalty applicable at the time when the offense was committed.

The principle of legality (legality in the definition of crimes and legality in the definition of penalties) is the main rule in Turkish criminal law and is considered a basic element of criminal offense s (the Element of Law) (*infra*, paragraph 105). This rule is laid down in the current Constitution (Article 38, AY) as a protection of individuals of the state and is the basis of Article 2, TCK.

Accordingly, a crime can only be created by a statute at the level of a *law*, and this law should also regulate the penalty for such a crime. The president is empowered to issue presidential decrees; but not in the field of criminal law (Article 104/17, AY). The legislature must define every crime and its penalty as clearly[56] as possible in the statutes, and a judge can apply a law to an act only if it is exactly the same as the one defined in the law (*nullum crimen sine lege certa*). No one can be punished for a deed that had not been identified as a crime at the time of its commission (Article 7/1, TCK) (*nullum crimen sine lege praevia*). However, a milder statute shall be applied retroactively (*infra*, paragraph 74).

64. Development of The Principle of Legality. The principle of legality was adopted in the eighteenth century to prevent arbitrary judicial behavior. Therefore, an individual's act may not be prohibited or subject to punishment except under the conditions openly regulated by written and published legislation.

Islamic law, which identifies some crimes and punishment and also sets the limits of certain punishment, has a different outlook on the principle of legality. For *divine* crimes (i.e., crimes against God) as defined by the Koran, the principle of legality is applied in a strict sense. However, for crimes committed against individuals (worldly affairs), the judicial authority has the power to determine and inflict the punishment.[57]

---

56. Turkish Penal Code now regulates clearly the acts of the crime of fraudulent bankruptcy (Arts. 161, 162 TCK) (İ. Özgenç, *Türk Ceza Hukuku Genel Hükümler,* Gözden Geçirilmiş ve Güncellenmiş 10. Bası, Ankara, Seçkin, 2014, p. 113).
57. S. Dönmezer & E. Sahir (Bayraktar, Kiziroğlu, Zafer, Sınar, Önok, Erman), *Nazari ve Tatbiki Ceza Hukuku, Genel Kısım, Cilt I,* 14. Bası, İstanbul: DER Yayınları, 2016, n. 53; T. Demirbaş, *Ceza Hukuku Genel Hükümler*, 15. Baskı, Seçkin, Ankara 2020, p. 88; H. Hakeri, *Ceza Hukuku Genel Hükümler*, 21. Baskı, Adalet, Ankara 2017, p. 9; M. Koca & İ. Üzülmez, *Türk Ceza Hukuku Genel Hükümler*, 13. Baskı, Seçkin, Ankara 2020, p. 38; D. Soyaslan, *Ceza Hukuku Genel Hükümler*, 8. Baskı, Yetkin, Ankara 2018, p. 81.

The first Turkish constitutional act to consider the principle of legality is the Decree of *Tanzimat* of 1839. The 1924 Constitution does not explicitly mention this principle.[58] But the 1961 Constitution (Article 33) and the 1982 Constitution (Article 38, AY) do mention it.

65. Turkish criminal law is a written, positive law. In Turkish law, a crime can only be created by written Acts of the TBMM and put into effect accordingly. Therefore, in Turkish law a crime cannot be created, nor may the punishment be assessed, by the case law (*nullum crimen sine lege scripta*) and by a presidential decree (*supra*, paragraph 63).

66. Restrictive Interpretation of Criminal Statutes. For a perfect application of the principle of legality, the rules of interpreting statutes must also be applied strictly.[59] In cases where the meaning is explicitly explained by the wording of the statute, there is no problem. However, if the meaning of words needs to be interpreted, such an interpretation should, as a result of the principle of legality, be narrowly considered. The meaning of a word cannot be extended, and the field of punishment cannot be expanded. Interpretation should favor the accused. The rule is that the accused benefits from any doubt (*in dubio pro reo*).[60] To this end, analogy is explicitly prohibited by the Penal Code (Article 2/3, TCK). In the interpretation of penal norms, the intention and the motives of the legislation should be studied.[61] The legislator's aim cannot be expanded by verbal interpretations. However, in cases where the analogy benefits the accused, it can be accepted. Analogy is restricted only under the circumstances where the penal liability is expanded (Article 2/3, TCK) (*nullum crimen sine lege stricta*). Because of the restriction of analogy, legal provisions are not retroactive. The only exceptions to this rule are more lenient statutes.[62]

67. The principle of legality only covers the field of substantive criminal law. This rule is not strictly applied in administrative law and other related fields. However, protective and educational measures are also considered in the sphere of criminal penalties.

There are some petty offense s for which the law does not provide a penalty. Article 526, of the old TCK was the general rule applied to such cases. The new

58. S. Dönmezer & S. Erman, *Nazari ve Tatbiki Ceza Hukuku, Genel Kısım*, Cilt I (Bayraktar, Kiziroğlu, Zafer, Sınar, Önok, Erman), *Nazari ve Tatbiki Ceza Hukuku, Genel Kısım, Cilt I,* 14. Bası, İstanbul: DER Yayınları, 2016, p. 55.
59. B. Öztürk & M.R. Erdem, *Uygulamalı Ceza Hukuku ve Güvenlik Tedbirleri Hukuku,* TCK Değişiklikleri̇ne Göre Yenilenmiş 20. Baskı, Ankara 2020, Seçkin Yayınları, p. 71.
60. Cass. CGK May 5, 2015, 2015/141 K.; Cass. 7. CD Nov. 26, 2015, 2015/23404 K.; Cass. 8. CD Oct. 14, 2015, 2015/22764 K.
61. Cass. CGK Oct. 22, 1984: K. İçel & K. Bayraktar, *Türk Ceza Hukukuna İlişkin Açıklamalar,* in Almanya Federal Cumhuriyeti Ceza Hukukuna Giriş, ed. H.-H. Jescheck, İstanbul, Beta, 1989, p. 134.
62. A. Önder, *Ceza Hukuku Genel Hükümler*, Cilt 1, Beta, İstanbul, 1991, p. 112.

criminal justice system now foresees a special statute for misdemeanors (*Kabahatler Kanunu*, KK, Act No. 2005–5326), which shall be applied as a general provision if a statute openly refers to this law (Article 32/2, KK). The principle of legality in the field of misdemeanors is provided by this statute (Article 4, KK) but is not as strict as in the field of crimes.[63] The legislator may give a very open definition to a certain misdemeanor, while the executive consequently works out the details. However, the law itself must determine the sanction.[64]

There has been a debate in Turkish law about the authority of administrative sources to create crimes and punishment. According to Article 91, AY, fundamental and political rights cannot be regulated through presidential decrees; therefore, presidential decrees cannot create a crime. This principle is now openly stated by the Penal Code (Article 2/2, TCK); *"no criminal offense or penalty shall be created by any regulatory provision adopted by the administration."*

In this sense, although an act of a criminal nature cannot be created, unlawful conduct may nevertheless be prohibited. Administrative provisions are expected to regulate police and administrative enforcement entities. The Constitutional Court held that the Council of Ministers has the authority to set maximum and minimum limits on fines for tax violations that are provided by criminal law. On March 28, 1983, the Constitutional Court ruled by way of Decision No. 4/71 that the administrative organ could create crimes by administrative regulations. This decision was criticized, as it does not comply with Article 91/1, AY. The administrative organ is entitled to apply any measures that do not restrict freedoms. However, the administrative organ may declare crimes so long as the law provides for it.

The principle of legality does not affect the law of disciplinary punishment. However, it will be applied to the security measures (*infra*, paragraph 295) (Article 38, AY; Article 2/1, TCK).

§4. The Principle of Guilt

68. The principle of guilt is an important aspect in Turkish criminal law. No one can be punished if there is no intentional guilt that can be condemned by law; for some crimes, however, negligence suffices. In the past, objective liability was applicable, and only the negative result was considered for the outcome of the crime and thus at objective liability. Today, in addition to the negative results, the accused's initial motive or ill intent is considered to determine the existence of the crime (resulting or, objective liability). In other words, the existence of the individual's guilty mind is now an essential condition of criminal liability.

Only individuals can be held criminally liable for the offenses committed by legal persons (corporations, organizations and associations), in particular the individuals

63. Here we use the term *crimes* meaning both very serious crimes and petty offenses, as opposed to misdemeanors. We cannot use the term *felonies*, as the distinction between misdemeanors and felonies has been abandoned by the 2005 legislation (B. Akbulut, *Türk Ceza Kanunu ile Kabahatler Kanunu Genel Hükümlerinin Yaptırım Hükümleri Dışında Karşılaştırmalı Olarak İncelenmesi*, 2. Baskı, Adalet, Ankara 2014).
64. İ. Özgenç, *Türk Ceza Hukuku Genel Hükümler*, Gözden Geçirilmiş ve Güncellenmiş 10. Bası Ankara, Seçkin, 2014, p. 119.

who constitute or make up the representative organs of such entities. Legal persons cannot be punished with criminal penalties, but they may be subject to other types of sanctions such as security measures (*güvenlik tedbiri niteliğindeki yaptırımlar*) (Article 20/2, TCK) (*infra*, paragraph 295).[65]

69. Individual Responsibility. Article 38, AY provides that penal liability is personal, and it accordingly adopts the principle of guilt.[66] Ignorance of the law was not accepted as a defense according to the previous Penal Code (Article 44, repealed TCK). For perfect application of the principle of guilt, this provision had to be interpreted broadly. The current TCK adopted a new approach in this regard: the new version of Article 4/1, TCK states that ignorance of the criminal statues is not an excuse. However, there is one exception to this rule in the chapter about mistake: The person who made an unavoidable mistake about the unjustness of his deed shall not be punished (Article 30/4, TCK).

A person who is not guilty cannot be punished. Likewise, a perpetrator cannot be punished with a penalty that is disproportionate to the degree of his guilt for the offense (*infra*, paragraph 68). Guilt should be identified in terms of the particular act of the accused, but not according to his general life style and behavior.

§5. The Principles of Proportionality and Equality

70. Since 2001, the Constitution applies the principle of proportionality to determine whether limitations on fundamental principles are justified (Article 13, AY).

The principle of proportionality is now explicitly laid down in the Penal Code: "*Penalties and security measures to be imposed on the perpetrator shall be proportional to the gravity of his deed*" (Article 3/1, TCK).[67]

Accordingly, the punishment should be in proportion to the degree of guilt and the importance of the result or harm. In 1965, the old TCK had accepted a rule that reduced the punishment of the offenses committed through negligence by one-eighth (1/8) (Article 455, repealed TCK). The current TCK does not make *a scaling of negligence*, but rules that each offender shall be punished according to the degree of his guilt (Article 22/4, 5, TCK). If the offender victimized himself personally or his family through his negligent deed, he shall not be punished if the infliction of a sanction is unnecessary (Article 22/6, TCK).

65. B. Öztürk & M.R. Erdem, *Uygulamalı Ceza Hukuku ve Güvenlik Tedbirleri Hukuku*, TCK Değişikliklerine Göre Yenilenmiş, 20. Baskı, Ankara 2020, Seçkin Yayınları, p. 601.

66. T. Demirbaş, *Ceza Hukuku Genel Hükümler*, 15. Baskı, Seçkin, Ankara 2020, p. 61.

67. This provision also entails the principles of justice and equality. Some legal experts argue that the notion of gravity rather belongs to the determination of the sentence and should have been included in Art. 61 TCK (V.Ö. Özbek, TCK *İzmir şerhi, Türk Ceza Kanununun Anlamı, Genel Hükümler (Madde 1–75)*; G. Geçirilmiş, Genişletilmiş 4. Bası, Ankara, Seçkin, 2010, p. 88. There is a strong relation between the concept of unlawfulness *(Unrecht, haksızlık)* and the concept of crime. In cases of petty crimes *(Bagatelldelikte)*, the punishment has to be proportional to the injustice of the conduct. While determining the punishment, the framework of *insignificance* may be relevant. In applying the abstract norm to the concrete case, the practitioner should make an interpretation by utilizing the concept of insignificance to determine the content of unlawfulness (S. Özkan, *Ceza Hukukunda Önemsizlik*, Onikilevha, İstanbul 2018).

The Penal Procedure Code (Article 100/1, CMK) explicitly regulates the principle of proportionality concerning the investigative stage. Accordingly, if the relationship between the probable punishment and the deprivation of liberty were disproportionate, then the examining judge shall not order the arrest of the suspect. Similarly, for crimes punished only with a criminal fine or with imprisonment fewer than two years, pre-trial detention is not permitted (Article 100/4, CMK) (*infra,* paragraph 467). Additionally, the Penal Procedure Code has introduced the concept of *judicial control* to meet the requirement of proportionality (Article 109/1, CMK) (*infra,* paragraph 479).

71. In addition to the Constitution (Article 10, AY), the TCK now explicitly mentions the principle of equality (Article 3/2, TCK). The Constitutional Court applied this principle to abolish the regulation in Article 104/2, TCK, which had criminalized this kind of behavior and aggravating the punishment for consensual sexual intercourse with a minor who has attained the age of fifteen if the suspect was older than the victim by five years or more.[68]

68. Decision of the Constitutional Court dated Nov. 23, 2005, 103/89, RG: Feb. 25, 2006/26091.

Chapter 2. Application of Criminal Law

§1. Principles Concerning the Application of Criminal Law in Relation to Time

72. It is possible for criminal law to be amended after an offense has been committed and before the judgment is rendered. Under such circumstances, the problem arises as regards the time of applicability of criminal statutes.[69] The first rule is the immediate application of criminal statutes. However, a more lenient statute may be applied retroactively if it favors the accused. In cases where there have been several changes in criminal law provisions between the time of the commission of the crime and the time of the judgment, the court has to apply the most lenient provision of all (Article 7/2, TCK).

I. The Rule of Immediate Application

73. The legal provisions contained in acts in force are automatically applied as of the date of enforcement.[70]

Retroactive criminal law is constitutionally prohibited (Article 38, AY) (*infra*, paragraph 74). Furthermore, according to Article 7 of the TCK, no one can be punished for actions that are not identified as a *crime* at the time the action was performed. There must be a legal rule that identifies the act as a crime before it occurs. This rule underlines the prohibition on retroactive criminal law under Turkish Law.

There must be a legal provision defining the offense when the punishable act is committed, and the person should be informed and aware of the restricted and prohibited acts. Therefore, acts that fall outside such limits do not constitute crimes. It would be unfair and unjust to punish the accused for an act that was not legally defined as a crime when he carried it out.[71]

II. Retroactivity of the Milder Statute

74. If the provision of a law in force when a crime is committed differs from the provision of a law enacted after it was committed, the law that benefits the accused is applied and executed (Article 7/2, TCK).[72] Likewise, if a law that favors the

69. İ. Özgenç, *Türk Ceza Hukuku Genel Hükümler,* Gözden Geçirilmiş ve Güncellenmiş 10. Bası, Ankara, Seçkin, 2014, p. 120; T. Katoğlu, *Ceza Kanunlarının Zaman Yönünden Uygulanması;* Ankara: Seçkin, 2008.
70. Z. Hafızoğulları & M. Özen, *Türk Ceza Hukuku Genel Hükümler, Gözden Geçirilmiş, İşlenmiş ve Yenilenmiş 2.* Baskı, Ankara, US-A Yayıncılık, 2010, p. 29.
71. S. Dönmezer & S. Erman (I), *Nazari ve Tatbiki Ceza Hukuku,* Genel Kısım, Cilt I, (Bayraktar, Kiziroğlu, Zafer, Sınar, Önok, Erman), *Nazari ve Tatbiki Ceza Hukuku, Genel Kısım, Cilt I,* 14. Bası, İstanbul: DER Yayınları, 2016, n. 388; R. Murat Önok, Penal Law, in Introduction to Turkish Law, ed. *Tuğrul Ansay, Don Wallance Jr., Işık Önay,* Seventh Edition, Ch. 10, Kluwer, Deventer 2020, p. 211.
72. İ. Özgenç, *Türk Ceza Hukuku Genel Hükümler, Gözden Geçirilmiş ve Güncellenmiş* 10. Bası,

accused comes into force during a trial, then that criminal law shall be applied. However, if a procedural rule that applies in a case is abolished during the trial, and then the new procedural rule shall immediately apply in the case.

After June 1, 2005, when the TCK came into force, there were many disputes about the distinction and retroactive application of the milder statute, as all crime definitions and punishments in the repealed Penal Code had been amended by the new Code. Different legal reasoning led to the reversal of some judgments of the first instance courts, which caused significant delays in the criminal justice system.

The rules regarding *measures of security* were also immediately applicable under the same rules under the old Penal Code (Article 2/1, repealed TCK). The current Penal Code has a different approach as a result of ECHR case law: measures of security shall also be applied and executed retroactively if they are in favor of the accused (Article 7/1, TCK).

In cases where the Constitutional Court has annulled a criminal law, the annulment of this criminal law provision shall be applied retroactively, although the decisions of this court do not affect the past.[73]

75. Article 7/2 of the Penal Code is not applied to the amendments of acts that are not criminal law acts.[74] For example, administrative regulations of the Council of Ministers[75] do not have a force of law, and, therefore, Article 7/2, TCK does not apply.

However, if a *United Decision of the Court of Cassation* (*supra,* paragraph 57) is changed, this change in opinion does not have a retroactive effect.[76]

76. Scope of the Application of Criminal Law Concerning Time. According to the repealed TCK and at the time of coming into force, according to the TCK (Article 7/3, TCK), laws concerning the enforcement of penalties were not applied retroactively.[77] Meanwhile, the TCK has been amended. It now makes the following distinction. On the one hand, statutes related to suspended imprisonment (*infra*, paragraph 339), conditional release (*infra*, paragraph 617) and recidivism (*infra*, paragraph 307) shall be applied retroactively, if in favor of the accused. On the other hand, legal provisions related to the regime of enforcement (of a prison sentence) shall be applied immediately (Article 7/3, TCK).

The application of *temporary statutes* shall continue for crimes committed within the period when they were in force (Article 7/4, TCK).

Ankara, Seçkin, 2014, p. 123; N. Kaçak, *Sanık Lehine Kanunun Tespitine İlişkin Emsal İçtihatlar*, Ankara: Seçkin Yayınları, 2005.

73. 5. CD 9.3.1998, E. 1998/82, K. 854; YKD 24 (1998), 455; Cass. 3. CD Mar. 24, 2015 2015/10507 K; Cass. CGK Mar. 17, 2015 2015/49 K.; Cass. 6. CD Nov. 27, 2015 2015/45467 K.
74. A. Önder, *Ceza Hukuku Genel Hükümler*, Cilt 1, İstanbul, Beta, 1991, p. 153.
75. Cass. CGK Oct. 1, 1984, 7–424/290, YKD 1984/12, 1837.
76. Cass. IçBK Jun. 15, 1949/11: Official Gazette, Sep. 20, 1949; B. Öztürk & M. Ruhan Erdem, *Uygulamalı Ceza Hukuku ve Güvenlik Tedbirleri Hukuku,* TCK Değişikliklerine Göre Yenilenmiş 20. Baskı, Ankara 2020, Seçkin Yayınları, p. 149.
77. F. Yenisey & A. Nuhoğlu, *Ceza Muhakemesi Hukuku,* 6. Baskı, Seçkin, Ankara 2018, p. 84; S. Dönmezer & S. Erman (Bayraktar, Kiziroğlu, Zafer, Sınar, Önok, Erman), *Nazari ve Tatbiki Ceza Hukuku, Genel Kısım, Cilt I,* 14. Bası, İstanbul: DER Yayınları, 2016, n. 406.

Procedural rules are automatically applicable after their enactment. However, after the amendment of the old Penal Procedure Code of November 18, 1992, by Act No. 3842 (RG December 1, 1992), there was a discussion about the retroactive application of the procedural statutes. Act No. 3842 introduced new rights for the accused, such as mandatory legal representation for an accused under the age of 18 (Article 138, CMUK), and it forbade certain methods of investigation (Article 135a, CMUK). When this new law came into effect, there were some cases at the Court of Cassation for appellate review. The Military Court of Cassation decided on December 10, 1992,[78] that new amendments in the Code of Penal Procedure were related to the public order and were regulations in favor of the accused. Therefore, new articles are to be applied to offenses committed before the law was enacted.[79]

If a crime was previously prosecuted directly by the prosecutor, but a new law makes this crime prosecutable only upon the complaint, the new law shall not apply until the new time limit for putting forward a complaint under the new law has expired.

With respect to the statute of limitations period, an act that favors the accused was applicable only during a pending trial, according to the Old Code of Application of Penal Code, Article 22. The new criminal justice system takes a different approach. A milder criminal statute is also retroactively applicable, even if there is a final judgment and the sentence is being enforced. In that case, the court of the first instance has to decide which statute is the *milder* or more lenient one in that specific case. While judging again, the court does not take into account the provisions of the statute of limitations regarding prosecution (Act on the Application of the TCK 2004–5252, Article 9/4). By contrast, the rules concerning the interruption of the statute of limitations and its lapsing (*infra,* paragraph 407) should be applied immediately.

III. The Time of Commission of the Crime

77. The time when the crime is committed plays an important role in deciding which rule favors the suspect. There are no difficulties for instant crimes that is, where the action and the result occur at the same time. However, with crimes where the action and the result are separate, the crime is committed at the time when the action is committed, and not at the time of the result.[80] An example of this is when an offender wounds an individual who later dies because of the act (at a different time and place).

In case of *ongoing, continuing offenses*, such as carrying a weapon, or a *chain of crimes*, for instance an employee of a bank who regularly steals some of the bank's

78. E. 1992/119, K. 1992/140; Cass. 4. CD Feb. 16, 2011, 2011/1865 K.; Cass. 12. CD Sep. 23, 2011, 2011/1740 K.
79. The General Assembly of the Court of Cassation has a different view of this legal point: if the amendment has been made after the Court of First Instance has ruled, the appellate court is not entitled to retroactively apply procedural rules in favor of the accused (CGK Apr. 12, 1993, E. 93/6–62, K. 93/94).
80. M. Koca & İ. Üzülmez, *Türk Ceza Hukuku Genel Hükümler,* Gözden Geçirilmiş ve Güncellenmiş 13. Baskı, Ankara, Seçkin, 2020, p. 80.

cash (Article 43, TCK), the offense is considered to be committed at the time of the termination of the ongoing act or the very last act. This determines the venue of the court as well (Article 12/2, CMK).[81]

IV. Determining the Milder Statute

78. A new law that abolishes a crime or results in more lenient penalties favors the accused.[82] But if the new law entails a shorter period of punishment than the old law, the former is also considered a more lenient statute.[83]

Formerly, if there were several punishments, such as a fine and imprisonment, contained in an old law, as well as others in a new law, the Court of Cassation would extract from each law the rules most favorable to the accused. Thus, favorable rules in different legislation were all applicable.[84] The Court of Cassation, however, changed its opinion in 1999 and since then regards the favorable total outcome of the consequences between two final judgments.

According to the provisions of the old Penal Procedure Code, if there was an amendment of the law in favor of the convict after the conviction had become final and enforceable, the prosecutor had to request the Court of Cassation of the first instance to reopen the case and decide on this matter and clear up the uncertainty (Article 402, repealed CMUK). The current criminal justice system has transferred this legal rule into the Code on Execution of Penalties and Security Measures, Act 2004–5275, Article 98: "*If there are changes in criminal law statutes in favor of the convicted individual or there are some legal problems related to the interpretation of conviction, then the court which had rendered the disputed judgment shall reopen the file and reconsider*" (Article 98/1, CGIK).

---

81. A. Önder (I), *Ceza Hukuku Genel Hükümler*, Cilt 1, İstanbul, Beta, 1991, p. 141; V.Ö. Özbek et al., *Türk Ceza Hukuku Genel Hükümler*, Ankara, Seçkin, 7. Baskı, 2016, p. 141; However, *Koca and Üzülmez* have a different approach for *chain of crimes* and argue that each crime committed during this period should be considered separately (M. Koca & İ. Üzülmez, *Türk Ceza Hukuku Genel Hükümler*, Gözden Geçirilmiş ve Güncellenmiş 13. Baskı Ankara, Seçkin, 2020, p. 82).
82. N. Centel, H. Zafer & Ö. Çakmut, *Türk Ceza Hukukuna Giriş,* 10. Bası, İstanbul, Beta, 2017, p. 101.
83. B. Öztürk & M.R. Erdem, *Uygulamalı Ceza Hukuku ve Güvenlik Tedbirleri Hukuku,* TCK Değişikliklerine Göre Yenilenmiş 20. Baskı, Ankara 2020, Seçkin Yayınları, p. 150; A. Önder (I), *Ceza Hukuku Genel Hükümler*, Cilt 1, İstanbul: Beta, 1991, p. 145.
84. Cass. CGK May 25, 1999, E. 1999/10–133, K. 1999/142; Cass. 13. CD Oct. 15, 2014, 2014/28213 K; Cass. 22. CD Apr. 15, 2015, 2015/132 K; Cass. 2. CD Oct. 13, 2014, 2014/23073 K.

§2. Principles Concerning the Application of Criminal Law in Relation to Place

I. Territorial Principle

79. A crime may be committed on or outside Turkish territory. Because of growing international interactions, human beings are more mobile. Accordingly, their crimes have become international.[85]

Turkish laws shall be applied for crimes committed within the territory of Turkey.[86] The crime shall also be considered as *committed within the territory of Turkey* if the criminal behavior was totally or partly conducted in Turkish territory, or if the result of action outside of Turkey had some results within Turkish territory (Article 8/1, TCK).[87]

A Turkish citizen sentenced in a foreign country for a crime committed in Turkey may be retried in Turkey. A foreigner (or *heimatlos*) who has been sentenced in a foreign country for a crime committed in Turkey according to local legislation may be tried in Turkey (*infra*, paragraph 84).

The TCK adopts the principle of territoriality as a general rule, with a few exceptions. In order not to let criminals go unpunished, a crime committed outside Turkish territory, by foreigners or against them, will be prosecuted (*aut dedere aut judicare*) and punished according to the TCK.

80. In terms of geography, the application of TCK reflects the system of territoriality as a basic rule. The land within the frontiers is considered a country's territory. The territorial application of criminal law comprises the rivers, lakes and the internal waters of the State. According to Act No. 2674 of May 20, 1982, the internal waters of Turkey extend six miles out to sea.

Some provisions of the Penal Code are related to the *fiction of territory*. Crimes are considered committed in the territory of Turkey when they are perpetrated in: (a) Turkish territory, air space and internal waters; (b) on board a ship or an airplane that flies under the Turkish flag, when that ship or airplane is in international waters or airspace; (c) in Turkish warships and military airplanes, if they are actually in international waters or international airspace; and (d) within the Turkish continent shelf, in or against the platforms within Turkish economic space (Article 8/2, TCK).[88]

---

85. M. Sur, *Uluslararası Hukukun Esasları*, İstanbul, Beta, 2007; F. Yenisey, *Milletlerarası Ceza Hukukunda Yeni Gelişmeler,* in *Ceza Hukuku Günleri*, İstanbul, 1998, p. 47; E.İ. Külçür, *Ceza Hukukunda Yer Bakımından Uygulama,* On İki Levha, İstanbul 2017.
86. K. İçel & S. Donay, *Karşılaştırmalı ve Uygulamalı Ceza Hukuku*, 2. Bası, İstanbul, Filiz, 1993, p. 157. For explanations of the meaning and the evaluation of the concept of sovereignty, *see*; A. Gündüz, *Eroding Concept of National Sovereignty: The Turkish Example*, *Marmara Journal of European Studies* 1, nos. 1–2 (1991): 99–154. M.R. Önok. *Penal Law*, in Introduction to Turkish Law, ed. *Tuğrul Ansay, Don Wallance Jr., Işık Önay,* Seventh Edition, Ch. 10, Kluwer, Deventer 2020, p. 212.
87. T. Demirbaş, *Ceza Hukuku Genel Hükümler*, 15. Baskı, Seçkin, Ankara 2020, p. 147; V.Ö. Özbek et al., *Türk Ceza Hukuku Genel Hükümler*, Ankara, Seçkin, 7. Baskı, 2016, p. 145.
88. N. Centel, H. Zafer & Ö. Çakmut, *Türk Ceza Hukukuna Giriş*, 10. Bası, İstanbul, Beta, 2017, p. 154;

81. A crime can be described as international[89] when it is committed in more than one state. The Court of Cassation decided in a case (in which an airplane was hijacked from Bulgaria) that the crime was committed in the state where the act was committed. This ruling was included in the Penal Code in 2004 (Article 8/1, TCK): Partly or wholly conducted actions in Turkey and actions in a foreign country causing any result in Turkey shall be considered as a crime committed in Turkey, even if they are attempted. For example, a parcel containing explosives, which is addressed to a receiver in Turkey but discovered and seized in Germany, shall be considered as a crime committed in Turkey.

II. The Principle of Personality

A. *The Active Principle of Personality*

82. The state follows its citizens in foreign countries. The Turkish state punishes crimes committed against its citizens and crimes committed against the Turkish State. In Turkish criminal law, the principle of personality[90] is not applied as a single rule. It is also supported by other principles.[91]

83. Civil servants who carry out a duty in the name of the Turkish Republic in a foreign country shall be tried in Turkey for crimes committed within their capacity as civil servants, even if they had been tried and convicted there (Article 10, TCK).

84. If a Turkish citizen commits a crime outside Turkey that requires imprisonment for more than one year (previously this was three years), upon his return to Turkey he will automatically be prosecuted by the public prosecutor at the lower level of the punishment if the imprisonment is furnished with upper and lower levels (Article 11/1, TCK).

If the crime is punished by imprisonment for less than one year, the prosecution may be initiated upon the complaint of the injured party or the foreign government. The complaint must be filed within six months after the suspected Turkish citizen returned to Turkish territory (Article 11/2, TCK).

If a citizen commits a crime outside Turkey; he will be tried in Turkey (Article 11, TCK) if the act is considered a crime according to Turkish aw.[92]

K. İçel & S. Donay, *Karşılaştırmalı ve Uygulamalı Ceza Hukuku,* 2. Bası, İstanbul, Filiz, 1993, p. 158.

89. İ. Özgenç, *Türk Ceza Hukuku Genel Hükümler, Gözden Geçirilmiş ve Güncellenmiş* 10. Bası, Ankara, Seçkin, 2014, p. 871.
90. V.Ö. Özbek et al., *Türk Ceza Hukuku Genel Hükümler*, Ankara, Seçkin, 7. Baskı, 2016, p. 154.
91. K. İçel & S. Donay, *Karşılaştırmalı ve Uygulamalı Ceza Hukuku,* 2. Bası, İstanbul, Filiz, 1993, p. 159.
92. According to the repealed Penal Code, if the act was a crime in Turkey, but not in the country where it was committed, the perpetrator could not be punished in Turkey (Art. 10a, repealed TCK). The

B. The Passive Principle of Personality (Principle of Protection)

85. The state naturally protects itself. Articles 12 and 13 of the new TCK lay down the principle of self-protection.

86. Crimes Committed by a Foreigner in a Foreign Country against Turkey. A foreigner in a foreign country who commits a crime other than those mentioned in Article 13, against Turkey, which entails punishment, restricting liberty for a minimum period of one year under Turkish law, shall be punished in accordance with the TCK, if the offender is present in Turkey. The prosecution can be made upon request (*istem*) of the Minister of Justice (Article 12/1, TCK).

87. Crimes Committed by a Foreigner in a Foreign Country against a Turkish Citizen or Legal Entity. A foreigner in a foreign country who commits a crime other than one mentioned in Article 13, against a Turkish citizen or a legal person founded under Turkish laws, and which entails punishment restricting liberty for a minimum period of one year under Turkish law, shall be punished according to the TCK if the offender is present in Turkey (Article 12/2, TCK). The prosecution can be made upon request of the Minister of Justice (Article 12/1, TCK). Act No. 2014-6545 abolished the requirement of the request of the Minister of Justice for crimes committed abroad related to bribery (Article 252, TCK) or trading with influence (Article 255, TCK). The legislator's objective was to ensure an efficient prosecution of bribing foreign officials in a foreign country (Article 12/5, TCK) (*infra*, paragraph 231).

88. Crimes committed by a foreigner in a foreign country against a foreigner. If the victim of a crime committed outside of Turkey is a foreigner, the offender will be prosecuted in Turkey at the request of the Minister of Justice, provided that the punishment for the act is not less than three years of imprisonment according to the Turkish law and that there is no extradition treaty between Turkey and the country concerned, or that extradition was refused by the government of the territory where the crime was committed or by the state where the offender is a citizen (Article 12/3, TCK).

III. The Principle of Universality

89. The Penal Code has adopted the principle of universality, taking into consideration certain types of crimes (Article 13, TCK).

The following serious crimes committed by a Turkish citizen or a foreigner in a foreign country shall be prosecuted ex officio (Article 13/1-a, TCK): Genocide, crimes against humanity (Articles 76, 77, TCK), smuggling of immigrants and

---

current Penal Code contains a different regulation in this regard, and now there is a border of punishment that cannot be exceeded; this border is the high level of the punishment foreseen by the foreign criminal provision (Art. 19, TCK).

human trafficking (Articles 79, 80, TCK). Additionally, some serious crimes committed by a Turkish citizen or a foreigner in a foreign country against a Turkish citizen shall be prosecuted ex officio (Article 13/1-b, TCK): (a) crimes against the symbols of the sovereignty of the state and crimes against the reputation of its organs (*infra*, paragraph 246), (b) crimes against the security of the state (*infra*, paragraph 247), (c) crimes against the constitutional order and the well-functioning of this order (*infra*, paragraph 248), (d) crimes against the national defense (*infra*, paragraph 249), (e) crimes against state secrets and spying (*infra*, paragraph 250), (f) crimes against the relationships with foreign countries (*infra*, paragraph 251).

The following serious crimes committed by a Turkish citizen or a foreigner in a foreign country shall be prosecuted in Turkey upon the request of the Minister of Justice (Article 13/2, TCK): (1) torture (Articles 94–95, TCK), (2) intentional pollution of the environment (Article 181, TCK), (3) production and trafficking of narcotic substances (Article 188, TCK) and promoting the consumption of narcotic substances (Article 190, TCK), (4) counterfeiting money (Article 197 TCK), production of and trading with the material used for the production of money and valuable seals (Article 200, TCK) and counterfeiting government seal (Article 202, TCK), (5) prostitution (Article 227, TCK), (6) hijacking or seizure of transport vehicles (Article 223/2,3, TCK) or damaging such vehicles (Article 152, TCK).

IV. Enforcement of Foreign Judgments and *Ne Bis in Idem*

90. Judgments delivered by a foreign state have a limited validity compared to judgments of Turkish courts. Foreign judgments shall be taken into account and under some circumstances shall bar a new trial in Turkey (*ne bis in idem*). Foreign judgments have different effects in Turkey according to the circumstances.

If anybody (a Turkish citizen or foreigner) commits a crime in Turkey and is adjudicated in a foreign country, the judgment of the foreign court has no legal value in Turkey: there shall be a new trial in Turkey (Article 9, TCK) (*supra,* paragraph 79).

Crimes committed by a civil servant in a foreign country shall be retried in Turkey, even if there has been a conviction (Article 10, TCK).

If a Turkish citizen commits a crime in a foreign country and has not been tried there, he shall be tried in Turkey. However, if there has been a final judgment rendered against him in the foreign country, there shall be no second trial in Turkey, if he is present in Turkey (Article 11/1, TCK). For the prosecution of crimes requiring imprisonment of less than one year, there must be a complaint (Article 11/2, TCK).

A foreigner in a foreign country who commits a crime other than those mentioned in Article 13, against Turkey, which entails punishment, restricting liberty for a minimum period of one year under Turkish law, shall be punished under the TCK if the offender is present in Turkey. The prosecution can be made upon request of the Minister of Justice (Article 12/1, TCK). In cases where the foreigner had been convicted in a foreign country, the Minister of Justice may request a new trial in Turkey (Article 12/4, TCK).

A foreigner in a foreign country who commits a crime other than those mentioned in Article 13, against a Turkish citizen or a legal person founded according to Turkish laws, and which entails punishment restricting liberty for a minimum period of one year under Turkish law, shall be punished under the TCK if the offender is present in Turkey (Article 12/2, TCK). The prosecution can be made upon request of the Minister of Justice (Article 12/1, TCK).

If the victim of a crime committed outside of Turkey is a foreigner, the offender will be prosecuted in Turkey at the request of the Minister of Justice, provided the punishment for the act is not less than three years of imprisonment according to the Turkish law, and that there is no extradition treaty between Turkey and the country concerned, or that extradition was refused by the government of the territory where the crime was committed or by the state where the offender is a citizen (Article 12/3, TCK).

Those who commit any of the crimes listed under Article 13 of TCK, except those crimes mentioned in Article 13/2 TCK, will, at the request of the Minister of Justice, be retried in Turkey even if the offender had previously been convicted in a foreign country.

Cases of counterfeiting foreign currency and bribing foreign officials shall be prosecuted ex officio (Article 252/10, TCK) (*infra,* paragraph 231).

There is always a new trial upon the request of the Minister of Justice in Turkey for crimes committed abroad mentioned in Article 13/3, TCK, even if the foreign judgment was a conviction or an acquittal and the principle of *ne bis in idem* does not apply.

91. Ne bis in idem. Under the previous Penal Code, there was no written law regarding second prosecutions in Turkey concerning Turkish citizens sentenced for a crime committed in a foreign country (Article 5, repealed TCK). Consequently, there was no possibility for an individual to be retried in Turkey. In addition, the decisions of the Court of Cassation demonstrate full acceptance of the *ne bis in idem* principle, except in cases of drug smuggling from Turkey to foreign countries.

The Penal Code now openly states that a judgment rendered in a foreign country constitutes an obstacle to Turkish prosecution (Articles 11/1, 12/1, TCK); exceptions to this rule are mentioned above (*supra*, paragraph 90).

V. Mutual Assistance in Criminal Matters

A. *Problems Related to the Application of Foreign Criminal Law in Turkey*

92. In Turkish Criminal Law, crimes committed outside Turkey make up a special category, and the development in this field began in 1965. Article 18/1 of the repealed Code on Enforcement of Punishments had provided that a foreigner sentenced in Turkey was liable to serve his sentence in his own country if the principle of reciprocity and the execution of the full sentence were guaranteed.

In 1984, Act No. 3002 (which was repealed in 2016; *infra*, paragraph 96) abolished the above-mentioned regulation and substituted it with a larger act: the judgments of foreign countries would need to be applied in Turkish prosecutions. To this end the procedure contained in the act is that: The factual findings of the foreign judgment were considered final. Upon this, the Turkish Court crafted a new Turkish judgment and rendered a punishment according to the TCK that would be executed in Turkey. However, the final punishment could not be more severe than the upper-level punishment as foreseen in the law of the foreign country where the crime had been committed (Article 19/1, TCK). The foreign judgment was still valid from the perspective of that foreign country. Foreigners who had committed crimes in Turkey and had been sentenced by a Turkish Court could serve the sentence in their own countries under the condition of reciprocity. Act No. 6706 on International Legal Cooperation in Criminal Matters introduced new legal concepts for transfer of prisoners (*infra*, paragraph 96).

93. Regulations in the Repealed Penal Code. In 1991, Article 10(a) was taken from the 1989 Draft Penal Code and added to the now-repealed TCK. According to this regulation, if a Turkish citizen or a foreigner committed a crime in a foreign country and was subject to Turkish criminal jurisdiction according to the regulations of the First Book, Part I of the repealed TCK, then the law favoring the accused was applicable. The Turkish judge had to choose the more lenient of the Turkish Code and the code of the place where the crime was committed.

The provisions of Article 10a of the repealed Penal Code were not applied to crimes that had been committed against and had damaged the Turkish Republic.

The second exception held that if the law of the place where the crime was committed infringes Turkish public order or violates Turkey's international obligations, that law would not be applied in Turkey. In Article 10a, the words *public order* meant the basic principles of Turkish procedural law and the basic principles of Turkish Criminal Law. For example, if there were an international agreement where a principle of Islamic law favoring the accused had been foreseen, the foreign rule would not be applied in Turkey.

94. Provisions in the Penal Code. The current Penal Code simplified[93] the above-mentioned provision. Turkish courts have now to consider the upper level of the punishment in the Penal Code of the country where the crime has been committed, and the punishment in the Turkish judgment shall not exceed this limit (Article 19/1, TCK). This consideration does not apply if the crime was committed against the security or to the disadvantage of Turkey, or against the interests of a Turkish citizen or a legal person formed under Turkish Law (Article 19/2, TCK).

B. The Act on Judicial Cooperation in Criminal Matters

95. The Act on International Legal Cooperation in Criminal Matters, promulgated in 2016, Act No. 6706, was published in the Official Gazette on May 5, 2016. This Act regulates the classical methods of international judicial cooperation, such as extradition and legal assistance, as well as modern methods of international criminal law, such as transfer of investigation and prosecution, transfers of enforcement on sentences, and transfer of sentenced persons (*infra*, paragraph 96):

93. İ. Özgenç, *Türk Ceza Hukuku Genel Hükümler,* Gözden Geçirilmiş ve Güncellenmiş 10. Bası, Ankara, Seçkin, 2014, p. 912.

(a) *General provisions.* Except for the international agreements on judicial cooperation in criminal matters to which Turkey is a party and the provisions of the TCK, this act shall regulate the procedure and principle of international judicial cooperation in criminal matters. The Ministry of Justice, which is the central authority, is charged with the implementation of this Act in conjunction with judicial authorities (Article 2, Act No. 6706). The central authority shall decide on excepting the request of foreign states and give consent to the use of the information within the scope of cooperation by the requesting state and may accept the conditions stipulated by the state or grant the guarantee requested (Article 3, Act. No. 6706). If Turkey's sovereignty, national security, public order or other fundamental interests are violated, or the offense is a pure military offense, an offense related to the freedom of expression or a political offense, or if the person subject to request would be exposed to torture or ill treatment (if extradited) or his fundamental guarantees of the right to defense is not granted in the requesting state, the central authority may reject the request for judicial cooperation (Article 4, Act. No. 6706).

(b) *Mutual legal assistance in criminal matters.* Mutual legal assistance in criminal matters is one of the oldest methods of International criminal law. Act No. 6706 regulates legal assistance from the aspect of Turkish judicial authorities (Article 7, Act No. 6706) and the point view of request received from judicial authorities separately (Article 8, Act No. 6706). The scope of legal assistance covers witness hearing, questioning of a suspect or accused by the judge, collection of evidence by search and seizure and all related proceedings conducted during a criminal procedure. Turkish law applies, in particular, Act No. 6706 and in cases where there is no regulation on the related matter, the provisions of the Turkish Procedure Code (Article 5, Act No. 6706).

There is a modern regulation permitting legal assistance through audiovisual communication techniques (Article 9, Act No. 6706). During the execution of a foreign request on audiovisual technique Turkish judicial authorities shall be present and observe that the principles of Turkish law are not violated.

(c) *Extradition.* Turkey is a party to the European Convention on extradition. The punishment that the offender faces in the requesting state should be at least one year of imprisonment.[94]

Extradition[95] from Turkey to a foreign state is regulated in Article 10, of Act No. 6706. The old Penal Code did not foresee the extradition of a foreigner to a foreign state for political or related crimes.[96] The concept of *extradition* is defined with the word *"iade"* in Act No. 6706 instead of *"geri verme"* in the repealed Article 18 of TCK. If the conduct that is the subject of the request is not a *crime* under Turkish criminal law; is a crime of the nature of *freedom of expression crime* or a political

---

94. K. İçel & S. Donay, *Karşılaştırmalı ve Uygulamalı Ceza Hukuku*, 2. Bası, İstanbul, Filiz, 1993, p. 216.
95. E. Özgen, *Suçluların Geri Verilmesi*, Ankara, 1962, 3; N. Centel, H. Zafer & Ö. Çakmut *Türk Ceza Hukukuna Giriş*, İstanbul, 10. Bası, Beta, 2017, p. 183; A. Akın, *İnfaz Hukuku*, Seçkin, Ankara 2014, p. 374.
96. K. Bayraktar, *Siyasal Suç*, İstanbul, 1982.

or military crime; is a crime against the security of Turkey or a crime against a Turk or a legal person founded according to Turkish law; is a crime that does not fall under the jurisdiction of Turkey; or is such that the statute of limitations for prosecution has expired or there has been an amnesty or pardon; then Turkey shall not accept the request of extradition.

Extradition[97] of a Turkish citizen to a foreign state for a crime committed there is not allowed (Article 18, Act No. 6706).[98] Under Article 38, AY, Turkey does not extradite its citizens, except in response to its obligations of the Statute of the International Criminal Court (Article 11/1-a, Act No. 6706). Extradition of a Turkish citizen will be applicable if in the future Turkey would be party to the UN Convention.[99]

Under the requirements of Article 11: A foreigner who is under investigation or prosecution in a foreign country, or who has been convicted for an offense, committed in a foreign country may be extradited to the requesting state (Article 10/1, Act No. 6706). This formulation makes it clear that Turkish citizens and persons committing crimes in Turkey shall not be subject to extradition.[100] Although extradition is prohibited, modern methods of judicial cooperation in criminal matters for such individuals is applicable. For example, transfer of proceedings, transfer of investigation of prosecution (Article 23, Act No. 6706), or transfer of enforcement of sentences (Article 26, Act No. 6706) and besides extradition of convicted persons, transfer of inmates (Article 30, Act No. 6706) is possible.

A foreigner may not be deported without taking the opinion of the central authority during the process of extradition (Article 12, Act No. 6706).

Request for extradition by a foreign state shall be examined by the central authority, if not rejected, it will be sent to the Chief Public Prosecutors Office at the competent court of assizes. The competent court is where the person subject to extradition is present, and if the place where the person is present is not known, the Ankara Court of Assizes is competent (Article 15, Act No. 6706). The court is entitled to issue a provisional arrest order against the person concerned, if there is a strong suspicion that he has committed the offense (subject to the request of extradition) applying other procedural rules of CMK related to pre-trial arrest (Article 14, Act No. 6706). The court of assizes is also competent for ordering evidence protective measures such as search and seizure (Article 16, Act No. 6706).

There is a new regulation related to *extradition based on consent.* This is an expedited procedure upon the person's acceptance of the extradition, subject to the confirmation of the Central Authority (Article 17, Act No. 6706). The court of assizes shall examine the application for the extradition and if the request is accepted, it will make a decision ruling that there is no legal obstacle to the extradition (Article 19,

---

97. F. Yenisey, *Suçluların Geri Verilmesi ve Ceza İşlerinde Adli Yardımlaşma,* in *Adalet Dergisi*, 1981, sayı 4, p. 590.
98. E. Özgen, *Suçluların Geri Verilmesi*, Ankara, 1962, 3; H. Zafer & Ö. Çakmut, *Türk Ceza Hukukuna Giriş*, İstanbul, 10. Bası, Beta, 2018, p. 192; A. Akın, *İnfaz Hukuku,* Seçkin, Ankara 2014, p. 374.
99. M.E. Artuk et al., *Ceza Hukuku Genel Hükümler* Ankara, Yenilenmiş Gözden Geçirilmiş 11. Baskı Adalet, 2017, p. 1065.
100. M.E. Artuk, et al., *Ceza Hukuku Genel Hükümler* Ankara, Yenilenmiş Gözden Geçirilmiş 11. Baskı Adalet, 2017, p. 1065.

Act No. 6706). This ruling does not result in an obligation to extradite the individual; in contrast, the Central Authority may apply discretion upon such decisions to extradite or not to extradite. In cases, however, where the court of assizes rules that the extradition is not applicable in that given case, this decision will be binding for all authorities after ex-posting legal remedies. The intervention of parties to a pending extradition procedure is not permitted (Article 18/3, Act No. 6706). Upon the decision of the court of assizes deeming the extradition permissible, the Ministry of Justice shall ask the opinions of the ministries of Foreign Affairs and Interior and submit the decision of extradition for approval to the President of Turkey (Article 19/1, Act No. 6706).

The decision of the court of assizes may be appealed on law. This is the only court decision that goes directly to the Court of Cassation; all other decisions of trial courts are subject to fact and law appeal (*istinaf*) since July 20, 2016 (*infra*, paragraph 530).

The extradition procedure ends with the surrender of the person concerned (Article 20, Act No. 6706).

The second form of extradition is *Turkey's request for extradition* of a person located in a foreign state (Article 22, Act No. 6706). Judicial authorities of Turkey may request extradition of suspects for whom a pre-trial arrest warrant has been issued or an accused or a convict for an offense punishable by imprisonment for a minimum period of at least one year. The request shall be sent after being approved by the central authority to the foreign state (Article 22, Act No. 6706). If a foreign state requests extradition, the court of assizes of the area in which the requested person is present at the moment determines the citizenship of the requested person and the nature of the crime allegedly committed. The decision of the court may be contested by way of cassation at the Court of Cassation. If upheld, the decision of the Court *to not extradite* is final and the government has no discretion in this matter. If it is determined that the extradition request is acceptable, the government (i.e., the president of the state) still has discretion over whether the court decision shall indeed be executed or not (Article 13, Act No. 2016-6706). If the request is accepted, a warrant of arrest against the requested person may be issued, according to the related provisions of the Penal Procedure Code (Article 19, Act No. 2016-6706).

96. Modern Methods of International Judicial cooperation in Criminal methods, other than extradition. There are recent developments in international criminal law regarding judicial cooperation in criminal matters. Turkish law has recognized these new instruments and regulated them in Act No. 6706 under subtitles: (a) transfer of investigation or prosecution, (b) transfer of execution of sentences and (c) transfer of sentenced persons:

(a) *Transfer of investigation or prosecution.* Investigations or prosecutions pending in Turkey may be transferred to a foreign state, or investigations or prosecutions conducted for offenses committed in a foreign state may be taken over by Turkey (Article 23, Act No. 6706).

However, problems arise with the transfer of the Turkish prisoners to such Western European countries as Germany, Austria and Switzerland, on account of the *conditional release* regulation (*infra*, paragraph 617) under Turkish law. A crime committed in the Turkish territory punishable by a minimum of one year imprisonment may be investigated or prosecuted in a foreign country under certain circumstances: If a foreigner is in a foreign state and cannot be present in Turkey or his defense cannot be obtained through legal assistance, or a Turkish citizen, who habitually resides in a foreign state or the evidence is located there pending investigations or prosecutions may be transferred to that state (Article 24/1, Act No. 6706).

Taking over an investigation or prosecution pending in a foreign state is also possible if the office committed abroad requires a minimum imprisonment term of one year under Turkish law and shall not be lapsed or pardoned under Turkish law. The transfer request shall not be granted, if the person is not habitually resident in Turkey, not a Turkish national, if the offense has not been committed in the territory of the requesting state or if the person has been tried in Turkey for the same offense previously (Article 25, Act No. 6706).

(b) *Transfer of execution of sentences; international validity of judgments.* If an individual has already been convicted in a foreign country and but is not yet serving the imprisonment terms, execution of this sentence may be taken over to Turkey (Article 26, Act No. 6706). In such cases the Ankara Court of Assizes renders a decision about the term and the way of execution and duration of the imprisonment term contained in the final decision of a court of the foreign state (Article 26/5, Act No. 6706).

Convictions rendered by a Turkish court resulting in imprisonment terms may be transferred to foreign states for execution (Article 28, Act No. 6706).

(c) *Transfer of sentenced persons.* The third instrument of modern international legal cooperation is the transfer of inmates who are serving imprisonment terms. A sentenced person, who is currently serving his imprisonment term in a foreign country based on a final decision of a foreign court, may be transferred to Turkey (Article 30, Act No. 6706). Accordingly, a convict who has been sentenced by a Turkish court and is serving his term in Turkey may be transferred to a foreign state under this regulation (Article 32, Act No. 6706).

§3. Principles Concerning the Enforcement of Criminal Law in Relation to Persons

97. Criminal statutes apply either from the moment they are published in the official gazette or from the date specified in the law. However, there are some exceptions related to the inviolability of the president and the members of the Grand National Assembly. In addition to these exceptions, there is some immunity based on national and international public law.

I. Criminal Responsibility of the State President

98. The president of the state was immune from criminal liability within the parliamentary governmental system until 2018.[101] Within the presidential governmental system, however, the president has full criminal[102] responsibility for crimes he allegedly committed while he was holding office (even if his term is terminated) there are special procedures for investigation and prosecution (Article 105/6 AY). The criminal investigation may be initiated by a request submitted by an absolute majority of the total members of the Grand National Assembly. The Grand National Assembly shall debate this request within one month (the latest) and may decide to open the investigation through a three-fifth majority in the secret ballot (Article 105/1 AY). In cases where a decision to open an investigation is rendered, an investigative committee of fifteen members will be formed that submits its report to the president of the parliament within two months. This period may be extended only one time for two months (Article 105/2, AY). The report that will serve as an indictment if the president is impeached will be distributed to the members of the parliament within ten days and debated within ten days in the parliament after its distribution. If the two-third majority of the total numbers of vote in the secret ballot is in favor of the prosecution, the Grand National Assembly shall refer the case the Constitutional Court that acts as a court of the first instance under the title of "Supreme Court" (*Yüce Divan*) (*infra,* paragraph 364). The Supreme Court conducts a regular trial and renders its judgment within three months; if the trial is not completed within this period, a further period of three months will be granted. The trial must be absolutely completed within that time (Article 105/3, AY). The president cannot decide to hold elections (Article 105/4, AY) when an investigation is launched against him, and the term of the president shall cease if convicted (Article 105/5, AY).[103]

By contrast, presidents of foreign states are immune from Turkish jurisdiction.

99. There is no regulation that prevents a civil action against the President of the Republic, but executing the judgment would not be possible.

---

101. Article 105/2 of the Turkish Constitution stated that the president was inviolable (T. Demirbaş, *Ceza Hukuku Genel Hükümler*, 15. Baskı, Seçkin, Ankara 2020, p. 152). All presidential decrees would be signed by the prime minister and the ministers concerned unless otherwise provided by the Constitution and other laws. The prime minister and the ministers concerned were accountable for these decrees. No appeal could be made to any legal authority, including the Constitutional Court, against the decisions and orders signed by the President on his own initiative.

102. After the 2017-6771 amendments, the Constitution does not differentiate between crimes related to the office and personal crimes of the president. Prior to this change there was an obstacle to prosecution during the presidential term for offenses that have no official character, and prosecution was only possible after the presidential office had terminated (T. Demirbaş, *Ceza Hukuku Genel Hükümler*, 15. Baskı, Seçkin, Ankara 2020, p. 156; M. Koca & İ. Üzülmez, *Türk Ceza Hukuku Genel Hükümler*, Gözden Geçirilmiş ve Güncellenmiş 13. Baskı Ankara, Seçkin, 2020, p. 831).

103. D. Soyaslan, *Ceza Muhakemesi Hukuku,* 7. Baskı, Yetkin, Ankara 2018, p. 129.

II. Inviolability of the Members of the Grand National Assembly

100. Turkish Law differentiates between inviolability and immunity (*infra*, paragraph 101). According to Article 83/1, AY, members of the Grand National Assembly of Turkey are not criminally responsible, unless the Grand National Assembly decides otherwise, for their votes and statements concerning parliamentary functions, for the ideas they express before the Grand National Assembly and for repeating these ideas outside of the Grand National Assembly.[104]

III. Parliamentary Immunity

101. According to the Constitution, members of the Grand National Assembly are not subject to public prosecution during their office: A deputy who is alleged to have committed a crime before or after the election shall not be arrested, interrogated, detained or tried unless the Grand National Assembly decides otherwise (Article 83/2, AY).[105]

This provision shall not apply in cases where a member is caught in the act of committing a crime punishable by a lengthy penalty or in cases subject to Article 14, AY if an investigation has been initiated before the election. However, in such situations, the competent authority shall notify the Grand National Assembly of Turkey immediately and directly (Article 83/2, AY).

With Act No. 2016-6718 a new article (provisional Article 20) has been added to the Constitution. This provision removed the parliamentary immunity of the members of the parliament against those who have pending investigations against them and the request for lifting the immunity has been sent to the prosecution authorities before this act came into force. As a consequence, this act of the Parliament will remove parliamentary immunity provided by the second paragraph of Article 83 of the Constitution for the abovementioned pending cases.

IV. The Immunities of Diplomatic Corps

102. Since 1961, the Republic of Turkey has been party to the Convention of Vienna on the Immunities of the Diplomatic Corps. Consuls are not considered diplomats, but according to the Vienna Convention of March 19, 1967, Concerning Consular Relationships, consuls are subject to Turkish jurisdiction only if they have committed an act that is tried by the court dealing with the most serious offenses.[106]

---

104. N. Centel, H. Zafer & Ö. Çakmut, *Türk Ceza Hukukuna Giriş*, Beta, İstanbul, 10. Bası, 2017, p. 140.
105. N. Centel, H. Zafer & Ö. Çakmut, *Türk Ceza Hukukuna Giriş*, Beta, İstanbul, 10. Bası, 2017, p. 131; H. Hakeri, *Ceza Hukuku Genel Hükümler;* 21. Bası, Adalet, Ankara 2018, p. 109.
106. N. Centel, H. Zafer & Ö. Çakmut, *Türk Ceza Hukukuna Giriş*, Beta, İstanbul, 10. Bası, 2017, p. 146.

V. Immunities Based on the International Treaties

103. According to Article 23 of the Treaty on Prevention of Torture, accepted by Turkey in 1988, according to Act No. 3441, the members of the European Committee for Prevention of Torture have immunities for the duration of their tasks in Turkey.

104. Certain agreements between Turkey and other countries regulate the extent of Turkish criminal jurisdiction over foreign military personnel in Turkey. According to the North Atlantic Treaty, members of foreign military forces have a special status with regard to jurisdiction. Article 7 of the Treaty states that military forces exercise their own national civil and criminal jurisdiction over military personnel who understand their laws. If a foreign country (the sending state) has final jurisdiction in cases of high treason, sabotage, spying, and offenses related to state secrets, the case will be tried by that state and its laws will be applied.

If that state has privileged jurisdiction, according to Article 7/3 of the North Atlantic Treaty Organization (NATO) Treaty, it may refuse to exercise its right of jurisdiction. Special treaties between the foreign state and Turkey will govern the principles of the application of this right.

Chapter 3. General Principles of Criminal Responsibility or Liability

§1. Introduction: The Basic Elements or Requirements of Criminal Offenses

I. The Basic Elements of Criminal Offenses

105. The theory of the General Principles of Criminal Liability deals with the basic elements of criminal offenses. The Penal Code does not define crime. However, there are general elements of a crime that are common to all crimes. For certain crimes such as murder or theft, the law has provided some specific elements. From the perspective of positive law, any action that is punishable by criminal law is a crime.

Turkish doctrine divides the basic elements differently. Taner[107] speaks of three elements: *the element of the law*, *the material element* and *the mental element.*

Kunter[108] divides the elements into two groups: *the elements demonstrated by the act* (requirement to be shown in the law, unlawfulness and punishability) and *the material element* (action, result and causation).

Dönmezer and Erman[109] suggest four groups: *the element of the law* (*supra*, paragraph 106), *the material element*, *the element of unlawfulness* (*infra*, paragraph 134) and *the mental element* (*infra*, paragraph 122). The material element consists of human acts or omissions, physical results of human conduct that are defined by the penal code, and the causal link.

The new generation of legal experts considers illegal human conduct as a material element of the crime. Other elements are the mental element and unlawfulness.

The perpetrator (*infra,* paragraph 310), who commits the crime is a natural, living person who may act alone, or together with other actors. However, where civil servants collectively leave their work illegally, there must be at least four of them acting together, in order to be punishable (Article 260/1, TCK).

Certain crimes have special characteristics. For example, there are those in which the perpetrator must be a civil servant (bribery; Article 252, TCK) or a soldier. Only persons placed in pre-trial arrest or inmates who are eligible to commit the crime of escaping from prison (Article 292, TCK). In Turkish criminal law, these are called *special crimes* (*özgü suçlar*).

In some crimes, however, the position of the perpetrator is a ground for the aggravation of the punishment, such as forgery of documents conducted by a civil servant (Article 204/2, TCK), or a drug offense committed by a medical doctor (Article 188/8, TCK).

---

107. T. Taner, *Ceza Hukuku, Umumi Kısım*, İstanbul, Üçüncü Basım, İstanbul Üniversitesi Hukuk Fakültesi, 1955, p. 131.
108. N. Kunter, *Suçun Maddi Unsurları Nazariyesi*, İstanbul, İstanbul Hukuk Fakültesi, 1954; N. Kunter, *Suçun Kanuni Unsurları Nazariyesi*, İstanbul, İstanbul Hukuk Fakültesi, 1949.
109. S. Dönmezer & S. Erman (Bayraktar, Kiziroğlu, Zafer, Sınar, Önok, Erman), *Nazari ve Tatbiki Ceza Hukuku, Genel Kısım, Cilt I,* 14. Bası, İstanbul: DER Yayınları, 2016, n. 12.

II. Subjects in Addition to the Basic Elements of Criminal Offenses

106. Subjects in addition to the basic elements of criminal offense are preconditions, the conditions of punishability, the conditions of criminal prosecution, and the reasons for setting aside the sanction.[110]

107. The preconditions of criminal offenses have to be present at the time of the commission of the act. An act does not constitute a criminal offense if not all specifically required preconditions are fulfilled. For example, in abortion, the woman should be pregnant. In reality, the basic elements and preconditions of criminal offenses are not different subjects, but the Turkish doctrine makes this differentiation only for the sake of practicability.[111]

108. Conditions of punishability must be present after the act has been carried out. If the conditions of punishability are not met, the perpetrator will not be punished. For example, a Turk in a foreign country who commits a crime punishable under Turkish law that restricts personal liberty for a minimum period of one year shall be punished according to Turkish laws. However, this is only true if he is in Turkey, if there is no conviction by the foreign country and if the crime can be prosecuted in Turkey (Article 11/1, TCK). In this case, the presence of the perpetrator in Turkey is a condition of punishability. There are no such conditions for the intent of the accused.[112]

109. Preconditions of criminal prosecution (*infra*, paragraph 387) are not related to the basic elements of the criminal offense such as immunities (*supra*, paragraph 103). They only prevent the criminal investigation or prosecution if they are not present.

110. The reasons for setting aside the prosecution and the sanction (*infra*, paragraph 633) are not one of the basic elements of criminal offenses. These include the death of the accused or the convicted person (Article 64, TCK), amnesty (Article 65/1, TCK), pardon (Article 65/2, TCK), expiry of the period set by the statute of limitations for prosecution (Article 66, TCK) and expiry of the period set by the statute of limitations for punishment (Article 68, TCK).

---

110. S. Dönmezer & S.E. Sahir (Bayraktar, Kiziroğlu, Zafer, Sınar, Önok, Erman), *Nazari ve Tatbiki Ceza Hukuku, Genel Kısım, Cilt I,* 14. Bası, İstanbul: DER Yayınları, 2016, n. 436.
111. N. Centel, H. Zafer & Ö. Çakmut, *Türk Ceza Hukukuna Giriş*, İstanbul, 10. Bası, Beta, 2017, p. 219.
112. N. Centel, H. Zafer & Ö. Çakmut, *Türk Ceza Hukukuna Giriş*, İstanbul, Sekizinci Bası, Beta, 2014, p. 204.

§2. *Actus Reus*: The Material Element of the Offenses

I. Forbidden Act

111. The Penal Code defines forbidden human conduct that violates a protected legal value.[113] As a result of the principle of legality (*supra*, paragraph 63) (Article 2, TCK), the legislature has created certain types of offenses.

Everything that may be an expression of will is considered human conduct;[114] human conduct is manifested in the form of either an act or an omission.

The repealed Penal Code defined some offenses as *offenses without movement, which do not require a result to occur in the world.* Under the current law, human conduct that creates danger may be punished before any harm has resulted (Articles 125 and 176, TCK).

Offenses that can be committed only with action are divided into groups. The first group of these offenses consists of *offenses with limited actions* and *offenses with free-typed actions.* If the offense can be committed only using the type of action described in the law itself, there is *an offense with limited actions,* as described in Article 225, TCK (sexual intercourse or exhibitionism in public places).

112. Offenses of action[115] require a positive effort on the part of the offender, whereas with offenses of omission, the offender does not act when he is obliged[116] to do so (intentional homicide and bodily injury by omission: Articles 83 and 88, TCK).[117] By offenses of commission by omission, the offender commits a crime that can be made by an action with his non-action, such as not helping a wounded person (Article 98, TCK), failing to report a crime that is being committed (Article 278, TCK), or failing to report hidden evidence (even if he knew where the evidence was located) (Article 284/2, TCK).

If only one action is sufficient to fulfill the requirements of the offense, then there is a *one-action offense.* However, if the perpetrator must carry out more than one action, then there is an *offense that is committed through more than one action.* For example, in forgery of private documents, the perpetrator has to *change* the contents of the document and also *use* that forged private document (Article 207/1, TCK).

In some offenses there is more than one action described in the law, but carrying out only one of the actions is enough. Then there is an *offense of selecting action* (Article 155, TCK).

---

113. Y. Ünver, *Ceza Hukukuyla Korunması Amaçlanan Hukuksal Değer*, Ankara, Seçkin Yayınları, 2003.

114. S. Dönmezer & S. Erman (I), *Nazari ve Tatbiki Ceza Hukuku Genel Kısım*, Cilt I, 10. Bası, İstanbul, Beta, 1987, n. 503; N. Centel, H. Zafer & Ö. Çakmut, *Türk Ceza Hukukuna Giriş*, Sekizinci Bası, İstanbul, Beta, 2014, p. 337.

115. H. Hakeri, *İhmal Kavramı ve İhmali Suçların Çeşitleri*, Ankara, Seçkin Yayınları, 2003.

116. This legal position of obligation *(garantörlük)* may emanate from a contract, or it may be a legal obligation.

117. For example, the superior of the civil servant, who neglects to act to prevent torture, shall be liable and his punishment shall not be reduced on this ground (Art. 95/5, TCK).

Perpetrators who repeat the same intentional offense more than twice within one year and at different times are *habitual offenders* (Article 6/1-h, TCK). But offenders who make a living, even if partially, out of committing crimes, are called *professional offenders* (Article 6/1-i, TCK). Both of them are subject to security measures (Article 58/9, TCK) (*infra,* paragraph 295).

II. Physical Results of the Human Conduct

A. Introduction

113. The effect of action is what causes change in the world, which is separate from the action but caused by that action. This change can be either physical or psychological.

Some offenses require that the perpetrator's action have an effect. The acts or omissions (*supra,* paragraph 112) have to be the cause of the result that is forbidden by the law.[118] If the effect did not occur, there may still be an attempt to commit a crime (Article 35, TCK).

For some offenses, the fulfillment of the result is not required.[119] Provocation to commit a crime (Article 214/1, TCK) shall be punished, even if the person in question does not commit the crime eventually.

For crimes related to a foreign country (*supra,* paragraph 79), the crime shall be considered as committed in Turkey, if the physical behavior was attempted or committed totally or partly in Turkey, or action outside of Turkey had some results in Turkish territory.

B. Classification of Crimes According to the Physical Behavior or the Results

114. Crimes are classified in Turkish Criminal Law with regard to the changes caused in the outside world. Momentary or immediate offenses are committed at one moment. If the criminal behavior concerns an enduring situation, then there is a continuing offense; unlawful possession of a weapon and transporting illegal drugs are continuing offenses.[120]

---

118. S. Dönmezer & S. Erman (I), *Nazari ve Tatbiki Ceza Hukuku Genel Kısım,* Cilt I, 10. Bası, İstanbul, Beta, 1987, n. 514; N. Centel, H. Zafer & Ö. Çakmut, *Türk Ceza Hukukuna Giriş,* Sekizinci Bası, İstanbul, Beta, 2014, p. 255.
119. For example, when escaping from prison or a detention center, carrying out the actions for escaping was enough for the offense. Successfully escaping would not be regarded as a requirement (Art. 298, repealed TCK). The New Penal Code does not include such a crime. A person under preliminary custody or an inmate must have successfully escaped in order to commit this crime (Art. 292, TCK).
120. S. Dönmezer & S. Erman (I), *Nazari ve Tatbiki Ceza Hukuku Genel Kısım, Cilt I, 10.* Bası, İstanbul, Beta, 1987, n. 519; N. Centel, H. Zafer & Ö. Çakmut, *Türk Ceza Hukukuna Giriş,* İstanbul, Sekizinci Bası, Beta, 2014, p. 252.

Offenses by which the effect is close to the action are carried out at the time and place where and when the action takes place; if someone violates the personal dignity of another person in his presence, it is a crime. If the victim is not present, at least three other persons must have received the information (Article 125/1, TCK). If the action is carried out at a place and the effect occurs at another place, then an offense of distance has occurred.[121]

The *chain of crimes* concerns the repeated violation of a provision of the law against the same person under the same intent. Although such violations occur at different times, they are considered a single crime.[122] This principle also applies to crimes whereby the victim is not an identified individual (Article 43/1, TCK).

Two different offenses combined may constitute a new offense. If one of the offenses is (according to the law) an element of the principal crime, or if it constitutes an aggravating circumstance, then it is a combined offense (Article 42, TCK), which is also considered a single offense (Articles 108 and 148, TCK). In contrast to the repealed Penal Code (Articles 495, 191/4, repealed TCK), the new Penal Code foresees two separate crimes in a case where the perpetrator kills, wounds or inflicts damage to the property during the commission of threat (Article 106/3, TCK) or robbery (Article 149/2, TCK). If there is no connection in the element of the crime or aggravating ground, each act is a separate offense and additional punishments will be added (Article 42, TCK).

If the action defined by the law necessarily includes a less serious offense (e.g., rape in Article 102/2 includes Article 108, compelling an individual by using force), then there is a *mixed offense*.

If the perpetrator has unavoidably committed a less serious crime in order to be able to commit a more serious offense, then there is an *offense of passage*. For example, to commit a homicide (Article 81, TCK) the perpetrator must first commit battery (Article 86, TCK). In such cases, the perpetrator will be punished with the most severe punishment.

115. Any individual who violates several provisions of the law by a single act, shall be considered to have committed one offense (*infra*, paragraph 335) and will be sentenced for the offense with the heaviest penalty (concurrence of laws) (Article 44, TCK).

III. Causation

A. Introduction

116. There should be a causal connection between the act committed by the perpetrator and the result of the act.[123] If there is one certain cause of the result, it is

121. N. Toroslu, *Ceza Hukuku Genel Kısım*, 21. Bası, Ankara, Savaş Yayınevi, 2015.
122. T.Y. Sancar, *Müteselsil Suç*, 1995; Cass. 11. CD Feb. 16, 2015, 2015/16133 K.; Cass. 8. CD Feb. 5, 2015, 2015/2496 K.; Cass. 21. CD Jun. 1, 2015, 2015/1559 K.
123. S. Dönmezer & S. Erman (I), *Nazari ve Tatbiki Ceza Hukuku Genel Kısım, Cilt I*, 10. Bası, İstanbul, Beta, 1987, p. 606; H. Hakeri, *Ceza Hukuku Genel Hükümler*, 21. Baskı, Adalet, Ankara, 2017,

easy to find the link of causation. However, if more than one cause has influenced the result, it is important to discover which cause had the effect.

There is no definition of causation in the law, but some crimes do mention the concept of causation (such as Articles 87, 95, 103, TCK). Turkish case law has developed some theories to solve the problem of defining causation under criminal law.[124]

B. Theories of Causation

117. Under the Theory of Equivalence, each condition that is necessary for an action is considered a cause (*conditio sine qua non*). According to this theory, there is no distinction between an important cause and a less important cause. The perpetrator who produces such a cause is responsible.[125]

The Theory of the Last Cause considers the actor of the last cause as criminally responsible. If there is another action between the behavior and its effect, then the link of causation is broken.[126] In 1983, the Court of Cassation decided that there was no causal link between the accused's act of pushing the victim and the victim's subsequent death three days after the incident because the victim was not bleeding after the incident.[127]

The Theory of Adequate Causation considers some acts as effective means for carrying out the crime, whereas some acts create a greater possibility. In such cases there must be a general link between the action and its result; this is what is required to be an adequate cause. In this respect, not each condition is considered a *cause.*

118. Negligence (*infra*, paragraph 138) shall be punished if a result occurs.[128] There must be an act without foreseeing the consequences, that resulted in harm and there must be a direct connection between the conduct and the harm (Article 22/2,

p. 195; M. Koca & İ. Üzülmez, *Türk Ceza Hukuku Genel Hükümler*, 13. Baskı, Seçkin, Ankara 2020, p. 120; V.Ö. Özbek et al., *Türk Ceza Hukuku Genel Hükümler*, 7. Baskı, Seçkin, Ankara 2016, p. 239.

124. S. Dönmezer & S. Erman (I), *Nazari ve Tatbiki Ceza Hukuku Genel Kısım, Cilt I*, 10. Bası, İstanbul, Beta, 1987, p. 608; D. Soyaslan, *Ceza Hukuku Genel Hükümler*, 8. Baskı, Yetkin Yayınları, Ankara, 2018, p. 351; N. Centel, H. Zafer & Ö. Çakmut, *Türk Ceza Hukukuna Giriş*, 8. Baskı, Beta, İstanbul, 2014, p. 255; H. Zafer, *Ceza Hukuku Genel Hükümler*, 4. Baskı, Beta, İstanbul, 2015, p. 198; İ. Özgenç, *Türk Ceza Hukuku Genel Hükümler*, 10. Baskı, Seçkin, Ankara, 2014, p. 171; M.E. Artuk et al., *Ceza Hukuku Genel Hükümler* Ankara, Yenilenmiş Gözden Geçirilmiş 11. Baskı Adalet, 2017, p. 255.

125. S. Dönmezer & S. Erman (I), *Nazari ve Tatbiki Ceza Hukuku Genel Kısım, Cilt I, 10.* Bası, İstanbul, Beta, 1987, p. 628; M.E. Artuk et al., *Ceza Hukuku Genel Hükümler* Ankara, Yenilenmiş Gözden Geçirilmiş 11. Baskı Adalet, 2017, p. 253; İ. Özgenç, *Türk Ceza Hukuku Genel Hükümler*, 10. Baskı, Seçkin, Ankara, p. 171; N. Centel, H. Zafer, & Ö. Çakmut, *Türk Ceza Hukukuna Giriş*, 8. Bası, Beta, İstanbul, 2014, p. 255.

126. S. Dönmezer & S. Erman (I), *Nazari ve Tatbiki Ceza Hukuku Genel Kısım, Cilt I*, 10. Bası, İstanbul, Beta, 1987, p. 637.

127. Cass., 1 CD Apr. 5, 1983; IKID 1983, 5. For a more recent decision about causation based on the same principles see. Cass. CGK Mar. 31, 2015 K. 2015/75.

128. T. Demirbaş, *Ceza Hukuku Genel Hükümler*, 15. Baskı, Seçkin, Ankara 2020, p. 395.

TCK). If there is more than one factor that influences the result, each factor is responsible according to the respective contribution of the factor (*infra*, paragraph 141).

119. Turkish case law generally favors the Theory of Equivalence.[129] The Court of Cassation examines the causal link first objectively and then subjectively. If the action is objectively effective for carrying out the crime, then the personality of the perpetrator becomes important. The judge considers whether adequate legal causation is fulfilled as per the mental status of the perpetrator and as per personal relationships.[130]

The Court of Cassation sometimes views *the last cause* as important.[131] In cases where intentional conduct causes severe results beyond the intent of the accused, the Code then requires a status of negligence for the excess outcome (Article 23, TCK).

C. *Interruption of the Causal Link*

120. If there is another cause between the offender's act and the result, then the link of causation is broken.[132]

121. Causal link in case of an omission. Negligence may cause a physical result. In cases of omission, if the act that should have been carried out by the accused is the necessary condition of the result, then the link of causation is present. Foreseeability is another important criterion of negligence.[133]

§3. *MENS REA*: THE MENTAL ELEMENT

122. Personal liability and moral responsibility are important principles in modern criminal law. No one can be punished for an act he did not commit because

---

129. *Some legal experts have different opinion.* M.E. Artuk et al., *Ceza Hukuku Genel Hükümler* Ankara, Yenilenmiş Gözden Geçirilmiş 11. Baskı Adalet, 2017, p. 255.
130. S. Dönmezer & S. Erman (I), *Nazari ve Tatbiki Ceza Hukuku Genel Kısım, Cilt I, 10.* Bası, İstanbul, Beta, 1987, p. 643; Cass., CGK Apr. 27, 1992, E. 92/1–109, K. 92/126.
131. Cass., 1 CD Nov. 17, 1987, E. 1987/3243, K. 1987/4006; YKD 1988, 554.
132. Cass., 9 CD Nov. 30, 1982, E. 1982/4226 K. 1982/4456; YKD 1983/3, 452: B had wounded A. The injury was not fatal, but A died because of a mistake in medical treatment; the negligence of the doctors broke the link of causation. However, according to the repealed Penal Code, the offender would be punished with a lesser punishment if the act of wounding was not committed with the intention to kill, but nonetheless results in the death of the victim (Art. 452 repealed TCK). The Penal Code does not accept *objective responsibility* (*infra,* para. 143). The perpetrator is only accountable for killing if the death of the victim was due to his negligent behavior. Otherwise, he is only responsible for wounding the victim (Art. 23 and Art. 87/4 TCK); T. Demirbaş, *Ceza Hukuku Genel Hükümler*, 15. Baskı, Seçkin, Ankara 2020, p. 255.
133. N. Toroslu, *Ceza Hukuku Genel Kısım,* 21. Bası, Ankara, Savaş Yayınevi, 2015.

criminal liability is personal (Article 38, AY). Free will and the ability to distinguish right from wrong are the basic elements of moral responsibility.[134]

The majority of Turkish scholars consider, like we do, the *mental element* as a form of culpability (*infra,* paragraph 132), whereas a minority classifies it under the subjective part of the elements of the crime.[135]

Subjective responsibility means that the offender must answer for his unlawful conduct. Criminal responsibility cannot be based on his lifestyle.

The existence of intent is required for all types of crimes and should be proven by the prosecution.

Formerly, the proof of intent was not necessary for misdemeanors (Article 45, repealed TCK). The Code on Misdemeanors (Article 9, KK) stipulates that, if there is no special regulation by an act, misdemeanors can only be committed with intent or negligence and the prosecution has to prove this.

Turkish criminal law divides the mental element into two parts: *criminal capacity*, which means that the offender can act in a guilty state of mind, and *culpability*, which means that the accused was guilty in a certain situation (Articles 20–34, TCK).

I. Criminal Capacity

123. Criminal capacity[136] is the ability of the offender to know or understand the results caused by his action and the ability to will the results of his action. Therefore, the capacity to be guilty consists of two elements: The ability to distinguish between good and bad and the ability to act accordingly.[137] In other words, criminal responsibility requires both criminal capacity and criminal intent.[138]

An action that is committed knowingly and willingly by a person who has criminal capacity is important for criminal liability. If there is no guilt, the action cannot be punished. The punishment cannot be more severe than the degree of guilt and cannot be less than what the perpetrator deserves.

Minority, mental disorder of the offender and deaf-muteness are factors that influence the criminal capacity or eliminate it.

Legal entities have no real criminal responsibility in Turkey. The law only provides measures for legal persons, no penalties (*infra,* paragraph 309).

---

134. Z. Hafızoğulları & M. Özen, *Türk Ceza Hukuku Genel Hükümler, Gözden Geçirilmiş, İşlenmiş ve Yenilenmiş 2.* Bası, Ankara, US-A Yayıncılık, 2010, p. 264; N. Centel, H. Zafer & O. Çakmut, *Türk Ceza Hukukuna Giriş*, İstanbul, Sekizinci Bası, Beta, 2014, p. 337; K. İçel et al., *İçel Suç Teorisi*, Beta, İstanbul, İkinci Bası, 2000, p. 198.
135. S. Tellenbach, Subjektive Tatseite in der Türkei, in *Nationales Strafrecht in rechtsvergleichender Darstellung, Teilband 3*, ed. Sieber & Cornils, Berlin, 2008, p. 787; M.E. Artuk et al., *Ceza Hukuku Genel Hükümler* Ankara, Yenilenmiş Gözden Geçirilmiş 11. Baskı Adalet, 2017, p. 294.
136. N. Toroslu, *Ceza Hukuku Genel Kısım,* 21. Bası, Ankara, Savaş Yayınevi, 2015.
137. T.T. Yüce, *Ceza Hukukunun Temel Kavramları*, Ankara, Turhan, 1985, p. 54; N. Centel, H. Zafer & Ö. Çakmut, *Türk Ceza Hukukuna Giriş*, Beta, İstanbul, Sekizinci Bası, 2014, p. 376.
138. Intent and negligence are modalities of commission of a crime. M.E. Artuk et al., *Ceza Hukuku Genel Hükümler* Ankara, Yenilenmiş Gözden Geçirilmiş 11. Baskı Adalet, 2017, p. 293.

A. *Criminal Responsibility of Children*

124. Anyone who has not attained the age of 12 at the time the act is committed (Article 31/1, TCK) shall not be prosecuted or punished. The Child Protection Act (*Çocuk Koruma Kanunu,* ÇKK) No. 2005–5395 considers any individual under the age of 18 a child (Article 3, ÇKK).

125. Criminal capacity of children aged under fifteen. Between the ages of (over) twelve and (under) eighteen, criminal capacity may vary according to mental development and age.[139] The punishment will be reduced in accordance with TCK, and some measures will be imposed.

Whoever has attained the age of 12 but has not attained the age of 15 at the time the act was carried out, shall not be punished if he lacks discretion or if he has the capability to comprehend the legal meaning and the result of the act and to control his behavior in this respect. Where the child was capable of knowing that his act was a crime, the punishment shall be reduced (Article 31/2, TCK). According to the previous law, only this age group was subject to the Juvenile Courts. The Protection of Child Act defines the concept of the *child* as an individual who has not attained the age of 18, even if he was legally considered an *adult* at an earlier age (Article 3/1-a, TCK). So, any person under the age of 18 is under the jurisdiction of *Juvenile Criminal Courts* (Articles 25–32, ÇKK).

126. Children aged 15–18. Children between (over) 15 and (under) 18 years of age at the time of the commission of an act are considered to have full criminal responsibility; however, the punishment will be reduced in accordance with Article 31/3, TCK. The prosecution has no obligation to prove the capacity to distinguish right from wrong.[140] The Penal Code did not improve the legal status of an offending juvenile at this point. The delinquent juvenile shall only be punished with a reduced sanction; but the Penal Code (Article 31/3, TCK) and the Protection of the Child Act do not allow the judge to apply any security measures (as a sanction) on the child who is over 15 years of age (Article 11, ÇKK). It is still possible to apply protective and supporting measures[141] to this group of children while the investigation and prosecution are pending (Articles 5, 7 and 13, TCK), but not after the conviction.

B. *Deaf-Mute Persons*

127. Deaf-mute persons are considered less capable of understanding the consequences of their actions. Therefore, age limits for this group of children are raised. No prosecution shall be conducted against deaf-mute persons who have not attained

---

139. Y.S. Balo, *Çocuk Ceza Hukuku*, 2. Baskı, Seçkin, Ankara, 2015.
140. F. Yenisey, *Juvenile Delinquency in Turkey*, H. Messmer & H. Otto; *Restorative Justice on Trial*, Dordrecht, Boston, London: Kluwer Academic Publishers, 1992, p. 409.
141. B. Öztürk & M.R. Erdem, *Uygulamalı Ceza Hukuku ve Güvenlik Tedbirleri Hukuku,* TCK Değişikliklerine Göre Yenilenmiş, 20. Baskı Ankara 2020, Seçkin Yayınları, p. 320.

the age of 15 years at the time of commission of the act. The provision of Article 31, subparagraph 1 may be applied to such persons (Article 33, TCK).

The Penal Code simplified the former regulation by explicitly making the provisions related to children (Article 31, TCK) applicable to deaf-mute persons. With respect to deaf-mute persons, however, the age limit is 21 (Article 33, TCK). If it is understood that the deaf-mute person acted with the capacity to discern the nature of his crime, and if he had not attained the age of 18 years at the time of the commission of the crime, the provisions of Article 31/2, TCK shall apply. A deaf-mute person, who has not attained the age of 21 years, shall be subject to the provisions of Article 31/3, TCK.[142]

C. Mental Disorder of the Offender

128. Complete loss of the ability of discretion. A mental disease either reduces or eliminates the ability of discretion or it does not play any role concerning criminal liability.[143]

Anyone afflicted with mental disease in the medical sense, or rather, mental disease that, at the time of the commission of the act causes a complete loss of his/her ability to sense the legal consequences of the act or considerably reduces his/her ability to control his/her actions,[144] cannot be held *criminally liable* and shall not be punished (Article 32/1, TCK). However, security measures may apply (Article 57, TCK). The mentally ill criminal will be put into custody and treated until he is cured.

The TCK made a significant change compared to the situation under the old Penal Code. Under the old regime, *the considerably reduced ability of discretion* (Article 46/2, repealed TCK) was a ground for reducing the punishment. The new TCK considers this situation a ground of impunity (Article 32/1, TCK). By contrast, the *reduced ability of discretion* is now a ground for reducing the punishment (Article 32/2, TCK).

129. Reduced ability of discretion. If the mental disease considerably reduces the ability of discretion (his/her ability to control his/her actions concerning the act he/she is committing), the accused is subject to Article 32/2, TCK.

The punishment shall be reduced in the following manner: Aggravated life imprisonment shall be reduced to imprisonment of twenty-five years; life imprisonment shall be reduced to twenty years. Other punishments shall be reduced by not more than one-sixth. The punishment may also be inflicted partly or as a whole as a security measure for mentally ill persons; the duration of the measure has to be the same as the prison term (Article 32/2, TCK).

---

142. D. Soyaslan, *Ceza Hukuku Genel Hükümler,* Yetkin Yayınları, Güncelleştirilmiş 8. Baskı, Ankara 2018, p. 417.
143. S. Bayındır, *Türk Ceza Hukukunda Akıl Hastalığı,* Legal, İstanbul 2016.
144. İ. Özgenç, *Türk Ceza Hukuku Genel Hükümler, Gözden Geçirilmiş ve Güncellenmiş* 10. Bası, Ankara, Seçkin, 2014, p. 385; H. Ulutürk. *Türk Hukukunda Akıl Hastalığı ve Akıl Hastalığının Kusur Yeteneneğine Etkisi*, Seçkin, Ankara 2014.

130. Procedural aspects of mental disorder. The accused must have had criminal capacity at the time of committing the crime. Any person who was criminally responsible at the moment of the commission of the crime but later loses this capacity can be punished. However, in order to defend himself/herself, the person should be mentally competent during the court proceedings.[145]

D. Extraneous Matters

131. A person who is criminally responsible may lose his criminal capacity for a certain period because of extraneous circumstances or alcohol. The provision of Article 34/1 TCK shall apply to anyone who during the commission of a crime was not in a state of capacity of guilt (a complete loss of his/her ability of sensing the legal consequences of the act he/she is committing or a considerably reduced ability to control his/her actions for extraneous reasons or for involuntarily consumed alcohol or narcotic substances).

Acts committed under the influence of voluntary intoxication or under the influence of narcotics taken voluntarily are excluded from this rule (Article 34/2, TCK). Any person who has deliberately (*actiones liberae in causa*)[146] put himself/herself in a state of losing his/her criminal capacity will be punished accordingly. A decision of the Court of Cassation states that where a morgue servant was accused of stealing three golden bracelets of the corpse, he defended himself, as he was drunk and unable to create a criminal intent. The first instance the court justified him but the Court of Cassation overturned the decision by saying that he was voluntarily intoxicated and in this condition, his criminal responsibility would remain.[147]

Actiones liberae in causa is a principle applicable in the continental legal system. There is a special provision related to this situation in the German Penal Code (Article 323 a, StGB).[148]

II. Culpability

132. Culpability is the mental relationship between the offender and his/her prohibited act. Anyone who acts knowingly and willingly to commit a crime is criminally responsible. Knowing and willing are physiological matters.

However, besides this physiological relationship, the act should be legally condemnable. This aspect of culpability is called *the normative theory of culpability.*[149] This form of guilt is considered either *intent* or *negligence.*

---

145. N. Kunter, F. Yenisey & A. Nuhoğlu. *Muhakeme Hukuku Dalı Olarak Ceza Muhakemesi Hukuku,* 18. Bası, Beta Yayınevi, İstanbul, 2010, p. 695.
146. T. Demirbaş, *Ceza Hukuku Genel Hükümler*, 15. Baskı, Seçkin, Ankara 2020, p. 368.
147. Cass. CGK May 6, 2003, 2003/148 K.
148. F. Yenisey & G. Plagemann, *Alman Ceza Kanunu Strafgesetzbuch (StGB) Turkish and German Texts, Explanations and Dictionary,* Extended 2nd edn., Beta, İstanbul, May 2015, p. 458.
149. S. Dönmezer & S. Erman (II), *Nazari ve Tatbiki Ceza Hukuku, Genel Kısım, Cilt II,* 9. Bası, İstanbul, Beta, 1986, p. 912; T. Demirbaş, *Ceza Hukuku Genel Hükümler*, 15. Baskı, Seçkin, Ankara

Strict liability is not accepted according to the principles of modern criminal law. However, it still exists in some exceptional cases in Turkish criminal law (*infra*, paragraph 143).

A. *Criminal Intent and Knowledge of Injustice*

133. Intent. The presence of intent is a requirement for an act to be constituted a crime (Article 21/1, TCK).

There was no definition of intent in the repealed Code. However, the Draft Penal Code provided a description: *Intent is the will of knowing the act and willing the unlawful result of this act* (Article 21, TCKT 2002). The Penal Code gives a different definition: *Intent is accomplishing the elements of the crime as defined in the statute, knowingly and willingly.* (Article 21/1, TCK).[150]

Knowledge of injustice[151] belongs to the concept of intent. But *ignorance of the law* is no excuse (*infra*, paragraph 165).

134. Theories explaining the concept of intent. In Turkish case law two theories explain the concept of intent. According to the theory of foreseeability,[152] it is important that the offender must be able to foresee his/her act before he/she committed it. According to the theory of will, however, it is important that the offender wanted the result. Mainstream Turkish doctrine accepts a mixed theory. The intent is the will that is directed to accomplish the unlawful conduct.[153] However, the Penal Code is closer to the theory of foreseeability.[154]

In Turkish terminology, some concepts are related to intent: *Aim* is the result that is shown in the legal description. *Purpose* is the interest of the offender that is beyond the legal description. *Leading purpose or motive* is the aim that causes the offender to act.

135. Kinds of intent. There are two main kinds of intent: General and specific. If the leading purpose is important according to the law, then a specific intent of the accused is required.[155] Furthermore, Turkish criminal law distinguishes between

---

2020, p. 351; V.Ö. Özbek et al., *Türk Ceza Hukuku Genel Hükümler*, Ankara, Seçkin, 7. Baskı, 2016, p. 364.

150. E. Günay, *Teori ve Uygulamada Olası Kast Bilinçli Taksir, Öldürme ve Yaralama Kastı*, Seçkin Yayınları, 2005.

151. *The ability of an individual of observing his social environment is called* the ability of perception; *the ability of making a judgment about the illegality of his conduct is called* knowledge of injustice. (İ. Özgenç, *Türk Ceza Hukuku Genel Hükümler*, Gözden Geçirilmiş ve Güncellenmiş 10. Bası, Ankara, Seçkin, 2014, p. 185).

152. T. Demirbaş, *Ceza Hukuku Genel Hükümler*, 15. Baskı, Seçkin, Ankara 2020, p. 376.

153. S. Dönmezer & S. Erman (II), *Nazari ve Tatbiki Ceza Hukuku, Genel Kısım, Cilt II*, 9. Bası, İstanbul, Beta, 1986, p. 925; N. Centel, H. Zafer & Ö. Çakmut, *Türk Ceza Hukukuna Giriş*, Sekizinci Bası, İstanbul, Beta, 2014, p. 346.

154. The new approach does not consider intent as a part of culpability (İ. Özgenç, *Türk Ceza Hukuku Genel Hükümler*, Gözden Geçirilmiş ve Güncellenmiş 10. Bası, Ankara, Seçkin, 2014, p. 230).

155. S. Dönmezer & S. Erman (II), *Nazari ve Tatbiki Ceza Hukuku, Genel Kısım, Cilt II*, 9. Bası, İstanbul, Beta, 1986, p. 940; Cass. 4. CD Mar. 19, 2008, 2008/4860 K.

definite and indefinite intent on the one hand, and direct and indirect intent on the other. Definite intent is present when the offender is acting with the knowledge of the consequences of his act or omission. When the offender is shooting towards a crowd, he is acting with an indefinite intent.[156] There is direct intent if the result is within the limits of the will of the offender. However, the results that could be foreseen by the offender are considered indirect intent or probable intent (*dolus eventualis; infra*, paragraph 136).

If there is a short period between the decision to carry out a crime and the act itself, the form of the intent is a *momentary intent*. If the perpetrator had acted after thinking the case over and after having made plans, then he is acting with *premeditation*.[157] The Turkish Court of Cassation considers the intent is premeditated if the offender acted *calmly*.[158]

136. Probable intent (dolus eventualis). The Penal Code has also defined a new concept of intent: Probable intent. If the individual has committed the act though he had foreseen that the elements of the crime as defined in the statute could occur, this state of mind is called probable intent (Article 21/2, TCK). In such cases, the punishment shall be reduced.

137. Proof of intent. The decision on the presence of intent must be made by the Court of First Instance. The Court of Cassation has no competence to consider this issue.

The principle of *in dubio pro reo* will be applied if the judge cannot decide about the proof of intent.[159]

B. Negligence

138. Negligence and foreseeable negligence. In principle, a crime cannot be punished if the offender had not acted with intent. However, there is an exception for those cases where the law clearly prescribes punishment for consequences of the perpetrator's negligent acts or omissions (Article 22/1, TCK).[160]

---

156. B. Öztürk & M.R. Erdem, Uygulamalı Ceza Hukuku ve Güvenlik Tedbirleri Hukuku, TCK Değişikliklerine Göre Yenilenmiş 20. Baskı, Ankara 2020, Seçkin Yayınları, p. 247.
157. S. Dönmezer & S. Erman (II), *Nazari ve Tatbiki Ceza Hukuku, Genel Kısım, Cilt II*, 9. Bası, İstanbul, Beta, 1986, p. 947.
158. Cass. CGK Sep. 23, 2014, 2014/390; B. Öztürk & M.R. Erdem, *Uygulamalı Ceza Hukuku ve Güvenlik Tedbirleri Hukuku,* TCK Değişikliklerine Göre Yenilenmiş 20. Baskı, Ankara 2020, Seçkin Yayınları, p. 257.
159. Cass. CGK May 5, 2015, 2015/141 K.; Cass. 7. CD Nov. 26, 2015, 2015/23404 K.; Cass. 8. CD Oct. 14, 2015, 2015/22764 K.
160. Negligence is considered as a concept belonging to culpability in Turkish Criminal Law doctrine. After the reforms in 2005, some authors classify negligence as a part of the definition of the crime *(tipiklik; Tatbestand),* S. Tellenbach, *Objektive Tatseite in der Türkei,* in *Nationales Strafrecht in rechtsvergleichender Darstellung, Teilband* 3, ed. Sieber & Cornils (Berlin, 2008), p. 629.

Turkish Criminal Law previously did not define negligence.[161] The Penal Code now provides a definition of negligence: *not foreseeing the result, which is described in the legal definition of an action, as a consequence of his carelessness or lack of diligence* (Article 22/2, TCK).[162]

Punishability of intent requires that there be an open regulation that punishes the negligence and that the act must have been carried out willingly by the offender. In addition to these requirements, the offender must have been able to foresee the consequences of his action and must have been able to prevent them.

139. Foreseeable negligence. The notion of foreseeable negligence was first incorporated into the repealed TCK on January 8, 2003, with the expectation of preventing traffic accidents, as some drivers were acting with gross negligence at high risk of accidents: If the perpetrator was able to foresee the outcome of his act that results in a crime, which he did not wish to commit, the punishment will be aggravated by one-third (Article 45, repealed TCK).

This concept of negligence has been carried over to the Penal Code with a different language: *If the result, which the perpetrator had foreseen, realizes, although he did not want it to happen, then there is a foreseeable negligence; in such cases the punishment attached to the negligent crime shall be aggravated by one third up to half* (Article 22/3, TCK).[163]

140. Negligent harm to family members. The repealed Penal Code did not contemplate a lenient punishment if the suspect or the suspect's family members suffered harm by his/her negligence. However, the Draft Penal Code had already made an exception in such cases (Article 22, TCKT 2002). According to present legislation, the punishment of the offender will be excluded if he/she has or his/her family has suffered any harm by his/her negligence, after the court has established the seriousness of the harm the offender caused to himself. This regulation is to the extent that this inclusive personal or family-related harm has made him/her a victim, so that the infliction of a punishment is unnecessary (Article 22/6, TCK).[164] For example, if the father had negligently caused the death of his child, an imprisonment punishment would put his family into additional difficulties.[165]

---

161. However, repealed Arts. 455 and 459, dealing with unintentional wounding and killing, provided some guidance; Whoever causes the death of a person through negligence, carelessness or inexperience in his profession or trade or disobedience to regulations, orders or instructions, shall be punished by imprisonment for two to five years and by a heavy fine. The punishment may be reduced by one-eighth according to the degree of the negligence (Y. Altus, *The Damages for Wrongful Death under Turkish Law*, in *Annales de la Faculté de Droit d'Istanbul* XXIV, No. 40, 1977; p. 201).
162. K. Bayraktar, *Hekimin Tedavi Nedeniyle Cezai Sorumluluğu*, İstanbul, 1971; Y. Ünver, *Ceza Hukukunda İzin Verilen Risk*, İstanbul, Beta, 1998.
163. Cass. 9. CD Jul. 8, 2014, 2014/8260 K.; Cass. CGK Sep. 23, 2014, 2014/389 K.; Cass. 5. CD Feb. 25, 2015, 2015/7594 K.
164. M. Koca & İlhan Üzülmez, *Türk Ceza Hukuku Genel Hükümler*, Gözden Geçirilmiş ve Güncellenmiş 8. Baskı, Seçkin, Ankara 2015, p. 228.
165. E. Artuk, A. Gökçen & C. Yenidünya, *Türk Ceza Kanunu Şerhi, 1. Cilt*, Turhan Kitabevi, Ankara 2009, p. 457; Cass. 12. CD Mar. 12, 2015, 2015/4706 K.; Cass. 12. CD Dec. 17, 2014, 2014/25872; Cass. CGK Apr. 29, 2014, 2014/216 K.

141. Concurrent negligence. According to the former Penal Code, if there were two or more causes influencing a result, negligence would be divided into eight portions, and each perpetrator would be penalized according to the degree of his negligence. The sum of all points could not be more than eight-eighths. The TCK abandoned this rule; each perpetrator is now responsible according the degree of his/her personal guilt (Article 22/5, TCK).[166]

The presence of the link of causation is another requirement.

C. Culpability by Misdemeanors

142. The Penal Code does not include misdemeanors. Misdemeanors are now regulated in a specific act (KK, Act No. 2005–5326). This act defines general principles that rule the principle of legality (Article 4, KK), application of the act with regard to the time (Article 5, KK) and place (Article 6, KK), as well as rules of the legal responsibility (between Articles 7 and 15, KK).

According to the repealed Penal Code, in the field of misdemeanors, everyone was responsible for his/her act or omission even in the absence of criminal intent (Article 45/2, repealed TCK). If a misdemeanor was committed by a person under the authority, administration or supervision of a third party, and the act was within the area of authority of the latter and against the rules which the latter should enforce, and if the commission of the act could have been prevented by the latter's care and prudence, then he/she as well as the (physical) perpetrator were punished (Article 60/1, repealed TCK).

The Act on Misdemeanors regulates merely administrative sanctions as administrative fines and administrative measures (Article 16, KK). Misdemeanors can be committed both with intent and negligence if not regulated otherwise in the statute (Article 9, KK). If the representative of a legal person commits a misdemeanor, the legal person may also be held responsible (Article 8/1, KK).[167] If a real person owns a business and the person working for him/her commits a misdemeanor related to that activity, the owner may be held liable for the administrative sanction imposed on his employee (Article 8/2, KK).

---

166. T. Demirbaş, *Ceza Hukuku Genel Hükümler*, 15. Baskı, Seçkin, Ankara 2020, p. 408; İ. Özgenç, *Türk Ceza Hukuku Genel Hükümler, Gözden Geçirilmiş ve Güncellenmiş 10.* Bası, Ankara, Seçkin, 2014, p. 263.

167. Z. Kangal, *Kabahatler Hukuku, XII Levha*, İstanbul, 2011, p. 216; N. Meran, *Kabahatler Kanunu ve Özel Kanunlarda İdari Para Cezaları*, 4. Baskı, Adalet, Ankara 2015; B. Akbulut, *Türk Ceza Kanunu ile Kabahatler Kanununun Genel Hükümlerinin Yaptırım Hükümleri Dışında Karşılaştırmalı Olarak İncelenmesi*, 2. Baskı, Adalet, Ankara 2014; C. Otacı & İ. Keskin, *Türk Kabahatler Hukuku*, 3. Baskı, HUKAB Yayınları, 2014; H. Zafer & G. Pamuk & K. Çakır, *Gerekçeli-Açıklamalı-İçtihatlı Kabahatler Kanunu*, Beta, İstanbul, 2014.

III. Strict Liability

143. Strict liability by offenses committed by the press. Turkish criminal law applies the principle of subjective responsibility. There were formerly some exceptions to this rule in matters of unintended physical consequences, crimes aggravated because of the physical consequence[168] and offenses committed by the press. The Penal Code made changes in this respect, except in the field of the press.

Article 16 of the repealed Press Code made the author and the responsible editor for periodical publications criminally responsible for offenses committed by their periodical publications (*infra*, paragraph 188). The editor was punished with the same punishment as the author. Turkish literature criticized this form of strict liability.[169]

However, the Press Code (Article 11, Act No. 2004–5187) did not deviate further from the principle of individual responsibility; the author has the principal criminal responsibility. But if the author cannot be punished, for various reasons, the Press Act holds another person responsible as defined in the Act. If the person who did not prevent the publication was liable for his deed, there would be no problem. But the new Press Act, like the old Press Act, inflicts on this person the same punishment that is foreseen for the author.

144. Strict liability for misdemeanors. The repealed Penal Code made an individual in a supervisory capacity liable for the consequences that were beyond his/her intention if through his own fault, he did not prevent them from occurring (Article 60, repealed TCK). Turkish scholars were opposed to this regulation. However, the new act on Misdemeanors did not improve the situation, it made it worse: the clause on the obligation of preventing was incorporated in the new act (Article 8, KK). Thus, a clear example of strict liability has been created.[170]

---

168. When an abducted person was injured during or as a result of abduction, the punishment was increased. If the victim died, the offender was sentenced to lifelong imprisonment (Art. 439 repealed TCK). The Turkish Penal Code makes the perpetrator accountable for unintended consequences only if the excessive consequence happened because of his negligence (Art. 23 TCK).

169. S. Dönmezer & S. Erman (II), *Nazari ve Tatbiki Ceza Hukuku, Genel Kısım, Cilt II, 9.* Bası, İstanbul, Beta, 1986, p. 1221; M. Özen, *Ceza Hukukunda Objektif Sorumluluk*, 1998; M.E. Artuk et al., *Ceza Hukuku Genel Hükümler* Ankara, Yenilenmiş Gözden Geçirilmiş 11. Baskı Adalet, 2017, p. 13.

170. There are attempts to insert the principle of guilt by requiring at least the negligence. Z. Kangal *Kabahatler Hukuku, XII Levha,* İstanbul, 2011, p. 116; M. Kayançiçek, *Ceza Hukuku ve Kabahatler Hukukunda Zamanaşımı,* Adalet, Ankara, 2014; A. Parlar, *Açıklamalı-İçtihatlı Kabahatler Kanunu,* Bilge Yayınevi, 2012.

Chapter 4. Grounds for Justification of Criminal Offenses and Defenses That Diminish or Excuse Criminal Responsibility or Liability

§1. General Principles

145. Grounds for justification. To constitute a crime, the act or omission should be unlawful. If there are grounds of justification,[171] then the material element is not considered a crime.[172]

The presence of justification is determined objectively; it is not dependent on the perpetrator being aware of the justification,[173] and the subjective thoughts of the offender are not relevant.

The element of unlawfulness (*supra*, paragraph 105) is a unified concept. If an act is justified by one branch of law, then it cannot be considered illegal by another branch of law.[174]

§2. Necessity

146. Necessity. The law does not punish persons who are faced with serious harm that can only be avoided by violating the criminal statutes. No punishment shall be imposed if an individual acted out of necessity, and if there was no other way to protect himself/herself, or another person, against a grave and certain danger (Article 25/2, TCK).

Property damaged in cases of necessity will be restored. However, a judge has discretion on this matter (Article 52/2, BK).

147. The person himself must not knowingly cause the danger. If the perpetrator had caused the danger with intent, then the provisions of necessity are not applied. The means used to rescue must be proportional to the gravity of the danger and the protected right (Article 25/2, TCK).[175] However, in a case of negligence, it is possible to consider the case as one of necessity.

The person should not be obliged to expose himself to danger. The necessary action to prevent the danger should be the only way to escape harm. If actions could have been taken which would have resulted in lesser damage or emergencies but were not taken as such, then the perpetrator will be punished.

---

171. T. Demirbaş, *Ceza Hukuku Genel Hükümler*, 15. Baskı, Seçkin, Ankara 2020, p. 453.
172. T. Katoğlu, *Ceza Hukukunda Hukuka Aykırılık*, Ankara, Seçkin Yayınları, 2003; A. Parlar & M. Hatipoğlu, *5237 Sayılı TCK'da Ceza Sorumluluğunu Kaldıran veya Azaltan Nedenler*, 2010.
173. N. Toroslu, *Ceza Hukuku Genel Kısım*, 21. Bası, Ankara, Savaş Yayınevi, 2015.
174. S. Dönmezer & S. Erman (II), *Nazari ve Tatbiki Ceza Hukuku, Genel Kısım, Cilt II, 9.* Bası, Beta, İstanbul 1986, p. 679.
175. Cass. 3. CD Apr. 27, 2015, 2015/14779 K.; Cass. 4. CD Mar. 9, 2015, 2015/24129; Cass. 1. CD Jun. 9, 2014, 2014/3418.

§3. Defense Against Crime

148. The Penal Code (Article 25/1, TCK) changed[176] the definition of self-defense:[177]

> Whoever commits any action with the necessity of defending against an unjust assault directed against his/her or a third party's right shall not be punished, if his/her action was proportionate according to the circumstances at the moment of the assault and the assault was about to happen, happening or it was certain that it would happen again.

The first condition of self-defense[178] is an unlawful assault. *Unlawful* means that the law does not permit that type of activity. It is not required that the act constitutes a crime in itself.[179]

The second condition of self-defense is an assault caused by a human being that is directed at a *legal good.* In contrast to the previous legislation, where only life and chastity were protected, now property is also protected.

The third condition of self-defense has also been extended by the Penal Code: Previously, it was the rule that *the unlawful attack had already taken place and did not come to an end* (Article 49/2, repealed TCK). Now the Penal Code has made it also possible to *prevent* a repeating unlawful assault (Article 25/1, TCK).

Self-defense against the attack must have been necessary. If it was possible to escape without danger, self-defense is not allowed.

Only the Court of the First Instance has discretion on this issue. The Court of Cassation is not competent to exercise this discretion.[180]

There should be a causal connection between the attack and the defense. Where the attacked person endangers or harms the property of the perpetrator, there can be no demand for restitution for damages.

149. Defense of property was regulated separately (Article 461, repealed TCK). If the defender had taken extreme measures to defend his property, then the punishment for the offender was reduced. The new Penal Code does not include this provision, as the definition of self-defense has been extended to any endangered legal good (Article 25/1, TCK) (*supra*, paragraph 148).

---

176. The previous definition was as follows: *No punishment shall be imposed if an individual acted out of immediate necessity to fend off an unjust assault against him or another person, or if he acted to protect his or another's chastity* (repealed TCK, Art. 49/2).
177. M. Özen, *Meşru Müdafaa*, Ankara, Seçkin Yayınları, 1995; F. Yenisey, Kolluğun Zor ve Silah Kullanma Yetkisi, Mukayeseli Hukuk, AİHM Kararları, in *Kolluğun Silah Kullanma Yetkisi*, İstanbul, 2005, p. 95.
178. N. Toroslu, *Ceza Hukuku Genel Kısım*, 21. Bası, Ankara, Savaş Yayınevi, 2015.
179. S. Dönmezer & S. Erman (II), *Nazari ve Tatbiki Ceza Hukuku, Genel Kısım*, Cilt II, 9. Bası, Beta, İstanbul 1986, p. 798.
180. S. Dönmezer & S. Erman (II), *Nazari ve Tatbiki Ceza Hukuku, Genel Kısım*, Cilt II, 9. Bası Beta, İstanbul, 1986, p. 810; M. Özen, *Türk Ceza Hukukunda Meşru Müdafaa*, 1995; Cass. 4. CD Nov. 2, 2015, 2015/36783 K.; Cass. 23. CD Sep. 17, 2015, 2015/4232; Cass. 3. CD Apr. 27, 2015, 2015/14779 K.; Cass. 4. CD Mar. 9, 2015, 2015/24129; Cass. 1. CD Jun. 9, 2014, 2014/3418.

§4. Consent of the Victim

150. A victim is a person who has been directly injured by the criminal act. It is possible that the victim may have given his consent[181] to the illegal acts directed against him.[182] The consent of the victim (Article 26/2, TCK) is considered a ground of justification if the protection of public interest is not very important, and the assault is directed at a right on which the victim can dispose without limitation.[183] With respect to some crimes, such as crimes against sexual inviolability (*infra*, paragraph 202), crimes against liberty (*infra*, paragraph 203) and some crimes against property (*infra*, paragraph 210), consent of the victim plays an important role.

The Penal Code now provides a definition of the consent of the interested person (it does not use the terminology of the victim): No one shall be punished if he/she acts within the scope of the consent that has been declared by an individual concerning a right, on which he has an unrestricted right of usage (Article 26/2, TCK).[184]

The consent of the victim is not valid for offenses directed against the state.

151. Suicide is not a crime under Turkish Criminal Law. But an individual cannot rely on the will of someone to be killed as a defense, and if a doctor kills his patient upon his request, then he is responsible for intentional murder. Euthanasia is not allowed under Turkish Criminal Law.

§5. Execution of the Provisions of a Statute and Obeying Orders

152. Execution of the provisions of a statute. No punishment shall be imposed if the perpetrator acts in order to execute the provision of a statute (Article 24/1, TCK). The term "statute" includes all forms of acts, and not just criminal statutes.[185]

153. Obeying orders. The perpetrator shall not be punished if he/she acted to execute an order given by a responsible authority, the execution of which is within

181. Ö. Çakmut, *Tıbbi Müdahaleye Rızanın Ceza Hukuku Açısından İncelenmesi*; Legal Yayıncılık, 2003.
182. N. Centel, H. Zafer & Ö. Çakmut, *Türk Ceza Hukukuna Giriş*, Sekizinci Bası, İstanbul, Beta, 2014, p. 312.
183. S. Dönmezer & S. Erman (II), *Nazari ve Tatbiki Ceza Hukuku, Genel Kısım*, Cilt II, 9. Bası, Beta, İstanbul 1986, p. 736; B. Öztürk & M.R. Erdem, *Uygulamalı Ceza Hukuku ve Güvenlik Tedbirleri Hukuku TCK* Değişikliklerine Göre Yenilenmiş, 14. Baskı, Ankara 2014, Seçkin Yayınları, p. 168. The practice of *consent search,* which was regulated by the Internal Regulation on the Search Powers of the Police of 2003, was stopped after the Council of State ruled that it did not have a legal ground (Danıştay 10. Dairesi Nov. 23, 2003).
184. T. Demirbaş, *Ceza Hukuku Genel Hükümler*, 15. Baskı, Seçkin, Ankara 2020, p. 334.
185. S. Dönmezer & S. Erman (II), *Nazari ve Tatbiki Ceza Hukuku, Genel Kısım, Cilt II, 9.* Bası, İstanbul, Beta, 1986, p. 764; T. Demirbaş, *Ceza Hukuku Genel Hükümler*, 15. Baskı, Seçkin, Ankara 2020, p. 285.

his duty (Article 24/2, TCK). But if the order given by the superior violates provisions of the law, regulations or the Constitution, a person employed in public services shall not carry it out and shall inform the person giving the order of the violation. However, if his superior insists that the order be carried out and reissues it in writing, this order shall be executed. In this case, the person executing the order shall not be held responsible.

There are exceptions to this rule in the military and police branches. If the statute prohibits the examination of the lawfulness of the order, the superior giving the order shall be held responsible (Article 24/4, TCK).

An order, which in itself constitutes an offense, shall under no circumstances be executed (Article 137, AY; Article 24/3, TCK).

154. Military orders. According to the *Act on Internal Regulations of the Army* (*İç Hizmet Kanunu* No. 211, Article 3), soldiers must obey their superiors without hesitation. The responsibility of the execution belongs to the superior (Article 14, Act No. 211). However, it is forbidden to execute an order that in itself constitutes a crime (Article 24/3, TCK).

155. Orders in the police. In 1963, the Constitutional Court abolished the requirement of obeying all orders without hesitation.[186] According to the current provisions of the Police Act (*Polis Vazife ve Salahiyet Kanunu,* PVSK), Article 2/2, when a police officer believes that an order given by his superior is contrary to the law; he shall not carry it out. However, he must execute the order if it is reissued in writing. In cases where the protection of life is at stake, he must obey without delay and is not entitled to ask for a written order (Article 2/3, PVSK).

156. Orders given to civil servants. There are no special regulations in the Act on State Officials, Article 11, relating to the execution of orders given to regular officials.

The Ministry of Justice is entitled to ask the Attorney General at the Court of Cassation to file a lawsuit for legal errors in cases that did not reach the inspection of the Court of Appeals or the Court of Cassation (Article 309, CMK) (*infra*, paragraph 559).

§6. Exercising a Given Right

157. Exercising a right. An individual who exercises his legal right[187] shall not be punished for that (Article 26/1, TCK).[188] If the law or case law has recognized

---

186. Official Gazette, Nov. 13, 1963.

187. T. Demirbaş, *Ceza Hukuku Genel Hükümler*, 15. Baskı, Seçkin, Ankara 2020, p. 320; U. Uruşak, *Ceza Hukukunda Hukuka Uygunluk Sebebi Olarak Bir Hakkın Kullanılması*, İstanbul, Vedat Kitapçılık, 2010.

188. This ground of justification was not mentioned in the repealed Penal Code, Art. 49, but was accepted by criminal law in the following cases: The owner of goods has the right to prevent unjustified assaults by using force (Art. 981, MK); the owner of goods may protect his property with some automatic mechanisms such as a fence, or flashing light.

a subjective right to an individual that can be exercised directly, there is no penal responsibility if this right has been used in a proper way and within its limits.[189]

158. Exercising a profession. Within the limits of exercising one's profession, medical interventions[190] are considered exercising a right and are justified, so long as there is consent (Article 26/2, TCK) or necessity to do so (Article 17/2, AY).

159. Freedom of press. In the context of freedom of speech (Article 28, AY), the press has the right to inform the public. Within limits, newspaper publications (*infra*, paragraph 188) do not constitute a crime.

160. Exceeding the limits. Anyone who exceeds the limits of the grounds for setting aside criminal responsibility shall be punished with a reduced punishment pursuant to Article 27/1 of the Penal Code if the limits were exceeded without intent and the crime may be sanctioned if committed with negligence and the perpetrator exceeded the limits of justification through negligence. The punishment stated by the Code will be reduced from one-sixth up to one-third (Article 27/1, TCK). Thus, there is no exclusion of penalty if the limits are exceeded.

However, in cases of an unavoidable mistake without guilt, there is no punishment (Article 30/3, TCK).

Further, if the limits are exceeded, only within the *legitimate defense* (Article 25/1, TCK) there is a new exception to the reduced punishment. If the limits of a legitimate defense were exceeded as a result of excitement, fear or agitation (and this can be regarded as excusable) then the perpetrator shall not be punished (Article 27/2, TCK).[191]

§7. Grounds of Excuse (Grounds that Exclude the Guilty Mind)

161. Grounds of excuse. Where the will of the offender cannot be considered free, he cannot be held criminally responsible. In cases of accident, force majeure, coercion and mistake, the offender's will is not a guilty one. Coercion exempts one from guilt because there cannot be blameworthy conduct under coercion. The offender is not acting voluntarily, as he has lost his freedom of choice.[192]

No penalty shall be imposed on the individual if the crime is committed as a result of intolerable or inevitable violence or serious menace or gross threat. However, the person involved in the use of force and violence, menace and threat shall be considered the perpetrator of the crime (Article 28, TCK).

189. S. Dönmezer & S. Erman (II), *Nazari ve Tatbiki Ceza Hukuku, Genel Kısım,* Cilt II, 9. Bası, Beta, İstanbul 1986, p. 702; B. Öztürk & M.R. Erdem, *Uygulamalı Ceza Hukuku ve Güvenlik Tedbirleri Hukuku TCK* Değişikliklerine Göre Yenilenmiş, 14. Baskı, Ankara 2014, Seçkin Yayınları, p. 225.
190. B. Erman, *Tıbbi Müdahalelerin Hukuka Uygunluğu*, Ankara, Seçkin Yayınları, 2003.
191. T. Demirbaş, *Ceza Hukuku Genel Hükümler*, 15. Baskı, Seçkin, Ankara 2020, p. 343.
192. S. Dönmezer & S. Erman (II), *Nazari ve Tatbiki Ceza Hukuku, Genel Kısım,* Cilt II, 9. Bası Beta, İstanbul 1986, p. 1040; T. Demirbaş, *Ceza Hukuku Genel Hükümler*, 15. Baskı, Seçkin, Ankara 2020, p. 434.

162. Accident. There are some major events in life that cannot be foreseen, or if foreseen, cannot be prevented.[193] In such cases there is no criminal responsibility.[194]

163. Force majeure requires the perpetrator to act against his own will. He has no other choice. In such cases, he is not responsible. This ground for the excuse that excludes the guilty mind is not mentioned in the Penal Code as a general principle, but it is accepted as a general principle of criminal law. For example, a strike during wartime may be considered as a force majeure under Article 322, TCK.

164. Suppression of free will. In cases in which the free will of an individual is suppressed by force, violence, menace or threat (Article 28, TCK) or in cases of a mistake of facts (Article 30/1), that person is not considered to have acted intentionally.

165. Mistake of law: Ignorance of Law. Mistake means ignorance, lack of knowledge or wrong knowledge. Ignorance of law is no defense under Turkish criminal law (Article 4, TCK). However, an individual who makes an inevitable mistake about the unlawfulness of his act shall not be punished (Article 30/4, TCK).

The provisions of the TCK related to the *ignorance of law* have been in the focus of discussions during preparations of the Code, and have been amended just after the Code came into force, by removing its exceptions from Article 4/2, TCK into the chapter related to *mistake* (Article 30/4, TCK). The *knowledge of injustice* (*supra,* paragraph 133) shall affect the punishment of the accused, if ignorance of the law is unavoidable. An unavoidable ignorance of law shall exclude the punishment.[195]

For example, it is regulated as a crime to have sexual intercourse with a child under the age of 15 even though he or she consents (Article 104/1, TCK). Yet if the perpetrator does not know the child's age and supposes that the child is older than fifteen, this situation shall be regarded as a mistake. For instance, there are Syrian refugees in Turkey who permit their daughters under the age of 14 to get married in a religious ceremony, which constitutes a crime of child molestation under Article 103, TCK. The parents of both brides and grooms are considered participants in this crime. In such cases, the courts of first instance try to apply the rule of unavoidable mistake, since such behavior is not considered a crime in the homeland of the refugees. The Court of Cassation however makes a very detailed examination and very rarely considers the existence of a mistake.[196]

On the other hand, the Constitutional Court cancelled the provision, which regulates performing sexual abuse by inserting an organ or an object into the victim's

---

193. R. Gülşen, *Ceza Hukukunda Sorumluluğu Kaldıran Nedenlerden Kaza, Mücbir Sebep, Cebir ve Tehdit*, Ankara, Seçkin, 2007.
194. S. Dönmezer & S. Erman (II), *Nazari ve Tatbiki Ceza Hukuku, Genel Kısım, Cilt II*, 9. Bası, İstanbul, Beta, 1986, p. 1027; M.E. Artuk et al., *Ceza Hukuku Genel Hükümler* Ankara, Yenilenmiş Gözden Geçirilmiş 11. Baskı Adalet, 2017, p. 220; T. Demirbaş, *Ceza Hukuku Genel Hükümler*, 15. Baskı, Seçkin, Ankara 2020, p. 454.
195. T. Demirbaş, *Ceza Hukuku Genel Hükümler*, 15. Baskı, Seçkin, Ankara 2020, p. 446.
196. Cass. CGK Jan. 14, 2014, 2014/8 K.

body as a crime (Article 103/2, Act 2004–5275,). The aim of this decision was to secure the family union of the victim and the perpetrator who married after the intercourse.[197] This decision is criticized for bringing back the provision of the repealed Penal Code which regulated dropping of prosecution after the marriage between a rape offender and rape victim (Article 434, repealed TCK).

166. Ignorance of facts. A factual mistake may exclude intent. Any individual who is unaware of facts that constitute the element of the crime while committing his/her act shall not be considered as having acted intentionally (Article 30/1, TCK).

If a person commits a crime against a person other than the one he intended, as a result of a mistake or a defect, the matters of aggravation arising from the status of the injured party shall not be imputed to the perpetrator. Such cases may be dealt with as if the crime had been committed against the person intended, but the perpetrator shall benefit from any mitigating factor applicable to the felony (Article 30/2, TCK).[198]

197. Constitutional Court, Nov. 12, 2015, 2015/11 K.
198. K. İçel et al., *İçel Suç Teorisi,* Beta, İkinci Bası, İstanbul 2000, p. 278.

Chapter 5. Criminal Attempt and Participation in Criminal Offenses

§1. Criminal Attempt

I. Punishment for Attempted Crime

167. Attempt to commit a crime. Criminal thoughts, in and of them, are not punishable.

To be punishable there must be a completed criminal act. However, an unsuccessful attempt to commit a crime can be a crime in itself.[199] An attempt is a special form of crime as compared to the completed offense.[200]

An individual who is unable to complete the crime that he had intended to commit due to circumstances beyond his control, but who has begun directly with appropriate acts of commission, shall be liable for an attempted crime (Article 35/1, TCK).

There are some crimes that are not suitable to attempt. For example, undertaking a coup against the government (Article 312, TCK) shall be an accomplished crime, as soon as the perpetrators attempt to overthrow the regime.

The type of punishment depends upon the nature[201] of the attempt, that is to say, upon the seriousness of the harm or danger that was realized (Article 35/2, TCK).[202]

168. Degree of danger. Anyone, who directly starts the execution of an intended crime by appropriate acts, and cannot complete the acts necessary to commit the crime for reasons beyond his control, is placed in the position of attempt (Article 35/1, TCK).[203] In such cases, depending on the degree of the harm or danger, the perpetrator shall be sanctioned with imprisonment for a term of thirteen to twenty

---

199. R.A. İpekçioğlu, *Yeni Ceza Hukukunda Suça Teşebbüs*, 2009; S. Balcı, *Suça (Cürme) Teşebbüsün Eski ve Yeni Ceza Kanunu'na Göre Karşılaştırmalı İncelenmesi,* Legal Hukuk Dergisi sayı: 25, Ocak 2005; A. Parlar & M. Hatipoğlu, 5237 *Sayılı TCK'da Suça Teşebbüs, İştirak İçtima ve Yaptırımlar*, 2010; S. Tellenbach, *Strafbares Verhalten im Vorfeld der Tatvollendung in der Türkei*, in *Nationales Strafrecht in rechtsvergleichender Darstellung, Teilband 3*, ed. Sieber & Cornils, Berlin, 2008, p. 949.

200. K. İçel et al., *İçel Suç Teorisi*, 2. Kitap, Beta, İstanbul, İkinci Bası, 2000, p. 295; E. Artuk, A. Gökcen & C. Yenidünya, *Türk Ceza Kununu Şerhi*, 1. Cilt, Ankara, Turhan Kitabevi, 2009, p. 854; İ. Özgenç, *Türk Ceza Hukuku Genel Hükümler, Gözden Geçirilmiş ve Güncellenmiş* 10. Bası, Ankara, Seçkin, 2014, p. 451; M.R. Önok. *Penal Law,* in Introduction to Turkish Law, ed. Tuğrul Ansay, Don Wallance Jr., Işık Önay, Seventh Edition, Ch. 2, Kluwer, Deventer 2020, p. 235.

201. The current Penal Code does not make the distinction between the *completed attempt* and the *incomplete attempt*, as it was defined in the repealed Code (Arts. 61, 62, TCK).

202. D. Soyaslan, *Teşebbüs Suçu*, 1994; A. Sözüer, *Suça Teşebbüs*, 1994; N. Centel, H. Zafer & Ö. Çakmut, *Türk Ceza Hukukuna Giriş*, Sekizinci Bası, İstanbul, Beta, 2014, p. 431; B. Öztürk, M.R. Erdem, *Uygulamalı Ceza Hukuku ve Güvenlik Tedbirleri Hukuku TCK Değişikliklerine Göre Yenilenmiş*, 14. Baskı, Ankara, Seçkin Yayınları 2014, p. 316.

203. This definition was the definition for *incomplete attempt* according to the repealed Code and the punishment would be reduced according to Art. 61. If the offender completed all the acts for the execution of the felony he intended to commit, but for reasons beyond his control the felony did not materialize, he was placed in the position of *completed attempt* and his punishment was reduced according to repealed Art. 62.

years where the committed crime required a penalty of aggravated life imprisonment or with imprisonment for a term of nine to fifteen years where the committed crime required a penalty of life imprisonment. In other cases, the penalty shall be reduced by one-quarter to three-quarters (Article 35/2, TCK).[204]

169. Voluntarily withdrawal. If the perpetrator voluntarily withdraws from the completion of the intended criminal act, or prevents the completion of the crime or its consequences, he will not be punished (voluntary abandonment as defined in Article 36, TCK).

However, if the completed part of an action does constitute a crime, he shall be liable for the sanction of this part of his act.

170. Attempt to commit a misdemeanor. As mentioned earlier (*supra*, paragraph 67), the rules on misdemeanors are laid down in the Act on Misdemeanors (KK). Therefore, the perpetrator will not be sanctioned if his deeds constitute an attempted misdemeanor, unless the statute foresees the contrary (Article 13, KK). If there is such explicit regulation[205] about the punishable attempt of a misdemeanor, then the provisions of the Penal Code about criminal attempt (Article 35, TCK) and voluntary abandonment (Article 36, TCK) shall apply.

II. Conditions of Criminal Attempt

171. Intent. The intention of the perpetrator must be to commit a crime (Article 35/1, TCK). This intent is not the intent to attempt, but the intent to commit a certain crime.

In cases of negligence and strict liability, an attempt is not punished.

172. Preparatory acts. The preparatory acts are acts that are shown in the legal definition of the crime. These activities are in preparation of the forbidden action. The preparatory acts made before the commencement of the execution shall not be punished.

However, Article 316 TCK makes it a special crime for two or more persons to agree to commit a crime against state security or constitutional order of the state by suitable means, thus incriminating the planning of such crimes. In the field of organized crime, just forming an organization is an independent crime if the organization is furnished with suitable means and personnel (at least three) in order to commit the aimed crimes (Article 220/1, TCK).

173. Acts of direct execution. The perpetrator should have directly started to execute an intentional crime by appropriate acts of commission.

---

204. T. Demirbaş, *Ceza Hukuku Genel Hükümler*, 15. Baskı, Seçkin, Ankara 2020, p. 474.

205. For example, *Smuggling Act* (2007–5607), Art. 3/18 rules that, attempted misdemeanors in Art. 3/10 shall be punished as a completed misdemeanor.

The acts of direct execution (Article 35/1, TCK) began where the perpetrator had undertaken the actions described by the statute as the last act, openly indicating his intent to commit a crime.

174. Circumstances independent of the perpetrator's scope of control must cause the acts of execution[206] of the intended crime to remain incomplete.

175. Attempting the impossible. Sometimes it is impossible to complete the acts of execution because of ineffectiveness of the means of execution or of the unsuitability of the object.[207] TCK does not regulate the attempt of the impossible. However, the Court of Cassation considers a case as attempted crime where the perpetrator stole an invalid traveler's check and brought it to the bank.[208]

§2. Participation

I. Conditions of Participation

176. When an offense that can be committed only by one person was committed with the cooperation of several persons, the principle of participation will be applied (Articles 37–41, TCK).[209] The first condition of participation is the presence of a crime (Article 37/1, TCK) or a misdemeanor (Article 14, KK).[210]

The second condition of participation is that the plurality of the offenders agreed upon the act before or during the commission of the act and they started performing the act.

The agreement between the offenders should have been made before committing the crime or at least during the commission of the act.

Anyone who takes part in a crime knowingly and willingly, either before or during the commission of the act, is called a *participant* (Article 37, TCK).[211]

---

206. For the now abolished distinction between incomplete attempt and completed attempt, it was important to discover when the acts of execution were completed. If the perpetrator had fulfilled all the necessary acts to commit the intended result, and he had lost all possibility of withdrawal, the acts of execution were considered as completed (S. Dönmezer & S. Erman (I), *Nazari ve Tatbiki Ceza Hukuku, Genel Kısım,* Cilt I, 10. Bası, İstanbul, Beta, 1987, p. 569).
207. S. Dönmezer & S. Erman (I), *Nazari ve Tatbiki Ceza Hukuku, Genel Kısım,* Cilt I, 10. Bası, İstanbul, Beta, 1987, p. 539; N. Centel, H. Zafer & Ö. Çakmut, *Türk Ceza Hukukuna Giriş,* Sekizinci Bası, İstanbul, Beta, 2014, p. 455.
208. Cass., CGK Jun. 25, 1990; E. 1990/157, K. 1990/200, YKD 1990, 1381.
209. N. Centel, H. Zafer, & Ö. Çakmut, *Türk Ceza Hukukuna Giriş,* Sekizinci Bası, İstanbul, Beta, 2014, p. 466.
210. M.V. Dülger, *Yeni Türk Ceza Kanunu'nda Suç Ortaklığı*, sayı: 2, Yeditepe Üniversitesi Hukuk Fakültesi Dergisi cilt: 1, 2005; F.S. Mahmutoglu, *Kusurluluk Prensibi Açısından Azmettirenin Ceza Sorumluluğu*, İstanbul Üniversitesi Hukuk Fakültesi, 2005, Ayrı Bası; Hukuk Fakültesi Mecmuası; vol. 63, H. 1/2.2005; M.R. Önok. *Penal Law*, in Introduction to Turkish Law, ed. Tuğrul Ansay, Don Wallance Jr., Işık Önay, Seventh Edition, Ch. 2, Kluwer, Deventer 2020, p. 237.
211. If the offender plays a role in revealing the unknown identity of the instigator, his punishment may be reduced.

177. Certain offenses, however, presuppose the cooperation of several persons. In such cases, there is no participation and the plurality of offenders constitute an element of the offense. For example, in organized crime there must be at least three or more members of the gang (Article 220/1, repealed TCK).

In jointly committed crimes, the accomplice who voluntarily abandons the attempt to commit a crime may benefit from the voluntary abandonment (Article 36, TCK) provisions (Article 41/1, TCK). The voluntary abandonment provisions shall only apply to the person who voluntarily abandons and the crime was not committed because of his efforts and not for any other ground; or if the crime was committed despite his efforts to prevent the commission of that crime (Article 41/2, TCK).

This is another provision parallel to Article 38/3, TCK, which is designed to combat organized crime.

II. Forms of Participation

178. The current Penal Code foresees three classifications for jointly committed crimes: Joint offenders (Article 37/1, TCK); incitement (Article 38/1, TCK); and a person who assists (Article 39/1, TCK).

Those who perform the act jointly are named *(fail)*, and those who incite or assist are named *(suç ortağı)* within the language of the current Code (Article 38/3, TCK).

The old Turkish Criminal Law doctrine classified participation[212] into four categories: Principal, secondary, material and moral.

179. If several persons participate in a crime and perform the act prescribed by law jointly, each of them shall be considered principal offenders, and each shall be subject to the punishment prescribed for that act (Article 37/1, TCK).

Any person, who has cooperated by committing the acts of execution, is an *offender of that act.* For example, in a homicide, when two people acting together fire fatal shots, both are principal actors.

A person who does not commit the acts of execution but aids in the execution of the crime in such a way that the crime could not have been committed without his assistance is considered as committing the crime directly together with the perpetrator. For example, the driver of a car involved in the abduction of a woman is in this position and can be subject to the punishment prescribed for abduction as well.

The Penal Code has introduced the concept of *using another as an instrument* (Article 37/2, TCK): in such cases, that individual who uses another as an instrument for the commission of a crime remains liable as *offender,* even if he did not perform the act by his own hand.

In order to prevent children from being misused in committing crimes, the punishment is increased one-third to one-half if the *offender behind the acting offender* has used those who do not have the ability of discretion, and therefore have no criminal liability (Article 37/2, TCK).

212. İ. Özgenç, *Suça İştirakin Hukuki Esası ve Faillik*, 1996; T.Y. Sancar, *Çok Failli Suçlar*, 1998.

180. Anyone who incites another to commit a crime shall be subject to the same punishment of the crime that is committed (Article 38/1, TCK).

However, the provision of the repealed Penal Code (Article 64/2, TCK), which regulated that *if it is ascertained that the person who perpetrated the act had a personal interest in its execution, the punishment of the abettor shall be reduced* is not included into the Penal Code.

Where the incitement was conducted by using the influence arising from kinship as the direct ascendant or descendent, the punishment of the instigator shall be increased by one-third to one-half (Article 38/2, TCK).

If a *child* has been incited to commit a crime, kinship is not necessary for the application of Article 38/2, TCK.

The current Penal Code has introduced a general rule of *effective remorse* for jointly committed crimes. Those who perform the act jointly and those who incite or assist shall receive reduced[213] prison sentences if they reveal the identity of the unknown instigator (Article 38/3, TCK).

181. Whoever participates in the crime of the principal offender with some material activities is considered as being in the position of a person who assists (Articles 39/1; 38/3, TCK).

The Penal Code has furnished a definition of *the person who assists* (Article 39/2, TCK). Anyone participating in a crime by: (a) abetting or encouraging another toward the commission of a crime or by promising him aid and assistance after the commission of the act; (b) giving instruction as to the manner of the commission of the crime or providing the means which are used by the commission of the act; or (c) facilitating the commission of the crime through rendering aid and assistance before or during the commission of the crime shall be liable as the person who assists.

The person who assists shall be punished by a maximum of eight years of imprisonment; if the committed crime requires aggravated life imprisonment, he shall be sanctioned with an imprisonment term of fifteen to twenty years; if the committed crime requires life imprisonment, he shall be sanctioned with an imprisonment term of ten to fifteen years. Other imprisonment terms may be reduced by one-half (Article 39/1, TCK).

In the previous repealed Penal Code (Article 65/2, repealed TCK), the assistor's punishment was not reduced if the commission of the crime was not possible without his participation. The Penal Code does not include this provision, as the assisting person shall be regarded as a *principal offender* according Article 37/1, TCK if he has *control on the commission of the crime.*

---

213. The punishment is *imprisonment for twenty to twenty-five years* instead of aggravated life imprisonment, and *imprisonment for fifteen to twenty years* instead of life imprisonment. For other prison terms, the penalty to be imposed may be reduced by one-third (Art. 38/3, TCK).

182. Under the *dependency rule,* participation in a crime requires the commission of an act that is unlawful and committed intentionally (Article 40/1, TCK). There is no criminal liability if at least an attempted crime does not exist (Article 40/3, TCK).[214]

Each individual who participates in the commission of a crime shall be liable according to his guilty act, irrespective of the individual circumstances that may prevent the imposition of a penalty on the other offender (Article 40/1, TCK).

Facts requiring aggravation of the punishment, even though of such a nature as to change the classification of the felony or misdemeanor, shall also aggravate the punishment for all accomplices who knew about such facts at the time of the commission of the act (Article 67, TCK).

Participation in a previous crime is not a general ground for a more severe penalty. In some cases, there are exceptions to this rule (e.g., Articles 417, 479, 491, repealed TCK).

183. Participation in misdemeanors has been regulated explicitly in the Act on Misdemeanors (KK 14). According to this provision, in case of participation in a misdemeanor, each participant shall be punished by an administrative fine as the principal offender. In cases where there is a specific status such as being a civil servant required to punish, the participant who does not have this quality shall also be sanctioned by an administrative fine as the principal offender. The existence of an unlawful and willful act is sufficient to be sanctioned as a participant in misdemeanors. The person shall be sanctioned by an administrative fine even if the other participants are not responsible.

214. In order to constitute a jointly committed offense, it is sufficient that the act is unlawful and committed intentionally (Art. 40/1 TCK). In order to be culpable for a jointly committed offense, there must have been at least an attempt to commit the offense (Art. 40/3 TCK) (V. Bıçak & E. Grieves, *Mukayeseli Gerekçeli Türkçe-İngilizce Türk Ceza Kanunu,* 2. Bası, Ankara, Seçkin, 2007, p. 127).

Chapter 6. Classification of Criminal Offenses

§1. General Classification of Criminal Offenses

184. Crimes. The Penal Code regulates crimes.[215] Misdemeanors are not included. From a procedural point of view, there are some differences between ordinary crimes punished with imprisonment, misdemeanors punished with administrative sanctions imposed by administrative authorities, crimes dealing with state security, crimes committed by state officials and crimes committed by the press.

The repealed TCK distinguished between felonies *(cürümler)* and misdemeanors *(kabahatler)*.[216] The category of offenses that were called contraventions (*cünha*) existed in the 1858 Criminal Act of the Ottoman Empire but was not carried over into new legislation during Atatürk's Law Reform (*supra*, paragraph 34) of 1926. Felonies and misdemeanors were defined by reference to the penalty. Punishments for felonies were: Death, lengthy imprisonment (requiring the court of assizes and imprisonment under more severe conditions), light imprisonment, heavy fine and disqualification from a profession or trade (Article 11/1, repealed TCK). *Banishment* (*sürgün*) was abolished in 1965. Punishments for misdemeanors were: Light imprisonment, light fine and disqualification from a profession or trade (Article 11/2, repealed TCK).

The Penal Code introduced a unified concept of *crime* (*suç*) for petty or severe offenses altogether.

185. Ordinary crimes. All crimes, including organized crimes, are tried by the regular criminal courts (*infra*, paragraph 350) according to regular criminal legislation since 2014.

186. Organized crimes. There was a distinction between ordinary crimes and organized crimes, as far as the existence of deviating regulations for organized crime required a special procedure, offenses listed under the repealed Article 250 of the Penal Procedure Code and in the Anti-Terrorism Act were tried by a special section of the Court of Assizes, and they were subject to a special procedure as far as the pre-trial detention period and the examination of witnesses during the trial were concerned. Law No. 2014-6526, however, abolished Article 10 TMK, which was regulating such special procedure (*infra*, paragraph 355). There is now no difference between organized crimes and ordinary crimes with regard to procedure.

187. Crimes committed by state officials. Preliminary investigation of offenses committed by state officials[217] while on duty will be made by a high official in his

215. B. Öztürk, *Hukuk Devletinde Suç Yaratılmasının ve Suçun Aydınlatılmasının Sınırları Sempozyumu* (Yeşilköy, İstanbul 1–3 Haziran 2008, 2009). N. Toroslu, *Cürümlerin Tasnifi Bakımından Suçun Hukuki Konusu*, Ankara, 1970; Y. Ünver, *Ceza Hukukuyla Korunması Amaçlanan Hukuksal Değer*, Ankara, Seçkin Yayınları, 2003; A. Polat & S.K. Gül, *Suçun Ölçümü*, Ankara, Adalet, 2010.

216. N. Toroslu, *Cürumlerin Tasnifi Bakımından Suçun Hukuki Konusu*, Ankara, 1970, p. 87.

217. The Constitutional Court has abolished Art. 102 of Act No. 1580 (Decision dated Feb. 2, 1993 E. 1992/44, K. 1993/7: RG. Jun. 19, 1993). Hence, employees of municipalities are not considered as *state officials* anymore.

official capacity, and not by the public prosecutor.[218] The final investigation, however, will be tried by the competent ordinary court (Article 1, Act on Adjudication of Civil Servants; MKYK).[219]

Law enforcement officers, accused of using firearms in situations of terrorism as described in Act No. 1481, dated September 15, 1971 (Article 3) will be investigated by the public prosecutor directly (instead of an investigation by their superiors).

Allegations of breach of Article 94, TCK (torture), as well as of Article 160, CMK (not obeying the orders of the public prosecutor) are exempted from the privileges of the initial investigation by the superior (Article 2, Act on Adjudication of Civil Servants; MKYK). The public prosecutor explores and prosecutes such allegations directly.

Since 2014, after the terrorism courts had been abolished by Act No. 2014-6526, Article 161 was supplemented with a new subsection, giving the public prosecutor ex officio investigation for crimes regulated by Articles 302, 309, 311, 312, 314 and 316, even if such crimes are committed while being on duty, or in connection to the duty of the civil servant (Article 161/8, CMK).

188. Crimes committed by the press: Freedom of press and broadcasting. Article 28, AY guarantees the freedom of the Press.[220] There is a ground of justification for publication in the mass media. According to the special status of the press, offenses committed through publication are under the jurisdiction of the Press Courts.

The repealed Penal Code provided aggravated penalties for those who insulted the President, the Parliament, or the army by means of publication (Articles 158 and 159 repealed TCK). The current Penal Code does not include this aggravating factor (Articles 299, 300, 301, TCK). However, the penalty for discouraging people from performing military service shall be increased by one-half if the act is committed through the press or broadcasting (Article 318/2, TCK).

Until 1993, Turkish Radio and Television (TRT) had a legal monopoly over broadcasting. With the increasing availability of satellite dishes and cable, however, many Turkish viewers may now watch foreign broadcasts, including several Turkish-language private channels. The constitutional rule of the monopoly of the state over broadcasting (Article 133, AY) was abolished July 8, 1993 by Act No. 3913 (RG. July 10, 1993). The way for private radio and television broadcasting was thereby opened.

The administrative enforcement of the misdemeanors regarded as freedom of press lies with the Information and Communication Technologies Authority. This authority is empowered to investigate infringements of such regulations and to impose penalties on operators.

---

218. E. Çetin, *Açıklamalı-İçtihatlı Ceza Hukukunda ve Özel Yasalarda Memur, Memurlar ve Diğer Kamu Görevlilerinin Yargılanma Usulü ve Memur Suçları*, Ankara, Seçkin Yayınları, 2003.
219. H. Gökcan & A.T. Mustafa, *Kamu Görevlisi ve Özel Soruşturma Usulleri*, 2008.
220. E. Çetin, *İçtihatlı Basın Hukuku*, Ankara, Seçkin Yayınları, 2004. C.H. Derneği Yayınları, *İfade Özgürlüğü ve Türk Ceza Hukuku*, İstanbul, Beta Yayınları, 2003; E. Günay, *Yayın Yoluyla Kişilik Haklarına Saldırı ve Basında Sorumluluk*, Ankara, Seçkin Yayınları, 1999; K. İçel, Yener Ünver, *Kitle Haberleşme Hukuku*, İstanbul, Beta, 2007; K. Şahin, *Terörizm ve İfade Özgürlüğü Paradoksu,* Türk Ceza Adalet Sisteminin Etkinliğinin Geliştirilmesi Programı, Ankara 2014.

189. Implementation of press-related criminal law. Article 301, TCK, which criminalizes defamation of the Turkish nation (*infra*, paragraph 246), remained pending until 2012, and the provision has not yet been amended. The 4th Judicial Reform Package adopted in April 2013, addresses several key issues as regards freedom of expression where the definitions of the crimes of publishing, printing or producing propaganda on behalf of a terrorist organization have been narrowed down significantly by the introduction of the necessary element of coercion, violence or threats. The scope of the offense of committing a crime in the name of an organization without being a member of that organization has been narrowed down to armed organizations only. The definition of the offense of praising a crime or a criminal has been narrowed with the introduction of the necessary element of clear and imminent danger to public order.

190. Website bans. The obligations and responsibilities of the Internet service providers and the procedure of Internet bans are regulated by the Act on Regulation of Internet Publications and Combating Crimes Committed by Publications on Internet (*infra*, paragraph 490).

191. Restrictions on radio and television broadcasting. The Supreme Board of Radio and Television (RTÜK) may issue warnings and fines to television and radio stations, in particular for broadcasting superstitious beliefs, denigrating morals and national values and damaging the family, broadcasting obscenity and praising terrorism. In June 2013, RTÜK issued warnings to a number of television stations that had transmitted live coverage of the Gezi Park protests on the basis that they were violating the principle of objective broadcasting and fined them for inciting violence. All stations concerned appealed to the courts.

§2. CRIMES

I. Crimes of the Penal Code

192. The structure of the TCK. Crimes are regulated by the TCK[221] and by some Special Criminal Acts.

The TCK (dated September 26, 2004, No. 5237) has been effective since June 1, 2005. Book One of the Penal Code includes a General Part (Articles 1–75, TCK), which deals with the basic institutions of criminal law. Book two of the Penal Code (Articles 76–345, TCK) deals with specific crimes. The first part deals with *international crimes* (Articles 76–80, TCK) (*infra*, paragraph 193). The second part deals with *crimes against individuals* (Articles 81–169, TCK) (*supra*, paragraph 179). In order to demonstrate the importance of individual protection, crimes against persons precede the crimes aimed at protecting the state, which have been placed at the end of Book Two. The third part of Book Two regulates the *crimes against the public* (*topluma karşı suçlar*) (Articles 170–246, TCK) (*infra*, paragraph 216). The

221. M. Özen, *5237 Sayılı Türk Ceza Kanunu'nun Özel Hükümlerine İlişkin Düşünceler*, Türkiye Barolar Birliği Dergisi, Mart/Nisan 2006, p. 63.

fourth and last part of Book Two deals with *crimes against the nation and the state* (Articles 247–345, TCK) (*infra*, paragraph 229).

The TCK does not include misdemeanors. There is a separate Act on Misdemeanors (KK).[222]

A. *International Crimes Regulated by Penal Code*

1. Genocide and Crimes against Humanity

193. Genocide (Book Two, Specific Provisions; Part 1. Subsection 1. Articles 76–80, TCK). Part 1 is subdivided into two subsections: Genocide and crimes against humanity[223] (Articles 76, 77, TCK), and smuggling of immigrants and human trafficking (Articles 79, 80, TCK). Genocide is defined as committing crimes that are listed in the statute with the aim of the total or partial destruction of individuals who comprise a national, ethnic, racial or religious group, with the means of executing a plan (Article 76/1, TCK).[224]

194. Crimes against humanity. These crimes[225] are defined as committing crimes that are listed in the statute against one part of the population with political, philosophical, racial or religious motives, systematically to execute a plan. (Article 77/1, TCK).[226]

---

222. A. Karagülmez, *Adli İdari Para Cezaları*, Seçkin Yayınları, 2001; F.S. Mahmutoglu (ed.), *Türk Ceza ve Ceza Muhakemesi Hukuku (idari işlemle suç ve ceza konulup konulamayacağı ile kabahatli suç olmaktan çıkarma ...)* proje yöneticisi: F.S. Mahmutoğlu, *Avrupa Birliği'ne Uyum Sürecinde Türk Ceza ve Ceza Muhakemesi Hukuku*, İstanbul Barosu, 2008; F.S. Mahmutoğlu, *Ekonomik Suçlar Bağlamında Kredi Hukukundan Kaynaklanan Suç ve İdari Suçlar*, Ankara, Seçkin, 2003; F.S. Mahmutoğlu, *Kabahatleri Suç Olmaktan Çıkarma Eğilimi ve Düzene Aykırılıklar Hukukunda (Idari Ceza Hukukunda) Yaptırım Rejimi*, İstanbul, Kazancı Kitap Ticaret, 1995; N. Meran, *Kabahatler Kanunu ve Kabahat İçeren Kanunlar, Ankara, Adalet, 2008;* C. Otacı & İ. Keskin, *Türk Kabahatler Hukuku*, 2. Bası, Ankara, Adalet Yayınevi, 2010; C. Taşkın, 5236 *Sayılı Kabahatler Yasası'nın Anayasa'ya ve Hukuka Aykırılık Yönünden İncelenmesi*, Türkiye Barolar Birliği Dergisi, sayı 61, Kasım & Aralık 2005; H. Yılmaz, *Yetkili Mercilerin Kararlarına Uymama*, Ankara, Seçkin Yayınları, 1999.
223. Y. Aksar, *Uluslararası Ceza Mahkemesi ve Uluslararası Ceza Usul Hukuku*, Seçkin Yayınları, 2003; C.A. Ekşi, *Uluslararası Ceza Mahkemesinin İnsanlığa Karşı Suçlar Üzerindeki Yargı Yetkisi*, Ankara, Seçkin Yayınları, 2004; A.N. Tütüncü, *İnsancıl Hukuka Giriş*, İstanbul, Beta, 2006; F. Yenisey (ed.) *Uluslararası Ceza Divanı*, İstanbul, Arıkan Yayınları, 2007; E. Şen, *Uluslararası Ceza Mahkemesi*, 2009; M.Y. Aslan, *Uluslararası Ceza Mahkemesi*, Bilge Yayınevi, Ankara 2017; M.C. Kul, *Uluslararası Ceza Mahkemesi ve Uluslararası Tecâvüz (saldırı) Suçu = International criminal court and the crime of aggression = Cour penale internationale et le crime d'agression*, On İki Levha Yayıncılık, İstanbul 2016.
224. K. Bayraktar, V.S. Evik & G. Kurt, *Özel Ceza Hukuku: Uluslararası Suçlar*, 2. Bası, On İki Levha Yayıncılık, İstanbul 2017.
225. S. Erman, *The Problem of the Procedural Rights of War Criminals and International Law, Annales de la Faculte De Droit*, XXII, No. 38 (1972–1974), p. 287.
226. F. Yenisey (ed.) *Uluslararası Ceza Divanı*, İstanbul, Arıkan Yayınları, 2007.

2. Migrant Smuggling and Traffic in Human Beings

195. Migrant smuggling. Migrant smuggling has been one of the most important problems in the Mediterranean area for decades. Turkey enacted a criminal law provision (Article 79, TCK) in order to address this problem. This provision was amended in 2010. The problem of how to handle attempted migrant smuggling arose. Migrants, transported to border areas, who were arrested during this transport before crossing Turkish borders did create a legal uncertainty as a result of the decisions of the Court of Cassation. The Legislature amended the structure of the crime in 2010. Attempted smuggling of migrants shall be punished as a completed crime (Article 79/1, TCK). If the lives of migrants are endangered, or if the crime has been committed by means of degrading treatment, imposed punishment will be increased up to two-third of the sentence (Article 79/3, TCK).[227]

196. Trafficking in human beings. As concerns trafficking in human beings, the Turkish National Police identified a limited number of victims and prosecuted a limited number of traffickers. The Act on Foreigners and International Protection provides for the issuing of residence permits to victims or those strongly suspected of being victims of trafficking. The law also provides for the creation of a Department for the Protection of Victims of Human Trafficking. However, the framework of the anti-trafficking law has yet to be adopted in line with the EU acquits. A comprehensive, multi-disciplinary and victim-oriented approach to trafficking still needs to be developed and victim identification needs to be improved. Victims need to have unhindered access to assistance, support and protection. The re-integration of victims upon their return and the cooperation with civil society are vital. Prevention needs to be stepped up and efforts are needed to effectively curb the demand for trafficking in human beings. The Council of Europe Convention on Action against Trafficking in Human Beings needs to be ratified.

There is a growing concern about an increase in human trafficking as a consequence of the Syrian crisis. The Turkish authorities have made significant efforts to cope with the Syrian refugee crisis. According to official Turkish data, the number of Syrians staying in fifteen tent cities, five container camps and a temporary reception center exceeded 200,000. As concerns migration, following a consultative process, progress was made with the adoption of the *Act on Foreigners and International Protection* in April 2013. This law introduces a comprehensive legal and institutional framework on the legal status of migrants, procedures and safeguards to be followed in the context of detention and expulsion of irregular migrants as well as the protection of vulnerable categories of migrants such as minors, with a view to bringing Turkey into line with EU and international standards. The establishment of the General Directorate of Migration Management to deal with foreigners, suggests a development in this field. The courts' capacity to handle migration cases and the bar associations' capacity to provide legal aid need to be enhanced.[228]

227. D. Tezcan, M.R. Erdem & M. Önok, *Teorik ve Pratik Ceza Özel Hukuku,* 18. Baskı, Seçkin, Ankara 2020, p. 90.
228. European Commission, Turkey 2015 Progress Report.

B. *Crimes Against Human Beings*

1. Crimes Against Life

197. Crimes against life. Subsection 1 is the first subsection of Part Two to deal with crimes against individuals (Articles 81–169, TCK).[229]

This subsection deals with *intentional killing*[230] (manslaughter) (Article 81, TCK), *aggravated intentional killing* (murder) (Article 82, TCK), *committing an intentional killing by omitting a conduct* (Article 83, TCK), *leading to commit suicide* (Article 84, TCK) and *negligent killing* (Article 85, TCK).[231]

The TCK does not allow euthanasia, as all forms of assisted suicide[232] are considered as intentional killings. The judge may, however, reduce the punishment according Article 62, TCK (*infra*, paragraph 318).

2. Crimes Against the Integrity of the Body

198. Crimes against the integrity of the body include fatal and non-fatal crimes (Part 2. Subsection 2. Articles 86–93, TCK).[233] Non-fatal crimes against the person include the following: Intentional wounding (battery) (Article 86, TCK), aggravated intentional wounding with regard to consequences (Article 87, TCK), where the perpetrator is only responsible for excess consequences if the perpetrator is liable at least by his negligence for this result beyond his intent (Article 23, TCK), committing an intentional wounding by omitting conduct (Article 83, TCK), negligent wounding (Article 89, TCK) and trading with human organs or skin (Articles 91–93, TCK).

---

229. I. Akbulut, *Kan Gütme Saiki ile Adam Öldürme*, İstanbul, Kazancı Hukuk Yayınevi, 2006; N. Centel, H. Zafer, & O. Çakmut, *Kişilere Karşı İşlenen Suçlar*, İstanbul, Beta, 2007; S. Dönmezer, *Kişilere ve Mala Karşı Cürümler*, 16. Bası, İstanbul, 2001. A.E. Ahmet Sevinç & Ö. Ramazan, *Kasten Adam Öldürme Suçları*, Ankara, Seçkin Yayınları, 1996; E. Göztepe, *Namus Cinayetlerinin Hukuki Boyutu: Yeni Türk Ceza Kanunu'nun Bir Değerlendirmesi*, Türkiye Barolar Birliği Dergisi, p. 29 Temmuz & Ağustos 2005; H. Hakeri, *Kasten Öldürme Suçları*, Seçkin Yayınları, Gözden Geçirilmiş 2. Baskı, Ankara 2007; M. Kaygısız & S. Katiller, *Paralel Cinayetler*, 2009; O.K. Keskin, *Taksirle Ölüme ve Yaralanmaya Neden Olma*, Ankara, Seçkin Yayınları, 1994; N. Meran, *Kişilere Karşı Suçlar; Genişletilmiş ve Gözden Geçirilmiş 2.* Baskı, Ankara, Seçkin, 2008; N. Meran, *Yeni Türk Ceza Kanununda Kişilere Karşı Suçlar*, Ankara, Seçkin Yayınları, 2005; C. Öztürkler, *Ölüm ve Bedeni Zarar Hallerinde Maddi Tazminatın Hesaplanması Teknikleri,* Ankara, Seçkin Yayınları, 2003.

230. A.C. Ruhi, *Türk Ceza Kanununda Kasten Öldürme Suçları: En Son Yargıtay İçtihatları İle,* On İki Levha, İstanbul 2017; D. Tezcan, M.R. Erdem & M. Önok, *Teorik ve Pratik Ceza Özel Hukuku,* 18. Baskı, Seçkin, Ankara 2020, p. 137.

231. H. Hakeri, *Kasten Öldürme Suçları*, Gözden Geçirilmiş İkinci Baskı, Seçkin, Ankara 2007.

232. S. Dönmezer, *Kişilere ve Mala Karşı Cürümler,* 16. Bası, İstanbul, 2001, p. 39.

233. M.R. Erdem, *Cinsel İlişki Yoluyla Başkasına HIV Bulaştırmanın Cezalandırılabilirliği Sorunu*, Erzincan Hukuk Fakültesi Dergisi Cilt 8 sayı: 1–2 p. 73, Erzincan 2004; S. Kaymaz, *5237 Sayılı Türk Ceza Kanunu'nun 87/4 Maddesinde Düzenlenen Neticesi Sebebiyle Ağırlaşmış Yaralama Suçu*, Türkiye Barolar Birliği Dergisi, sayı 58 sayfa 73, Mayıs & Haziran 2005.

3. Torture and Harassment

199. The crime of torture by state officials[234] and torture by civilians (Part 2. Subsection 3. Articles 94–96, TCK) have been separated. The Penal Code has a new approach to the crimes of torture.[235] In contrast to international regulations, torture is not a crime that can only be committed by state officials. Civilians may also be offenders.

A state official, who commits acts that are incompatible with human dignity and lead to the suffering of bodily or mental pain, which influences the perception capabilities or the abilities to form will by the victim, and which degrade him, shall be liable for *torture* (Article 94, TCK).

Aggravated torture with regard to consequences (Article 95, TCK) is a new crime; the perpetrator is only responsible for excess consequences if he is liable at least by the negligence of the result beyond his intent (Article 23, TCK).

Torture by civilians (harassment) is also a new crime (Article 96, TCK). Any conduct that leads to the suffering of heavy pain is considered a crime.

Torture is an ordinary crime in contrast to *torture* within offenses against humanity in Article 77, TCK. However, because of some procedural obstacles, torture prosecutions against civil servants, specifically law enforcement officers, were delayed in the past. To avoid running out of the statute of limitations in prosecution, the legislature added a new provision to Article 94 TCK. Like in crimes against humanity (Article 77/4, TCK), the statute of limitations does not apply to the ordinary crime of torture since 2013 (added paragraph 6 to Article 94, TCK by Act No. 6459).

The prevention of torture, ill treatment and excessive use of force during demonstrations and arrests and in official detention places, as well as in prisons, continues to be a matter of concern. The excessive use of force during largely peaceful protests across the country in May-June 2013, and other cities raised serious concerns.

The EctHR in the case of *Yaşa and Others v. Turkey* considered that the safeguards surrounding the proper use of tear-gas grenades needed to be strengthened in order to minimize the risk of death and injury resulting from their use. In June 2013, following the demonstrations across Turkey and accusations of the excessive use of force by the police, the Ministry of the Interior issued a circular detailing stringent rules governing the use of tear gas and pepper spray by the police. The Council of Europe Secretary-General called for a change of mentality in the police and the judiciary.

Several trials remain ongoing in connection with the allegations of ill-treatment of conscientious objectors in military prisons. EctHR judgments in this area remain to be executed.[236]

---

234. V. Akay, *Folter und die türkische Gerichtsbarkeit*, Zambon, Frankfurt a. M. 2001. Giffard, Camile, *İşkencenin Rapor Edilmesi* (2001); V.Ö. Özbek et al., *Türk Ceza Hukuku Özel Hükümler*, 8. Baskı, Seçkin, Ankara 2015, p. 263.
235. M. Önok, *Uluslararası Boyutuyla İşkence Suçu*, 2006.
236. Turkey, despite being a member of the European Council, has refused to recognize the right to conscientious objection. ECtHR examined such cases in the context of Art. 9 of ECHR and found that

4. Neglecting the Obligation of Protection

200. Violation of the obligations of protection, help and notification (Part 2. Subsection 4 Articles 97, 98, TCK). A person who abandons any individual for whom he has an obligation of care has committed the crime of abandonment (Article 97, TCK). If the abandoned individual suffers an illness or dies, the perpetrator is responsible for these excessive consequences under the provisions of Article 23, TCK.[237]

Whoever omits to help an individual who was not able to rescue himself, as he was in a state of helplessness because of his age, illness or because he was wounded or whoever does not give notice of this state of affairs to the respected authorities, shall be punished by imprisonment of up to one year or with a criminal fine (Article 98, TCK).

5. Abortions and Sterilization

201. The person who conducts an abortion without having received the consent of the women shall be punished by imprisonment between five and ten years (Article 99, TCK). If the pregnant woman wanted the abortion, and the duration of the pregnancy was more than ten weeks, she shall be punished with imprisonment for up to one year or with a criminal fine (Article 100, TCK). The one doing that abortion shall be punished as well.[238]

Sterilization (Article 101, TCK) without receiving the consent of the subject is punishable by imprisonment between three and six years.

6. Crimes Against Sexual Inviolability

202. Crimes against the sexual inviolability (Part 2. Subsection 6. Articles 102–105, TCK). The title of subsection 6 indicates a significant change in the approach of the lawmaker.[239] Instead of protecting public decency, the protection is now on sexual[240] liberties.

Turkey has violated the Convention (*Erçep v. Turkey, Tarhan v. Turkey, Savda v. Turkey, Feti Demirtaş v. Turkey, Buldu and others v. Turkey*).

237. E. Yılmaz, *Yardım veya Bildirim Yükümlülüğünün Yerine Getirilmemesi Suçu,* Seçkin, Ankara 2020; D. Tezcan, M.R. Erdem & M. Önok, *Teorik ve Pratik Ceza Özel Hukuku,* 18. Baskı, Seçkin, Ankara 2020, p. 350.

238. D. Tezcan, M.R. Erdem & M. Önok, *Teorik ve Pratik Ceza Özel Hukuku,* 18. Baskı, Seçkin, Ankara 2020, p. 365; S. Oktar, *Türk Ceza Kanunu'nda Çocuk Düşürtme ve Çocuk Düşürme Suçları,* Seçkin, Ankara 2016.

239. N. Abadan, *Social Change and Turkish Women*, Ankara Üniversitesi 1963; M.E. Artuk & A.C. Yenidünya *Türk Ceza Hukukunda Kız, Kadın ve Erkek Kaçırma Suçları*, Türkiye Barolar Birliği Dergisi sayı 54, Eylül & Ekim 2004; E. Doğramacı, *Rights of Women in Turkey*, Ankara, Universal Bookstore 1982; E. Doğramacı, *Status of Women in Turkey,* 2nd ed., Ankara, 1984; A.H. Evik, *Ceza Kanunumuz ve Kadın*, İstanbul, Prof. Dr. Çetin Özek Armağanı, Galatasaray Üniversitesi Yayını, 2004; H.Y. Sevük, *5237 Sayılı Türk Ceza Kanunu'nda Cinsel Saldırı ve Cinsel Taciz Suçları*, Türkiye Barolar Birliği Dergisi, sayı 57, Mart & Nisan 2005; A.C. Yenidünya, *5237 Sayılı*

Act No. 2014–6545 introduced a big change in the field of sexual crimes: The whole chapter on sexual crimes was rewritten and the new law imposed more severe punishments.[241]

The main crime in this area is sexual assault (Article 102, TCK), which can only be committed by at least touching the victim. Child abuse (Article 103, TCK), sexual intercourse with a minor (Article 104, TCK)[242] and sexual molestation (Article 105, TCK) are the other sexual crimes.

The new wording of *sexual assault* (Article 102, TCK) reads as follows:

(1) Any person, who violates the sexual integrity of a person by a sexual behavior, will be sentenced to imprisonment from five years to ten years.[243] In cases where the sexual behavior has stayed at the stage of molestation, imprisonment will be two to five years.

(2) In case of the commission of offense by inserting an organ or instrument into a body shall punish the offender by minimum imprisonment of twelve years. In case of the commission of this offense against a spouse, the commencement of investigation and prosecution is bound to the complaint of the victim.

(3) If the offense is committed;

(a) Against a person who cannot protect himself because of corporal or spiritual disability,

(b) By undue influence based on public office, tutorship or work conditions,

(c) Against a person with whom he/she has a third-degree blood relation or kinship, or by a person who is a stepfather, stepmother, sister or brother-in-law, adoptive father or mother and adopted child,

(d) By using a weapon or participation of more than one person in the offense,

---

Yeni Türk Ceza Kanunu'nda Cinsel Dokunulmazlığa Karşı Suçlar, Legal Hukuk Dergisi sayı: 33, Eylül 2005; P.M. Kartal, *Türk Ceza Hukukunda çocukların Cinsel İstismarı*, DER Yayınları, İstanbul 2014; S. Bakıcı, *Açıklamalı, İçtihatlı Genel Adap ve Aile Düzenine Karşı Cürümler*, 1994; C. Otacı, *Genel Adap ve Aile Düzenine Karşı İşlenen Suçlar*, 2000; S. Selçuk, *Kızlık Bozma Suçu*, 1996, Mustafa Arslantürk, *Türk Ceza Kanunu Uygulamasında Cinsel Suçlar: Yargılamadan Uygulamalarla, Somut Olaylarla, Pratik Çözümlerle*, 3. Baskı, Seçkin, Ankara 2017; F.G. Taner, *Türk Ceza Hukuku'nda Cinsel Özgürlüğe Karşı Suçlar*, 2. Baskı, Seçkin, Ankara 2017.

240. N. Karadağ, *Cinsel Azınlıkların Bireysel Hakları*, 2008.

241. Violation of sexual integrity carried imprisonment term of two to seven years. After the amendment, imprisonment term is now from five to ten years (Art. 102/1). Accordingly, punishments in other provisions have also been increased such as for child abuse the imprisonment term was three to eight years and now the same crime carries imprisonment term from eight to fifteen years (Art. 103/1, TCK).

242. N. Kantarcı, *Türk Ceza Hukukunda Reşit Olmayanla Cinsel İlişki Suçu*, Adalet, Ankara 2016; R. Gündüz, *Türk Ceza Kanununda Cinsel Dokunulmazlığa Karşı suçlar: Cinsel Saldırı (TCK 102), Çocukların Cinsel İstismarı (TCK 103), Reşit Olmayanla Cinsel İlişki (TCK 104), Cinsel Taciz (TCK 105)*, 2. Baskı, Bilge Yayınevi, Ankara 2017.

243. The requirement of compliant of the victim and lesser punishment of two years to seven years for cases where the crime is committed by a sudden act, has been abolished.

(e) In a place where individuals have to live together, by taking advantage of this circumstance, the punishments imposed according to above subsections are increased by one half.

(4) In cases where the use of force during the commission of offense causes aggravated results of intended injury, provisions related to the intended injury will be applied additionally.

(5) In cases where the victim enters into a vegetative state or dies as result of the offense, the offender will be sentenced to aggravated life imprisonment.[244]

The new definition of *child abuse* (Article 103, TCK) is now as follows:

(1) Any person who sexually abuses a child shall be punished by imprisonment for a term of eight to fifteen years. In cases where the sexual abuse has stayed at the stage of molestation, imprisonment will be three to eight years. If the offender of the crime at the stage of molestation is a child, investigation and prosecution requires the complaint of the guardian or tutor of the victim. Sexual abuse means:

(a) Any act of a sexual nature against a child who has not completed fifteen years of age or, though having completed fifteen years, lacks the competence to understand the meaning and consequences of such acts,

(b) Sexual acts conduct against any other child only by using of force, threat, deception or any other method, which affects the willingness of the child.

(2) Where the sexual abuse is committed by inserting an organ or a similar object into the body, imprisonment term shall be not less than sixteen years. If the victim did not attain the age of twelve, the prison term shall not be less than eighteen years.

(3) If the offense is committed;

(a) By more than one person jointly,

(b) In a place where individuals have to live together by taking advantage of this circumstance,

(c) Against a person with whom he has third degree blood relation or kinship, or by a person who is a stepfather, stepmother, sister or brother-in-law, adoptive father or mother, adopted child,

(d) By the tutor, educator, teacher, caretaker, by persons who deliver services as protecting family or health care or by persons who have an obligation to take care or oversight,

(e) By undue influence based on public office or work conditions, the punishments indicated in the above paragraphs will be doubled.

244. As the determining of *the deterioration of corporal and spiritual health* created big problems, the previous subs. 5 has been deleted. The deleted provision was as follows: *In case of the deterioration of the corporal and the spiritual health of the victim as a result of the offense, the offender shall be sentenced to imprisonment not less than ten years.*

(4) Where the sexual assault is committed against children described in section (a) by force or threat, or against children described in section (b) by using a weapon, the punishments indicated in the above paragraphs will be increased by one half.
(5) Where any force or violence, used with the aim of sexual assault, leads to any aggravated injury on account of its consequences, the provisions of that offense shall apply in addition.
(6) Where the offense leads the victim to enter a vegetative state, or if the victim dies, a penalty of aggravated life imprisonment shall be imposed.

The Penal Code has divided the former provisions related to *public decency* in two parts. Some of the crimes are considered more *individual related* and, therefore, have been regulated in Part 2, Subsection 6. But pornography[245] is deemed more *public related* and has been taken to Part 3, Subsection 7 (*infra,* paragraph 254).

Child pornography is a new type of crime, committed when children are used in the production of pornographic material (Article 226/3, TCK).

Raping a prostitute (Article 438, repealed TCK) formerly was subject to a mitigated penalty. This provision was abolished in 1990 by Act No. 3679.

Formerly, the Constitutional Court had abolished *adultery* (Articles 440–444, repealed TCK) on the basis of being against the principle of equality. The Penal Code does not include adultery. However, there have been some efforts to make it a crime again. This caused big discussions during the promulgation of the Penal Code.

The current Penal Code made *rape within a marriage*[246] a crime, punishable by imprisonment of minimum twelve years (it was imprisonment between seven and twelve years before the 2014-6545 amendment). The investigation of the crime and the prosecution can only be done if the spouse files a *complaint* (Article 102/2, TCK).

Complaint crimes are subject to *mediation* and cannot be prosecuted before an attempt to mediate fails or turns out to be unsuccessful. However, *complaint crimes against sexual inviolability* are exempted (Article 253/3, CMK).

7. Crimes Against Liberty

203. Crimes against liberty (Part 2. Subsection 7. Articles 106–124, TCK)[247] are restructured within the new Code in the following manner: threat (Article 106, TCK), extortion (Article 107, TCK), deprivation of personal liberty (Article 109,

245. Pornography was forbidden by Art. 426 of the repealed Turkish Penal Code, Act No. 3266 of Mar. 3, 1986; Act No. 3506 of 1988 had amended this article, increasing the applicable fines.
246. Previously, *rape within a marriage* was not considered a crime according to Turkish case law. However, if the husband forced anal intercourse on his wife, this act was considered an *illegal act against family members* and was punishable under Art. 478 repealed TCK (S. Dönmezer, *Kişilere ve Mala Karşı Cürümler,* 16. Bası, İstanbul, Beta, 2001, p. 260).
247. O. Yaşar, *Uygulamada ve Öğretide Hürriyet Aleyhinde İşlenen Suçlar* (2001); M.E. Artuk, A.

TCK), obstructing of education (Article 112, TCK), obstructing the use of political rights (Article 114, TCK), obstructing the use of the rights of religion, thought and belief (Article 115, TCK), violation of dwelling immunity[248] (Article 116, TCK), violation of the freedom of labor (Article 117, TCK), conducting an illegal search on a person (Article 120, TCK), apartheid (Article 122, TCK), disturbing the tranquility of an individual (Article 123, TCK) and obstructing the communication between individuals[249] (Article 124, TCK).[250] These are regulated in the seventh subsection of Part 2.

Obstructing education (Article 112, TCK) was amended in 2014 by Act No. 6529:

> Whoever by using violence or threat, or by any illegal manner obstructs the education in an educational facility that is established by, or operated upon, a permission granted by the state, or violates the right of individuals to give an education, or prevents students from entering, or leaving educational buildings, shall be punished by imprisonment of two to five years.

Obstructing the Use of the Rights of Utilizing Public Services (Article 113, TCK) was amended in 2014, by Law No. 6529:

> Whoever by using violence or threat, or by any illegal manner, obstructs the running of a public activity, or other services provided by public authorities, or by professional establishments, or services offered upon a permission of a public authority, shall be punished with imprisonment of two to five years.

Obstructing the Exercise of the Right of Religion, Thought And Belief (Article 115/2, TCK) was amended in 2014 by Act No. 6529:

> Whoever by using violence or threat, or by any illegal manner obstructs the fulfilling of the requirements of a religious belief, or religious worship or ceremonies, shall be punished according to subsection 1, Article 115, TCK. Whoever by using violence or threat, or by any illegal manner interferes with the way of living that is a consequence of his/her religious, political, social and philosophical belief or thought, or forces him/her to alter this, shall be punished according to subsection 1, Article 115, TCK.

Gökçen & A.C. Yenidünya, *Ceza Hukuku Özel Hükümler,* 14. Bası (Ankara, 2014), p. 259. Smuggling Immigrants (Art. 201a, repealed TCK) and forcing them to work (or slavery), organ donations under duress, gaining consent of vulnerable individuals (Art. 201b, repealed TCK) were introduced to the Turkish Penal Code on Aug. 3, 2002, and regulated within the group of crimes against liberty. However, these new types of crimes have now been regulated in the first Part of the Penal Code as *international crimes* (Arts. 79 and 80, TCK). D. Tezcan, M.R. Erdem & M. Önok, *Teorik ve Pratik Ceza Özel Hukuku,* 18. Baskı, Seçkin, Ankara 2020, p. 506.

248. A.R. Çınar, *Konut Dokunulmazlığını İhlal Suçları*, 1999.
249. E. Şen, *Devlet ve Kitle İletişim Araçları Karşısında Özel Hayatın Gizliliği ve Korunması*, 1996.
250. S. Keskin-Kiziroğlu, *Konut Dokunulmazlığının İhlali Suçu*, Ankara, Adalet Yayınevi, 2010; İ. Üzülmez, *Şantaj Suçu*, Erzincan Hukuk Fakültesi Dergisi, Cilt 8 sayı: 1–2, Erzincan 2004, p. 173; O. Yaşar, *Hürriyet Aleyhinde Cürümler*, Ankara, Seçkin Yayınları, 2001.

Hate crimes are incorporated into the crime of apartheid (Article 122, TCK) in 2014, by Act No. 6529:

> Whoever prevents by the cause of a feeling of hate which emanates from the difference of language, ethnicity, nationality, color, gender, disability, political thoughts, philosophical beliefs, religion, or sect, the offering of sale of a movable or immovable property that was publicly announced for sale, or as to rent, or prevents the utilizing of a service that was offered to the public, the hiring of such an individual, or the ordinary economic activities of such a person, shall be punished by imprisonment of 1 to 3 years (Article 122, TCK).

Crimes against freedom of religion were changed on January 9, 1986, Act No. 3255, and the penalties were made more severe. The Constitutional Court abolished Articles 175 and 176 of the repealed TCK on November 4, 1986.[251] After this, Articles 175 and 176 had been reformulated on May 5, 1987 by Act No. 3369.

8. Crimes Against Honor

204. Crimes against honor (Part 2. Subsection 8. Articles 125–131 TCK) include several categories.[252] The law on defamation (Article 125, TCK) includes two types of *actus reus*. The first conduct is: Attaching a concrete act or state of affairs to an individual, which is eligible to disrupt his honor, dignity and reputation.[253] The second conduct is: Aattacking his honor, dignity and reputation by cursing.[254] The repealed Penal Code considered these two types of conducts as two separate crimes, and punished them differently (Articles 480 and 482, repealed TCK). The TCK foresees the same punishment.

Defamation of a deceased person is a crime if at least three persons were present at the time of the act (Article 130, TCK).

There is a special Act for Protection of Atatürk against Defamation. Crimes of defamation can only be investigated and prosecuted if the victim files a criminal complaint (Article 131, TCK). They are subject to mediation (Article 253, CMK). However, defamation of a public servant with regard to his office shall be prosecuted ex officio.

---

251. Decision of the Constitutional Court, Nov. 4, 1986, E. 1986/11, K. 1986/267.
252. H. Bulut, *Kişilik Hakları ve Kişilik Haklarına Saldırıdan Kaynaklanan Hukuk Davaları*, Beta, İstanbul, 2006; E. Çetin, *Yeni Türk Ceza Yasasındaki Hakaret Suçları*, Ankara, Seçkin Yayınları, 2005; A. Gündel, *Atatürk'e ve Cumhurbaşakanına, Cumhuriyete, Hükümete Hakaret Suçları Yasadışı Yakalanan ve Tutuklananlara Tazminat Verilmesi Davaları*, Ankara, Seçkin Yayınları, 1997; T.Y. Sancar, *Alenen Tahkir ve Tezyif Suçları*, Ankara, Seçkin Yayınları, 2004; A.O. Onar, *Türk Ceza Hukukunda Hakaret Suçu,* Adalet, Ankara 2016.
253. D. Tezcan, M.R. Erdem & M. Önok, *Teorik ve Pratik Ceza Özel Hukuku,* 18. Baskı, Seçkin, Ankara 2020, p. 627.
254. H. Sınar, *Hakaret;* in K. Bayraktar (Ed.)*, Özel Ceza Hukuku, Cilt III, Onikilevha, İstanbul 2018,* p. 423.

9. Crimes Against Private Life

205. Crimes against private life and the confidential sphere of life are found in Part 2. Subsection 9. Articles 132–140, TCK.[255] Crimes against property are found in Part 2. Subsection 10. Articles 141–169, TCK.

TCK has introduced some new types of crimes in the field of the protection of private life.

206. Confidentiality of communication. The digital revolution is one of the profound changes experienced by the industrialized world in the last generation and these changes are mirrored in the world at large. As a result of cell phones, individuals can be and are connected to each other wherever they go.[256] These changes have created amazing easiness in people's lives but on the other hand they have also simplified interventions in the confidentiality of communication as well..

Violation of the confidentiality of communications between individuals is a crime (Article 132, TCK). Recording and revealing the content of the communication are aggravated forms of this crime.

Violation of confidentiality of communication has been one of the most important legal concerns of citizens because of expanding wiretap practices in Turkey and the world. Private individuals as well as the law enforcement community have frequently disregarded the confidentiality of individuals' communications.[257]

The legislature redesigned Part 9 of the Penal Code by Act No. 6352, dated 2012, protecting privacy and confidentiality. Violating the confidentiality of communications between individuals by telephone or mail (Article 132, TCK) shall be punished more harshly since the amendment by Act No. 2012-6352; providing for imprisonment by one to three years (instead of six months to two years) and criminal fine.

If the violation of confidentiality occurs through a recording of the content of the communication, the penalty to be imposed shall be doubled (Article 132/1, TCK, as amended in 2012). Any person who unlawfully publicizes the contents of a communication between the parties of conversation shall be sentenced to a penalty of imprisonment for a term of two to five years (Article 132/2, TCK).

Any person who unlawfully discloses in public the content of a communication between himself/herself and others without obtaining their prior consent shall be sentenced to a penalty of imprisonment for a term of one to five years. Where the disclosed data is published by the press or broadcasted, the same punishment shall be applied (Article 132/3, TCK).

207. Oral conversations. Listening to non-public oral conversations without the consent of either one of the parties of the conversation, using a device for recording

---

255. K. Bayraktar, *Özel Hayata ve Hayatın Gizli Alanına Karşı Suçların Genel Özellikleri;* in K. Bayraktar (Ed.), Özel Ceza Hukuku, Cilt III, Onikilevha, İstanbul 2018, p. 465.
256. D.J. Gottlieb, *The Fourth Amendment and the Digital Revolution;* in Prof. Dr. Feridun Yenisey'e, Armağan, Beta, İstanbul 2014, p. 852.
257. H. Zafer, *Haberleşmenin Gizliliğini İhlal;* in K. Bayraktar (Ed.), Özel Ceza Hukuku, Cilt III, Onikilevha, İstanbul 2018, p. 471.

the voice is a crime (Article 133, TCK). It shall nevertheless be investigated or prosecuted only upon the complaint of the victim, and it is subject to mediation (Article 253, CMK).

Article 133 TCK sanctions the third party's eavesdropping by an instrument or recording by means of a sound device of private conversations between other individuals. The amendments introduced by Act No. 2012-6352 have increased the punishments for this crime, as well as changed the elements of it and created a new type of crime.

Any person who listens to confidential conversation between other individuals through a tapping device or who records such conversations using a sound recording device without their consent shall be punished by imprisonment for two to five years (Article 133/1, TCK).

Whoever records by means of a sound recording device a non-public conversation, in which he is one of the parties, without the consent of the other speaker, shall be punished by imprisonment for six months up to two years or by a criminal fine (Article 133/2, TCK).

Whoever unlawfully and publicly discloses the data collected through recording of non-public conversations between individuals shall be sentenced to a penalty of imprisonment for a term of two to five years or of a criminal fine of four thousand days (*infra,* paragraph 290).

Where the press or broadcasting channels publish the disclosed data, the same punishment shall be applied (Article 133/3, TCK).

208. Protection of private life. Violation of the confidentiality of private life (Article 134, TCK) is a crime. If the confidentiality of an individual's private life has been violated by taking pictures or recording the voice, imprisonment is for one year up to two years.

Criminal Law protects private life more efficiently since 2012. By the amendment in the first paragraph, the punishment has been increased from six months to two years' imprisonment or a criminal fine of imprisonment from one year to three years.

For the qualified version of the crime, the punishment will be doubled: *Any person who violates the confidentiality of another person's private life shall be punished by imprisonment of one to three years. Where the violation of privacy occurs as a result of recording images or sound, the penalty shall be doubled* (Article 134/1, TCK). Whoever discloses the images or sounds of another person's private life unlawfully, shall be punished by imprisonment of two to five years.

Where the disclosed data is published by the press or broadcasted, the same punishment shall be applied (Article 134/3, TCK).

All crimes mentioned in Articles 132, 133 and 134 are, however, investigated and prosecuted only upon the claim of the victim (Article 139, TCK), and therefore are subject to a mediation procedure (Article 253, CMK).

209. Protection of personal data. Collecting and storing personal data in an illegal way is a crime (Article 135, TCK).[258] Act No. 2014-6526 has increased the lower level of punishment of this crime from six months to one year.

Act No. 2014-6526 also increased the lower level of the punishment for illegal transfer of personal data to another person from one year to two years.

The person who neglects his legal obligation of deleting stored personal data, after the term as foreseen in an act has expired, is criminally responsible (Article 138, TCK). The imprisonment term for this crime was increased from one to two years (before it was six months to one year), and a second subsection was incorporated: *in cases where the personal data to be destroyed was collected under the provisions of Penal Procedure Code, the punishment shall be doubled* (Article 5 of Act No. 2014-6526).[259]

The Act on Protection of Personal Data (Act No. 2016-6698) has been published in the Official Gazette dated April 7, 2016. The purpose of the Act on Protection of Personal Data is to regulate the protection of privacy, fundamental rights and freedoms of people and also to enumerate the procedures and principles needed to be followed by real and legal persons who are processing personal data. This Act on Protection of Personal Data defines personal data on par with international regulations as *any information relating to an identified or identifiable natural person* and also defines many concepts related to personal data. Article 17 of this Act refers to TCK for the implementation of punishments. However, there are also misdemeanors regulated in Article 18 as a special provision. There is a Personal Data Protection Board acting as the executive body monitoring the compliance of data processing and transferring (Article 21).

This act amended some articles of the TCK. One of these changes is about obscenity (Article 226, TCK). Formerly, it was a crime to use only a human being who is a child; now, it is a crime to use a real child and representative images of children or persons looking like children in the manufacturing of obscene images, writings or words.

Furthermore, this Act added a new Article to TCK. This new Article (Article 245A, TCK) makes it a crime to produce computer programs that facilitate committing further crimes; it is also a crime to make or to create a device, computer program, password or other security codes with the aim of committing crimes regulated in the tenth section of TCK dealing with information technology (IT)-systems crimes.

---

258. K. Bayraktar, *Kişisel Verilerin Kaydedilmesi, Verilmesi, Ele Geçirilmesi ve Yok Edilmesi;* in K. Bayraktar (Ed.), Özel Ceza Hukuku, Cilt III, Onikilevha, İstanbul 2018, p. 627.
259. H. Sınar, *Data Protection in Turkish Criminal Law,* in Prof. Dr. Feridun Yenisey'e Armağan, Beta, İstanbul 2014, p. 635; K.M. Burch, *Protecting Privacy in the Digital Age,* in Prof. Dr. Feridun Yenisey'e Armağan, Beta, İstanbul 2014, p. 1713; J.M. Burkoff, *Law Enforcement Use of Drones & Privacy Rights in the United States*, in Prof. Dr. Feridun Yenisey'e Armağan, Beta, İstanbul 2014, p. 1733.

10. Crimes Against Property

210. Classification of crimes against property. The crimes against property[260] are as follows: theft (Article 141, TCK), qualified theft (Article 142, TCK), theft for use (Article 146, TCK), robbery (Article 148, TCK), qualified robbery (Article, 149 TCK), damage to property (Article 151, TCK), qualified damage to property (Article 152, TCK), damaging places of worship and cemeteries (Article 153, TCK), trespass (Article 154, TCK), abuse of trust (Article 155, TCK), fraud (Article 157, TCK), qualified fraud (Article 158, TCK), bankruptcy (Article 161, TCK), bankruptcy by negligence (Article 162, TCK) and benefiting without payment (Article 163, TCK). Also discussed are personal grounds that reduce or abolish the punishment (Article 167, TCK), effective remorse (Article 168, TCK) and security measures on legal entities (Article 169, TCK).[261]

211. Theft of energy. Act No. 2014–6545 introduced more severe punishments for crimes against property. The provisions in Article 141/2 TCK related to theft of energy (any kind of energy which has an economic value shall be deemed movable property) and the provision of Article 142/1-f about the theft of electrical energy have been repealed by Act No. 2012-6352.

The reason for this amendment was the big number of pending prosecutions related to theft of electrical energy, which had occupied dockets of criminal courts. Parallel to the amendment to Articles 141 and 142 TCK, the structure of the offense *gratuitous benefit* in Article 163 TCK has been changed by the same act:

> Whoever spends electrical energy, water or natural gas which may be utilized on the basis of subscription, without the consent of the owner in such a way that prevents the determination of the quantity of those consumed items, shall be punished with 1–3 years of imprisonment.

In cases where the suspect compensates the damages to the victim to the full extent, before investigations are finalized, there shall be no prosecution. If the suspect shows *effective remorse* after the prosecution and before the judgment has been rendered, the punishment will be reduced up to one-third (Article 168/5, TCK). The suspect may avail of this opportunity only twice.

In cases of suspected electric energy theft, water or natural gas, the consumer pays all damages within six months after this tacit amnesty law is in force (July 7,

260. D. Tezcan, M.R. Erdem & M. Önok, *Teorik ve Pratik Ceza Özel Hukuku*, 18. Baskı, Seçkin, Ankara 2020, p. 733.

261. M.E. Alşahin, *Yargıtay Kararları Işığında Mala Zarar Verme Suçları (5237 Sayılı TCK. m. 151 vd.)*, Ankara, Turhan Kitabevi, 2010; M. Ekinci & S. Esen, *Hırsızlık, Yağma, Güveni Kötüye Kullanma, Dolandırıcılık, Hileli ve Taksirli İflas, Karkılıksız Yararlanma, Belgelerde Sahtecilik ve Bilişim Alanında Suçlar*, Ankara, Yetkin Yayınları, 2005; A. Gündel, *Açıklamalı İçtihatlı 765 ve 5237 Sayılı Türk Ceza Kanunlarındaki Hırsızlık ve Dolandırıcılık Suçları*, Ankara, Seçkin Yayınları, 2005; K. İçel & Y. Ünver (eds.), *Malvarlığına Karşı Suçlar ve Ekonomik Suçluluk*, Ankara, Seçkin, 2009; N. Meran, *Sahtecilik - Malvarlığı, Bilişim Suçları ile Ekonomi ve Ticaret Alanında Suçlar*; Genişletilmiş ve Gözden Geçirilmiş 2. Bası, Ankara, Seçkin, 2008; N. Meran, *Yeni Türk Ceza Kanununda Sahtecilik-Malvarlığı Bilişim Suçları ile Ekonomi ve Ticaret Alanında Suçlar*, Ankara, Seçkin Yayınları, 2005; S. Selçuk, *Dolandırıcılığın Kimi Suçlardan Ayrımı*, Ankara, 1993.

2012); he shall not be punished, and if a sanction had been imposed earlier, it will be abolished, including all consequences of the punishment (provisional Article 2/2, of Act No. 2012-6352).

All decisions rendered against a person who has benefited from the provisions related to effective remorse at the offense of *gratuitous benefit* (Article 163, TCK) shall be registered at the National Criminal Record system and kept for fifteen years (Article 6/2, Criminal Records Act).

Where the object of theft is gas or a liquid form of energy or if the crime is committed in a factory, which stores, refines or transfers such forms of energy, the offender shall be punished by imprisonment for five to twelve years. Where the crime has been committed within the framework of the activities of a criminal organization, the penalty shall be increased by one-half (Article 142/3, TCK).

212. Trespass. The crime of trespass reads as follows:

> Any person who partially or completely occupies an immovable property, or its associated property belonging to someone else, without relying on any ownership right, as if he were the owner or alters or destroys the boundaries of such places, or prevents, even partially, the owner from using such, shall be sentenced, upon the complaint of the victim, to a penalty of imprisonment for a term of six months to three years and a criminal fine up to one thousand days (Article 154, TCK).

The investigation and prosecution of occupying public or private real property without having a legal right on it, or preventing the utilization by the owner, has been redesigned as a *complaint crime* by Act No. 2009-5841. The mediation procedure is applicable to this crime.

213. Qualified fraud. Imprisonment terms for some types of qualified theft by deception have been increased in 2005 and in 2013. If the offense of theft by deception is committed by causing loss to a public institution or corporation by using electronic data processing systems, a bank or lending institution, by obtaining a loan which would not otherwise be obtainable from a bank or other financial institution or to collect an insurance payment, the imprisonment term shall not be less than three years and the criminal fine shall not be less than double the benefit obtained from the offense (Article 158/1, TCK).

214. Benefiting without payment. In rural areas there is a common usage of electric energy by illegal methods, which leads to a great number of investigations and prosecutions. The caseload of criminal courts has been tripled in the past years. In order to reduce such cases, provisional Article 2 of the Act No. 2012-6352 has introduced a tacit amnesty: suspects paying the damage shall not be prosecuted, pending cases shall be dropped. A third paragraph has been added to the Article 163 TCK, which regulates the crime benefiting without payment by the same Act No. 2012-6352: Any person who uses electricity, water or natural gas that can only be consumed through a subscription, without having a prior consent of the owner or in a way that the consumption amount cannot be quantified shall be sentenced to a penalty of imprisonment for a term of one to three years. As a consequence of this amendment, Article 141/2 TCK, which had established that any form of energy, which has an economic value, was considered to be movable property, was repealed in 2012, by the same Act.

For the offense of benefiting without payment if the offender, inciter or assistor, however, shows remorse and compensates completely the loss of the victim, the state or a private legal person prior to the commencement of an investigation, there will be no prosecution. Where the losses are compensated before the verdict, the penalty to be imposed shall be reduced by one third. The same person can, however, cannot make use of the provision of this paragraph more than two times (Article 168/5, TCK).

215. Purchasing contraband goods or other assets obtained through the commission of a crime. This conduct had already been defined as an offense at Article 165 TCK. The amendment by Act No. 2009-5918 introduced the concept without participating at the commission of that particular crime, into the structure of this crime.

If the first crime is money laundering (Article 282, TCK), the money launderer and his accomplices shall not be punished for purchasing, possessing etc., the *contraband*, but only other individuals, who did not participate in money laundering, are liable under these provisions (Article 282/3, TCK).

The structure of the *crime of purchasing or accepting property acquired through the commission of an offense* (Article 165, TCK) has been amended by Act No. 5918 dated 2009: The wording *without being an accomplice of such offense* has been added. The new structure reads as follows: *Any person who sells, hands over, purchases or accepts a property or any other kind of asset which was acquired through the commission of an offense, without being an accomplice of such offense, shall be sentenced to a penalty of imprisonment for a term of six months to three years and a criminal fine of up to ten thousand days.*

C. Crimes Against the Public

1. Creating Danger

216. Crimes creating a general danger for the public. TCK has changed the order of the listing of crimes; in order to indicate the value of the individual, crimes against persons are at the beginning of the special part of the Penal Code. Crimes against the public and the state are in the second half of the Penal Code.[262]

These crimes[263] (Part 3. Subsection 1. Articles 170–180, TCK) include the following: intended endangering of public security with regard to fires, floods and

262. D. Tezcan, M.R. Erdem & M. Önok, *Teorik ve Pratik Ceza Özel Hukuku*, 18. Baskı, Seçkin, Ankara 2020, p. 955.
263. M.E. Artuk & İ. Üzülmez, *Yangına, İnfilaka, Batmaya, Deniz Kazasına veya Bir Tehlikeye Taksirle Sebebiyet Verme Suçu*, Türkiye Barolar Birliği Dergisi, sayfa 181, Mart, Nisan 2005.

other serious dangers (Article 170, TCK, Articles 369–383, repealed TCK); negligent endangering public security (Article 171, TCK); causing radiation (Article 172, TCK); causing a nuclear explosion (Article 173, TCK); unauthorized possession of dangerous substances (Article 174, TCK); neglecting the custody obligations for a mentally ill person (Article 175 TCK); endangering public safety (Article 170, TCK); endangering safety in traffic (Article 179, TCK)[264] and negligently endangering traffic (Article 180, TCK).

2. Crimes Against the Environment

217. Crimes against the environment. These crimes (Part 3. Subsection 2. Articles 181–184, TCK) include the new crime of intended pollution of the environment, punishable by imprisonment (Article 181, TCK). Negligent pollution is also a crime (Article 182, TCK). Causing a noise that is likely to harm the health is a newly listed crime (Article 183, TCK). There are also specific laws on the protection of the environment (*infra*, paragraph 255).

218. Construction pollution. Any person who constructs a building without getting the necessary permissions shall be punished with imprisonment. Supplying such buildings with city water or electricity is also a crime. The lawmaker here intended to prevent construction pollution[265] (Article 184, TCK).[266]

3. Crimes Against Public Health

219. These crimes (Part 3. Subsection 3. Articles 185–196, TCK) include contaminating drinking water or poisoning food with (Article 185, TCK) and trading in decayed food or falsified medicaments (Article 186, TCK), or production of such medicaments (Article 187, TCK). Production of and trading with narcotic substances[267] (Article 188, TCK), promoting their consumption (Article 190, TCK) and possession of narcotics for personal use (Article 191, TCK) are regulated in more detail in the TCK.[268] In this context, penalties were increased, scope of the criminal

---

264. Ö.M. Aynural, *Soyut Tehlike Bağlamında Trafik Güvenliğini Tehlikeye Sokma Suçu,* İstanbul Arşivi, Onikilavha, İstanbul 2018.
265. N. Meran, *İmar Kirliliğine Neden Olma*, Ankara, Adalet Yayınevi, 2010.
266. M.A. Karasu, *Kente Karşı Suç: İmar Uygulamaları Bağlamında Kente Karşı İşlenen Suçlar*, 2009; Orta Elif, *İmar Hukukunda Plan Hiyerarşisi ve Planların çatışması*, 2006; Ö. Köroğlu, *İmar Hukukunda Planlama Süreci ve Arazi ve Arsa Düzenlemeleri*, On İki Levha Yayıncılık, İstanbul 2016; H. Kalabalık, *İmar Hukuku Dersleri*, 7. Baskı, Seçkin, Ankara, 2015; M.L. Çelik & C. Altıparmak, *İmar Kirliliğine Neden Olma Suçu*, 2. Baskı, Seçkin, Ankara 2015; M. Genç, *İmar Hukuku*, Seçkin, Ankara, 2015.
267. A.C. Ruhi, *Türk Ceza Kanunu'nda Uyuşturucu ve Uyarıcı Madde Suçları: En Son Yargıtay İçtihatları İle,* On İki Levha, İstanbul 2017.
268. Ö. Çakmut, *Türk Ceza Kanununa Göre Uyuşturucu Madde Kullanımının Yasal Sonuçları ve Iptila Halinde Verilecek Hüküm*, in Prof. Dr. Çetin Özek Armağanı, Galatasaray Üniversitesi, 2004; S.N. Deda, *Gıda Mevzuatı ve Tatbikatı*, Ankara, Seçkin Yayınları, 1994; E. Günay, *Uygulamalı Uyuşturucu veya Uyarıcı Madde Suçları ve İlgili Mevzuat*, Ankara, Seçkin Yayınları, 2005; E. Günay,

acts were extended and in line with current social developments, new substances were added to the list of drug coverage. One of these new substances is phenazepam (bonzai), a drug that has come under the spotlight recently following a number of deaths linked to its abuse.

Purchasing, receiving or possessing narcotic or psychotropic substances with the aim of consuming them is punishable by imprisonment from two years up to five years (Article 191/1, TCK).

220. The crimes against public health at the repealed TCK. These crimes were changed by Act No. 2891 of September 22, 1983, and penalties were increased. In addition to the 1981 and 1990 amendments, Articles 403–406 of the repealed TCK were completely changed in 1991 to prevent double jeopardy for drug related crimes committed in foreign countries. The greater punishments were reduced to be in conformity with European standards (Act No. 2370 of January 7, 1981; Act No. 3679 of 1990 and Act No. 3756 of June 6, 1991).

4. Crimes Against Public Confidence

221. These crimes (Part 3. Subsection 3. Articles 197–212, TCK) include the following: counterfeiting money (Article 197, TCK), counterfeiting valuable seals (Article 199, TCK), counterfeiting government seals (Article 202, TCK), breaking a seal[269] (Article 203, TCK), forgery of official documents[270] (Articles 204–206, TCK), forgery of private documents (Articles 207–208, TCK) and misusing a blank signature (Article 209, TCK). Forgery of identification cards, passports, and so forth were explicitly regulated in the repealed Penal Code (Articles 350–357, TCK). These provisions now exist partly regulated (Articles 204, 207, 210 and 268, TCK). The provisions of the repealed Code related to using fraud or deceit in commerce, industry and auctions (Articles 358–368, TCK) are partly regulated in the new Code (Articles 235–239, TCK).[271]

5. Crimes Against Public Peace and Freedom of Speech Issues

222. The crimes in Part 3. Subsection 5. Articles 213–222, TCK include such crimes as: Threat with the aim of creating fear and panic in public (Article 213, TCK), inciting to commit a crime[272] (Article 214, TCK, Article 312, repealed TCK),

---

Uyuşturucu Madde Suçları ve Cezaları, Ankara, Seçkin Yayınları, 1999; S. Kaymaz & H.T. Gökçan, *Gıda Suçları ve Yeni Gıda Mevzuatı*, Ankara, Seçkin Yayınları, 2002.

269. H.T. Gökcan, *Mühür Bozma, Yedieminlik Yükümlülüğüne Uymama, İhtiyati Tedbir Kararlarına Aykırılık Suçları ve Zarara Yol Açan Yediemin ile Haksız Tedbir Uygulatana Karşı Tazminat Davaları* (2001).

270. G.Ö. Dörtgöz, *Tapu ve Kadastro İşlemlerinde Sahtecilik Suçları ve Alınması Gerekli Tedbirler* (1993).

271. D. Tezcan, M.R. Erdem & M. Önok, *Teorik ve Pratik Ceza Özel Hukuku*, 18. Baskı, Seçkin, Ankara 2020, p. 1033.

272. A. Gökçen, *Halkı Kin ve Düşmanlığa Açıkça Tahrik Cürmü* (2001).

praising a committed crime or the perpetrator (Article 215, TCK), incitement of hate and enmity between the different groups in the society and degrading some sections of the population[273] (Article 216, TCK), incitement not to obey the rules of a statute (Article 217, TCK), misusing the religious services while in office (Article 219, TCK), forming an organization for the purpose of committing crimes (Articles 220–221, TCK, Articles 313–314 repealed TCK).

The offenses consisting in the violation of the reform laws of the Turkish Republic related to wearing a hat, and writing in Latin alphabet (Article 222, TCK) were repealed in 2014, by Act No. 6529, as p^{ar}t of the 5th Reform Package, in order to facilitate social unification in the South East of Turkey, permitting the usage of letters (x, q, w) in Kurdish language. The *ratio legis* of enforcing writing in Latin alphabet was banning the usage of Arabic alphabet in the early years of the Republic. Since the reforms of Atatürk are well established since that time, there should be no danger of a backwards change.

One of the crimes related to restrictions in freedom of speech is, *praising an offense and offender*, which is regulated in Article 215 TCK. To narrow down the scope of the crime, new wording *(clear and imminent danger to public security)* has been included in the definition of the crime. According to the new structure, if that act *creates a clear and imminent danger to public security, then the perpetrator shall be punished by imprisonment of up to two years* (Article 215, TCK).

Crimes related to freedom of speech, such as Articles 213, 214, 215, 216, and 217 TCK, are endangerment offenses.

Inciting hatred and enmity amongst different segments of the population regarding social class, race, religion or region has already been structured as a *concrete danger crime*, where the perpetrator is punished, only if the incitement created a clear and present danger for the public order (Article 216/1, TCK).

The amendment by Act 2013–6459 has introduced the same requirement for publicly praising a committed crime or offender for committing a certain crime: Only if the praising of the crime or the perpetuator has created a clear and present danger for the public order will the conduct be considered criminal (Article 215).

The amendment to Article 218 TCK by Act No. 2005-5377 (*explanation of thought which is within the limits of informing the public and criticism which does not constitute a crime*) did not provide for sufficient relief. The increased number of crimes, committed by using media, led the legislature to introduce another *tacit amnesty* in the field of crimes related to freedom of speech.

As a consequence, the Act No. 2011-6352, a provisional Article 1 has been enacted, which requires the *postponement of the indictment*, even if the conditions at Article 171 CMK are not met, and *suspension of prosecution* at the prosecution phase, and after the sanction has been finalized, the *suspension of the execution of the punishment* for crimes committed through publication in the media or through other methods of explanation of thought if the *basic punishment* does not exceed criminal fine, or imprisonment of not more than five years at the upper level (Provisional Article 1, Act No. 2011-6352). The suspended sanction shall not carry consequences related to loss of rights.

---

273. U. Karan, *Yeni Türk Ceza Kanunu 216. Maddesi ve Anlatım Özgürlüğü*, İstanbul Barosu Dergisi, cilt: 79, sayı: 2005/5.

In cases where the individual in question does not commit another crime within three years as specified at Provisional Article 1/1, the case shall be dropped (Provisional Article 1/2). Otherwise, suspended investigation or prosecution will resume.

Another freedom of speech-related amendment has been achieved for the *propaganda of crime organizations*. According to Article 220/8 TCK, it is an act of criminal conduct to make propaganda of a crime organization (or of its aims). Act No. 2013-6459 has limited the scope of this crime while adding new requirements into the structure of the crime: The words *of its aims* have been replaced by *in a way that would justify or praise or encourage the application of the methods of violence, coercion or threat* (Article 220/8, TCK).

There is a similar change in the Anti-Terrorism Act (*Terörle Mücadele Kanunu,* TMK), with respect to the crime of *propaganda of terrorism organizations*, where the same wording has been incorporated into Article 7/2 TMK by the Act No. 2013-6459.

Since the basic punishment imposed by the Anti-Terrorism Act, Article 7/2 is *up to five years imprisonment*, perpetrators are eligible to benefit from the *tacit amnesty* provided by Provisional Article 1 of Act No. 2011-6352. This applies also to terrorism propaganda crimes committed through media, where the basic punishment will be increased by half. Editors with legal responsibility, who are not accomplices, will be sanctioned by judicial fine from 1,000 up to 5,000 days and may enjoy the *suspension of prosecution* as well.

Some specified conduct occurring during a demonstration, defined in the Anti-Terrorism Act, is considered as the *propaganda of a terrorism organization* (Article 7/2, sub-paragraph a, and b TMK). The prohibited conduct includes: Covering the face in order to hide the identity, exposing the emblems or symbols of a terrorism organization, shouting out slogans or wearing uniforms with symbols of a terrorism organization, thus revealing being a member or supporter of that terrorism organization. After the amendment was effected by Act No. 2013-6459 (which has limited the scope of propaganda) subparagraphs (a) and (b) of Article 7/2 TMK have lost their contents since it is not clear whether such conduct may trigger or encourage the neutral participants of the demonstration to apply methods of violence, coercion, or threat of the terrorism organization, or not.

223. Organized crime. Whoever establishes an organization, in order to commit crimes, which are defined in law, or is leading such a crime organization, comprised of at least three individuals, shall be punished by imprisonment for two to six years, if the number of members, its structure and equipment are suitable for the commission of indented crimes (Article 220/1, TCK).[274]

There are three categories of crime organizations according to the purpose: (a) the first group is regular crime organizations (Article 220/1, TCK); (b) the second group engages in conduct which constitutes political crimes as specified in Articles

274. V. Gültaş, *5237 Sayılı Türk Ceza Kanununda Suç İşlemek Amacıyla Örgüt Kurma Suçu ve Etkin Pişmanlık (TCK 220-221),* 4. Baskı, Bilge Yayınevi, Ankara 2017. M.E. Tulay, *Kriminelle Vereinigungen im deutschen Strafrecht im Vergleich zum türkischen Strafrecht unter besonderer Berücksichtigung der Beteiligungsdogmatik*, Holzkirchen, 2018.

314, 315, 316 TCK; and (c) the third group is terrorism organizations intending to engage in conduct which constitutes terrorism crimes specified by the Anti-Terrorism Act (Article 7, TMK). Inflicted punishments are different for each group.

Membership in criminal organization is an independent crime (Articles 220/2, 314/2, TCK, Article 7/1, TMK).

Each single crime committed within the activities of the criminal organization shall be subject to an additional punishment (Article 220/4, TCK).

The leaders of the criminal organization will be also be additionally punished for each single crime, committed by its members (Article 220/5, TCK). Organizing the activities of a terrorism organization shall be considered as *leadership*.

An individual who does not belong to the hierarchical structure of the criminal organization, but knowingly and willingly aids and abets it, shall be punished as if he were a member of the organization by one to three years of imprisonment; according to the extent of his help, the punishment may be reduced by up to one-third (Article 220/7 TCK).

Another *implied membership* is regulated in Article 220/6 TCK, but is valid only for *armed criminal organizations*, as defined in Articles 220/3, 314/3 TCK and in Article 7/1 TMK: If a non-member commits a crime on behalf of the criminal organization, he shall be additionally punished for *membership* as well, but this punishment may be reduced by up to one half (Article 220/6, TCK).

Paragraphs 6 and 7 of Article 220 TCK are amended. Actually, a sentence is added to each paragraph to make a reduction in the sentence. Also, the scope of the application of paragraphs 6 and 8 was limited by adding further requirements for act constituting this crime:

> "Any person, who commits an offense on behalf of an organization although he is not a member of that organization, shall be punished by an additional imprisonment penalty as if he were a member of that organization. The punishment to be imposed for the membership to the organization may be reduced up to half. This paragraph is applicable only to armed organizations" (Article 220, subparagraph 6, TCK).
>
> "Any person who knowingly and willingly aids and abets a criminal organization, although he does not belong to the structure of that organization, shall be punished as if he were a member of such an organization. The punishment for the membership may be reduced by up to one third, based on the nature of the aid provided" (Article 220/7, TCK).
>
> "Whoever makes propaganda about the criminal organization in a way that reflects the methods used by the criminal organization that consist of extortion, violence and threat as legitimate, or praises them or promotes the employment of such methods, shall be punished by imprisonment from one up to three years. If this crime is committed through the press or broadcasting, the punishment shall be increased by one half" (Article 220/8, TCK).

Turkey adopted the Action Plan against Organized Crime (2013–2015) implementing the National Strategy against Organized Crime (2010–2015). Turkey is also a party to the main international conventions in the area of police cooperation and the fight against organized crime but a lack of data protection legislation limits police cooperation at the international level and an operational cooperation agreement with Europol cannot be concluded. Europol and Turkey have been preparing a memorandum of understanding on confidentiality and information security. The assignment of a police liaison officer in The Hague would improve bilateral cooperation. Inter-agency cooperation needs to be strengthened.

6. Crimes Against Means of Transportation and Platforms

224. These crimes (Part 3. Subsection 6. Articles 223, 224, TCK) include hijacking or seizure of transport vehicles (Article 223, TCK), and occupation of a platform on territorial land or industrial zone (Article 224, TCK). The repealed Penal Code had regulated crimes arising as a result of the criminal misuse of transportation and communications in the subsection against public health (Articles 384–393, TCK). Some important changes have been made to this section. Article 384 was rewritten in 1979 and incorporated into Chapter 2 to regulate hijacking airplanes (Act No. 2245 of 1979 and Act No. 2248 of 1992).

7. Crimes Against Public Morals

225. These crimes (Part 3. Subsection 7. Articles 225–229 TCK) include: indecent acts (Article 225, TCK), obscenity[275] (Article 226, TCK), prostitution (Article 227, TCK), providing an environment for gambling (Article 228, TCK) and begging (Article 229, TCK).

In Turkey, the crime of *prostitution* is regulated in Article 227 of TCK. Encouraging, facilitating or providing a place for prostitution is decriminalized. An individual who is forced into prostitution is considered as a victim and it is indicated by the Article 227/8 that this person may be subjected to a treatment or a psychological therapy. If the victim of this crime is a child, the penalty must be increased heavily and preparatory acts shall be punished as a completed crime.[276]

8. Crimes Against Family Order

226. These crimes (Part 3. Subsection 8. Articles 230–234 TCK) include: Polygamy, marriage by deception and religious ceremonies (Article 230, TCK), altering the lineage of a child (Article 231, TCK), maltreatment (Article 232, TCK), breach of obligations derived from family law (Article 233, TCK) and kidnapping and detention of a child (Article 234, TCK).[277]

---

275. V.Ö. Özbek, *Müstehcenlik Suçu (TCK m. 226)*, Ankara, Seçkin, 2009; D. Soyaslan, *Ceza Hukuku Özel Hükümler*, Yetkin Yayınları, Güncelleştirilmiş 12. Baskı, Ankara 2018, p. 571.
276. A.Ö. Atalay, *Türk Ceza Hukukunda Fuhuş Suçu*, XII Levha, İstanbul 2013.
277. A. Nuhoğlu, *Aile Düzenine Karşı Suçlar*, İstanbul, Beta, 2009; I. Andrejew, *Ailenin Ceza Hukuku Yönünden Korunması;* İstanbul Üniversitesi Mukayeseli Hukuk Enstitüsü Mukayeseli Hukuk Araştırmalari Dergisi, Yeni seri, Yıl 3, No. 4, Garanti Matbaası, İstanbul 1969; C. Otacı, *Genel*

Family violence and *honor killings* have been among the major legal issues that Turkey has confronted in the past years. As a consequence, Act No. 6284, Protection of the Family and Prevention of Violence against Women was enacted in 2012. There is an internal regulation attached to this act published in the Official Gazette (RG 10 January, 2013). (*supra,* paragraph 319)

9. Crimes Against Economy, Industry and Commerce

227. These crimes (Part 3. Subsection 9. Articles 235–242 TCK) include: Fraud during a tender (Article 235, TCK); fraud during the discharge of contractual obligations (Article 236, TCK); price manipulation (Article 237, TCK), causing shortage of items required by the public (Article 238, TCK); disclosure of confidential documents relating to commerce, banking or private customers (Article 239, TCK); restriction of supply of goods and services (Article 240, TCK); and unlawful money lending (Article 241, TCK).[278]

Mass housing projects (TOKİ) and land regeneration plans (*kentsel dönüşüm*) against risks of a future earthquake created a big market for contractors, where municipalities open competitive biddings for undertakers. As a consequence, there have been many allegations and cases against public officials, related to *fraudulent bidding* (Article 235, TCK). As the definition of this crime did not include *bidding for building*, Act No. 2005-5328 added this element. Act No. 2013–6459 lowered the punishment for *fraudulent bidding* (Article 235/1, TCK) from imprisonment for a period of five to twelve years to a period of three to seven years. If there is *no public loss* as a consequence of a *fraudulent bidding*, the punishment has also been reduced (one to three years imprisonment; Article 235/3-b, TCK). In contrast, if the *fraudulent bidding* is committed by using *violence and threat*, the punishment has been increased (minimum five years' imprisonment at the lower level). Further, physical injury inflicted through violence now shall be punished as an independent crime (Article 235/3-a TCK).

10. Cyber Crimes

228. These crimes (Part 3. Subsection 10. Articles 243–246, TCK) include:[279] Accessing a data processing system (Article 243, TCK), preventing the functioning

Adap ve Aile Düzenine Karşı Suçlar, Ankara, Seçkin Yayınları, 2000.

278. Y. Aslan, *Rekabet Hukuku Dersleri*, İstanbul, Vedat Kitapçılık, 2010; D. Cengiz, *Türk Rekabet Hukukundaki Uyumlu Eylem ve Bu Eylemin Hukuki Sonuçları*, İstanbul, Beta, 2006; M. Delmas-Marty, (eds.) çevirenler, S. Keskin, H. Zafer & Ü. Kocasakal, *Avrupa Birliğinin Mali çıkarlarının Korunmasına İlişkin Ceza Hukuku Kuralları (Corpus juris)*, Ankara, Seçkin, 2001; H. Dursun, *Ekonomik Suçlar ve Türkiye'deki Sürdürülebilir Kalkınmaya Etkileri*, Türkiye Barolar Birliği Dergisi, sayı 58, p. 215, Mayıs & Haziran, 2005; Y. Ersoy, *Çalışma Hürriyetine Karşı Suçlar*, Ankara, 1973; A.P. Hatipoğlu, *Özel Ceza Yasaları Uygulamalarında Ekonomik ve Ticari Suçlar*, Ankara, Yetkin Yayınları, 2005; S. Keskin, H. Zafer & U. Kocasakal, *Avrupa Birliğinin Mali çıkarlarının Korunmasına İlişkin Ceza Hukuku Kuralları*, Ankara, Seçkin Yayınları, 2001.

279. O. Değirmenci, *Türk Ceza Kanunu'nun Bilişim Suçları Bakımından Değerlendirilmesi*, Türkiye

of a system and deletion, alteration or corrupting of data (Article 244 TCK), misusing of bank or credit cards (Article 245, TCK) and implementation of security measures on legal entities (Article 246 TCK).[280] Computer crimes had been incorporated into the repealed Penal Code (Articles 525a–525d, TCK) by Act No. 3756 of 1991 as technology had developed.[281]

D. Crimes Against the Nation and the State

1. Crimes Against the Administration of Government

229. Part 4 of the TCK (Articles 247–343, TCK) is dealing with mainly crimes against the administration of government and crimes against criminal administration. This part is subdivided into nine subsections.

These crimes (Part 4. Subsection 1. Articles 247–266, TCK) include:[282] Embezzlement[283] (Article 247, TCK), extortion (Article 250, TCK), bribery[284] (Articles 252–254, TCK), excessive use of force (Article 256, TCK), misconduct in office (Article 257, TCK), revealing a secret of the office (Article 258, TCK), trade by a public official (Article 259, TCK), abandoning or not fulfilling a public duty (Article 260, TCK), usurpation of public office or title or reputation (Article 262, TCK), resistance to government forces (Article 265, TCK) and the use of material preserved for official use while committing a crime (Article 266, TCK).[285]

Barolar Birliği Dergisi, sayı 58, p. 195, Mayıs & Haziran, 2005; M.V. Dülger, *Bilişim Suçları*, Seçkin Yayınları, 2004; Eker, Ö. Umut, *Türk Ceza Hukukunda Bilişim Suçları – Eski TCK Bağlamında Hukukumuzda Yer Alan İlk Düzenlemeler ve 5237 Sayılı TCK'nın İlgili Hükümlerinin Yorumu*, Türkiye Barolar Birliği Dergisi sayı 62, Ocak & Şubat 2006; A. Karagülmez, *Bilişim Suçları ve Soruşturma Kovuşturma Evreleri*, Seçkin Yayınları, 2005; L. Kurt, *Açıklamalı İçtihatlı Tüm Yönleriyle Bilişim Suçları ve Türk Ceza Kanunundaki Uygulaması*, Ankara, Seçkin Yayınları, 2005; A. Önder, *Şahıslara ve Mala Karşı Cürümler ve Bilişim Alanında Suçlar*, İstanbul, Filiz Kitabevi, 1994; A.P. Hatipoğlu, *Türk Ceza Hukukunda Bilişim Suçları*, İstanbul, Vedat Kitapçılık, 2010.

280. D. Tezcan, M.R. Erdem & M. Önok, *Teorik ve Pratik Ceza Özel Hukuku*, 18. Baskı, Seçkin, Ankara 2020, p. 1175.

281. A. Önder, *Şahıslara ve Mala Karşı Cürümler ve Bilişim Alanında Suçlar* (1994); K. Taşdemir & R. Özkepir, *Uygulamada Öğretide Belgelerde Sahtecilik, Mala Karşı Suçlar ve Bilişim Alanında Suçlar* (1998); R.Y. Yazıcıoğlu, *Bilgisayar Suçları* (1997); H. Sınar, *İnternet ve Ceza Hukuku* (2001).

282. C. Alver, *Memur Suçları ve Memur Soruşturması*, Açıklamalı, İçtihatlı, 1997.

283. İ. Özgenç, *Zimmet Suçu*, Seçkin, Ankara, 2009; C. Kütük, *Türk Ceza Hukukunda Zimmet Suçu*, Seçkin, Ankara 2016.

284. I. Malkoç, M. Güler & I. Zimmet, *Rüşvet ve Başlıca Memur Suçları* (1993); I. Malkoç & M. Güler, *Memurlar – Suçlar* (1998); M.E. Artuk, A. Gökcen & A.C. Yenidünya, *Ceza Hukuku Özel Hükümler*, 14. Baskı Ankara, Seçkin 2014, p. 935.

285. I. Akçin, *Kamu İdaresinin Güvenilirliğine ve İşleyişine Karşı Suçlar*, Ankara, Seçkin, 2007; H.T. Gökcan, *Avukatlık Yasası, Görev Suçları, Kovuşturma ve Hukuki Sorumluluk*, Ankara, Seçkin Yayınları, 2001; E. Günay, *Hakim, Savcı, Avukatlar ve Diğer Adli Personelin İşlediği Suçlar ve Soruşturmalar*, Seçkin Yayınları, 1997; A. Gündel, *Zimmet, Sahtecilik, Hırsızlık, Gasp, Dolandırıcılık ve Emniyeti Suistimal Suçları*, Ankara, Seçkin Yayınları, 2002; N. Meran, *Zimmet-Rüşvet-İrtikap ve Görevi Kötüye Kullanma Suçları, Kamu Görevlisi Kavramı, Kamu İdaresine Karşı İşlenen Diğer Suçlar*, Ankara, Seçkin, 2008.

The provisions related to crimes against the administration of the government were changed in 1990 by Act No. 3679 in order to combat corruption. Articles 220–227 of the repealed TCK were abolished.

230. Bribery. The crime of bribery is completely rewritten in 2012, by Act No. 6352. The aim of the amendment is to broaden the extent of the Turkish provisions against bribery which previously covered only foreign public institutions or public corporations in order to include: (a) elected or appointed civil servants of a foreign state; (b) judges or jury members of international or supranational courts or of a foreign state; (c) members of an international or supranational parliament; (d) individuals who run a public activity for a foreign state to include public institutions or corporations; (e) arbitrators, nationals or non-nationals, who have been appointed for resolving a legal dispute through arbitration; and (f) officials or representative of an international or supranational organization established by an international agreement.

The second enlargement of the scope of the crime is related to the offender. Previous definition of the crime included only offering bribe to foreign public officials. Receiving a bribe was not included. The new definition introduced by the Act No. 6352 now includes both the offering and receiving of a bribe and makes foreign public officials as defined in TCK paragraph 9 of Article 252 punishable in Turkey as well.

In cases where the act of bribing occurs (in any case as defined in paragraph 9 of Article 252) has been committed in a foreign country by a foreigner against the interests of the Turkish state or against interests of a Turkish citizen or a private legal entity, the offender shall be investigated and prosecuted in Turkey, if the offender is in Turkey. This is a mandatory prosecution (Article 252/10, TCK). In relation to offering bribes to foreign public officials, the provisions of effective remorse as defined in Article 254 of TCK have not been applicable since 2009 (Article 254/4, TCK). This amendment was necessary in order to overcome the critics of the inefficiency of punishment for bribing foreign public officials. After the amendment, however, there is no equality between bribing Turkish public officials and foreign officials, a situation that might raise constitutionality issues.

The first eight subsections of Article 252 TCK, which regulate domestic bribery read as follows:

(1) Whoever provides a benefit to a person in charge of a public duty directly or by means of a middleman in order to influence the behavior of the recipient in a positive or negative way for an interaction that is within his public powers shall be punished by imprisonment 4-12 years.

(2) In order to fulfill or to refrain from doing an interaction within his public powers, the Public officials who obtain benefits directly or by means of a middleman shall also be punished by the same sanctioned.

(3) Where the parties have reached an agreement the crime of bribery is considered as completed.

(4) The punishment foreseen for the perpetrator shall be decreased by half, if the public official demands a bribe, but the demand is not accepted, it applies for the other party.

(5) The middleman, even if he is not a public official, shall be punished. Since this crime is a special regulation for civil servants only, the Law makes this distinct regulation.
(6) Even if he is not a public official, entity shall be punished as co-offender, if he receives indirect benefits thru a bribe interaction.
(7) In cases where the receiver of the bribe or the person demanding a bribe or entering into a bribe agreement is a person who charged with judicial duties an arbitrator, a court appointed expert, public notary or certified financial advisor, the punishment shall be increased from 1/3 to one half.
(8) The provisions of the crime of bribery shall be applicable for the following persons, if they are acting as a middleman, even if they are not public officials:
  a) Chambers of professions which are considered as public entities,
  b) Companies which have been established by public entities or by institutions considered as public entities,
  c) Foundations which are operating within public entities or in institutions considered as public entities.
  d) Associations which are operating for public benefit,
  e) Cooperatives,
  f) Joint stock companies.

231. Bribing foreign civil servants. Bribing civil servants was regulated in Article 252/5, TCK.[286] This provision was amended right after the enactment of the Penal Code by Act No. 2005–5377, aiming to extend the scope of the provision to include the public officials of international organizations. Act No. 2012-6352 introduced a new structure:

> Article 252/9: Offering bribe or giving benefits to foreign public officials, elected or appointed in a foreign country has been a crime in Turkey according to the convention on prevention on bribing foreign officials.

The amendment in 2012 by Act No. 6352 extended this crime to receiving or requesting bribes by foreign public officials as well (Article 255/9, TCK).

The act has also extended the scope of the recipients of bribe to include judges, jury members or other officials, who serve in international or supranational courts or in a court of a foreign country, members of an international or supranational parliament.

Also included are individuals who serve a public activity in the name of a foreign country, including public entities or public business, arbitrators who are Turkish citizens or foreigners who have been appointed to resolve a legal dispute through arbitration, and officials or representatives of international or supranational organizations, which have been established based on an international agreement:

---

286. Bribing foreign civil servants in international transactions was introduced as a new crime on Jan. 2, 2003 by Act No. 4782. This act alsoamended Art. 4 repealed TCK. If the accused has been tried in a foreign country, there will be no new trial in Turkey; legal persons face a fine even if the individual representative has been punished separately (Art. 220, repealed TCK).

In cases where a crime of bribery within the scope of Article 252/9 TCK has been committed outside of Turkey by a foreigner, and the crime is committed in order to achieve the commission of an interaction or neglecting of an interaction, by which the state of the Turkish Republic, a public entity established in Turkey, a private legal entity, which has been established according Turkish law or a Turkish citizen is a party to the transaction, and the person who provides the bribe, offers it, receives the bribe, asks for the bribe, their middleman or the person who obtains indirect benefit from bribe is in Turkey, such individuals shall be investigated and prosecuted ex officio in Turkey (Article 252/10, TCK).

The universality principle for prosecuting bribery offenses committed outside of Turkey was regulated in Article 13/1-h TCK. Act 2009–5918 moved this provision to Article 252/9, TCK in connection with other amendments related to bribing foreign civil servants and others.

232. Bribery by extortion. The elements of bribery by extortion includes a civil servant forcing someone to provide or promise to provide a benefit for himself or for another person, using the influence provided him by his office (Article 250/1, TCK).

The structure of the crime of extortion has been amended: A presumption of extortion is introduced. If the citizen is forced by unjustified behavior of the public officer to provide a benefit, the existence of extortion will be presumed. The Act No. 2012-6352 added a new element to this crime: If the victim gets an impression from the unjustified behavior of the civil servant that his legal request may not be fulfilled and thus if he feels himself obliged to provide benefit to him, this shall constitute an *implied bribery by extortion.* (Article 250/1, TCK).

However, while fixing the punishment, the amount and value of the benefit, as well as the financial situation of the victim, shall be taken into consideration and the punishment may be reduced up to half (Article 250/4 TCK).

233. Effective remorse. The effective remorse provision in Article 254 TCK is extended. Under the previous provision, a person in receipt of the bribe would not be punished if he presented the thing he took as bribe to the authorities in its original state before the commencement of the investigation. Now this must be done before the officials find it out. Similar provision is envisaged for those who offer bribes and their accomplices as well.

Effective remorse in bribery crimes is defined in Article 254 TCK. In cases where the recipient of the bribe surrendered the bribe before a criminal investigation had been initiated, that recipient would not have been punished under previous regulation. The same rule applied for the public official who entered into a bribe agreement but who informed official authorities prior to the initiation of a criminal investigation. The amendment in 2012, by Act No. 6352, has introduced a new and prior time setting for effective remorse. According to the new regulations both parties are benefit from effective remorse, if they surrender the benefit, or inform the official authorities before the authorities learn about a bribing case, they shall not be punished (Article 254/1, 2, TCK).

234. Trading with influence. The elements of crime regulated at Article 255 TCK were totally restructured in 2012. The repealed provision defined it as a crime if a public official pretended that he was authorized to accomplish an interaction, thus obtaining a benefit, and the punishment upon conviction was imprisonment of one year to a maximum of five years and a criminal fine.

The 2012 amendment changed the name of the crime in Article 255 TCK from *securing a benefit for a task outside the scope of authority* to *trading with influence*. The basic type of crime deals now with an ordinary person: Any person pretending that he has some influence with a public official obtaining direct benefit, or indirect benefit through a middleman, in order to accomplish an unjustified interaction, shall be punished by two to five years' imprisonment and up to 5,000 days criminal fine. In cases where the perpetrator is the public official himself, the punishment will increase by one-half. The person who expects the fulfillment of interaction and provides benefits will be punished by imprisonment of one year to three years (Article 255/1, TCK).

This new type of crime is also applicable for crimes related to bribing foreign public officials, as listed in Article 252/9 TCK. Such perpetrators will be investigated and prosecuted ex officio if they are in Turkey, regardless of their citizenship. Act No. 2014-6545 abolished the requirement of the request of the Minister of Justice for crimes committed abroad related to bribery (Article 252, TCK) or trading with influence (Article 255, TCK). As indicated before, the aim is to ensure an efficient prosecution of the bribery of foreign officials in a foreign country (Article 12/5, TCK).

235. Misconduct in office. Misconduct in office is a general definition for crimes committed by public officials.[287] If an action of a public official does not constitute a specific crime defined in criminal laws, the public official still may be punished by imprisonment from one year to three years (Article 257/1, TCK), because of the misuse of powers if private individuals are victimized, or there is a public damage or if the public official has caused an unjustified profit for himself or others. If neglecting or delaying the public duties commits the same crime, the sanction is imprisonment from six months to two years (Article 257/2, TCK). This form of regulation crimes does not meet the main requirements of the Constitution, as it is not a clear definition of what constitutes a crime.

With the apparent intent of protecting public officials from heavy sanctions, the lawmaker replaced the word "profit" in both paragraphs of Article 257 with the word "benefit" and reduced the imprisonment term making it six months to two years for misusing the power and imprisonment of three months up to three years for neglecting or delaying of official duties (Article 257 TCK/1 and 2, TCK).

Additionally, Article 257/3 TCK has been repealed by Act No. 6352 in 2012. The prior provision made wrongful conduct of public officials, which does not constitute extortion by bribery a crime, punishable by the same punishment as in paragraph one of Article 257, TCK.

Misuse of public duty was amended in 2010 by Act No. 6008. The wording *unjust financial gain* was replaced by *benefit* in paragraph 1 of Article 257 TCK,

287. V.S. Evik, *Görevi Kötüye Kullanma Suçları (TCK m. 257)*, Onikilevha İstanbul 2019.

and the possible punishment was reduced from a range of one to three years' imprisonment to a range of six months to two years. This amendment helped suspected mayors who had been prosecuted for misuse of public duty. The new definition and decrease in the punishment made it possible to use the provisions of Article 231 of the Penal Procedure Code in delaying the pronouncement of the judgment.

In 2012, Act No. 6312 repealed the third paragraph of Article 257 TCK criminalizing the securing of financial benefit for himself/herself, or another in return for fulfilling the requirement of his/her duty as a public officer.

236. Operating of illegal education establishments was repealed. Internal security issues and the national education system have been under the responsibility of the central government in Turkey since the foundation of the Republic. During the recent years there have been some tendencies underway, in order to strengthen local governments and furnish them with powers related to both these sensitive issues. In this respect, it is important to note that Article 263, TCK, which criminalized the act of establishing and operating educational institutions in a way that is contrary to the existing regulations, or the act of teaching knowingly at such establishments, was repealed in 2013, by Act No. 6460. Previously, these crimes had been punishable by imprisonment from six months up to three years.

Operating private preparation courses for university examinations is a very profitable field of business in Turkey and has been the cause of political disputes between the ruling party and a religious movement since the spring of 2013.

Repealing Article 263 of TCK reflects the movements of the government in securing religious ideas. In 1924, a secular state was established in Turkey; religious courts and sharia were abandoned. A secular education has been one of the most important priorities of the Republic. Principles for protecting the Republic's reforms are still incorporated in Article 174 of the Turkish Constitution. The provision of Penal Code (Article 263, TCK) establishing illegal education institutions was, however, abolished by Act No. 6460.

237. Other crimes related to the administration of government. The offenses in the repealed Penal Code involving imams, religious orators or preachers and spiritual leaders (Articles 241–242, repealed TCK) have been transferred to Article 219 TCK. Maltreatment of individuals by public officers (Articles 243–251, repealed TCK) has been abolished and regulated as regular injury (Articles 94, 95 TCK). Offenses against persons having official titles (Articles 266–273 repealed TCK) were abolished and were not replaced. The offenses of breaking seals and stealing property in government custody (Articles 274–277, repealed TCK) have been transferred to Articles 203, 205, 281, 289 and 290 TCK. Securing benefit through influencing government officials (Article 278, repealed TCK) has been transferred to Article 158 TCK.

2. Crimes Against Judicial Administration

238. The structure of crimes against judicial administration. These crimes (Part 4. Subsection 2. Articles 267–298, TCK) include:[288] False accusation (Articles 267–271, TCK); perjury (Articles 272–274, TCK);[289] false swearing (Article 275, TCK); influencing a person who is fulfilling a judicial duty (Article 277, TCK, which has been amended in 2014 by Act No. 6545, due to the decision of the Constitutional Court dated April 10, 2013 K: 2015–31); failing to report a crime while it is being committed (Article 278, TCK);[290] public servants' failure of reporting crimes (Article 279, TCK); harboring felons and removing evidence of felonies (Article 281, TCK); money laundering (Article 282, TCK); protecting an offender (Article 283, TCK); not reporting where a wanted suspect or where some evidence is a crime (Article 284, TCK); violation of the confidentiality of investigations (Article 285, TCK); making a video or audio recording during investigation or trial (Article 286, TCK); genital medical examination without a judge's order (Article 287, TCK); public submissions with the aim of tampering with the fairness of the procedures (Article 288, TCK); abuse of custodial powers in detention (Article 289, TCK); escape from prison or detention house (Article 292, TCK); importing forbidden goods into a correctional facility (Article 297, TCK); and preventing the inmates from exercising their rights and from taking nutrition (Article 298 TCK). A major hunger strike by prisoners convicted for terrorism crimes came to an end on its 68th day, on November 18, 2013. There were 683 strikers in 66 different prisons across the country. The Ministries of Health and Justice provided adequate healthcare to the hunger strikers. The transfer of some hunger strikers to other prisons after the strikes was criticized for hampering the rights of defense and the right of family visits.[291]

239. False accusation (Article 267, TCK). False accusation is regulated as a crime and punishes a person who despite knowing that someone is innocent causes him or her to be sentenced by slandering. This article has been subject to Constitutional Court decisions in 2011.[292]

---

288. I. Döner, *Suçu Bildirmeme Suçu TCK 278*, Erzincan Hukuk Fakültesi Dergisi Cilt 9 sayı 3–4, p. 63, Erzincan, 2005; H.T. Gökcan, *Mühür Bozma, Yedieminlik Yükümlülüğüne Uymama, İhtiyati Tedbir Kararına Aykırılık Suçları ve Zarara Yol Açan Yediemin ile Haksız Tedbir Uygulatana Karşı Tazminat Davaları*, Ankara, Seçkin Yayınları, 2001; S.A. Hızal, *Türk Ceza Hukukunda Sağlık Personelinin İhbar Yükümlülüğü*, İzmir, İzmir Tabip Odası Yayını, 2010; N. Meran, *Hakaret – İftira, Yargılamayı Etkilemeye Teşebbüs ve Soruşturmanın Gizliliğini İhal Suçları*, Ankara, Seçkin, 2009; N. Meran, *Kamu Görevlisine ve Adliyeye İlişkin Suçlar*, Ankara, Seçkin, 2006; Y. Ünver, *Adliyeye Karşı Suçlar (TCK. m. 267–298)* 2. Bası, Ankara, Seçkin, 2010.
289. A.İ. Tunçer, *Yalan Tanıklık Suçu,* Seçkin, Ankara 2020.
290. This article was repealed by the decision of the Constitutional Court dated Jun. 30, 2011. E. 2010–52. K. 2011–113 and then amended in 2012 with the Act No. 6352.
291. D. Tezcan, M.R. Erdem & M. Önok, *Teorik ve Pratik Ceza Özel Hukuku,* 18. Baskı, Seçkin, Ankara 2020, p. 149.
292. Decision of the Constitutional Court, Nov. 17, 2011, E. 2010–115, K. 2011–154. Formerly, para. 7 of Art. 267 was regulating the defamer's punishment, but it was higher than the punishment of the person who is sentenced because of the defamer, although being innocent. The Constitutional Court cancelled this paragraph on the ground that it was unjust.

240. Influencing an individual who is performing judicial duties (Article 277, TCK). The crime of influencing an individual who is performing judicial duties (Article 277, TCK) has been restructured in 2012, by Act No. 6352. This crime had been a big problem for individuals who would make statements about pending prosecutions. The repealed definition of this crime included attempting to influence a person who is performing a judicial duty by any means, and was therefore very vague.

The new definition limits the scope of application in the direction as foreseen by the Constitution Article 38: "*Attempting to influence any person, who performs judicial duties, or a court appointed expert, or a witness, with the aim of obstructing justice, or for causing injustice, in order to achieve a profitable outcome for one of the parties of the case, shall be punished by imprisonment 2-4 years*" (Article 277, TCK).

With the amendment, the Article was almost entirely rewritten. The title of the Article was amended as well. In addition to persons charged with a judicial duty, such attempts towards expert witnesses and witnesses are covered by the new provision. With the amendment the investigation phase is also covered. Additionally, with the new provision an addition is made to clarify the offense. In this regard under the new wording, the attempt to influence a person charged with a judicial duty must be done *in order to prevent the truth from coming out, or to do someone an injustice.* Under the old version of the provision, in addition to attempt using force, instructing/giving orders used to be a constituent element of the crime.

The second paragraph added to the article stated that if the act of a person constituting this crime does constitute another crime at the same time the punishment to be given shall be increased up to one-half in accordance with the provisions of conceptual aggregation under Article 44 of the Penal Code.

241. Failure to report an offense (Article 278, TCK). Not reporting a crime, which is in progress, or a crime, which is completed, but the consequences of which would be limited, if reported, is a crime (Article 278, TCK). The Constitutional Court has annulled this provision, as it would also potentially be punishable for parents who neglected reporting crimes of their own children.[293]

The legislator responded to this decision with a limitation on the definition of crime: *Individuals who are eligible to refrain from taking the witness stand, shall not be punished; but they are obliged to prevent the crime* (Article 278/4, TCK).

Additionally, a cosmetic change was made to replace the Turkish word *özürlü* (disabled) (used for a handicapped person) with *engelli*, which is much more politically correct.

242. Offense of the laundering of assets and legislation related to money laundering. With this amendment two things were changed. First of all, under the previous provisions, in order for actions for money laundering to constitute a crime, it was required that the underlying offense carries a minimum penalty of one-year imprisonment. With this amendment the penalty for the underlying offense is decreased to six months. The second major change is that the penalty for violation

293. Decision of the Constitutional Court, dated Jun. 30, 2011.

of Article 282 TCK is raised from a term of two years to five years' imprisonment to a term of three to seven years. The criminal fine of up to 20,000 days was not changed. A new paragraph two was added after paragraph one, and the subsequent three paragraphs are renumbered. In the added paragraph knowingly buying, accepting, holding or using of those assets, which constitute the subject of this crime but without being an accomplice to the underlying crime is criminalized.

Apart from the crime in the TCK mentioned above, there is a statute regulating money laundering issues that was introduced in Turkey on November 13, 1996 by Act No. 4208.[294] The TCK regulates *laundering assets emanating from a crime* (Article 282, TCK) and has altered the previous definition of this crime.

Since October 11, 2006, there is a special Act on Laundering Assets Emanating from Crime (Act No. 5549), which regulates the preventive measures against money laundering such as identifying and reporting of suspicious money transfers (Article 4). The act also provides administrative or criminal fines, imprisonment or security measures for violation of its rules (Articles 13, 14, 15).

Turkey has signed and ratified the 2000 UN Convention on Prevention of Financing of Terrorism. With regard to the fight against terrorism, Turkey adopted the Act on the Prevention of the Financing of Terrorism, which addresses certain shortcomings identified by the Financial Action Task Force (FATF). The Act No. 6415 on *"Prevention of Financing Terrorism"* dated February 7, 2013, and the Act No. 7262 on "*Prevention of Financing and Dissemination of Mass Destruction Weapons*" dated December 27, 2020, are pieces of legislation in order to address such shortcomings.

Turkey has signed but not yet ratified the Council of Europe's Convention on the Laundering, Search, Seizure and Confiscation of the Proceeds from Crime and on the Financing of Terrorism for some political reasons.

Turkey's active counter-terrorism dialogue with the EU has intensified. However, police and judicial cooperation with the EU Member States and EU Agencies in this area is limited given the absence of a data protection law and the difference between the norms defining and sanctioning terrorism in Turkey, in the EU and its Member States.

243. Breach of Confidentiality (Article 285, TCK). Violation of confidentiality of criminal investigations was regulated as a new type of crime in the TCK in 2005.[295] The aim of this provision is to protect the suspects' rights to be presumed innocent. Until the court has approved the indictment, the investigation phase is secret from the public and from the suspect (Article 157, CMK). If the suspect is aware of the direction of investigations, he would wish to obscure evidence and this would be a ground for his custody in pre-trial detention. There have been many incidents, however, where the contents of investigations conducted in secret have been revealed in

---

294. O. Değirmenci, *Mukayeseli Hukukta ve Türk Hukukunda Suçtan Kaynaklanan Malvarlığı Değerlerini Aklama Suçu*, Ankara, Turhan, 2007; E. Ergül, *Kara Ekonomi ve Aklama Suçları*, Ankara, Yetkin Yayınları, 2005; E. Ergül, *Hukuki, Mali, Ekonomik, Aktüel Boyutları ve İlgili Mevzuatıyla Karaparanın Aklanması ve Suçları*, 1998; H. İpek, *Önemli Bir Sorun: Karapara ve Karaparanın Aklanması*, 2000; E. Ergül, *Karapara Endüstrisi ve Aklama Suçu*, 2001.

295. E. Günay, *Uygulamada Hakim, Savcı, Avukatlar ile Diğer Adlî Personelin İşledikleri Suçlar ve Soruşturmalar* (1997).

the mass media and the public might have thought that the suspect under investigation was guilty. In light of this difficulty, the crime in Article 285, TCK has been amended in 2012, by the Act No. 6352. The new wording of the crime states the definition of the violation of the secrecy of an investigation. In order to be a crime, it is now necessary that revealing the contents of an interaction, conducted during the investigation phase should violate the presumption of the innocence of the suspect, or violate the confidentiality of his communications, or his private life, and must be suitable to obstruct the revealing of factual truth (Article 285/1, TCK). Revealing of the confidential information must additionally happen publicly. However, decisions, such as wiretap orders by a judge or a search warrant, which should be kept secret from the suspects, shall be punished, even if the contents are not revealed publicly (Article 285/2, TCK).

If a court renders a decision to conduct a trial in a closed session, and puts a restriction on revealing the testimony given during the trial, such information shall also be punishable under the same provision (Article 285/3, TCK).

Another aspect of protection of the presumption of innocence is the ban on the publication of the pictures of the suspects and the accused, which would create an impression of guilt. Such publication is punished by imprisonment of six months to two years (Article 285/5, TCK). But if the publication is within the limits of informing the public about contemporary events, such publication shall not constitute a crime (Article 285/6, TCK).

244. Attempting to influence a fair trial (Article 288, TCK). The Legislature changed the structure of this crime in 2012, in Act No. 6352.[296] The new wording of Article 288, TCK reads as follows: Whoever makes an oral or written statement about a pending prosecution or investigation with the aim of inducing a person who performs a judicial duty, a court appointed expert, or a witness to render an illegal decision or engage in an illegal interaction, shall be punished by judicial fine, not less than fifty days.

This new structure and punishment of the crime falls under the provisions of Article 75 TCK, which regulates a pre-payment of criminal fine: If the perpetrator pays the amount of the criminal fine in advance, there shall be no prosecution at all. On the other hand, the aggravating factor in Article 288/2 had already been abolished by Act No. 5377 (if the crime was committed by means of mass media), thus protecting the freedom of press.

With the amendment, the wording of the article was almost completely rewritten to clarify the application of the article. In this regard, the public statement, oral or written made by the offender with the aim of influencing a public prosecutor, judge, court, expert witness is made to make them render an unlawful decision or take an unlawful act or give a false statement.

296. Attempting to influence a fair trial was one of the crimes related to freedom of speech: Whoever attempted to influence the prosecutor, judge, court appointed expert or a witness by making public oral and written explanations would be punished by imprisonment of six months to three years. If the crime was committed using a publication by mass media, the punishment would be increased by one-half. This wording resulted in a big number of investigations and prosecutions against some politicians who were talking about pending high profile cases in public.

245. Forbidden substances in correctional facilities. It is a crime to smuggle in weapons, narcotic substances or electronic means of communication into a correctional facility (Article 297, TCK). The second paragraph of this provision was punishing smuggling in of substances, which has been forbidden by the correctional administration. The Constitutional Court annulled the second paragraph in 2011, on the basis that criminal statutes must contain clear definitions of the crime, not depending upon an administrative decision to provide the definition of what is forbidden.[297]

3. Crimes Against the Symbols of Sovereignty of the State and Crimes Against the Reputation of its Organs

246. Defamation of the Turkish Nation. The crimes in Part 4. Subsection 3 (Articles 299–301) include crimes that permit the state to limit the freedom of expression, such as insulting the President of the Republic (Article 299, TCK), discrediting the symbols of the state sovereignty (Article 300 TCK) and discrediting the Turkish nation, the Republic, the organs and institutions of the state (Article 301, TCK).[298]

Defamation of the Turkish Nation, Republic, Grand National Assembly, government,[299] ministries, army, security forces or judiciary was already penalized by Article 159 of the repealed Penal Code. Previously, the punishment for such *defamation* was lengthy imprisonment for one year to six years. Act No. 2002–4744 reduced the punishment to imprisonment for one to three years, and Act No. 2002-4771 made it clear that *critics* are not to be punished if there is no specific intent of defamation (Article 2, Act No. 4771 of August 3, 2002).[300]

One of the most disputed provisions of the TCK regarding of freedom of speech has been *degrading Turkishness, the Turkish Republic and instructions of the state* (Article 301 TCK). The amendment in 2008, by Act No. 5759 replaced the wording *Turkishness* with the words *Turkish Nation*, and required the permission of the Minister of Justice in order to start any investigation related to this crime (Article 301 TCK).

The provision of the Penal Code (Article 301, TCK) now contains the following wording: "(1) *Whoever publicly discredits the Turkish Nation, the Republic of Turkey, the Turkish Grand National Assembly, the Government of the Republic of Turkey or the judicial organs of the State shall be punished with imprisonment from six months up to two years.* (2) *Whoever publicly discredits the military or the security*

297. Decision of the Constitutional Court dated Jul. 7, 2011, K. 2011/116.
298. A. Gökçen, *Halkı Kin ve Düşmanlığa Açıkça Tahrik Cürmü* (2001). O.D. Aydın, *Üç Demokraside Düşünce İfade Özgürlüğü*, Ankara, Seçkin Yayınları, 2004.
299. D.B. Belli, *Basın Yoluyla Kişilik Hakkına Saldırıdan Doğan Hukuki Sorumluluk* (2008).
300. A. Gündel, Açıklamalı, *İçtihatlı Atatürk'e, Cumhurbaşkanına, Cumhuriyet'e, Hükümete Hakaret Suçları* (1997).

organizations of the State shall be punished according to the provisions of subsection one. (3) *Expressing ideas with the aim of criticism does not constitute a crime.* (4) *The investigation of this crime requires the permission of the Minister of Justice.*"

4. Terrorism Crimes

247. Crimes against the security of the state. Any person who commits an act aimed to place the land of the state, partly or as a whole, under the sovereignty of a foreign state, or aimed to disrupt the unity of the state or to weaken the independence of the state, or commits an act aimed to separate part of the territory of the state that is under the sovereignty of the state from the state administration, shall be punished by aggravated life imprisonment (Article 302/1, TCK) (*See infra*, paragraph 279 for definition of aggravated life imprisonment).

Alliance with the enemy (Article 303, TCK), incitement to war against a state (Article 304, TCK), activities against the fundamental national interests for benefit (Article 305, TCK), recruitment of soldiers against a foreign state (Article 306, TCK), destruction of military facilities (Article 307, TCK) and material, financial aid to enemy states (Article 308, TCK) are the other crimes in this subsection (for other crimes related to terrorism *see infra* paragraph 264).

The Anti-Terrorism Act of April 12, 1991 (Act No. 3713) introduced several types of crimes (Articles 6, 7, 8, TMK).[301]

The Anti-Terrorism Act is used to detain terrorists and people who *threaten the indivisible unity of the state.* The Constitutional Court, upon the examination of the constitutionality of several provisions of the Anti-Terrorism Act, reduced the fines imposed on the press, returned the assets and properties of the Turkish Confederation of Revolutionary Workers Unions (DISK) on March 31, 1992, struck down a regulation concerning the ban on communication between prisoners involved in acts of terrorism and their lawyers and annulled a provision which limited to three the number of attorneys permitted to follow a given case in the state Security Court.[302]

Subsequent to the 2001–4709 amendments to the Constitution, the Anti-Terrorism Act was amended: Article 7(2) TMK provides that incitement to terrorism is only punishable if the declaration is a *call to use terrorist methods* that can incite violent action or applying methods of terrorism. Article 7 has been supplied

301. E. Akın, *Terör ve Terörün Finansmanı Suçu*, Ankara, Adalet, 2009; C. Akkaya, *Terör Suçları ve Cezalarının İnfazı*, Ankara, Adalet, 2009; Y. Alexander, E. Brenner & S.T. Krause, *Turkey, Terrorism, Civil Rights, and the European Union*; London and New York: Routledge, 2008; H. Çakmak & Atunok Taner, *Terörizmin Finansmanı ve Ekonomisi*, 2009; M. Gemalmaz, *Historical Roots of Martial Law Within the Turkish Legal System*, 1991; K. İçel & Y. Ünver, *Terör ve Düşman Ceza Hukuku*, Ankara, Seçkin, 2008; O.K. Keskin, *Devlet Güvenlik Mahkemelerinin Yapısı, Görevleri ve Yargılama Usulleri*, Ankara, Kazancı Matbaacılık Sanayii, 1987; S. Kurt, *Terör Suçları* Ankara, Seçkin Yayınları, 1998.

302. I. Akbulut, *Gerekçeli Terörle Mücadele Kanunu ve Açıklaması* (1993); C. Bardak, *Açıklamalı İçtihatlı Terörle Mücadele Kanunu ve Devlet Güvenlik Mahkemeleri Kanunu* (1997); S. Kurt, *Uygulamada Terör Suçları ve İlgili Mevzuat* (1998); H. Zafer, *Ceza Hukukunda Terörizm* (1999); S. Tellenbach, *Einige Betrachtungen zu den Staatsschutzdelikten im Entwurf eines türkischen Strafgesetzbuches* (2001); E. Bose, *Terörizm, Avrupa Birliği ve İnsan Hakları* (2002).

by the third subsection in 2019 by Act No. 7188, saying that "explanations of views which are within the borders of news reporting or critics shall not be punished."

Under Turkish Law, the financing of terrorism was first addressed as a criminal offense in the Anti-Terrorism Act. The Act No. 2006-5532 had amended Article 8 of this Act; the Act No. 6415 on the Prevention of Financing of Terrorism, however, repealed this provision. The new regulation provides the principles and procedures on the implementation of the United Nations Security Council Resolutions 1267 (1999), 1988 (2011) and 1989 (2011) through the decisions of the Council of Ministers.[303]

There are specialized courts dealing with terrorism and organized crimes (*infra*, paragraph 355).

5. Crimes Against the Constitutional Order

248. Whoever attempts to abolish, replace or prevent the implementation of the constitutional order of the Turkish Republic through force and violence, shall be sentenced to a penalty of aggravated life imprisonment (Article 309/1, TCK).[304]

Assassination of and physical attack on the President (Article 310, TCK), offense against a legislative body (Article 311, TCK), offenses against the government (Article 312, TCK), armed revolt against the government of the Turkish Republic (Article 313, TCK), armed organization (Article 314, TCK), supplying arms (Article 315, TCK) and agreement to commit an offense (Article 316, TCK) are crimes regulated in this subsection.

6. Crimes Against National Defense

249. Discouraging people from performing military service. These crimes include: Usurping military command (Article 317, TCK), discouraging people from performing military service (Article 318, TCK), encouraging soldiers to disobey (Article 319, TCK), enlistment of soldiers in foreign service (Article 320, TCK), disobeying orders during war (Article 321, TCK), obligations during wartime (Article 322, TCK), dissemination of false information in wartime (Article 323, TCK), failure in the performance of a duty during mobilization (Article 324, TCK), acceptance of title and similar awards from the enemy (Article 325, TCK).

Encouraging or advising or making propaganda in order to discourage citizens from military services was a crime under Article 318, TCK, and was under the jurisdiction of military courts. Since the jurisdiction of military courts over civilians is

---

303. E. Aksoy Retornaz, *Countering the Financing of Terrorism in Turkish Law*, in Prof. Dr. Feridun Yenisey'e Armağan, Beta, İstanbul 2014, p. 561; P.B. Heymann, *Terrorism, Freedom and Security*, in Prof. Dr. Feridun Yenisey'e Armağan, Beta, İstanbul 2014, p. 1877.

304. E. Grieves & V. Bıçak, *The Turkish Penal Code, Translation of the Turkish Penal Code Has Been Realised with Funding from the Foreign and Commonwealth Office Global Opportunities Fund* (Re-Uniting Europe Programme, September 2007).

against the principles of fair trial set by Article 6/1 European Convention on Human Rights, the structure of this crime has also been amended in 2013 by Act No. 6459.

The offense is now an endangerment type of offense: "*whoever encourages or advises the serviceman or woman in the army in a suitable way, that would make them refuse serving in military, or run away from their military base, shall be punished by imprisonment from six months to two years.*"

The previous wording of the article stating "*[a]ny person who encourages, uses repetition or conducts propaganda which would have the effect of discouraging people from performing military service* is replaced by the wording stating *[a]ny person who encourages or uses repetition in way to incite those who are in service to desertion or discourage/dissuade those who will join military service from serving in the military.*" The punishment is kept the same.

7. Crimes Against State Secrets and Spying

250. These crimes[305] include: Revealing documents relating to state security (Article 326, TCK), securing information relating to state security (Article 327, TCK), political or military espionage (Article 328, TCK), disclosure of information relating to the security and political interests of the state (Article 329, TCK), disclosure of information which must be kept confidential (Article 330, TCK), entering military zones (Article 332, TCK), exploitation of state secrets and disloyalty in government services (Article 333, TCK), securing prohibited information (Article 334, TCK), securing prohibited information for espionage (Article 335, TCK), disclosure of prohibited information (Article 336, TCK), disclosure of prohibited information for political or military espionage (Article 337, TCK), espionage through recklessness (Article 338, TCK) and possession of documents concerning state security (Article 339, TCK).

8. Crimes Against the Relationships with Foreign Countries

251. Crimes under this subsection are: offenses against the head of a foreign state (Article 340, TCK), offenses against the flag of a foreign state (Article 341, TCK) and offenses against the representative of a foreign state (Article 342, TCK). Reciprocal conditions (Article 343, TCK), entering into force (Article 344, TCK) and execution (Article 345, TCK) are also discussed.

II. Specific Crimes Defined Outside of the Penal Code

252. Specific criminal law. There are a large number of special laws outside the Code that deal with criminal offenses. Some of them deal with minor offenses when

305. V.S. Evik, A. Evik, *Devlet Sırrını ve Yayılması Yasaklanan Bilgileri Açıklama ve Elde Etme Suçları*, Erzincan Hukuk Fakültesi Dergisi Cilt 8 sayı 3–4, Erzincan, 2004.

compared to offenses under TCK.[306] These minor offenses make up the majority of pending cases. Few of the criminal offenses in specific criminal law are of great importance.[307] We will review only those specific laws that have been changed recently.

Article 5 TCK indicates that general principles laid down in the TCK apply to specific criminal law as well.

253. Drug control. Drug control legislation was amended by Code No. 2236, of May 22, 1979, and planting cannabis was forbidden (Article 3). The Penal Code Articles (Articles 190–192, TCK) were amended accordingly.[308]

As concerns cooperation in the field of drugs, the final evaluation of the 2nd National Action Plan against Drugs and Drug Addiction (2010–2012), implementing the National Strategy (2006–2012), was carried out in February 2013. The updated 2013–2018 National Strategy and the 2013–2015 Action Plan have been adopted.

254. Pornography. Act No. 1117, of June 21, 1927, protects children against pornography. This Act was amended by Act No. 3266 on March 6, 1986, and by Act No. 3445 on May 11, 1988. Fines relating to pornographic printings were increased. The related Articles of TCK (*supra*, paragraph 202) were amended accordingly.

255. The Criminal Law of Environment. The Environmental Law was enacted on September 8, 1983 by Act No. 2872, and introduced administrative sanctions against pollution.[309] This Code was amended on June 4, 1986, Act No. 3416 and in 1988, Act No. 3416 (RG. March 4, 1988). The related ordinances were put in force in 1993 (RG. February 7, 1993).[310]

---

306. A.A. Küçükbayrak, *Sulh Ceza Davaları* (1998); S. Kaymaz & H.T. Gökcan, *Uygulamada Sulh Ceza Davaları* (1998); H.T. Gökcan & S. Kaymaz, *Türk Ceza Kanunu ve Özel Yasalardaki Önödemeye Bağlı Suçlar* (1998).
307. V. Gültaş, *Uygulamada Türk Ceza Kanunu ve Özel Kanunlarda Ağır Cezalık Suçlar* (1998).
308. E. Ergül, *Uyuşturucu Madde Alışkanlığının Hukuki ve Cezai Yönleri* (1993); E. Ergül, *Hukuki, Adli, Tıbbi, Kriminolojik, Aktüel Boyutları ve İlgili Mevzuatıyla Uyuşturucu Maddeler ve Suçları* (1997); E. Günay, *Uyuşturucu Madde Suçları ve Cezaları* (1999).
309. K. Anadol, *Termik, Santrallere Hayır* (1991). İ.Ö. Kaboğlu, *Çevre Hakkı* (1992, 1996); R. Keleş & E. Uluğ, *İnsan, çevre, Toplum* (1992); çevre Eğitimi (1993); Gap ve Çevre (1993); Türkiye'nin Sulak Alanları (1993); O. Uslu, *Çevresel Etki Değerlendirmesi* (1993); E. Şen, *Çevre Ceza Hukuku* (1994); N. Erdoğan, E. Önen & B. Balkız, *Kırda Demografik Hareketlilik, Toplumsal Değişme ve Bergama Köylerinde Çevre Bilinci* (1994); M. Abacıoğlu, *Açıklamalı İçtihatlı Çevre Kanunu ve Çevre Sağlığı Mevzuatı* (1995); S. Güneş, *Orta Bakırçay Havzasında Pamuk, Tütün Tarımının Toprak ve İklim Sorunları* (1995); F.D. Yaşamış, *Çevre Yönetiminin Temel Araçları* (1995); B. Cantürk, *Çevre Kanunu ve İlgili Mevzuat* (1996); O.S. Kocahanoğlu, *Türk Çevre Mevzuatı, çevre Sağlığı ve çevre Güvenliği* (1996); S. Tellenbach, *Türkei*, in *Umweltstrafrecht in mittelund südeuropäischen Ländern, edition iuscrim, Freiburg i.Br.* (1997).
310. E. Memiş, *Çevre ve Çevre İdare Hukuku* (2006). S. Boşça & S.C. Çiğdem, *Enerji Hukuku ve Mevzuatı* (2005). I. Aslan, Yılmaz, *Enerji Hukuku* (2009).

Penalties in the *Code on Water Resources and Marine Life* (March 22, 1971, Act No. 1380) were increased on May 15, 1986 (Act No. 3288).[311]

The Act concerning the Protection of the Coast (April 4, 1990, Act No. 3621) was amended on July 1, 1992 (Act No. 3830) and the protected coastline was extended to one hundred meters from the shore.

The environment is also protected by the Penal Code (*supra,* paragraph 217). Additional protection is aimed by the Turkey's Agency of Environment: The Act No. 7261 dated 24.12.2020 has created a new independent authority, consisting of an executive committee, presidency, and advisory committee, which have the duties of executing the strategic decisions of the Ministry of Environment and especially foresees a recycling program by establishing a mandatory deposit administration system and of raising the awareness of the public about environmental issues.

256. Protection of cultural and natural property. There is High Council for the Protection of Cultural Property attached to the Ministry of Culture and Tourism. The Act Protection of Cultural and Natural Resources dated July 21, 1983 (Act. No. 2683), contains both regulatory as well as criminal provisions.[312]

257. Check-related Crimes. Check crimes[313] and other economic crimes are the most frequently committed crimes in Turkey.[314] There is a new Check Act *(Çek Kanunu)* since December 14, 2009 (Act No. 5941).[315] The aim of the legislation is to prevent uncovered checks (Article 1). Banks have to make an investigation about the ability of their customers to make payment before issuing a checkbook printed only for that customer (Article 2). In cases where the check is not covered, the bank has the responsibility of covering payment up to a certain sum (Article 3).[316]

The customer who has issued the uncovered check shall be punished with a criminal fine, if there is a complaint against him (Article 5). There is a new procedural institution: The judge at the investigation phase and the court at the prosecution phase are entitled to rule on a *prohibition on issuing checks*, upon the request of the public prosecutor (Article 5/4).

Where a merchant uses the checkbook of a non-merchant person for the commercial purposes of his business, he shall be punished with imprisonment from six months up to two years (Article 7/1).

---

311. A.M. Acabey, *Sınıraşan Sular*, İstanbul, Beta, 2006; S.N. Deda, *Orman Kanunu ve Tatbikatı,* Ankara, Seçkin Yayınları, 1994.
312. S. Kanadoğlu, *Kültür ve Tabiat Varlıklarını Koruma Kanunu* (Ankara: Seçkin Yayınları, 2003).
313. Y. Aker, *Çekten Cayma ve Ödeme Yasağı*, İstanbul, Beta, 2006; G. Erik, *Çek Hukuku*, Ankara, Seçkin Yayınları, 2004; S. Selçuk, *Çek Suçları, Öğreti, Mevzuat İçtihat*, Ankara, Hatiboğlu Yayınları, 1993.
314. T. Uyar, *Gerekçeli, Notlu, İçtihatlı İtcra ve İflas Kanunu,* 2 cilt.; M.N. Ünver, *İcra ve İflas Kanununda Suç Sayılan Fiiller* (1997); E. Çetin, *Kamu İktisadi Teşebbüsleri Personelinin ve Kooperatif Görevlilerinin Ceza Sorumluluğu* (1994); A. Kendigelen, *Çek Hukuku* (2007).
315. Prior this legislation Act No. 3167 of Mar. 19, 1985 regulated protection of recipients of checks. Anyone who issued an uncovered check was punished with a prison term of up to five years (Art. 16, Act No. 3167). Amendments of Jan. 14, 1993 and of 2003 stated that this crime would be prosecuted if the victim filed a complaint even though the accused did not appear at the trial.
316. G.S. Soyer, *Borç İçin Hapis Yasağı ve Karşılıksız Çek Keşide Etme Suçu*, 2007.

Bank personnel who do not register the uncovered check upon request shall be punished with imprisonment up to one year if there is a complaint (Article 7/4).

258. Tax related crimes. There are some crimes that are related to taxation.[317] These crimes are regulated under Article 331 of Tax Procedure Act *(Vergi Usul Kanunu).* According to this Article, those who violate the provisions of tax law shall be punished with tax penalties. These penalties are divided into two groups: Tax loss and tax fraud. If the crime is related to tax evasion the penalty shall be imprisonment under Article 359 of Tax Procedure Act.

259. Corruption. The high officers of the state and the leaders of the political parties are obliged to submit information about their property holdings.[318] According to Act No. 3628, of April 19, 1990, anyone who fails to do so shall be punished by imprisonment (Article 10, Act No. 3628). As mentioned earlier, bribery of foreign civil servants is a new crime in the Penal Code (*supra*, paragraph 231).

There is a National Anti-Corruption Strategy in Turkey. Working groups on corruption-related issues are following up the policy proposals and engage effectively with civil society. However, a greater political will is needed to achieve concrete results. Group of States Against Corruption (GRECO) recommendations remain a priority. In this context, the financing of political parties needs to be addressed, finding sources, donation ceilings and obligations on candidates to disclose assets and submit financial information during a campaign should be introduced. Measures are required to reduce the broad scope of parliamentary immunity in corruption cases and to define objective criteria for the lifting of immunity. Arrangements to verify assets declared by political figures and public officials need to be strengthened. Turkey collects the statistics on court decisions in corruption cases, but investigations, indictments and convictions are not cited in those statistics.

Turkey collects certain statistics on court decisions in corruption cases, with a breakdown of figures for bribery, embezzlement, extortion and misuse of power. Efforts are needed to develop a thorough track record of investigation, indictment and conviction. Following up on the policy suggestion to establish comprehensive tracking of data on corruption is of crucial importance in this respect.[319]

260. Law and Medicine. Medical law has been an important issue in recent years.[320] Act No. 2238, of 1979, on Organ Transplantation governs taking human organs from a corpse and lists penalties for violations.[321]

---

317. B. Baykara, *Teori ve Pratik Yönleriyle Vergi ve Vergi Ceza Hukuku*, 2008; N. Ok & A. Gündel, *Ceza Mahkemeleri Görevine Giren Vergi Suçları*, Ankara, Seçkin Yayınları, 2002; D. şenyüz, *Vergi Ceza Hukuku, Vergi Kabahatleri ve Suçları*, 2008; F. Yenisey & G. Güneş, *Prof. Dr. Adnan Tezel Günleri: Vergi Hukuku*, Arıkan Yayıncılık, 2006.
318. H. Ökçesiz, *İstanbul Barosu Çevresi Adli Yargıda Yolsuzluk Araştırması* (2001).
319. European Commission, Turkey 2015 Progress Report.
320. H. Petek, *İlaç Üreticisinin Hukuki Sorumluğu* (2009); H. Sarıtaş, *Hasta Hakları Açısından Hekimin Sorumluluğu* (2005). K. İçel, Y. Ünver & B. Tag (ed. Yener Ünver), *Organ Nakli ve Organ Ticareti Suçu* (Ankara: Prof. Dr. Utr. Brigitte Tag'a Armağan, Seçkin, 2009). K. İçel, *Tıp ve Ceza Hukuku* (Seçkin Yayınları, 2004). H. Özkan, S.Ö. Akyıldız, *Hasta Hekim Hakları ve Davaları* (2008). O.

261. Banking Crimes. The Bank Code (Act No. 7129 of June 23, 1958) was replaced by a new Code of April 25, 1985, which regulates crimes related to banking transactions.[322] The Bank Code was renewed in 1999. There was a loophole in the law and private banks were excluded from the scope of criminal responsibility. This Code has been replaced by the Banking Act (*Bankacılık Kanunu*) (October 19, 2005, Act No. 5411).[323]

262. Smuggling. The repealed Code on Prohibition of Smuggling dated January 7, 1932 (Act No. 1918) was amended by Act No. 2867 of July 26, 1983, which changed some of the imprisonment penalties into fines. Act No. 3217, of June 9, 1985 removed some more of the custodial penalties of that code.[324] The following Act on Combating Smuggling (*Kaçakçılıkla Mücadele Kanunu,* KaçK), effective July 10, 2003 (Act No. 4926) replaced the 1932 Act.[325]

However, this *new* act was also repealed by 2007–5607 *Combating Smuggling Act.* This act defines crimes and misdemeanors in the field of smuggling (Articles 3/1–16) and adds an *intent* requirement for those misdemeanors (except for Article 3/16). In addition, it punishes the attempted conduct as if finalized (Article 3/18).

263. Protection of Turkish Currency. The Act for Protection of the Value of Turkish Money (Act No. 1567) was amended on May 5, 1985 (Act No. 3196). The custodial penalties were abolished and only criminal fines remain.[326] According to this act, possessing foreign currency (which required imprisonment) is no longer a crime. This amendment has been an important step on the way to privatization.

264. Crimes related to terrorism. Within the area of special criminal laws, there are some acts that deal with combating terrorism (*supra*, paragraph 247). On July 10, 2014, the Turkish Parliament adopted a new Act to bring an end to terrorism and to strengthen the social integrity (Act No. 6551, entitled *"Terörün Sona Erdirilmesi ve Toplumsal Bütünleşmenin Güçlendirilmesine Dair Kanun"*). The aim of

---

Polat, *Tıbbi Uygulama Hataları*, Ankara, Seçkin Yayınları, 2005. M. Sevtap, *Biyo-Tıp Etiği ve Hukuk* (2010); Y. Ünver, *Tıp ve Ceza Hukuku*, Ankara, Seçkin Yayınları, 2004.

321. A. Taşkın, *Organ ve Doku Nakillerinde Hekimin Cezai Sorumuluğu* (1997).

322. Y. Alıcı, *Bankacılık Kanunu şerhi*, İstanbul, Beta, 2007; S. Donay, *Bankacılık Ceza Hukuku*, İstanbul, Beta, 2007; S. Dursun, *Ekonomik ve Suçlar ve Bankacılık Suçları Bağlamında, Bankacılık Düzenine Karşı İşlenen Suçlar*, Ankara, Yetkin Yayınları, 2006; S. Erman, *Bankacılık Suçları*, İstanbul, 1984; S. Erman, *Döviz Suçları*, İstanbul, 1983; A.H. Evik, *Sermaye Piyasası Araçlarının Değerini Etkileyebilecek Aldatıcı Hareketler Yapma (Manipülasyon) Suçları*, Ankara, Seçkin Yayınları, 2004.

323. RG. 1.11.2005/25983. H. Yasaman, *Banka Hukuku ile İlgili Makaleler, Hukuki Mütalaalar, Bilirkişi Raporları* (2005).

324. E. Günay, *Uygulamalı Kaçakçılık Suçları* (1996); M. Ertuğrul, *Kaçakçılık Suçları 1918; sayılı Kaçakçılığın Men ve Takibine Dair Kanun* (1998); M. Danışman, *Açıklamalı Kaçakçılıkla Mücadele Kanunu, Kaçak Petrol ve Ulusal Marker: 5607 Sayılı Kaçakçılıkla Mücadele Kanunu, 5015 Sayılı Petrol Piyasası Kanunu, Yönetmelikler Tutanak Örnekleri* (2010); E. Günay, *Kaçakçılıkla Mücadele Kanunu*, Ankara, Seçkin Yayınları, 2004; E. Yurtcan, *Yeni Kaçakçılıkla Mücadele Kanunun şerhi*, İstanbul, Beta, 2007.

325. L. Başöz & R. Çakmakçı, *Gerekçeli Kaçakçılıkla Mücadele Kanunu ve İlgili Mevzuat* (2003).

326. K. Bakal & I. Kürümoğlu, *Açıklamalı İçtihatlı Türk Parasının Kıymetini Koruma ve Kambiyo Mevzuatı*, Ankara, Seçkin Yayınları, 2002.

this law was to bring legal foundations to the social unification and reintegration of those who leave the terrorist organization, but did not achieve its goal.

265. Demonstration Law. The alleged violations of human rights in the context of the protests in May and June 2013, across the country, underline the need for far-reaching reforms in order to ensure respect for the freedom of assembly in line with European standards.

The Internal Security Package numbered 2015-6638 provides for changes to the Law on demonstrations. According to this regulation Article 33 of Act on Demonstrations has been changed and punishments increased in case of attending a meeting armed. If there are some damages caused by demonstrators, state will pay the damages but the demonstrator will have to pay back to the state (Additional Article 1 of Act on Demonstrations).[327] It notably foresees that authorities need to consult stakeholders before making decisions on rallies and demonstrations, it extends the time periods within which rallies and demonstrations can be held and it gives authority for monitoring and terminating the rallies to anybody including representatives of demonstrators.

266. Law on weapons. There is a special Act on Weapons (1953–6136: *Ateşli Silahlar ve Bıçaklar ile Diğer Aletler Hakkında Kanun*).[328] This Act prohibits producing, selling and buying of weapons and have designated weapons that are prohibited and regulates places where carrying weapons is prohibited as well as other important issues related to this topic.

267. Military crimes. The AsCK, enacted by Act No. 1632 dated May 22, 1930 regulates special crimes for military personnel.[329]

Disciplinary sanctions applicable for military personnel are regulated in Act No. 6412, dated January 1, 2015. This statute is still applicable even if the military courts have been abolished (*infra*, paragraph 357).

268. Sport Law. Sport has many aspects of law, some of which are enforced under criminal law.[330] For the purpose of preventing incidents of violence at sport

---

327. İç Güvenlik Kuvvetlerinin Sivil Gözetimi ile İlgili Mevzuat, Improvement of Civilian Oversight of Internal Security Sector Project, Phase II.
328. K. Ekşioğlu, *Açıklamalı – Yorumlu– İçtihatlı Bütün Boyutlarıyla Uygulamalı Silah Hukuku* (1993); Y. Alasu, *Hukukumuzda Ateşli Silahlar Bıçaklar ve Patlayıcı Maddeler* (1995); N. Tankut, *Ateşli Silahlar, Bıçaklar Patlayıcı Maddeler, Av Tüfekleri* (1997); M. Güler, *Ateşli Silahlar ve Bıçaklar Hakkında Kanun* (1998); B. Özer, *Silah Hukuku ve Mevzuatı* (1998); E. Doğan, *Tabanca ve Tüfek Ruhsatları* (1998).
329. Z. Kangal, *Askeri Ceza Hukuku,* 2. Baskı, Seçkin, Ankara 2012. D. Karaca, *Askeri Personel için Hukuk Rehberi* (2007). Ü. Kardaş & M. Çıngı, *Disiplin Mahkemeleri Kuruluşu, Yargılama Usulü ve Disiplin Suç ve Cezaları Hakkında Kanun* (2005). M. Akkurt, *Er, Erbaş ve Yedek Subaylar İçin Ceza Hukuku Rehberi*, Ankara, Adalet Yayınevi, 2010.
330. K. Erkiner, *Uluslararası Spor Tahkim Mahkemesi C.A.S.*, İstanbul, Vedat Kitapçılık, 2010; Y. Ünver, *Çocuklar ve Spor – Ceza*, Ankara, Seçkin Yayınları, 2005; Y. Ünver, *Spor ve Ceza Hukuku*, Ankara, Seçkin Yayınları, 2004; H. Karaahmetoğlu, *Sporda Şiddet Şike ve Teşvik Primi,* İstanbul 2015.

events a new Act entered into force on April 14, 2011. Its name is Act on Prevention of Disorder and Violence in Sports (Act. No. 6222). This Act designates the order of the places where sport events will be held, their round-trip routes, and places where hooligans are found in groups, permanently or temporarily. In order to fulfill the tasks assigned by this act a new police unit has been established. This act has brought really serious penalties for actions such as match-fixing, incentive payments, insulting cheers and bringing banned objects inside the sports arena.

269. Traffic offenses. The Road Traffic Act (*Karayolları Trafik Kanunu,* KTK) and related regulations have created a traffic law.[331] According to the Road Traffic Act No. 1983-2918, the following actions are defined as traffic offenses: Violating traffic rules, driving a vehicle under the influence of alcohol, drugs or psychotropic substances, violating speed limits, disobeying driving time periods.

270. Crimes against intellectual property.[332] Intellectual Property Act No. 1951-5846 is the main source of protecting intellectual and artistic works. Infringement of moral or financial rights and other related rights are regulated as crimes.

331. H.T. Gökcan & S. Kaymaz, *Trafik Suçları ve Trafik Mevzuatı*, Ankara, Seçkin Yayınları, 2000; E. Günay, *Uygulamada Trafik Kazalarında Kusur*, Ankara, Seçkin Yayınları, 2004; B. Karakaş, *Karayolları Trafik Kanunu'ndaki Ceza Hükümleri ve Uygulaması*, Ankara, Seçkin Yayınları, 2002; C. Ülgen, *Plakaya Düzenlenen Trafik Para Cezalarının İptali Davaları*, İstanbul, Beta, 2007.

332. M. Aksu, *Bilgisayar Programlarının Fikri Mülkiyet Hukukunda Korunması*, İstanbul, Beta, 2006; S. Keskin, *Patent ve Markanın Ceza Normları ile Korunması, Fikri (Düşünsel) Mülkiyet Hakları*, Ankara, Seçkin, 2003; O. Öncü, *Fikir ve Sanat Eserleri Hukukunda İktibas Serbestisi ve Sınırları*, İstanbul, Vedat Kitapçılık, 2010.

Chapter 7. The Sanctioning System

§1. The General System

271. Principles of sanctions. The principles of the sanctioning[333] system (crimes and penalties) are provided by Article 38 of the Constitution.

272. No one shall be punished for any act which does not constitute a criminal offense under the law in force at the time committed; no one shall be punished with a more severe punishment for any act which is heavier than the punishment at the time it was committed (Article 38/1, AY).

The same principle applies to the statute of limitations for prosecution and punishment, as well as to the consequences of the criminal conviction (Article 38/2, AY). Punishments and security measures shall only be imposed by an Act (Article, 38/3). Criminal responsibility is personal (Article 38/4, AY). Death penalty and general confiscation are forbidden. The executive shall not impose any sanction resulting in restriction of personal liberty.

Sanctions (*yaptırım*) are divided into two sections: Penalties (*cezalar*) (Articles 45–52, TCK) and measures (*güvenlik tedbirleri*) (Articles 53–60, TCK). The penalties (or punishments) and security measures of the Turkish sanctioning system are governed by two sources: The current *TCK* and the *Code of Enforcement of Punishments and Security Measures* (*Ceza ve Güvenlik Tedbirlerinin İnfazı Hakkında Kanun, CGIK*).[334]

Committed crimes require penalties, either *imprisonment* or a *criminal fine* (Article 45, TCK). Criminal fines are always imposed by a criminal court, as opposed to administrative fines which are imposed by an administrative authority. According to the principle of the legality of punishment (Article 2, TCK), these two penalties are the only applicable punishment under contemporary Turkish criminal law.

The repealed TCK provided different penalties for crimes and misdemeanors, but the new TCK regulates only *crimes* and no longer includes misdemeanors. Some of the previous misdemeanors were transferred into the Misdemeanor Act of 2005.

273. Classification of penalties under the repealed Code. The repealed Penal Code divided the penalties into principal, accessory, and auxiliary penalties. Accessory penalties were automatically added to the principal penalty; for example, lengthy imprisonment for more than five years disqualified the convicted person from holding public office for life (Article 31, repealed TCK). Auxiliary penalties were added to the principal penalty at the discretion of the judge. For example, if a public officer learned of the occurrence of an offense related to his duty, he had to notify the authorities. If he failed or neglected to report it, a penalty of imprisonment would be imposed as the principal penalty, and he was subject to the auxiliary penalty of possible disqualification from holding public office, at the judge's discretion (Article 235, repealed TCK).

---

333. K. Grzybowski, *Penalties under Turkish Criminal Law*, Washington, 1954.

334. K. İçel et al., *İçel Yaptırım Teorisi*, 3. Kitap, İstanbul, Beta, 2000, p. 3.

The current Penal Code does not make any distinction in this regard. The previous accessory or auxiliary penalties are considered *security measures* in the new criminal justice system.

274. Classification in Code of Enforcement of Penalties. The TCK identifies the punishments (Articles 45–52) and security measures (Articles 53–60, TCK), while the Code on the Execution of Penalties and Security Measures (Act No. 5275, dated December 13, 2004) (Articles 109, 110, CGIK) and the Act on Controlled Liberty (2005–5402) regulate the mode of application thereof.

§2. PENALTIES

I. Death Penalty

275. There is no death penalty in Turkey.[335] In practice, the death penalty has not been used in Turkey since 1984. After being the subject of debate,[336] the death penalty existed in the Constitution until 2004 for wartime crimes, crimes committed in the status of clear and present threat of war and crimes of terrorism (Article 38, AY). The Act of August 3, 2002–4771 accepted a narrower concept and abolished the death penalty for crimes of terrorism as well. The Act No. 2004-5170 removed the death penalty from the Constitution.[337]

276. Turkey ratified the 6th Protocol to the ECHR concerning the abolition of death penalty on January 15, 2003. An amendment to the Constitution was made (Act No. 5170, dated 2004) to bring Turkish law in line with the 13th Protocol of the ECHR concerning abolition of death penalty in all circumstances, which Turkey signed on January 9, 2004. This Protocol was ratified on October 12, 2005 and has been in force in Turkey since June 1, 2006.[338]

335. İ. Özgenç, *Türk Ceza Hukuku Genel Hükümler,* Gözden Geçirilmiş ve Güncellenmiş 10. Bası, Ankara, Seçkin, 2014, p. 631; T. Demirbaş, *Ceza Hukuku Genel Hükümler*, 15. Baskı, Seçkin, Ankara 2020, p. 594.
336. T.T. Yüce, *Ceza Hukukunun Temel Kavramları*, Ankara, Turhan, 1985, p. 111; S. Tellenbach, Todesstrafe in der Türkei, ZAR (1991): 87–89; Kleinjahns & Artuk, Das türkische Strafvollzugssystem, ZStW 107 (1995): p. 662. In 1963, the Constitutional Court refused to hear a death penalty case (Decision of the Constitutional Court, Jul. 1, 1963, E. 1963/207, K. 1963/175).
337. After the 2001 amendment of Art. 38 of the Constitution (*supra*, para. 11), the death penalty for crimes of terrorism was abolished by Art. 1, Act No. 4771 of Aug. 3, 2002.
338. Article 6 of the International Covenant on Civil and Political Rights recognizes a state's right to impose the death penalty in exceptional circumstances. Additional optional Protocol No. 2, adopted by Resolution 44/128 on Dec. 15, 1989, however, requires each signatory party to abolish the death penalty within its jurisdiction. Turkey ratified this Protocol on Dec. 27, 2005, without any reservation for the right to impose the death penalty in wartime military crimes. This Protocol has been in force for Turkey since Jun. 2, 2006. Thus, there is no exception to the death penalty ban in Turkey.

277. The current TCK therefore does not include the death penalty.[339] Act No. 2006-5530 to remove the death penalty has also amended the Military Courts Act. Sometimes after children have been raped and killed, there have been loud voices urging reintroduction of the death penalty.

II. Imprisonment and Alternatives to Imprisonment

278. TCK contains two categories of penalties as sanctions for crimes: imprisonment and criminal fine (Article 45, TCK).

There are three types of imprisonment: *Aggravated imprisonment for life, imprisonment for life* and *temporary imprisonment* (Article 46, TCK). Temporary imprisonment cannot be shorter than one month and not longer than twenty years if not specifically stated in the Penal Code (Article 49/1, TCK). Short-term imprisonment is regulated in the Penal Code (not in the Act of Execution of Punishments and Measures, as it was before): if the final judgment of the court carries a term of imprisonment of one year or less, this imprisonment is considered as *short-term imprisonment* (Article 49/2, TCK).

Given the disillusionment with the result of prison as a means of crime prevention, it comes as no surprise that alternatives to the classical approach to crime and criminals have become more prevalent.[340]

The alternatives to short-term imprisonment (*infra*, paragraph 281) are shown in the Penal Code (Article 50, TCK).

A. *Aggravated Imprisonment for Life*

279. Aggravated imprisonment for life is the most severe modality and has replaced the death penalty of the previous legislation. This type of imprisonment lasts as long as the inmate lives and shall be enforced under the tight security regime as regulated in Act No. 5275 (CGIK), Article 25 (Article 47, TCK): The prisoner shall be placed into a cell, in solitary confinement, but shall be given the right to stay at least one hour in the open air during his/her period of cell term, while later on, the convicted prisoner may talk on the telephone to the people mentioned in Article 25, paragraph (f) CGIK, once in fifteen days, for a ten minute-period of time, the prisoner shall enjoy the right to receive a visit by his/her spouse, those in lineal consanguinity, his/her brothers and sisters and his/her tutor. The convicted prisoner shall not be allowed to leave the institution. The enforcement of the sentence shall not be interrupted by any means. Treatment of the ill will be conducted in high security institutions.

---

339. According to Art. 87 of the 1982 Constitution, enactment of a specific law was needed for the execution of each death penalty decision of any court. There was a possible constitutional challenge of the *Execution Law* in each case. The promulgation of this law was a requirement for the execution of the death penalty (Art. 2/4, repealed CIK). Law No. 5170 dated 2004 removed these words from the text of Art. 87 of the Constitution while abolishing the death penalty.

340. H. Kury & E. Shea, *Are Prisons an Effective Means of Crime Prevention? The Importance of Alternatives*, in Prof. Dr. Feridun Yenisey'e Armağan, Beta, İstanbul 2014, p. 53.

B. Imprisonment for Life

280. The current Penal Code includes imprisonment for life, which lasts as long as the inmate lives (Article 48, TCK). The inmate displaying good behavior, however, may be eligible for parole after serving a minimum of twenty-four years (Article 107/2, CGIK) (*infra*, paragraph 617).

C. Imprisonment for a Specific Term and Alternative Sanctions for Short-Time Imprisonment

1. Imprisonment Term Specified by the Court

281. Imprisonment for a specific term is regulated in various articles of the Penal Code. If the Code does not indicate the length of imprisonment, it cannot be shorter than one month or longer than twenty years (Article 49/1, TCK).

An inmate's good behavior may make him/her eligible for parole after serving at least half of his/her prison term (Article 107/2, CGIK) (*infra*, paragraph 619).

If the imprisonment term as decided in the judgment of the court is one year, or less than one year, this is considered as a *short-term imprisonment* (Article 49/2, TCK) and may be converted into an alternative sanction as regulated in Article 50 TCK.

2. Commutation of Short-Time Imprisonment into Alternative Sanctions

282. According to Article 50 of Penal Code, the court may commute a short-time imprisonment by taking into account the personality[341] of the individual, his/her social and economic situation, his/her feelings of regret expressed during the trial and the manner of the commission of the crime.[342] In any further legal application, the commuted criminal fine or measure is considered as the final conviction (Article 50/5, TCK).

A *long-term imprisonment* may also be commuted if the crime has been committed through negligence. However, if the accused acted with *foreseeable negligence*, this provision does not apply (Article 50/4, TCK).

Although it has been argued that the commutation of imprisonment to other punishments or measures is an infringement of the Constitution, the Constitutional Court decided otherwise.[343]

---

341. İ. Özgenç, *Türk Ceza Hukuku Genel Hükümler,* Gözden Geçirilmiş ve Güncellenmiş 10. Bası, Ankara, Seçkin, 2014, p. 675.
342. For example, commuting imprisonment to a fine contravenes the law when the convicted individual had negligently killed another person while using a gun that he possessed without permission: Cass. 1 CD Dec. 26, 1977; YKD 1987/7, 1202.
343. Decision of the Constitutional Court dated 1971, E. 42/K. 30; S. Dönmezer & S. Erman I, *Nazari ve Tatbiki Ceza Hukuku, Genel Kısım*, Cilt I, 11. Bası, Beta, İstanbul 1994, p. 76.

If the convicted individual is punished with imprisonment for the first time and his/her term is not more than thirty days, and if the convicted individual has not attained 18 years of age or has attained the age of 60 when he/she commits the crime (Article 50/3 TCK), a commutation is obligatory.

The commutation of punishments is within the competence of the court, and as such, it is a means of the individualization of punishment. The judge must fix a custodial punishment and then determine whether it should be commuted into another punishment or measure. Even if there is no request for such a commutation, the judge must consider this matter ex officio. The judge must explain the decision in the reasons for judgment.

In cases of commutation to alternative sanctions, short- (or long-) term imprisonment is considered as the fundamental conviction (*infra*, paragraph 322) (Article 50/5, TCK). After the commuted criminal fine or alternative measure is finalized, public prosecutor's office notifies the convicted person about his/her obligations to fulfill the sanction within thirty days. If the individual does not comply with his/her obligations or interrupts their performance, the enforcement judge (before 2020-7242 amendment it was the court that rendered the judgment) makes a new decision about the execution of the short-term imprisonment, which shall be executed immediately (Article 50/6, TCK).

283. Commutation of short-term imprisonment imposed for military crimes is forbidden. There is another ban on the commutation of short-time imprisonment to alternatives in the special criminal law (Act No. 3628, Article 16; Act on Combating Bribery and Corruption).

The court can choose a fine (Article 50/1-a, TCK), or one of the five measures (Article 50/1-b, c, d, e, f, TCK) as listed below (*infra*, paragraphs 284–290). However, if the definition of the crime indicates *imprisonment or criminal fine* as alternative punishment, and the court has imposed a short-term imprisonment, commutation into a fine is no longer permitted (Article 50/2, TCK).[344] In cases of recidivism, if the statute foresees the option of imprisonment and a fine, the court is not entitled to choose criminal fine (Article 58/3, TCK).

When the alternative sentence has not been complied with due to reasons beyond the control of the convicted person, the enforcement judge, shall amend the alternative measure (Article 50/7, TCK).

3. Commutation to a Fine

284. Short-time imprisonment (imprisonment of a duration of one year or no more than one year) and long-term imprisonment imposed for crimes committed

344. Prior to this regulation, the High Court of Cassation ruled that it was possible to commute the imprisonment term into a fine, even if the judge had decided the option of imprisonment (İçBK 4.2.1974, No. 3/5; Ali Rıza Çınar, *Türk Ceza Hukukunda Cezalar* (Ankara, 2005), p. 46).

negligently may be commuted into criminal fines. The judge may commute imprisonment, without asking the consent of the convicted individual, into a fine, by multiplying the identified number of days by the daily amount (Article 52/1, TCK). The daily amount shall be determined with regard to the personal and economic conditions of the individual.

Commutation of short-term imprisonment to a fine for crimes committed with intent (Article 50/1-a, TCK), and crimes committed with negligence (Article 50/4, TCK), are different from one another: Long-term imprisonment imposed for crimes committed negligently may also be commuted into a criminal fine. This provision does not apply if the perpetrator had acted with *foreseeable intent* (Article 50/4, TCK).

If the accused had suffered terms of deprivation of freedom prior to commutation of his conviction of imprisonment to a fine, each day shall be calculated for 100 Turkish Lira and reduced from the imprisonment term (Article 63, TCK).

If the law provides for short-term custodial punishment or a fine at the discretion of the judge and the judge prefers short-term custodial punishment, then he cannot later commute it to a fine (Article 50/2, TCK).

Some Turkish laws prohibit commuting imprisonment into fines, such as those relating to military crimes committed by officers.[345] Furthermore, prison terms in these cases cannot be commuted to disciplinary punishments.

Short-term custodial punishments may be commuted into criminal fines and can be replaced by making reparation, attendance at a school or an educational center, prohibition of access to certain places or association with certain people, the suspension of a driving license or other licenses or by community service (Article 50, TCK).

If a short-term imprisonment has been commuted into a fine or another form of alternative sanction, that sanction is regarded as the *principal* or *fundamental conviction* (Article 50/5, TCK). Execution of short-term imprisonment may take one of several forms, and which form it will take depends on the applications made by the convicted individual (Article 109, CGIK).

4. Commutation to an Alternative Sanction

285. A short-term imprisonment may be commuted into an alternative measure, as indicated in Article 50/1-b, c, d, e, f, TCK, such as restitution or compensation. These are measures, in contrast to the fine in Article 50/1-a, TCK that is a penalty, and the convicted person is not under supervision.

The first alternative measure is *restitution* or *compensation*. The law provides rules for restitution of damages or *full* compensation for losses (Article 50/1-b,

345. Article 16. Act No. 3628, dated Apr. 19, 1990.3. However, a review in the Court of Cassation depended on the amount of the fine (Art. 305, repealed CMUK), which often would not be reached in the case of a commutation. Fines resulting from a commutation would be barred from such a review. The amended Art. 4/4 of the repealed Code of Enforcement of Punishments provided that this is not an obstacle for such a review. The current Penal Code has adopted the same approach.

TCK). Restitution is limited to offenses involving property. Damage compensation can be for physical and non-physical damage.

The ideas of restitution and compensation are also regulated by the concept of mediation (Article 253, CMK) (*infra*, paragraph 393).

286. Commutation to education. The offender may be ordered to attend a school or an educational institution, which may be a boarding school, for at least two years (Article 50/1-c, TCK).

287. Commutation to restrictions. Restrictions like prohibition from visiting certain places or carrying on certain activities or occupations (Article 50/1-d, TCK), which may not exceed half of the imposed imprisonment term, serve the purpose of improving the delinquent. The judge fixes the details of these prohibitions. In this way, the judge can prepare an educational curriculum for the delinquent. If the delinquent does not comply with the prohibitions, he/she will be forced to do so, and the general principles of penal law will be applied.

288. Commutation to limitations. The law provides for the revocation of driving licenses and other licenses, or deprivation of the right to carry out a profession or to operate in a certain area of activity (Article 50/1-e, TCK). Any license or right can be withdrawn for a period of one-half of the imposed imprisonment term up to double the imprisonment term. Such a withdrawal is imposed if the crime was committed by failing to discharge a duty of care and attention or by abusing authority or a right.

289. Commutation to publicly beneficial work (or community service). A short-time imprisonment may be commuted into a measure of publicly beneficial work for a minimum term of between one-half and two times the terms of imprisonment, although only with the consent of the offender (Article 50/1-f, TCK).

The execution of this measure is regulated in the Code on Corrections (Article 105/2, CGIK). Parole centers make a list of the institutions that have available works, and the court chooses a workplace from this list.

290. Suspension of imprisonment. The TCK avoids restriction of liberty for relatively short periods in the following circumstances: An imprisonment term of two years or less may be suspended if the accused has not been previously sentenced to a penalty for a term of more than three-months imprisonment for commission of a prior intentional crime, and the court is convinced that, as a result of remorse seen at the time of the trial, he will not commit further crimes in the future (Article 51, TCK) (*infra,* paragraph 339).

III. Criminal Fine

291. The criminal fine,[346] or the so-called day-fine system, is a sum of money that the offender pays to the state Treasury. The court calculates this sum by multiplying the number of days as indicated by the Code with a daily amount. The number of days shall be more than 5 but not more than 730 (Article 52/1, TCK).

The daily amount, which shall be at minimum 20 and at most TRY 100. The number of full days and the daily amount shall be stated separately in the judgment (Article 52/3 TCK).

It is permitted to pay the fine within one year or by installments. Taking into account the personal and economic conditions of the convicted person, the judge may decide upon an installment period of up to two years and upon the number of installments. For the sake of caution, if any installment has not been paid on time, the full amount of the remaining unpaid fine shall be due immediately and shall be converted into imprisonment (Article 52/4, TCK).

As the new Penal Code has adopted the day-fine system and regulated *confiscation of gains*, it does not include relative fines (e.g., the sum of the fine for smuggling was five times the value of the smuggled goods; Article 18, repealed Act No. 1918).[347] In contrast, Banking Act No. 5411, Article 160/2 foresees a *relative fine* for bribery in bank transactions.

292. Fines of the repealed Code. According to the repealed Penal Code, fines were adjusted annually. Due to inflation, a system of adjustment of fines was introduced to Turkish Criminal Law in 1988. A basic multiplier applied to the salary of state officials, which was set every year with the budget, has been taken as a constant value. In 1988, the multiplier was eighty-four. According to this regulation, every sevent-five points over this multiplier was considered one unit, and the fine shown in the related article of the Code would be multiplied by this unit (added Articles 1–5, repealed TCK). In 1999, however, the former multiplier for the salaries was replaced by Act No. 4421 with the taxation index.[348] The current Penal Code has abolished this difficult way of calculation and introduced the day-fine system, similar to that of the German Penal Code.[349]

293. Fixing the criminal fine. Some fines are listed in the related articles and are fixed. There are other fines having upper and lower limits. The court has discretion in these latter cases and decides the amount of the fine according to the accused's

346. O. Erdoğan, *Para Cezaları ve İnfazı* (İstanbul: Beta, 2007). K. Keskin, *Para Cezaları, Ön Ödeme Ceza Tabloları, Erteleme, Paraya çevirme, Harçlar* (Ankara: Desen Ofset, 1996).

347. İ. Özgenç, *Türk Ceza Hukuku Genel Hükümler,* 10. Bası, Ankara, Seçkin, 2014, p. 734. The previous law did not fix the upper limit of certain fines. These were so-called relative fines.

348. İ. Malkoç, *Açıklamalı Türk Ceza Kanunu, Son Değişiklikler ve İçtihatlarla* (Ankara, 2002), 180. The author gives examples of the amount of the fines relating to years 2000, 2001 and 2002, which are relevant to the application of Art. 7/2 TCK, as the judge is not entitled to impose a more severe punishment at the time of the judgment compared to the punishment when the crime was committed.

349. F. Yenisey & G. Plagemann, *Alman Ceza Kanunu (StGB)*, Gözden Geçirilmiş ve Genişletilmiş 2. Baskı, Beta, İstanbul 2015.

financial situation and other personal status such as his family responsibilities, his profession, age, health and the social effects of the fine, in accordance with the circumstances of the offense, or the offender's blameworthiness (Articles 52/2, 61/8, TCK).

294. Administrative fines. There was another category of fines in Turkish Law, namely compensatory fines. The new Penal Code does not include this type of fine, but the Act of Misdemeanors (Article 17, KK) does under the form of administrative fines.[350]

Technically, administrative fines are not considered a *punishment*; rather, they are designed as a warning to the wrongdoer. Administrative fines may also be used to compensate the losses of the public.

295. The current Penal Code has changed the system of punishments and reduced the number of penalties to two: Imprisonment and criminal fine (Article 49, TCK).[351] All other penalties have been abolished: disqualification to hold public office (either for life or temporary), temporary disqualification from exercising a profession or trade that requires an official license or certification, revocation of a driving license, civil disqualification of persons sentenced to more than five years' lengthy imprisonment during the period of punishment, public announcement of judgments, confiscation and forfeiture as a penalty, criminal admonition instead of a penalty that does not exceed one month of imprisonment, and light imprisonment or a heavy or a light fine of TRY 3,000.

§3. Measures of Security

296. Security measures do not have the repressive function of penalties, but they are subject to the principle of legality (Article 38, AY).[352] Security measures relate to dangerous offenders and the purpose is to protect society against dangerous individuals and to reform offenders. However, administrative authorities may apply any type of preventive police measures that do not restrict basic personal freedoms.[353]

Certain measures are designed to prevent crime. These include: confiscation (Articles 54 and 55, TCK); custody and treatment of mentally ill persons (Article 57, TCK); commitment to an institution or placing children who do not have criminal capacity into the custody of their parents (Article 56, TCK); and custody and treatment of drug addicts and alcoholics (Article 191, TCK) (*supra,* paragraph 219).

---

350. R. Çağlayan, *İdari Yaptırımlar Hukuku*, 2006; M. Karabulut, *İdari Yaptırımların Hukuki Rejimi*, 2008.

351. F. Erem, *Memnu Hakların İadesi* (Ankara, 1948); H.H. Sümer, *Sakat ve Eski Hükümlü Çalıştırma Yükümlülüğü,* in *AdD,* No. 3 (1989), 22; E. Günay, *Dava ve Ceza Zamanaşımı, Memnu Hakların İadesi, Adli Sicil Kayıtlarının Silinmesi* (1998).

352. İ. Özgenç, *Türk Ceza Hukuku Genel Hükümler, Gözden Geçirilmiş ve Güncellenmiş* 10. Bası, Ankara, Seçkin, 2014, p. 760.

353. K. İçel & S. Donay, *Karşılaştırmalı ve Uygulamalı Ceza Hukuku,* 2. Bası, İstanbul, Filiz, 1993, p. 81.

The Penal Code has introduced the criminal fine and alternative measures as potential substitutes for short-term imprisonment.

Measures restricting personal freedom are only valid if a judge has ordered their enforcement. During the preliminary investigation, the decision regarding measures must be rendered by the criminal peace judgeship (Article 74/1, CMK), and, during the prosecution phase, by a competent court (Article 57, TCK).

The Juvenile Judge and Juvenile Courts have jurisdiction over measures for children who have not attained 18 years of age (Article 3/1-c, 25) ÇKK (*supra*, paragraph 124).

Security measures are not sufficiently regulated by the current TCK. In the repealed TCK, the expression *security measure* was not even mentioned. The existing regulations are considered below.

I. Deprivation of Exercising Certain Rights

297. The deprivation of the exercise of certain rights as a legal consequence. The TCK currently regulates two categories of deprivation of rights: (1) deprivation of exercising rights for the duration of the imprisonment; and (2) deprivation of exercising rights after the completion of the prison sentence, if the sentence of imprisonment had been imposed for a crime related to the abuse of that right.

The deprivation of the exercise of certain rights is a legal consequence for convicts who have been sentenced to an imprisonment term for an intentional crime (Article 53/1, TCK). It shall be applied until the completion of the convict's prison term (Article 53/2, TCK).

Until the completion of the term of the convict's imprisonment (Article 53/2, TCK), the following rights shall continue to be restricted as the legal consequence of a conviction leading to imprisonment:

> *The right to serve as a civil servant.* The right to serve as a civil servant permanently, temporarily or for a fixed period of time. This includes becoming a member of the TBMM, serving as a civil servant, serving as an employee at a public institution, and serving as an appointed or elected public officer within the administration of the state, a province, a municipality or a village or as one at an institution or entity under their control or supervision (Article 53/1-a, TCK).
>
> *Political rights.* The eligibility to vote or to be elected, and to exercise other political rights (Article 53/1-b TCK). This restriction is not applicable to a convict whose sentence of imprisonment has been suspended, or who has been conditionally released, with respect to acting as a guardian or being appointed in the role of guardianship or as a trustee (Article 53/3, TCK).
>
> Except as mentioned in the proceeding subsection, the right to act as a guardian: The right to serve in the role of guardianship or as a trustee (Article 53/1-c, TCK).
>
> The right to be the administrator or inspector of a legal person, namely, of a foundation, association, labor union, company, cooperative or political party (Article 53/1-d, TCK).

The right to conduct any profession or trade in which conducting in general is subject to the permission of a professional organization (which is in the nature of a public institution or organization), under his own responsibility as a professional or a tradesman (Article 53/1-e, TCK).

Where an offender has been subject to a suspended prison sentence, this prohibition may not apply (Article 53/3, TCK).

298. The deprivation of the exercise of certain rights as an additional prohibition. Where a sentence of imprisonment has been imposed for a crime related to the abuse of one of the rights or authorities defined in Article 53/1, TCK, the convict shall be prohibited from exercising such right for a period of one-half to two times the length of imprisonment imposed. This restriction comes into effect after the prison term is served.

Where only a fine has been imposed for a crime related to the abuse of one of these rights or authority, the exercise of this right shall be prohibited for a period of one-half to double the number of days stated in the judgment.

The prohibition comes into effect once the judgment is finalized, and the duration of the prohibition period starts when the criminal fine has been completely executed (Article 53/5 TCK).

299. Restoration of prohibited rights. The provisions of the repealed Penal Code related to the restoration of rights are not included in the current Penal Code because of the regulations in Article 53, subsections 2 and 5, TCK. As a consequence, all previously convicted individuals should be able to enjoy full rights in political and social life. However, Article 76/2 of the Constitution states that in order for a person to be eligible to run as a candidate in parliamentary elections, that person must never have been convicted of a crime listed in that Article.

The Act on Criminal Register has been amended by Act No. 2006-5560, and restoration of rights for penalties imposed on crimes regulated in special criminal statutes has been regulated by the Added Article 13A. In some instances, this has affected the eligibility to run for public office mentioned in the preceding paragraph.

300. Suspension of licenses. Where an offender is convicted of a reckless offense on the grounds of failing to discharge a duty of care and attention while performing a certain profession or trade, or while observing the necessities of traffic safety, it may be determined that the offender shall be prohibited from performing such profession or trade, or that his driver's license shall be suspended for a period of not less than three months and not more than three years as a measure of security[354] (Article 53/6, TCK).

The prohibition or the suspension shall be enforced once the judgment is finalized, and such period starts once any sentence is completely served.

---

354. *Revocation of driving license* and *ban of professional activities* may also be utilized in cases of commutation of short-term imprisonment as an *alternative sanction* (Art. 50/1-e, TCK).

II. Confiscation

301. Confiscation of property. The legal nature of confiscation has been totally changed in the TCK: confiscation is one of the security measures, and not a penalty.[355] There are two categories of confiscation: (1) confiscation of property (Article 54, TCK); and (2) confiscation of gains (Article 55, TCK).[356]

On the condition that the property does not belong to any third party acting in good faith, the property that is used for committing an intentional offense or is allocated for the purpose of committing an offense, or property that has emerged as the result of an offense shall be confiscated. Property that is prepared for the purpose of committing a crime shall be confiscated if it presents a danger to public security, public health or public morality.

Where the property defined in section 1 cannot be confiscated because it has been destroyed, given to another, consumed or because of any other reason, an amount of money equal to the value of this particular property shall be confiscated.

Where the confiscation of property used in an offense would lead to more serious consequences than the offense itself, and these would be unfair, confiscation may not be ordered.

Any property the production, possession, usage, transportation, buying and selling of which has constituted an offense shall be confiscated.

When only a certain part of a property needs to be confiscated, then only that part shall be confiscated, if it is possible to do so without harming the whole, or if it is possible to separate that part of it from the whole.

Where property is shared by more than one person, only the share of the person who has taken part in the crime shall be confiscated (Article 54, TCK). Good faith of the person who subsequently acquired the goods is protected under the provisions of the Civil Code dated November 22, 2001, No. 4721.

302. Confiscation of gains. Material gain obtained through the commission of a crime, forming the subject of a crime, or obtained for the commission of a crime, and the economic earnings obtained as a result of its investment or conversion, shall be confiscated. Confiscation under this section should only be ordered where it is possible to return the material gain to the victim of the crime.

Where property and material gain are subject to confiscation and cannot be seized or provided to the authorities, then the value corresponding to such property and gains shall be confiscated (Article 55, TCK).

The provisions about confiscation (Article 55, TCK) were supplemented by a new third paragraph in order to reflect the good faith rule of the person who after the crime has been committed acquired a property according to the rules of Turkish Civil Code: if the person benefits from the *good faith rules*, confiscation is not permitted (Article 55/3, TCK).

---

355. İ. Özgenç, *Türk Ceza Hukuku Genel Hükümler,* Gözden Geçirilmiş ve Güncellenmiş 10. Bası, Ankara, Seçkin, 2014, p. 775.

356. D. Gedik, *5237 sayılı Türk Ceza Kanunu ve 5271 sayılı Ceza Muhakemesi Kanunu'na Göre Müsadere,* 2. Bası, Adalet, Ankara 2016.

III. Measures of Security Against Children, Mentally Ill Persons and Drug Addicts

303. Measures of security against children. Children who have not reached the age of 12 are not capable of being criminally responsible (*supra*, paragraph 124), and they cannot be punished for a crime.[357] Children under the age of 12 will be placed in an institution under government administration or supervision until they reach 18 years of age.

Children who have attained the age of 12, but have not yet attained the age of 15 at the time of the commission of an act, are nevertheless criminally responsible if they have the capability to comprehend the legal meaning and the result of the act and to control their behavior according to their action (Article 31/2, TCK).

Children and adolescents who have attained the age of 15, but have not yet attained the age of 18 at the time of the commission of an act, shall be punished with a reduced penalty pursuant to Article 55/1 of the TCK.

The legal status of minors is regulated under Article 31, TCK. Minors under the age of 12 are exempt from criminal responsibility. The Penal Code does not include *Measures Against Children*, though it gives a direction to the legislature: *Types of security measures and their enforcement procedures, specific to children shall be defined in relevant statute* (Article 56, TCK).

The ÇKK No. 2005–5395 incorporates protective and supportive measures for children.[358] These measures are considered as *Measures Against Children* (Article 11, ÇKK). The ÇKK is applicable to all *children* (until the age of 18).

304. A deaf-mute person who was not capable of understanding that his act was an offense and who was older than 15 years of age (*supra*, paragraph 127) at the time of the commission of the act shall not be punished (Article 33, TCK).

305. If the offender is afflicted by a mental disease that causes a complete loss of consciousness or of freedom of action at the time of the act (completely mentally ill offenders) (*supra*, paragraph 128), he shall not be punished (Article 32/1, TCK). The custody and medical treatment will continue until the offender is cured. There is no mandatory term of treatment under the current Penal Code, which was also same under the repealed Code. If the defendant was accused of a crime that entailed lengthy imprisonment, he was not released before one year of custody in a medical institute[359] (Article 46/3, repealed TCK).

If the offender was afflicted with a mental disease that considerably reduced his awareness or his freedom of action (partially mentally ill offenders), his punishment shall be reduced pursuant to Article 32/2, TCK (*supra*, paragraph 129).

---

357. B. Aksay, *Ceza Hukukunda Yaş Küçüklüğü, Kusur Yeteneğine ve Sorumluluğa Etkisi* (İstanbul, 1990); Kurşun, *Jugendkriminalitat in der Türkei* (München, 1957).

358. H.Y. Sevük, *Çocuk Yargılaması Hukukunda Hazırlık Soruşturması* (Erzincan Hukuk Fakültesi Dergisi Cilt 8 sayı: 1–2, p. 199, Erzincan, 2004); E. Yurtcan, *Çocuk Koruma Kanunu ve Yorumu* (2006).

359. Ö. Tosun, *Suçluların Gözlemi*, İstanbul, İstanbul Üniversitesi, 1958.

306. In respect of any criminal proceedings initiated as a result of the crime of buying narcotic or psychotropic substances for consuming (Article 191/1, TCK) the public prosecutor shall delay the investigation phase and determine whether the offender should be subject to a measure to undergo treatment and a probationary period (Article 191/2, TCK) (*supra*, paragraph 219).

Alcoholics, who are habitually drunk, according to Articles 571 and 572 of the repealed TCK, were kept and treated in a hospital until it was medically ascertained that they were completely recovered (Article 573, repealed TCK).[360]

IV. Recidivism

307. Recidivism calls for a security measure under the current TCK for repeating offenders and dangerous criminals (Article 58, TCK), in particular a probationary measure. Previously, recidivism was a general aggravating circumstance (Article 81, repealed TCK).[361]

The provisions regarding the repeat offender shall be applied where there has been the commission of another offense subsequent to a previous finalized conviction. For this provision to apply it is not necessary that any penalty is enforced.

The repeat offending provisions shall not apply to offenses committed five years after the completion date of the sentence for the previous conviction, where such sentence was for a period greater than five years, or three years after the completion date of the sentence for the previous conviction, where such sentence was for a period of imprisonment of five years or less or was a criminal fine.

In cases of repeat offending, if penalties of imprisonment or a fine are prescribed as alternatives of the most recent offense committed, a penalty of imprisonment shall be given. It is not possible to commute imprisonment to a fine in case of repeat offending.

The sentence, in cases of repeat offending, shall be enforced in accordance with the Enforcement Code. Furthermore, for the repeat offender, a probationary measure shall be applied following the completion of the term of imprisonment.

The judgment of the court should clearly state what the applicable enforcement regime for repeat offenders is and should state what probationary measures will apply following the completion of the term of imprisonment.

The provisions in TCK pertaining to repeat offenders, including the aforementioned probationary measure, shall also apply to habitual offenders, career offenders or members of a criminal organization.

360. Drug addicts were kept and treated in a hospital until it was medically ascertained that they had recovered (Art. 404 repealed TCK). If there was no hospital in the district or town where the crime was committed, the addicts were sent to a place where there was one.

361. İ. Özgenç, *Türk Ceza Hukuku Genel Hükümler,* Gözden Geçirilmiş ve Güncellenmiş 10. Bası, Ankara, Seçkin, 2014, p. 795; M.S. Altunç, *Ceza Hukukunda Tekerrür*, İstanbul, Yayınlanmamış Doktora Tezi, 2010; C. Arslan & M. Kayançiçek, *Suçta Tekerrür*, Ankara, Seçkin, 2009; Ilhan Üzülmez, *Türk Hukukunda Tekerrür*, Ankara: Turhan, 2003.

308. As explained above, the current TCK has amended the structure of regulating recidivism, but keeping the same terminology, it has introduced a new measure (Article 58, TCK) based on the danger posed by the repeat offender and has applied special rules for conditional release and forms of execution of imprisonment for repeat offenders and dangerous offenders (Articles 107/12, 108, CGIK).

The repeat offender provisions shall not be applied where an offense of negligence follows an offense of intent or vice versa, and where a strict military offense follows any other offense or vice versa (Article 58/4, TCK).

The judgments of foreign courts shall be not be considered in applying the regulations related to recidivism, excluding the offenses of intentional killing, intentional injury, robbery, deception, production and trade of narcotics or psychotropic substances or counterfeiting money or valuable stamps (Article 58/4, TCK).

The repeat offender provisions shall not be applicable to offenses committed by any person who was under 18 years old at the time of the commission of the act.

The measure of police supervision provided for by Articles 28 and 42 TCK was abolished in 1987.[362] The TCK does not include this measure, but rather has introduced modalities of *controlled liberty.*

V. Deportation

309. Deportation is a measure under the Penal Code (Article 59, TCK). Foreigners who have been convicted and sentenced to a period of imprisonment in Turkey shall be deported after completing their sentence, should the Ministry of Interior decide in this respect. Deportation was mandatory when the Penal Code came into force in 2005, but since then this provision has been amended by Act No. 2005-5328, and the decision by discretion of the Ministry of Interior has been added.

VI. Responsibility of Legal Entities

310. The TCK does not inflict any punishment on legal entities (Article 20/2, TCK), but has foreseen security measures specific to private legal entities (Article 60, TCK).[363] Security measures for legal entities are only applicable if the definition of that specific crime specifically states it (Article 60/4, TCK).

In cases where an intentional crime has been committed for the benefit of a private legal person jointly by the representatives of the legal person misusing the power granted by the license, that license shall be cancelled. This provision applies only to those legal entities that are incorporated under Turkish civil law (thus excluding public law legal entities) and operating under a license granted by a public institution.

The provisions on confiscation (Articles 55, 56, TCK) are also applicable for legal entities of civil law when the crime has been committed for their benefit (Article 60/2, TCK).

---

362. Act dated 1987, No. 3352; RG Apr. 24, 1987.
363. Z.T. Kangal, *Tüzel Kişilerin Cezai Sorumluluğu*, Ankara, Seçkin Yayınları, 2003.

However, if the application of a security measure leads to consequences more serious than the crime itself, the judge under his discretion may, or may not impose this measure (Article 60/3, TCK).[364]

Special legislation contains some provisions, which allow sanctioning by closing down some legal persons, such as associations and political parties. In such cases, the public prosecutor is entitled to prosecute the legal persons together with the associated individuals. Accordingly, natural persons and legal persons have criminal liability.[365]

§4. Sentencing

I. The Perpetrator

311. The person committing a crime is called a perpetrator.[366] In the terminology of Turkish criminal law, this term originally meant a convicted person only. However, it is used for the defendant as well. This is the correct term, and it should be used before the judgment becomes final.

Because of the constitutional principle of the individuality of punishments, only a living, natural person can be brought to trial. The mental element that must be present in a crime is criminal intent, and only living persons can have such intent.

The criminal responsibility of legal persons has been debated.[367] There are sanctions that can be imposed on legal persons, such as closing an association or a political party. However, these are more administrative punishments, whereas most criminal punishments cannot be applied to legal persons. An association cannot be put into prison. The current Penal Code does not include punishments for legal entities; only *security measures specific to legal entities* (*supra*, paragraph 309) are applicable (Article 60, TCK).

---

364. A. Nuhoğlu (ed.), *Sanktionen gegen juristische Personen (Tüzel Kişiler Hakkında Uygulanan Yaptırımlar),* Series of the Max-Planck-Institute for Foreign and International Criminal Law and Bahçeşehir University Joint Research Group, Volume T2, Bahçeşehir Üniversitesi Yayınları, Istanbul 2013.

365. M.E. Artuk et al., *Ceza Hukuku Genel Hükümler* Ankara, Yenilenmiş Gözden Geçirilmiş 11. Baskı Adalet, 2017, p. 274; İ.S. Teorisi, 2. Kitap, Beta, İstanbul, İkinci Bası, 2000, p. 59.

366. S. Dönmezer & S. Erman (II), *Nazari ve Tatbiki Ceza Hukuku, Genel Kısım, Cilt II,* 9, İstanbul, Bası Beta, 1985, p. 1145; H. Hakeri, *Ceza Hukuku Genel Hükümler*, 18. Baskı, Adalet, Ankara, 2015, p. 134; V.Ö. Özbek et al., Türk Ceza Hukuku Genel Hükümler, 6. Baskı, Seçkin, Ankara, 2015, p. 549; T. Demirbaş, *Ceza Hukuku Genel Hükümler*, 15. Baskı, Seçkin, Ankara 2020, 741; M. Koca & İ. Üzülmez, *Türk Ceza Hukuku Genel Hükümler*, 8. Baskı, Seçkin, Ankara, 2015, 104; D. Soyaslan, *Ceza Hukuku Genel Hükümler*, 8. Baskı, Yetkin Yayınları, Ankara, 2018, 528; H. Zafer, *Ceza Hukuku Genel Hükümler*, 4. Bası, Beta, İstanbul, 2015, p. 148; N. Centel et al., 8. Bası, Beta, İstanbul, 2014, p. 474.

367. S. Dönmezer & S. Erman (II), *Nazari ve Tatbiki Ceza Hukuku, Genel Kısım, Cilt II,* 9, İstanbul, Bası, Beta, 1985, p. 1148; İ. Özgenç, *Türk Ceza Hukuku Genel Hükümler*, 10. Bası, Seçkin, Ankara 2014, 480; M.E. Artuk et al., *Ceza Hukuku Genel Hükümler* Ankara, Yenilenmiş Gözden Geçirilmiş 11. Baskı Adalet, 2017, p. 272.

II. Determining the Sentence

A. Principles in Fixing the Sanction

312. Discretion of judge. Unless the law explicitly provides, punishments can be neither decreased nor changed (Article 61/10, TCK).[368] However, a judge can set[369] the punishment[370] at the level that seems to be appropriate for the convicted individual. Apart from increasing or decreasing the punishment, the question of suspension of the punishment (*supra*, paragraph 289) must be considered as well.[371]

313. Range of punishments. There are some cases in which the law does not provide for a definite punishment, but it sets a range of punishments. The provision that a crime must be punished with a prison term between twenty-four and thirty years is an example of a range of punishments. The power of the judge to impose punishment within certain limits is to some extent controlled by the obligation to give reasons for the judgment (Article 34, CMK).

There is no judgment without certain limits on the penalty in Turkish law.[372] Only security measures against mentally ill offenders can be fixed without a time limitation (Article 57/2, TCK).[373]

314. Individualization of punishment. To reach the goal of criminal law, the sanction against the perpetrator must be a punishment appropriate to his personality. Therefore, the judge should have an informed idea of the criminal's personality. The legislature has provided different punishments for the same crime (i.e., imprisonment and fine, from which the judge can choose the punishment that seems more suitable to the personality of the perpetrator). Unfortunately, psychological explorations that serve that purpose are very rare in Turkey.

If the law contains provisions that require an aggravated or mitigated punishment, the general punishment will first be fixed, and then it will be aggravated or mitigated (Article 61/4, TCK).

315. Unjust provocation. Unjust provocation (*haksız tahrik*) is a general mitigating factor. If a person commits a crime in the heat of anger caused by an unjust action against him, we speak of provocation (Article 29, TCK).[374] Provocation is a personal and general mitigating ground. It is, however, not a ground of justification. A crime committed by a person as a result of a provocation always remains illegal.

---

368. İ. Özgenç, *Türk Ceza Hukuku Genel Hükümler,* Gözden Geçirilmiş ve Güncellenmiş 10. Bası, Ankara, Seçkin, 2014, p. 820.
369. C. Akkaya, *Cezaların Belirlenmesi ve Ceza ve Güvenlik Tedbirlerinin İnfazı ve İnfaz Hukuku;* 2. Baskı, Ankara, Kartal Yayınevi, 2007.
370. M. Artuç & T. Hırslı, *Hüküm Kurma Esasları*, Ankara, Adalet Yayınevi, 2010.
371. E. Günay, *Uygulamada Suçların Tesbiti ve Cezaların* Tayini, Ankara, Adil Yayınevi, 1995.
372. S. Dönmezer & S. Erman (II), *Nazari ve Tatbiki Ceza Hukuku, Genel Kısım, Cilt II,* 9. Bası, İstanbul, Beta, 1985, p. 1359.
373. T.T. Yüce, *Ceza Hukukunun Temel Kavramları*, Ankara, Turhan, 1985, p. 111; Silvia Tellenbach, *Todesstrafe in der Türkei,* ZAR (1991): p. 135.
374. T. Demirbaş, *Türk Ceza Hukukunda Özel Haksız Tahrik Halleri*, İstanbul, 1985; M.H. Tutumlu, *Türk Ceza Hukukunda Haksız Tahrik* (1999).

Honor killings committed against women started a movement in Turkey in order to exclude the provisions of unjust provocation and discretionary mitigation of punishment (*infra,* paragraph 318).

316. Simple and serious provocation. In cases where the offender has committed the crime in a state of anger or severe distress caused by an unjust act, the penalty shall be eighteen to twenty years imprisonment instead of aggravated life imprisonment; or twelve to eighteen years instead of life imprisonment. Other punishments shall be reduced by one-quarter to three-quarters (Article 29, TCK).

The Court of Cassation has accepted the existence of provocation even if the crime was premeditated.[375]

The repealed Penal Code had divided the unjust provocation into *simple* provocation (*adi tahrik*),[376] and *grievous and serious* unjust provocation (*ağır tahrik*).[377] The current TCK does not make this distinction.[378]

A judge at the Court of First Instance has the discretion to decide whether a crime was provoked. A provocation can consist of an action against a person, an animal or any other object.[379]

317. Reduced punishments for minority, deaf-muteness and mental disease. Persons of diminished mental capacity who commit crimes are punished by a reduced punishment (Articles 49, 57 and 61, TCK).

318. Punishment for attempt. For incomplete crimes (*supra*, paragraph 167), the punishment will be reduced (Article 35, TCK).

319. Grounds for discretionary mitigation. Discretionary grounds of mitigation (Article 62, TCK) are recognized but not listed in the Penal Code. These are left to the discretion of the judge, who is competent to consider special circumstances as grounds for a reduction of punishment.[380]

If the court accepts the existence of mitigating factors, then it imposes life imprisonment instead of aggravated life imprisonment, or twenty years imprisonment instead of life imprisonment. Other punishments shall be reduced by up to one-sixth.[381]

This legal institution is used in Turkey in order to reduce the high number of prison sentences provided in the repealed Penal Code, and it was used to avoid the

375. Cass., 1. CD Apr. 19, 1988; E. 1779/K. 1697, YKD 1988, 1285.
376. The criminal was sentenced to life imprisonment instead of with the death penalty. If life imprisonment is provided by law, sentencing is to lengthy imprisonment for twenty-four years; other penalties shall be reduced by one-fourth (Art. 51/1 repealed TCK).
377. The criminal was sentenced to twenty-four years lengthy imprisonment instead of to the death penalty; other punishment prescribed for the crime shall be reduced by one half to two-thirds (Art. 51/2 repealed TCK).
378. İ. Üzülmez, *Yeni Ceza Kanunun Sisteminde Cezanın Belirlenmesi ve Bireyselleştirilmesi*, Erzincan Üniversitesi Hukuk Fakültesi Dergisi, cilt X, sayı 3–4, yıl 2006, 203.
379. CGK May 22, 1989; YKD 1989, 2468.
380. Originally it was reduced by up to one-fifth; however, the Act No. 2005-5328 amended the rule.
381. S. Dönmezer & S. Erman (II), *Nazari ve Tatbiki Ceza Hukuku, Genel Kısım, Cilt II,* 9. Bası, İstanbul, Beta, 1985, p. 1106.

death penalty before it was abolished.[382] Some examples of the factors considered by courts to mitigate the punishment may be cited as follow: Confession of the offender,[383] or the amount of the confiscated drug being minor.[384] Now, however, the TCK openly lists the grounds for discretionary mitigation as follows: *background of the offender, his social relations, his behavior after the commission of the crime and during the trial, and the potential effects of the penalty on the future of the offender* (Article 62/2, TCK).

Even if every factor has the potential to be a mitigating ground in Turkish Criminal Law, the court must explain the reasons for its decision (Article 62/2, TCK). The scope of the control of the Court of Cassation has been extended in issues of discretionary mitigation since 1998. Formerly, the Court of Cassation would accept the proper application of law;[385] the court now inspects whether, by recognizing the grounds for discretionary mitigation, the motives in the decision are also *logical, admissible and fair* and whether the aim of this legal concept has been met.[386]

A mitigating factor that is provided for by the law cannot be a discretionary mitigating ground.[387] Furthermore, the Court of Cassation does not allow both mitigating factors and provocation (*supra*, paragraph 315) at the same time.[388]

Substantial efforts have been undertaken to effectively protect women's rights by enacting the Act No. 6284 to *Protect Family and Prevent Violence against Women* in March 2012. Unfortunately, the number of women murdered in Turkey is very high.[389] Act 6284 regulates some provisions to prevent violence against women. For this reason, following measures are enacted: Housing and nursery assistance, temporary financial aid, consultancy service and temporary protection if there is a life-threatening danger. By the size of the danger these measures become more serious.

---

382. B. Öztürk & M.R. Erdem, *Uygulamalı Ceza Hukuku ve Güvenlik Tedbirleri Hukuku*, TCK Değişikliklerine Göre Yenilenmiş, 14. Baskı, Ankara 2014, Seçkin Yayınları, 287.
383. CGK Nov. 12, 1987, 1-329/506; Savaş, Mollamahmutoğlu, *Türk Ceza Kanununun Yorumu,* 4 Cilt, 3. Bası (Ankara, 1999), p. 1123.
384. CGK Apr. 24, 1972, 175/205; S. Mollamahmutoğlu, *Türk Ceza Kanununun Yorumu,* 4 Cilt, 3. Bası (Ankara, 1999), p. 1135.
385. CGK Apr. 26, 1976, 204/208, S. Mollamahmutoğlu, *Türk Ceza Kanununun Yorumu,* 4 Cilt, 3. Bası (Ankara, 1999), p. 1134.
386. CGK Jun. 9, 1998, 8-163/216: S. Mollamahmutoğlu, *Türk Ceza Kanununun Yorumu,* 4 Cilt, 3. Bası (Ankara, 1999), p. 1129.
387. S. Dönmezer & S. Erman (II), *Nazari ve Tatbiki Ceza Hukuku, Genel Kısım,* Cilt II, 9 Bası, İstanbul, Beta, 1985, p. 1110. For detailed explanations of mitigating factors provided by the law, such as in Art. 485 TPC (unjust behavior of the victim in defamation), *see* T. Demirbaş, *Türk Ceza Kanununda Özel Tahrik Halleri*, İstanbul, 1985.
388. Cass., CGK Nov. 16, 1988; B. Öztürk, *Uygulamalı Ceza Muhakemesi Hukuku*, Ankara, 1994, p. 222.
389. Turkey has been a party to the European Convention on Preventing and Combating Violence Against Women and Domestic Violence, which was approved and opened for signature in Istanbul in 2011, was signed by Turkey in 2012 and became effective in 2014. The application of this convention required changes in domestic law which were achieved in the succeeding years, but violence against women and murder or killing of woman was not prevented. The Convention requires a risk assessment prior to application of measures foreseen in the Convention but the Turkish law maker did not include the "risk assessment" provisions in the domestic law. As a consequence, protective and preventive measures have been applied widely in Turkey but provoked more violence. As a consequence, Turkey withdrew from the Convention by the Executive Order (Cumhurbaşkanı kararı; *supra*, paragraph) No. 3718 of Mar. 19, 2021 (RG Mar. 20, 2021).

320. Effective remorse. TCK has openly[390] regulated voluntary abandonment (Article 36, TCK) as a ground for not punishing attempted crimes if, the offender voluntarily abandons the performance of the acts necessary to commit the crime, or prevents the completion of the crime or its consequences.[391]

As far as the accomplished crimes are concerned, the New Penal Code has incorporated several provisions of *effective remorse,*[392] such as Article 221 TCK, which is either a *ground of personal impunity* or a *ground for mitigation of punishment.*

Grounds of personal impunity in cases of effective remorse give the public prosecutor the discretion of prosecution (Article 171/1, CMK). If the prosecutor drops the case under his discretion, there is no opposition to this decision (Article 173/5, CMK).

B. The Authority of the Judge to Determine the Sentence

321. Limits of the discretion of the judge. The judge must fix the punishment within the limits prescribed by the law. He must consider such circumstances as the way in which the crime had been committed, the means used, its importance, the time and scene of the crime, the gravity of damage and danger, the degree of intention or negligence, and the motives and reasons for the crime, as well as the perpetrator's goals, his background, his personal and social situation, his behavior after the commission of the crime and so on (Article 61, TCK). The reasons for the punishment ordered must be explained in the judgment, even if only a minimum penalty was ordered (Article 34, CMK).

322. Discretion in fixing fines. Article 52/4 of the Penal Code offers guidance for judges imposing fines on the convicted individual according to the latter's ability to pay. Thus, the judge will take into account the economic and personal status of the convicted individual.

323. Fundamental punishment. In some articles, the Law provides for only the minimum or the maximum penalty. In these cases, the minimum penalty results from the general provisions of Articles 13 and 15 of TCK. Most of the penal provisions prescribe a minimum and a maximum penalty. If the punishment has to be set between two limits, then the judge will do this. This punishment is called the principal or fundamental punishment (Article 61/1, TCK), which is the first step of the commutation of punishments (*supra*, paragraph 281), if it applies.

---

390. The government offered the members of political and ordinary organized crime groups an opportunity to withdraw from their illegal groups. Act No. 3419 of Mar. 25, 1988, the application of which has been extended several times (the last extension was by Act No. 4450 of Aug. 26, 1999), allowed for reduction of or even exemption from punishment for those gang members who did not participate in crimes committed by the gang under certain circumstances (such as surrendering without resistance or providing information). This legislation is called the *Act on Reintegration into the Society* (*Topluma Kazandırma Kanunu*) of Jul. 29, 2003, Act No. 4959, expired in March 2004.

391. R. Keklik, *5237 sayılı Türk Ceza Kanunu'nda Etkin Pişmanlık,* Adalet, Ankara 2016.

392. E. Günay, *Öğreti ve Uygulamada Yeni Türk Ceza Kanunundaki Etkin Pişmanlık ve Gönüllü Vazgeçme* (Ankara: Yetkin Yayınları, 2005).

324. Determining the fundamental punishment. The judge considers the following factors while determining the fundamental punishment: The manner in which the crime has been committed, the means used while committing the crime, time and place where the crime has been committed, the importance and value of the subject of the crime, the gravity of the damage or danger, the degree of intent or negligence, and the motives and aim of the offender (Article 61/1, TCK). However, if one of these factors is an element of the crime, this factor shall not be taken into account while determining the fundamental punishment (Article 61/3, TCK).

The punishment determined according to these factors shall be mitigated or increased if the offender acted with probable intent or foreseeable negligence (Article 61/2, TCK).

Once the fundamental punishment has been determined, the aggravating and then mitigating grounds are considered (Article 61/4, TCK).

325. Final punishment. After the punishment has been determined according to the above-mentioned rules, the final punishment shall be fixed, taking into account the following factors in this order: attempt, conspiracy, successive committed crimes, unjust provocation, the age of minority, mental illness, personal circumstances that require the reduction of penalty and, lastly, the grounds for discretionary mitigation (Article 61/5, TCK).

The *final punishment* determined under Article 61 shall not exceed thirty years (Article 61/7, TCK) for a crime that requires a specific term of imprisonment (Article 49/1, TCK).

The duration of the final punishment plays a significant role in Turkish Penal Procedure Law since the amendment of Article 231, CMK in 2010, which has opened the possibility of the *delayed announcement of the judgment*, if the final punishment is imprisonment of two years or less, or is a criminal fine (*infra*, paragraph 519).

Another important consequence of the *final punishment* is related to the right to appeal for convictions involving *criminal fines commuted from a short-term imprisonment*: Whereas there is no right to appeal against some criminal fines, the legislation in 2011 opened it for such commuted sentences.

326. Individualization of criminal fine. In cases of determining the fine, the increase and decrease of punishment in order to individualize the sanction shall be fixed according to the number of days, as indicated by the relevant article; the final fine shall be calculated by multiplying the designated final number of days by the amount the convict is able to pay (Article 61/8, TCK).

If the criminal fine is to be imposed as an alternative sanction, the minimum days related to such penalty shall not be less than the minimum imprisonment term for that crime, and the maximum limit of such shall not exceed the maximum imprisonment penalty for such a crime (Article 61/9, TCK).

327. Suspension of Imprisonment. Suspension of imprisonment (*infra*, paragraph 339) means that at the time of sentencing, the judge decides that the imprisonment shall not be executed at once. If during the probationary period the convicted individual commits another crime, probation will be revoked and both sentences (i.e., the suspended one and the one imposed for the new offense) will have to be served (Article 51, TCK). The delayed announcement of the judgment (*infra*, paragraph 519) has a similar effect as the suspension of imprisonment.

328. Deduction of Periods of Detention. Article 63 of the Penal Code provides that prison terms will be reduced by any period of detention and all cases limiting personal freedom before the final judgment.

Reduction of periods of custody from criminal fine shall be made with the assumption that one day corresponds to TRY 100 (Article 63, TCK).

329. Paying Fines by Installments. Fines can be paid in installments over a period of no more than two years, or the court may grant a period of payment, not exceeding one year from the date of the finalization of the judgment (Article 52/4, TCK).

It is a ground for reversing the judgment if the convicted individual requested installment payment and the court did not consider it. An individual convicted of a crime can also request installment payment at a later time.

The decision of the court should also contain a statement indicating that if any of the installments have not been paid when due, the entire balance of the criminal fine becomes due immediately (Article 52/4, TCK).

330. Imprisonment in Default of Payment of Fine. If the convicted individual does not pay the fine, it can be converted to prison time by the decision of the public prosecutor for a period equivalent to the full days of the fine (Article 52/1, TCK) (Article 106/3, CGIK).

This kind of imprisonment, however, cannot exceed three years; in cases of convictions resulting in more than one criminal fine, however, the total days of imprisonment cannot exceed five years (Article 106/7, CGIK).

Fines imposed on minors cannot be converted to prison time (Article 106/4, CGIK).

C. Commuting Punishments to Other Punishments

331. In some cases, punishment can be commuted to another punishment if it is provided for in the law or if the judge has the authority to commute the punishment.

332. Commutation of short-term imprisonment. As a rule, the commutation of short-term imprisonment into measures (*supra*, paragraph 281) is optional. The discretion of the judge in this respect is very important.

333. Commutation of long-term custodial sentences. According to Article 50/4 of the Penal Code, long-term imprisonment for crimes committed through negligence (except foreseeable negligence; *supra*, paragraph 139) may be exceptionally commuted to other measures in Article 50/1, TCK.

334. Commutation to Admonition. Commutation to admonition is no longer permitted under the current Penal Code. However, the repealed Code had included this legal concept.

III. Multiplicity of Crimes and Punishments

A. Multiplicity of Crimes

335. Concurrence of Laws. If a punishable act violates more than one law or if several punishable acts violate one law, there are special regulations for each situation.

If more than one wrongful act of a person is combined with another, we speak of a multiplicity of crimes. Multiplicity of crimes was dealt with in Articles 42–44 of the repealed TCK: if a person was convicted of several crimes, or if the same person was convicted of another crime after a judgment, all the punishments had to be added up (Articles 68 and 69, repealed TCK). However, the current TCK does not include provisions in this respect.

If someone commits a crime to commit or conceal another crime, each crime is an independent crime and the punishments are joined. But if such a crime is an element or a ground of aggravation of another crime, only one penalty is imposed on the perpetrator[393] (Article 42, TCK). This collection is called a *compound crime* (*bileşik suç*) or concurrence of laws (*gerçek içtima*).[394]

336. Concurrence of Offenses. If a single act constitutes several crimes, the most severe punishment of those provided by law *(fikri içtima)* will be imposed on the perpetrator (Article 44, TCK): for example, imprisonment is more severe than criminal fine, and aggravated imprisonment for life is the most severe punishment.[395] The number of acts is important. If there is more than one physical result, criminal liability will be assessed according to the most severe result.[396]

337. Continuation of Offenses. If various punishable acts are committed against the same individual, they violate the same law and are the result of the same intent, we speak of a continuation of offenses (now: *zincirleme suç;* Article 43/1 TCK, previously: *müteselsil suç* Article 80, repealed TCK).[397] The punishment provided for such a crime is increased by one-fourth up to three-fourths (previously one-sixth).

The principal form of a crime and its aggravated form shall be considered as the *same crime* (Article 43/1, TCK). This provision is also applicable, if there is no

393. K. İçel et al., *İçel Suç Teorisi*, 2. Kitap, İstanbul, İkinci Bası, Beta, 2000, p. 414.
394. A. Önder (II), *Ceza Hukuku Genel Hükümler*, Cilt 2, İstanbul, Beta, 1989, p. 524.
395. O. Keskinsoy, *Yeni Ceza Kanunundaki Ceza Düzenlemeler Doğrultusunda Fikri İçtima Müessesesinin Analizi*, Ankara Barosu Dergisi, Sayı: 2005/3; S. Dönmezer & S. Erman (II), *Nazari ve Tatbiki Ceza Hukuku, Genel Kısım*, Cilt II, 9. Bası, İstanbul, Beta, 1985, p. 1129.
396. A. Önder (II), *Ceza Hukuku Genel Hükümler*, Cilt 2, İstanbul, Beta, 1989, p. 533.
397. O. Keskinsoy, *Yeni Türk Ceza Kanunu'nun Müteselsil Suçla Alakalı Hükümlerinin Değerlendirilmesi*, Türkiye Barolar Birliği Dergisi, sayı 61, Kasım, Aralık 2005; T.Y. Sancar, *Müteselsil Suç*, Seçkin Yayınları, 1995.

identified victim of the crime (Article 43/1, TCK), and also in cases where several crimes have been committed against more than one person through one action (Article 43/2, TCK). Crimes of intended killing, intended wounding, torture and plundering are exempted from the privilege of punishment reduction by considering them as a continuation of offenses (Article 43/3 TCK), and the punishments of these crimes shall be added up.

B. Multiplicity of Punishments

338. Joining punishments for more than one crime was called 'multiplicity of punishments' (Articles 68–78, repealed TCK), a legal concept that was not included in the current TCK.

In cases where one accused has committed several crimes, all punishments shall be added up during the execution of the punishment for the purposes of determining the day of conditional release (*infra,* paragraph 617).

§5. Suspension of the Imprisonment

339. Suspension of punishment is understood to mean suspending the execution of a punishment for a certain time.[398] It is a completely different measure from conditional release (*infra*, paragraph 617). The TCK regulates suspending sentences of imprisonment only; criminal fines (*supra*, paragraph 291) are excluded (Article 51/1, TCK).

A sentence of imprisonment for a term of two years or less may be suspended. However, the upper limit of this term is three years for those under 18 years of age or above 60 years at the time of the commission of the offense.

Further, in order to decide to suspend the sentence, the person may not have been sentenced in a prior proceeding arising from a prior offense to a penalty for a term of more than three months imprisonment for an intentional offense, and the court should be convinced, as a result of hearing the remorse expressed during trial, that the offender will not commit new crimes in the future (Article 51/1, TCK).

The suspension of the penalty may depend upon the condition that compensation is provided to the victim or public. This restores property harmed by the crime to the previous condition before the crime was committed (*in integrum restitutio)* or restores all damage caused. In such a case, the enforcement of the penalty shall continue until the requirements are fulfilled. Once the condition is met, the offender shall be released immediately, upon the decision of the enforcement judge (Article 51/2, TCK).

---

398. A. Önder, *Ceza Hukukunda Tecil ve Benzeri Müesseseler*, İstanbul, 1963; F. Turhan, *Yeni Türk Ceza Kanununa Göre Cezaların Ertelenmesi ve Uygulamada Ortaya Çıkan Bazı Sorunlar*, Erzincan Üniversitesi Hukuk Fakültesi Dergisi, cilt X, sayı 3–4, yıl 2006, p. 28.

For an offender whose sentence has been suspended, a probation period shall be imposed that shall not be less than one year and not more than three years. The lower limit of this period shall not be less than the term of sentence (Article 51/3, TCK).

The court may decide that an offender, who does not have a profession or trade, shall attend an educational program for educational purposes during the probation period. An offender who possesses a profession or trade shall work in a public or private institution under the supervision of another person who has the same profession or trade in return for remuneration. An offender under the age of 18 shall attend an educational institution, which provides accommodation when necessary, in order to acquire a profession or trade (Article 51/4, TCK). The court may decide not to impose any obligation or may authorize an expert for the probation period (Article 51/6, TCK).

The court may appoint an expert to counsel the offender within the probation period. This expert shall guide the offender, confer with the authorities of the educational institution or workplace of the offender and prepare a report for the enforcement judge, every three months, on the development of the offender (Article 51/5, TCK).

In cases where the convict commits an intentional offense or does not follow his obligations within the probation period, despite the warning of the enforcement judge, the court shall decide to fully or partly enforce the suspended sentence in an enforcement institution (Article 51/7, TCK).

If a period of probation has been spent in compliance with the requirements and in a good manner, the sentence shall be regarded as served (Article 51/8, TCK) and thus registered.

The current regulation differs significantly from the repealed law. Previously if the convicted individual did not commit another punishable act during the probation period (one year for a misdemeanor, five years for a crime) (Article 95, repealed TCK), the first effect of the suspension was that the punishment was not executed, and the second effect was that the convicted individual was regarded as though he had never been punished, and there would be no record of a conviction. If he did commit another crime, the punishments for both crimes would be executed and recorded.

340. Previous provisions. According to the repealed law, the condition for suspension of a punishment was that the court expected that the offender would not re-offend in the future. The execution of the decision regarding the suspension of punishment could be postponed until the victim had recovered his damages (Article 93, repealed TCK). If all these conditions were met, the sentence could be suspended. The reasons for suspension were to be given in the decision (Article 32, repealed CMUK). Repeating the facts of the law is not accepted as reasons.

341. The sanction to be suspended refers to the fundamental punishment (*supra*, paragraph 323).[399]

342. According to prevailing opinion, fines that are commutations from imprisonment (*supra*, paragraph 282) can be suspended. If a total punishment, which was combined from various single punishments, exceeds the maximum period of imprisonment that can be suspended, then every single punishment must be regarded and can be suspended independently from the others, so long as they do not exceed the maximum period that can be suspended.[400]

343. Exceptions to the suspension of punishments. TCK takes into account the concrete term of imprisonment in order to give way to its suspension. Criminal fines are excluded from suspension, unless they are commuted into prison sentences.

There were some other exceptions: Punishments for military offenses in AsCK (Article 47/1, AsCK) and sanctions for disciplinary violations were excluded from suspension. The Constitutional Court abolished this exception on January 23, 2013.

In cases of a conviction based on a crime in the Anti- Terrorism Act, imprisonment shall not be suspended and the duration of the imprisonment term shall not be taken into account (Article 13, TMK). This exception has been lifted for children who did not attain the age of 18 while committing a crime under the Anti-Terrorism Act (Act of July 22, 2010, No. 6008).[401]

A judgment issued by a foreign court does not prevent the suspension of another sentence in Turkey. Provisions in international conventions are reserved.

344. Exceptions related to the age. A sentence of imprisonment for a term of two years or less may be suspended. The upper limit of this term is three years for those under 18 years of age or above 60 years at the time of the commission of the offense (Article 51/1, TCK).

Imprisonment of children, who did not attain the age of 18 while committing a crime based on Anti-Terrorism Act, may be suspended exceptionally (Article 13, TMK).[402]

---

399. In practice, however, the fine or measure that resulted from a commutation according to Art. 4/4 of the repealed Code of Enforcement of Punishments was regarded as *principal or fundamental punishment.* When the fundamental punishment was suspended, the accessory punishment was automatically suspended as well. The court could, however, decide that this would not be suspended.
400. F. Erem, A. Danışman & E. Artuk, *Ceza Hukuku Genel Hükümler*, 14. Baskı, Ankara, Seçkin, 1997, p. 818.
401. İ. Özgenç, *Türk Ceza Hukuku Genel Hükümler,* Gözden Geçirilmiş ve Güncellenmiş 10. Bası, Ankara, Seçkin, 2014, p. 627.
402. İ. Özgenç, *Türk Ceza Hukuku Genel Hükümler,* Gözden Geçirilmiş ve Güncellenmiş 10. Bası, Ankara, Seçkin, 2014, p. 627.

Part II. Criminal Procedure

Chapter 1. Principles, Institutions, Stages

§1. The Judicial Organisation

345. The rules of criminal procedure law, substantive criminal law, the administration of justice, the rights of the accused, and the powers of the prosecution services are interconnected with each other; thus, they constitute a system of criminal justice.

The repealed Turkish Code of Penal Procedure (*Ceza Muhakemeleri Usulü Kanunu, CMUK*) was enacted on April 20, 1929, by Act No. 1412. It was a translation of the 1872 German Code of Penal Procedure, adopted with few changes. The Code of Penal Procedure replaced this Code in 2005 (*Ceza Muhakemesi Kanunu, CMK*).

The 2005 Turkish Penal Procedure Code adopted the *mixed system* of criminal procedure. On the one hand, the preliminary investigation and the preparation of the public prosecution are conducted in camera (Article 157, CMK), in accordance with the *inquisitorial system.* On the other hand, the trial inquiry stage is conducted publicly, in the presence of the accused, and orally, according to the accusatorial system.[403]

Since 2012, the Penal Procedure Code regulates electronic communication between the various criminal actors during the criminal process (Article 38/A, CMK, added by Act No. 6352). The decisions and judgments as well as all interactions shall be signed by electronic signature (Article 38A/3, CMK).

I. Trial Jurisdictions

A. *Subject Matter Jurisdiction and Venue of the Courts*

1. Jurisdiction of Courts

346. A sovereign country has three branches of power, one of which is the jurisdiction of independent courts. Taken as a whole, the jurisdictions of the different

403. N. Gürelli, *The Recent Development of Turkish Criminal Procedure and the Practice of the Turkish Judiciary,* Annales de la Faculte De Droit Istanbul, XXIX, No. 45, Tome (1983): 113, p. 149.

courts cover the entire territory of Turkey, with a few exceptions related to crimes committed outside the Turkish territory (*supra*, paragraph 82).

There exists a *unity of jurisdiction*. Within the state there is a single jurisdiction divided into branches: constitutional, civil and criminal. The law governs the field of jurisdiction of each branch.[404]

The structure of the courts was designed along the French model in 1879. There have been unsuccessful efforts for decades to change this system. Finally, in 2005, a new Code on Courts brought a major reform (*Adli Yargı İlk Derece Mahkemeleri ile Bölge Adliye Mahkemelerinin Kuruluş, Görev ve Yetkileri Hakkında Kanun; Act No. 5235*).

The courts in Turkey are divided into ordinary courts and administrative courts. The courts of ordinary jurisdiction are divided into two branches: Civil[405] and criminal courts. The civil and criminal courts are different and separate.

Distinguishing the competence of the administrative courts and that of the ordinary civil courts is not easy. A special court, the Court of Conflicts, resolves conflicts between ordinary civil courts and administrative courts (*infra*, paragraph 356).

2. Subject Matter Jurisdiction

347. The courts such as courts of general jurisdiction (*infra*, paragraph 351) and courts of assizes (*infra*, paragraph 352), or terrorism courts (*infra*, paragraph 355) cannot hear cases that are outside of their subject matter jurisdiction (*görev*).[406] This kind of jurisdiction of the court is related to the public order; hence the rules on jurisdiction are mandatory.

Exceptionally, as a matter of procedural economy, a court of higher jurisdiction may not reverse a case from a lower court when the indictment has been approved (Article 5/1, CMK): the higher court provides better protection for the rights of the accused compared to the lower court. As a result of the joinder of cases, connected offenses are tried by a court of higher jurisdiction (Article 16, CMK).[407]

---

404. D. Soyaslan, *Ceza Muhakemesi Hukuku,* 7. Baskı, Yetkin, Ankara 2018, p. 47.

405. The lower courts of civil jurisdiction are the Courts of First Instance, Peace Court in Civil Matters (criminal peace judge) and Commercial Courts, Execution Officers, Bankruptcy Officers and Investigation Authorities. The Investigation Authorities also act as judges in certain cases with the capacity to settle monetary disputes by means of summary procedures (A.C. Budak & M.O. Yağcı, *Law of Civil Procedure,* in: Introduction to Turkish Law, ed. *Tuğrul Ansay, Don Wallance Jr., Işık Önay,* Seventh Edition, Ch. 2, Kluwer, Deventer 2020, p. 256.

406. E. Yurtcan, *Ceza Yargılaması Hukuku,* 4. Bası, İstanbul, Kazancı, 1991, 85; N. Centel & H. Zafer, *Ceza Muhakemesi Hukuku*, 14. Bası, İstanbul, Beta, 2017, p. 582.

407. N. Kunter, *Fikri İçtima Sebebiyle Suçların Birleştirilmesi,* İHFM (1948): I, II, p. 369.

3. Venue

348. The courts of the Turkish Republic are competent for crimes committed on Turkish territory (Article 8, TCK). There are some exceptions for crimes committed outside of the Turkish territory (*supra*, paragraph 82).[408]

The Turkish Penal Procedure Code grants jurisdiction to only one court: "*The trial of a criminal conduct shall be held in the place where the offence was committed*" (Article 12/1, CMK). In cases of attempted offenses, the court of the place where the last act was committed has jurisdiction, and in cases of continuing offenses and successive offenses (Article 43, TCK), the court of the place where the last crime was committed has jurisdiction.[409]

If the place where the crime was committed is not known, the court of the place where the accused was arrested, or, if he is not arrested, the court of the place of his domicile will have venue. If the accused does not reside in Turkey, as per the court where he last resided in Turkey will act as the venue (Article 13, CMK).

There are some exceptions to this rule. Juvenile courts (Article 25, ÇKK) (*infra,* paragraph 358) have a wider venue, as these courts have many cities under their jurisdiction. Therefore, a crime committed in one city may be tried in another location if there is no juvenile court in that particular city.

349. Some special courts might have jurisdiction according to the status of the accused in the society. For example, if the President must be tried, he or she will be tried by the Constitutional Court (Article 148/3, AY) (*infra*, paragraph 363) in its function as the Highest Criminal Court.

Crimes committed by state officials (*supra*, paragraph 187) form another exception. Under the *Act on the Adjudication of Civil Servants* (*Memurlar ve Diğer Kamu Görevlilerinin Yargılanması Hakkında Kanun*) of April 12, 1999 (No. 4483), the public prosecutor is not directly competent in such cases.[410] The supervisor of the alleged civil servant makes the preliminary investigation and decides whether to give the public prosecutor permission to bring the case to the competent criminal court for that specific crime.

B. Criminal Courts of First Instance

350. The criminal courts of first instance fall into three categories: general criminal courts, special chambers (or sections) of the general courts and the criminal

408. N. Centel & H. Zafer, *Ceza Muhakemesi Hukuku*, 14. Bası, İstanbul, Beta, 2017, p. 591.

409. D. Aydın Okur, *Deniz Hukukunda Liman Devleti Yetkisi ve Denetimi: Gemi Kaynaklı Deniz Kirliliğinin Önlenmesinde Değişen Yetki Dengeleri Bağlamında Liman Devleti Yetkisinin Artan Önemi* (2009).

410. Formerly, local governmental commissions, and not the public prosecutor, were competent to bring the case to court under the 1913 Act, abolished in 1999 *(Memurin Muhakematı Kanunu)*; S. Pınar, *Memur Suçlarında İdari ve Adli Soruşturma Yöntemi* (Ankara, 1984), p. 43; Ö. Tosun, *Memurların Suçlarında Özel Muhakeme Kuralları* (YD, January 1984), pp. 9–32; A. Gökçe, *Memurların Yargılanmalarına Ilişkin Yasada Öngörülen Itiraz Süresi ve Danıştayın İlginç Kararları* (YD 1981), No. 3, p. 255.

courts founded on a special statute. There are two categories of general criminal courts: Court of general jurisdiction in criminal matters and court of assizes. Peace courts have been repealed.[411] Investigating judges no longer exist in Turkey, as judicial inquiries were abolished in 1985.[412]

1. Court of General Jurisdiction

351. The court of general jurisdiction is competent to hear cases that do not fall under the jurisdiction of other criminal courts (Article 11, Act No. 5235).[413] This court applies "simplified procedure" for crimes carrying two years or less imprisonment (*infra,* paragraph 400).

There is a court of general jurisdiction in each district. This court has one judge (Article 9/2, Act No. 5235).[414] From May 2011, until the end of 2013, the public prosecutor was removed from the proceedings at the court of general jurisdiction in order to speed up the procedure. The aim was to allow prosecutors to concentrate on the investigation phase of the proceeding, and the collection of evidence, so that the trial proceedings could be conducted in a speedy way. As of September 2020, the public prosecutor has returned to the court-room.

2. Court of Assizes

352. Courts' jurisdictions in Turkey are composed of the limited jurisdiction of the court of assizes and the comprehensive jurisdiction of the court of general jurisdiction: Crimes that do not fall under the court of assizes will be tried by the general jurisdiction.

The court of assizes is composed of two associate justices and one president (Article 9/3, Act No. 5235).

The court of assizes has jurisdiction on crimes that bring *aggravated life imprisonment, life imprisonment and imprisonment more than ten years.* Additionally, it has jurisdiction over certain crimes which are listed in the Code: Theft by force (Article 148, TCK), bribery by force (Article 250/1 and 2, TCK), forgery of official documents (Article 204/2, TCK), qualified swindling (Article 158, TCK) and fraudulent bankruptcy (Article 161, TCK). Designated chambers of this court have jurisdiction on terrorism and organized crime cases.

---

411. In order to achieve an accelerated procedure, the legislator repealed the peace courts in 2014. Previously peace courts had jurisdiction on cases that dealt with crimes carrying imprisonment up to two years, two years included, and it could impose criminal fines and security measures as well. Only one judge sat in the peace court (Art. 9/2, Act No. 5235) and there was no public prosecutor.
412. Feridun Yenisey, *Law of Penal Procedure,* in Introduction to Turkish Law, ed. *Tuğrul Ansay, Don Wallance Jr., Işık Önay,* Seventh Edition, Ch. 2, Kluwer, Deventer 2020, p. 276.
413. A. Parlar & M. Hatipoğlu, *Asliye Ceza Davaları,* 2008. A. Gündel, *Asliye Ceza Davaları,* Ankara, Seçkin Yayınları, 2000.
414. M. Görgün, *Uygulamada Asliye Ceza Davaları* (1999).

In cases where another legislation recognizes the jurisdiction of the Constitutional Court, the Court of Cassation as a first instance court or juvenile courts, the case will be tried in that court and not by the court of assizes (Article 12, Act No. 5235).

3. Specialized Courts

353. Press courts. Within the organization of Turkish courts there are special chambers of the general courts that are specialized in certain subject matters. In particular, the special chambers of the criminal courts include press courts, smuggling courts, and traffic courts (*infra*, paragraph 354) and organized crime courts. According to the Press Code, the second chamber of the court of assizes or the court of general jurisdiction is competent for offenses committed by the press (Article 27/2, Act No. 5187) (*supra*, paragraph 188).

354. Smuggling courts and traffic courts. Since March 21, 2007, with the implementation of the Combating Smuggling Act 2007 No. 5607 (KaçK), courts dealing with smuggling have been operational.[415] In cases of misdemeanors, the public prosecutor is empowered to rule on administrative fines. If the case is dealing with administrative confiscation in Article 14, KK, the criminal peace judgeship has jurisdiction upon the request of the public prosecutor. Legal remedies against these decisions are governed by the Act on Misdemeanors (Article 17/1, KaçK). In cases of crimes regulated in the Combating Smuggling Act, cases shall be tried by smuggling courts, established by the Council of Judges and Prosecutors, upon the request of the Ministry of Justice (Article 17/2, KaçK).

Some traffic offenses are subject to the jurisdiction of the criminal peace judgeship. In each district, one chamber of the criminal peace judgeship is appointed to deal with these offenses (Article 112, Act No. 2918).

355. Terrorism courts. When terrorism attacks started in Turkey first, the legislator created state security courts by a special act. Later in 2004, this special act was repealed and a designated chamber of general criminal courts was assigned for adjudication of terrorism crimes by Act No. 6526. Therefore, there were no specialized courts for organized crimes and terrorism crimes, and no special procedural rules for such crimes in Turkey; the ordinary courts of assizes were competent just before the failed coup of July 15, 2016; however, the court of assizes at the city where terrorism crimes and crimes against the state were committed had been appointed as competent for adjudicating these crimes (Article 15, Act on Courts). The Council for Judges and Prosecutors determines the places where such terrorism courts are to be established. These courts were applying special procedural rules enacted during the period of OHAL after 2016. There are still few exceptional rules related to the pre-trial arrest (Provisional Article 19, TMK, added by Act No. 7145, dated July 25,

---

415. Before this legislation, the first chamber of the court of general jurisdiction was appointed to deal with smuggling offenses (Art. 26/2, repealed Act 2003-4926).

2018) still applicable, even after the OHAL has been lifted. These special procedural rules will be discussed in the relevant chapter (*infra,* paragraph 470).

356. Court of Conflicts. If there is a conflict of competence between the ordinary courts and administrative courts, the Court of Conflicts decides which court is competent. This court is depending on its own special status (Act No. 2247).

357. (Abolished) military courts. Military courts were regulated by Article 145 of the Constitution for military offenses. These courts were repealed by Act No. 6771 on April 16, 2017, and only military disciplinary courts remained.

358. Juvenile courts. There are juvenile courts and juvenile courts of assizes. The juvenile courts are established in the center of each city, where there is one judge. The public prosecutor is not present at the court (Article 25/1, Act No. 5395). This court acts as a Court of General Jurisdiction in juvenile matters (Article 26, Act No. 5395).

Juvenile courts of assizes consist of one president and a sufficient number of members. The court hears cases with one president and two members, and it has regional jurisdiction (Article 25/2, Act No. 5395) within the same city (Article 27/2, Act No. 5395) in cases that would originally fall under the competence of the court of assizes (Article 26/2, Act No. 5395).

Juvenile courts were formerly regulated by the 1979, Act No. 2253 and suspects from 11–15 years of age were tried in juvenile courts. The Protection of the Child Act (Act No. 5395) has extended the jurisdiction of the juvenile court to all persons until they attain the age of 18 (Article 3/1, Act No. 5395).

Suspects under 18 years of age must have a lawyer (Article 150/2, CMK). Pretrial detention of a child is forbidden if the child is under the age of 15 and the alleged crime carries an imprisonment of less than five years as the upper level of punishment (Article 21, Act No. 5395).[416] There are special procedural rules in juvenile matters aimed at the protection of a child suspect who has been *instigated* to commit a crime *(suça sürüklenen çocuk).* This is the new terminology used by the Protection of the Child Act for describing child suspects. Police are not empowered to interview a child instigated to commit a crime.

359. Family courts. Family courts are competent civil courts to handle all matters arising from divorce applications, including settling the disputes. This institution was established on January 9, 2003, by Act No. 4787, in order to strengthen the family unit and thereby prevent juvenile delinquency. If the settlement attempt fails, only then the family court decides on the merits of the case (Article 7, Act No. 4787). Family court may order a child to be placed in another family if the members of his family are not fulfilling their duties toward their child (Article 6, Act No. 4787). The family court is also competent to order child protection measures regulated by the Protection of the Child Act (Article 5, ÇKK). As family courts have

416. The former Act of Juvenile Courts contained a similar provision: The pre-trial detention of a child under eighteen years of age was forbidden if the committed crime was punished by a custody of less than three years (repealed Art. 19/3, ÇMK).

also jurisdiction in juvenile matters, experts have been appointed to family courts who are from the field of psychology, pedagogy or are social workers, have attained 30 years of age, are married and have children and have made Master of Law in the field of family relations (Article 5, Act No. 4787).

C. Courts of Legal Remedies

1. Regional Courts of Appeal

360. The courts of appeal in facts and law had been established during the Ottoman Empire in 1879, but were abolished in 1924. Since that time, there have been plenty of unsuccessful attempts to create these intermediate courts and to establish a remedy of appeal in relation to the facts of the case. The Turkish Criminal Justice System offered only one ordinary legal remedy: That is cassation against the final decisions of the trial courts (Act of Court of Cassation, No. 2797). The legally existing Courts of Appeal for the past eleven years, were established as of July 20, 2016.

The Act on the Establishment, Duties and Powers of the Ordinary Courts of the First Instance and the Regional Courts (Act No. 5235) regulates the organization of the Court of Appeals and their rules of procedure are in the Penal Procedure Code (Articles 272–285, CMK).

Ordinary regional courts are founded upon the decision of the Council of Judges and Prosecutors, by the Ministry of Justice (Article 25, Act No. 5235). These courts are established regionally, based upon the geographical location and the caseload. Ordinary regional courts consist of an office of presidency, an assembly of presidents, chambers, office of public prosecutor, justice commission of the ordinary regional court and directorships (Article 26, Act No. 5235).

The chambers of the ordinary regional courts are divided into *civil chambers* and *criminal chambers*. There are at least three civil chambers and two criminal chambers at each ordinary regional court. The Council of Judges and Prosecutors is entitled to increase or decrease the number of the chambers according to the proposal of the Ministry of Justice. The chambers consist of one president and a sufficient number of members (Article 29, Act No. 5235).

2. Court of Cassation

361. The Court of Cassation reviews petitions related to mistakes in the application of the law in final judgments of regional Court of Appeal. The Court of Cassation is comprised of twenty-three chambers for civil matters, and twenty-three chambers for criminal matters.[417]

---

417. According to the provisional Art. 14, which has been added to the act on the Court of Cassation by Act No. 6572, new elections have been organized for the recently established civil and criminal chambers, and the First Presidential Chairmanship has been newly formed. Accordingly, as of the first days of January 2015, all chambers have been given new jurisdiction, and pending cases have

The General Assembly of the Court of Cassation (CGK) acts as the High Commission of the Court of Cassation. If, for example, the Attorney General (i.e., the Chief Prosecutor at the Court of Cassation; *Yargıtay Cumhuriyet Başsavcısı*) disagrees with the decision of the Chamber of the Court of Cassation, then the case shall be brought before the General Assembly (Article 308, CMK).

3. Repealed Military Court of Cassation

362. There was a Military Court of Cassation to review decisions and judgments rendered by the Military Courts (Article 156, AY) (*supra,* paragraph 357), which were abolished in 2018. The fact that there existed a Military Court of Cassation and the Supreme Military Administrative Court (Article 157, AY) in addition to the civilian Court of Cassation characterized the multiplicity of the supreme judicial authorities of Turkey's criminal justice system. The ECtHR addressed this issue of multiplicity of supreme judicial authorities in the case of *Nejdet Şahin and Perihan Şahin v. Turkey* (2010). Although it did not find a violation of the fair trial rights (Article 6/1, ECHR), it emphasized the problem of conflicting case law, which would undermine the legal certainty.[418] This legal argument and some political views resulted in abolishing the Military Court of Cassation.

4. The Constitutional Court

363. The Constitutional Court has several functions. Besides its powers as the court that controls the laws adopted by Parliament, it may hear petitions related to individual complaints, and function as a criminal court of the first instance.

a. Constitutional Court as Criminal Court

364. The Constitutional Court, when functioning as Supreme Court, has the power to try high-ranking officials, including the President (*supra*, paragraph 98), members of the Council of Ministers, as well as judges and prosecutors of the high courts. In addition to that, since the 2010 amendment (*supra*, paragraph 12), the Speaker of the TBMM and the Chief of Staff, the Commanders of the Land, Naval and Air Forces and the Commander of the Gendarmerie shall also be tried by the Constitutional Court in its capacity as the Supreme Court.

The Constitutional Court has also jurisdiction if the case deals with the closing down of a political party.[419]

---

been reassigned to the newly occupied chambers. The aim of these amendments may be the desire of the legislator to change the judges of some chambers.

418. E. Svanidze, *A Comparative Analysis of Military Justice System in the Council of Europe Member States*, Council of Europe 2012, p. 112.

419. In August 1993, the Constitutional Court closed down the People's Labor Party (HEP), a pro-Kurdish political party, on the grounds that it advocated separatism. Its successor, Democracy Party, was investigated on the same charges.

b. The Structure of the Constitutional Court

365. The 2012-5982 amendment of the Constitution changed the structure of the Constitutional Court (Article 146, AY). The number of members of the court increased from eleven to seventeen, but was reduced to fifteen in 2017, by Act No. 6771.[420] The members of the Constitutional Court shall serve for a single term of twelve years, without the possibility of renewal.

c. The Individual Constitutional Complaint

366. The constitutional amendment of 2012-5982 introduced a constitutional complaint procedure, which enables individuals to access the Constitutional Court directly. There are three cumulative application conditions: (a) One may apply to the Constitutional Court on the grounds that one's fundamental rights and freedoms has been violated by public authorities. (b) The concerned right or freedom, which is guaranteed by the Constitution, must be enumerated in the European Convention on Human Rights. (c) Before making the individual application, ordinary legal remedies must be exhausted.

Regarding the length of pre-trial detention or proceedings, the Constitutional Court may hear the individual applications while the case is still pending at first-instance level.

This remedy is modeled after the procedure before the ECtHR. For this reason, the ECtHR declared the application in the *Hasan Uzun v. Turkey* case inadmissible: The Court reiterated that the rule of the exhaustion of domestic remedies was an indispensable part of the functioning of the ECtHR mechanism. After having examined the main aspects of the individual application to the Constitutional Court, the ECtHR found that the Turkish Parliament had entrusted the Constitutional Court with powers that enabled it to provide, in principle, direct and speedy redress for violations of the rights and freedoms protected by the ECHR.

The Human Rights Compensation Commission started working in February 2013 following the adoption of the relevant legislation in the same year. The total number of the pending applications concerning Turkey is 11,150 as of the date of 30 November, 2020.[421] This law provided for a domestic remedy in front of the Human Rights Compensation Commission with respect to the length of judicial proceedings and the non-enforcement or delayed enforcement of judicial decisions.

420. The new law provides that three judges of the Constitutional Court shall be elected by the Turkish Grand National Assembly, two of which from among the candidates nominated by the Court of Accounts and a third one from among the candidates nominated by the presidents of the bar associations. In addition, fourteen members of Constitutional Court shall be elected by the president, who shall wield his appointing power directly for four members and indirectly for ten members. In particular, the president shall elect the former four members of the Constitutional Court on his own discretion among senior administrative officers, lawyers, judges and public prosecutors of the first degree, and reporting judges of the Constitutional Court. He shall elect the other constitutional judges from among the three candidates nominated by the following institutions: The Court of Cassation (three members), the Council of State (two members), and the Council of Higher Education (three members).

421. https://www.echr.coe.int/Documents/Stats_pending_month_2020_BIL.PDF.

5. European Court of Human Rights

367. Turkey has accepted the jurisdiction of the ECtHR[422] with respect to the ECtHR (Article 25/2, IHAS).[423] According to the amendment of Article 90 of the Turkish Constitution (in 2004 by Act No. 5170), international conventions related to substantive human rights are superior if there is a conflict with the internal codifications.[424]

II. Investigating Authorities and Pre-trial Judges

A. *The Public Prosecution Service*

368. The public prosecution service has a quasi-judicial, quasi-administrative function.[425] According to regulations relating to the organization of the courts, there is a chief public prosecution office attached to each court of general jurisdiction in every district, with a chief and public prosecutor under his supervision (Article 30, Act No. 5235).

There is also a separate chief public prosecutor at the level of the appeal courts on facts and law (Article 40, Act No. 5235).

The Attorney General at the Court of Cassation brings cases at this court. He is not superior to the other public prosecutors.

Turkey is divided into eighty-one provinces *(il)* and each province is composed of districts *(ilçe)*. Each district is under the jurisdiction of the court of that district, and there is an office of the chief public prosecutor in that district. As a consequence of this geographic division, every chief public prosecutor's office has its own venue. If a crime has been committed in another place, the public prosecutor shall decide that he has no jurisdiction and send the case file to the district of jurisdiction. If there is a dispute between two public prosecutors, the nearest court of assizes renders a decision that resolves this dispute (Article 161/7, CMK).

---

422. F. Yenisey & E. Cihan, *Menschenrechte im Strafverfahren, AIDP National Report,* Spain 1993.

423. N. Kunter, F. Yenisey & A. Nuhoğlu, *Muhakeme Hukuku Dalı Olarak Ceza Muhakemesi Hukuku*, 18. Bası, İstanbul, Beta, 2010, p. 1864.

424. O. Doğru, *Anayasa ile Karşılaştırmalı İnsan Hakları Avrupa Sözleşmesi ve Mahkeme İç Tüzüğü*, İstanbul, Vedat Kitapçılık, 2010; O. Doğru, *İnsan Hakları Avrupa Mahkemesi İçtihatları* 2004–2008; M.S. Gemalmaz, *Ulusalüstü İnsan Hakları Belgeleri*, 2010; R. Özmen, *İnsan Hakları Mevzuatı,* 2010; S. Unal, *Turkish Legal System and the protection of Human Rights*, Ministry of Foreign Affairs Center for Strategic Research, Sam Papers No: 3/99, Ankara, 1999; Y. Ünver, *Adil Yargılanma Hakkı ve Ceza Hukuku*, Ankara, Seçkin Yayınları, 2004.

425. M. Önder & S. Önder, *Savcıların Teşkilat İçindeki Yerleri ve Görevleri*, Ankara, Yarı Açık Cezaevi Basımevi, 1968; S. Keyman, *Ceza Muhakemesinde Savcılık*, Ankara, 1970, p. 216; Ö. Tosun, *Hazırlık Soruşturması* (İstanbul: Ümit Doğanay Armağanı, 1983), p. 91; C. Koyuncu, *Savcısının Takdir Yetkisi, AdD* (1985/4), p. 87.

All offenses are prosecuted in the name of the state.[426] The public prosecution office represents the executive branch of the government.[427]

The private prosecution of offenses laid down by Article 344 of the repealed Penal Procedure Code were not incorporated into the current 2004 Code. For these crimes only, the injured party could prosecute; the public prosecutor did not have any power.

The public prosecutor has the duty of making the necessary investigation in order to decide whether it is necessary to file a public prosecution, and if there are *factual findings which indicate that a crime has been committed* (Article 160/1, CMK).

If the preliminary investigation, based on sufficient evidence, justifies the opening of a public prosecution, the public prosecutor submits an indictment to the competent court by making an accusation (Article 170, CMK). However, the case shall be opened only if the court accepts the indictment (Article 175/1, CMK).

Practical arrangements at courthouses and during trials regarding judges, prosecutors and the defense do not guarantee that the principle of equality of arms is respected or perceived to be. This continues to cloud the perception of the impartiality of judges.

The public prosecutor was removed from the court of general jurisdiction in 2011. Therefore, there was no public prosecutor between 2011 and 2014. The Act No. 6572 extended this situation until December 31, 2019, by adding the Provisional Article 9 to CMK (*supra*, paragraph 351). As of September 2020, public prosecutors are present in the courtroom.

Public prosecutors in big cities are empowered to act as *terrorism prosecutors* since 2016.[428]

B. Police

1. Organisation of Security Forces

369. The police, in the broader sense of the word, are divided into two groups in Turkey: The general police and the special police, such as traffic police or village lookouts. The general police consists of those who are under the supervision of the Ministery of Interior, that is, the military police and watchmen or security men.[429]

---

426. Ö. Tosun, *Türk Suç Muhakemesi Hukuku Dersleri, Muhakemenin Yürüyüşü*, Cilt 2 (İstanbul, 1976), p. 10.
427. According to the old law, the Minister of Justice was entitled to give an order to the Chief Public Prosecutor to initiate a public prosecution for a certain case (Art. 148/3, CMUK), and the Provincial Governor would request the Public Prosecutor to initiate a public prosecution. This nevertheless did not oblige the Public Prosecutor to sue. These powers have not been included in the current Penal Procedure Code. Presidential Decree No. 1, dated Jul. 10, 2018, related to the infrastructure of the Office of the President regulated in its Arts. 38 and 41 a new power for the Minister of Justice: *The Minister of Justice is entitled to initiate a public prosecution.*
428. The chief public prosecution office of organized crime courts had special jurisdiction with respect to organized crime until 2012 (repealed Art. 250, CMK) (*supra*, para. 361). In March 2014 terrorism courts and the related public prosecution positions were abolished, and special prosecutors lost their special powers.
429. N. Kunter, F. Yenisey & A. Nuhoğlu, *Muhakeme Hukuku Dalı Olarak Ceza Muhakemesi Hukuku,*

The military branch of the police consists of gendarmes and coast guards, who are under the supervision of the Minister of Interior in the course of recent reforms. Gendarmes are regulated by the 1983 Act on the Gendarmerie. It functions in rural areas where the municipalities have not yet been formed; the police have no jurisdiction in such locations. The gendarmes serve 90% of the geography and 50% of population. This percentage increases in summer months, when the population of the seacoast resorts increases significantly because of tourist influx.

2. Administrative Police

370. The police function in two capacities: As administrative police and as judicial police.[430] In their duties as administrative police, the police are under the supervision of the Ministry of Interior.[431] In events when the police and gendarmerie are not able to suppress riots, the governor is entitled to ask for backup from the army (Act on the Administration of Cities (*İl İdaresi Kanunu*), dated June 18, 1949, No. 5443, Article 11/d). After the OHAL was lifted on July 18, 2018, a new law granted the governors larger powers in order to compensate the lack of authority emanating from OHAL (Act No. 7145 dated July 25, 2018): The governor is empowered to ban certain persons from entering and leaving certain places or jaywalking and assembling in certain places at certain times and to prohibit carrying all kinds of guns in cases where there are serious indications that public order has been destroyed or is going to be destroyed; these powers are limited in time, with a maximum of fifteen days.

3. Judicial Police

371. In the exercise of their judicial duties, the police are under the order of the public prosecutor (Articles 160/1 and 164, CMK).[432] As the regulation in repealed Code did not render control over the police investigation effectively, the 2004 Legislature decided to put the judicial police under the orders of the public prosecutor. According to the current Penal Procedure Code, the police have no authority to conduct any investigation unless there is a specific order of the public prosecutor (Article 160/1, CMK). The provision of the old Penal Procedure Code, which entitled the police to investigate in urgent cases (Article 156, CMUK) does not feature in the new Code.

The Regulation on the Judicial Police was adopted in 2005 under Article 167 of the Penal Procedure Code.

---

18. Bası, İstanbul, Beta, 2010, p. 347.

430. F. Yenisey, *Kolluk Hukuku*, İstanbul, Beta, 2015.

431. There is a branch of Turkish Police that is affiliated with INTERPOL (N. Bilecen, *Ceza Davalarında Usul ve Tatbikat,* 4. Bası, Ankara, Seçkin, 1982, p. 233.

432. N. Kunter, F. Yenisey & A. Nuhoğlu, *Muhakeme Hukuku Dalı Olarak Ceza Muhakemesi Hukuku,* 18. Bası, İstanbul, Beta, 2010, p. 353.

In Turkey, all police forces are competent to fulfill judicial duties, if ordered so. Public prosecutors have to rely on police units working for the Ministry of the Interior and have to develop their capacity to guide police investigations effectively and keep strict control of police activity.[433]

C. Criminal Peace Judgeship and Enforcement Judgeship

372. There is a distinction between "court" and "judgeship" in Turkey. "Court" has jurisdiction in criminal matters in prosecution phase. "Judgeship" in contrast has jurisdiction in preparatory inquiry or in correctional issues. Since 1985, there has been no judicial inquiry and investigating judge *(sorgu hakimi)* in Turkish Penal Procedure (*infra,* paragraph 376).

(a) The criminal peace judgeship. This office was established in 2014 by Act No. 6545 which replaced the previous "criminal courts of the peace" (*supra,* paragraph 351).[434] The criminal peace judgeship only has jurisdiction over rendering decisions during the preliminary investigation if they involve the deprivation of the rights to freedom or privacy, such as search and seizure, pre-trial detention and wire-taps. Additionally, this judgeship has the power to judicially review the decisions of the public prosecutor not to prosecute (*supra,* paragraph 382), removing the content and closing down of the Internet websites (*supra,* paragraph 490), and to remove a lawyer from a criminal case (Article 151/3 CMK). In addition, it should be noted that he also renders decisions on the merits of traffic offenses (*supra,* paragraph 269).

As a legal remedy against decisions of the criminal peace judgeship, the way of opposition is available. Not applying the general rule in the way of opposition, where the inspection is conducted by a higher degree court, the lawmaker of 2014 made an exception by designing a closed circle of appeals: Decisions of criminal peace judgeship shall be inspected by the criminal peace judgeship which has the following number in its jurisdiction (*infra*, paragraph 528). This appeal system has negative practical consequences for the independent review of judicial decisions on detention or other pre-trial measures. There are justified concerns about this regulation.

---

433. On Dec. 19, 2013, the Internal Regulation on Judicial Police was amended, requiring the judicial police investigators to notify their police hierarchy about any criminal notices or criminal complaints. The Council of State suspended the implementation of this amendment on Dec. 27, 2013, for being contrary to judicial independence.

434. The 2012 Reform Package (Act No. 2012-6352) had introduced the so-called freedom judge, who was empowered to render all decisions relating to measures restricting rights and freedom of individuals in cases of terrorism crimes. Political developments of Dec. 17 and 25, 2013, resulted in changes of the jurisdiction of judges in ruling secret investigation techniques; one chamber of the local court of assizes was empowered to issue rulings on interception of telecommunication, undercover investigation and surveillance (Arts. 135, 139 and 140, CMK), thus the "freedom judge" was abolished (Act dated Feb. 21, 2014; No. 2014-6526). Later, the Act dated Jun. 18, 2014 (No. 2014-6545) changed to a whole structure for decision making during the preliminary investigation, and introduced an office of "criminal peace judgeship" *(sulh hakimliği)* by amending the Art. 10, of the Code on Courts No. 5235.

(b) Enforcement judgeship. Disputes between inmates and the correction facility shall be decided by the enforcement judgeship. The powers of this judgeship have been extended in 2020 (*infra,* paragraph 615).

§2. The Stages of Penal Process

I. Two Basic Distinctions

373. The Penal Procedure Code foresees a penal process in two phases (Article 2/1-e and f, CMK): The investigation phase *(soruşturma evresi)* and the prosecution phase during the court inquiry *(kovuşturma evresi).*

Between the *investigation phase* and the *prosecution phase*, there is an *intermediate phase*, which consists of a decision-making about the admission of the charges (Article 174, CMK). This *intermediate phase* starts with the submission of the indictment to the court, and ends when the court decides on admitting the case to go to trial (Article 175/1, CMK). The court is also entitled to reverse the indictment (Article 174, CMK).

The *court inquiry* is divided into three parts: *Preparation of the trial session, course of the trial* and *deliberation of the final judgment.*

Criminal procedure has to be in conformity with three major fields of constitutional law; fundamental rights, rule of law and the specific guarantees of justice.[435]

II. The Preparatory Inquiry

A. *Similarities and Differences Between the Preliminary and Judicial Inquiry*

1. Characteristics of the Preliminary Inquiry

374. The Code calls the first phase of criminal process *the investigation phase* (Article 160, CMK). Investigations during the preparatory inquiry are written, non-adversarial and, in principle, secret (Article 157, CMK). However, the attorney of the accused is entitled to see (with some exceptions) all the records in the file and make free copies of them (Article 153, CMK).

375. All legal interactions conducted during the investigation and prosecution shall be recorded, signed, with complete identification of the participants (Article 169/2, CMK). However, in cases of crimes against the state and in terrorism crimes, the complete identity of law enforcement officers shall be replaced by their service numbers (Article 169/7, CMK).

---

435. R. Arnold, *European Constitutionalism and Criminal Law,* in Prof. Dr. Feridun Yenisey'e Armağan, Beta, İstanbul 2015, p. 799; J.W. Head, *Criminal Procedure in Transition*, in Prof. Dr. Feridun Yenisey'e Armağan, Beta, İstanbul 2015, p. 861.

2. Abolition of Judicial Inquiry

376. Judicial inquiry *(ilksoruşturma)* and the office of the investigating judge *(sorgu hakimi)* had been implemented in Turkey since 1876, following the French model until 1985, when it was abolished. It was argued that the actions conducted by the investigating judge were repeated by the trial court, which caused a delay in proceedings. The existing criminal peace judgeship (*supra,* paragraph 372), as a rule, does not conduct the criminal investigation, but only supervises the public prosecutor's investigation, intervening punctually to authorize (*ex ante*) certain intrusive investigation measures and controlling (*ex post*) the public prosecutor's decisions.

B. The Preliminary Inquiry

1. The Beginning of the Preliminary Inquiry

377. When a public prosecutor is informed of a fact that creates an impression that a crime has been committed either through a report of crime or any other way, he is required to undertake an investigation in order to determine whether there is a necessity for commencing a prosecution (Article 160/1, CMK).

In cases, however, where it is obvious that the content of the report does not constitute a crime, or where it is an abstract and general information, not supported by facts, the public prosecutor does not conduct any investigation and makes a ruling which has a new name: No need to initiate an investigation *(soruşturmaya yer olmadığı kararı)* (Article 158/6, CMK, added by Article 145 of KHK 694 dated August 25, 2017, approved by Act No. 7078 dated February 1, 2018). This new regulation protects the individual from acquiring the title of the suspect, as the investigation has not started yet. The public prosecutor's decision that there is no need to initiate an investigation shall be served to the person who reported the crime, and he may ask for the application of legal remedies available against the dropping of prosecution.

If there are factual basis supporting a simple suspicion *(basit başlangıç şüphesi)* according to the definition of Article 160/1, CMK, the preliminary inquiry begins when the public prosecutor or the police (upon his orders) start to investigate a case.[436] The police (even in urgent cases) have no power to begin an investigation on their own initiative.

According to Article 332 of the Turkish Penal Procedure Code, there is an obligation to answer, within ten days, the written questions of the public prosecutor related to matters of the investigation. If a civil servant fails to do so, he or she can be punished (Article 257, TCK).

378. Under Turkish Law, private individuals are not obliged to report a criminal offense. However, there are some exceptions to this rule. It is a crime not to report

436. B. Öztürk, *Ceza Muhakemesi Hukukunda Koğuşturma Mecburiyeti, Hazırlık Soruşturması*, 9. Bası, Ankara, 9 Eylül Üniversitesi, 1991, p. 52.

a crime that is presently being committed (Article 278/1, TCK); same applies with regard to crimes already committed, in which there are still consequences that could be minimized by reporting them (Article 278/2, TCK). State officials must report criminal offenses that they have learned of that relate to their duties. Failing to do so is a crime (Article 279, TCK).

The identity of the person who gives information to the police may not be kept secret from the accused. Since it is not mentioned in the Code of Penal Procedure, Turkish scholars are of the opinion that the police must reveal the identity of the informant to the accused.[437]

There are some provisions in the field of crimes against the state and profit-oriented organized crime that give the judge discretion to keep the identity of the witness out of the court records (Article 58/2, CMK; Article 20, TMK). Informants and investigators are also protected.

2. The Closing of the Preliminary Inquiry

379. The public prosecutor concludes the preliminary investigation as soon as the level of information is sufficient to enable prosecution. Only the public prosecutor has the discretion to decide whether the investigation is complete.[438] The public prosecutor must be satisfied with the outcome of the investigation. There is no direct review of this decision. The lawyer for the accused, during the preliminary investigation, has had the right to consult the file (with some limitations by Article 153/2, CMK). In this indirect way, the defense has gained a measure of control over the situation.

If the public prosecutor considers that additional investigations should be undertaken in a given case, he may order the police to conduct further investigations.

380. For closing the preliminary investigation, there are four options: (a) The public prosecutor may decide to drop the prosecution (*infra*, paragraph 381); (b) he may prepare an indictment (*infra*, paragraph 383) for the appropriate court if it appears that there is sufficient evidence against the accused; (c) he may apply a suitable "out of court settlement procedure," such as pre-payment of criminal fine, mediation, suspending the prosecution or speedy adjudication (*infra*, paragraph 397); or (d) he may also consider his own subject matter jurisdiction or the existence of a preliminary dispute such as with respect to the venue (*supra*, paragraph 348). If he concludes that such facts exist, he may temporarily stop the prosecution. In such cases, the file will be sent to the competent district or court.

437. Ö. Tosun, *Türk Suç Muhakemesi Hukuku Dersleri, Muhakemenin Yurüyüşü*, 2. Cilt, İstanbul, 1976, p. 13.

438. N. Centel & H. Zafer, *Ceza Muhakemesi Hukuku*, 14. Bası, İstanbul, Beta, 2017, p. 504; T. Kitapçıoğlu, *Ceza Muhakemesi Hukukunda Soruşturmanın Sonuçlandırılması*, Legal, İstanbul 2014.

a. Dropping the Prosecution

381. If no criminal offense was committed or if there was insufficient evidence or if the right to prosecute no longer exists, the public prosecutor may decide to drop the prosecution (Article 172/1, CMK).[439]

Public prosecutor's decision to drop the prosecution equals res judicata if finalized; there shall be no criminal prosecution about the same conduct after the decision on dropping the prosecution, unless new evidence is acquired, sufficient to support the prosecution, and the criminal peace judgeship renders a decision in this regard (Article 172/2, CMK).

An investigation must be re-opened within three months if the ECtHR finds that the decision for non-prosecution has been taken as a result of an ineffective investigation (Article 172/3, CMK). This obligation was originally applicable only for judgments of ECtHR, finding a violation against Turkey. Article 17 of Act No. 7145, dated July 25, 2018 extended the wording in Article 172/3: Two sided friendly settlements, and one-sided declarations of dropping an application, prior to the decision of the ECtHR shall re-open the investigation as well. In cases where the Constitutional Court finds a violation of basic constitutional rights upon an individual petition, based on ineffective investigation, there applies a different procedure: The Constitutional Court rules on opening an investigation, and there is no need for an application by the injured party (Act No. 6216, Article 50/2) (similar rules apply for re-opening a trial after established human rights violations either by the Constitutional Court or by the ECtHR; *supra,* paragraph 366).

b. Opposition to Dropping the Prosecution

382. If the public prosecutor decides to drop the prosecution, the injured party who had filed the complaint may oppose on grounds of new evidence. The opposition shall be filed with the criminal peace judgeship (*supra,* paragraph 372), which is on duty at the court of assizes district where the prosecutor has his jurisdiction (Article 173/1, CMK). Facts and proof that justify the opening of an official claim must accompany the opposition (Article 173/2, CMK). The requirement that an attorney must sign the petition has been repealed.

If the grounds set out in the petition are not sufficient to justify the commencement of a public prosecution, the criminal peace judgeship will refuse the petition. After a decision on dropping the prosecution, and after the refusal of the opposition by the criminal peace judgeship, public prosecution may only be re-opened if there are newly discovered evidence, supporting sufficient suspicion for an indictment and the criminal peace judgeship renders a decision for reopening (Articles 172/2 and 173/6, CMK).

If the *criminal peace judgeship* is of the opinion that the petition is valid, he will order the commencement of a public prosecution. The public prosecutor shall comply with this decision (Article 173/4, CMK).

---

439. N. Centel & H. Zafer, *Ceza Muhakemesi Hukuku*, 14. Bası, İstanbul, Beta, 2017, p. 521.

C. The Procedure of Approval and Reversal of Indictment

1. The Bill of Indictment

383. The principle of legality forces the prosecutor to prosecute with few minor exceptions (Article 170/2, CMK). If the prosecutor is of the opinion that there is sufficient evidence for commencement of a public prosecution, he prepares a bill of indictment and submits it to the court (Article 170, CMK). When the bill of indictment is ready and is signed by the authorized prosecutor, then the court that shall decide on the merits of the case, shall investigate the validity of the indictment and rule to approve it (Article 175/1, CMK). Thus, the prosecution of the case begins officially. At the same time, an inquiry in court begins as well.

The bill of indictment must contain a description of the relevant offense and shall describe the facts and circumstances that may increase or reduce the punishment. The identity of the accused must also be mentioned (Article 170, CMK); if not, the court shall return the indictment (Article 174, CMK).

2. Return of Indictment

384. Since 2005, the court is entitled to return an indictment under the provisions of Penal Procedure Code.[440] The trial court shall examine the whole document related to the investigation phase within fifteen days of the delivery of the indictment and in cases where the following missing parts and errors are discovered, shall return the indictment with a decision thereof, describing them and forwarding it to the public prosecutors' office:

(a) The indictment was produced in violation of the provisions of Article 170 CMK.
(b) The indictment was produced without collecting evidence that would prove the crime with certainty.
(c) The indictment was produced in crimes that are, according to the file of investigation, clearly falling under the provisions of *the settlement of the case on the pre-payment of the fine,* (*infra*, paragraph 391), *mediation* (*infra*, paragraph 393), or *speedy adjudication* (*infra*, paragraph 397) without applying these mentioned procedures (Article 174, CMK).
(d) In cases where the investigation or prosecution of the crime shall only be conducted upon an authorization or request and the indictment was produced without obtaining the authorization or request.

The indictment shall not be returned because of errors in the legal description of the crime.

---

440. N, Centel & H. Zafer, *Ceza Muhakemesi Hukuku*, 14. Bası, İstanbul, Beta, 2017, p. 561; F. Yenisey & A. Nuhoğlu, *Ceza Muhakemesi Hukuku,* 6. Baskı, Seçkin, Ankara, 2018.

In cases where the indictment has not been returned within the fifteen-day time limitation, as indicated in subsection 1 of Article 174, it shall be considered as accepted.

If an indictment has been returned, the public prosecutor shall complete the missing points and correct the errors as shown in the decision and if there is no situation that requires the issuing of a decision to not prosecute, he shall issue a new indictment and send it to the court. The indictment shall not be returned again based on reasons that had not been indicated in the first decision.

A public prosecutor may file a motion of opposition against the decision to return the indictment.

The courts reject very few indictments, which sometimes leads to trials taking longer, as evidence still has to be collected. All of this also applies to high-profile cases.

III. The Prosecution

A. Attribution of the Right to Prosecute

1. Mandatory Prosecution

385. In the Turkish system of Penal Procedure, the public prosecutor has a duty to prosecute criminal cases (Article 170/2, CMK), however there are some exceptions to this rule in relation to out-of-court settlement procedures (*infra*, paragraph 388).[441]

The public prosecutor does not have a monopoly on prosecution. The Treasury and some other agency officials are also competent to prosecute.[442] Private individuals who have been injured through crimes may intervene in a criminal case (Article 237, CMK).

The prosecutor's office is a hierarchical institution under the Ministry of Justice (*supra*, paragraph 27); however, the prosecutor's office conducts investigations independently. The use of personnel in the prosecutor's office is interchangeable, with one prosecutor being easily substituted for another.

There is a public prosecutor attached to the Court of Cassation, also called Attorney General. The Minister of Justice, by a *written order*, can ask him to make an *extraordinary appeal by way of cassation* (*infra*, paragraph 559) to the Court of Cassation (Article 309, CMK).

386. Public prosecutors have jurisdiction over investigations related to offenses committed within the local district of the Court of First Instance (Article 12, CMK). If that court does not have jurisdiction over a specific case, the prosecutor also has no jurisdiction to prosecute.

441. N. Centel & H. Zafer, *Ceza Muhakemesi Hukuku*, 14. Bası, İstanbul, Beta, 2017, p. 110.
442. Y. Hızlı, *Türk Vergi Hukukunda Kaçakçılık Suçu* (Ankara, 1984), 20; K. Mutluer, *Vergi Ceza Hukuku* (Eskişehir, 1979), p. 5.

2. Conditions of Criminal Prosecution

387. The public prosecutor may only bring a case to the court of competent jurisdiction if the conditions of the criminal prosecution required by law are present. For example, some offenses can only be prosecuted upon the complaint of the injured person or with the permission of the authorized state office.[443]

Furthermore, immunities (*supra*, paragraphs 101–103) are obstacles to prosecution. In such cases, the prosecution depends on the fulfillment of the precondition that the complaint has been made or permission has been obtained, or that parliamentary immunity has been lifted by the Parliament.[444] The court is also entitled to end the prosecution when the conditions of criminal prosecution have not been met and there is no possibility that they will be fulfilled.

B. The Suspension of the Right to Prosecute and Out-of-Court Settlement Procedures

388. There are few exceptions to the principle of mandatory prosecution in Turkey, such as discretion in filing the public claim (*infra*, paragraph 389) and suspension of prosecution (*infra,* paragraph 390). Alternative dispute resolution (ADR) options, which aim to diminish the case-load of courts of the first instance by enhancing the out-of-court settlement procedures, have been broadened in 2019. Existing procedures of pre-payment of criminal fine (*infra,* paragraph 391) and mediation (*infra,* paragraph 393) have been supplemented by two the new instruments, speedy adjudication (*infra,* paragraph 397) and simplified adjudication (*infra,* paragraph 400). Each alternative is only applicable to specified crimes. As a consequence, there are now several procedural rules embedded in Penal Procedure Code.

1. Discretion in Filing a Public Claim

389. When it came into force in 2005, the Turkish Penal Procedure Code had given the prosecutor a limited permission to utilize discretion for suspending the prosecution under certain conditions.[445] Prior to the extension of the prosecutorial discretion in 2006, the public prosecutor had only discretion to drop the prosecution in cases where the requirements for the application of the provisions of effective remorse that lifts the punishment as a personal ground (e.g., Article 221/2, TCK), or

443. N. Kunter, *Şikayetin Mevzuu*, IHFM (1950), 460; T. Taner, *Ceza Muhakemeleri Usulü*, 3. Bası (İstanbul, 1955), p. 94; D. Tezcan, *Türk Hukukunda Diplomatik Yargı Bağışıklığı*, BMTDY (1985): p. 141; B. Öztürk, *Uygulamalı Suç Muhakemesi Hukuku,* Cilt 1, 9 (Ankara: 9 Eylül Üniversitesi, 1987), p. 25.

444. N. Kunter, F. Yenisey & A. Nuhoğlu, *Muhakeme Hukuku Dalı Olarak Ceza Muhakemesi Hukuku,* 18. Bası, İstanbul, Beta, 2010, p. 650.

445. The only example under the repealed Penal Code was that of the kidnapper who married the girl he kidnapped. He could only have been prosecuted after the marriage was abolished and after being found at fault (Art. 434, repealed TCK).

the provisions of personal impunity (e.g., Article 22/6, TCK) were met (Article 171/1, CMK).[446] The 2006-5560 legislation broadened this provision by inserting the subsection 2 and introduced a new concept under the title Suspension of Prosecution Under Some Conditions, to be explained below.

2. Suspension of Prosecution

390. In cases of suspended prosecution under Article 171/2, CMK, if the suspect fulfills the requirements and obligations imposed on him by the public prosecutor, there shall be no prosecution and the case shall be dropped.[447]

The prosecutor may suspend the prosecution under the below mentioned conditions for crimes that are punished with imprisonment by up to three years (Article 171/2, CMK). Crimes that fall under the mediation procedure are an exception.[448]

In order to suspend the prosecution, the following requirements have all to be fulfilled:

- The suspect has not been convicted previously with an imprisonment.
- The conducted investigation reveals that in case of a non-prosecution, the suspect will refrain from committing further crimes.
- That the suspension of prosecution is more in favor of the society and of the suspect, compared to a prosecution.
- The losses of the victim or society may be recovered to the full extent (Article 171/3, CMK).

3. Pre-payment of Criminal Fine

391. Another ground for dismissal of a case recognized by the Turkish Penal Procedure Code is *pre-payment of a criminal fine*, which is applicable for any offense punishable by a criminal fine, or by imprisonment of not more than six months at the upper level, or by crimes listed in Article 75/6, TCK.[449]

---

446. In cases, where the public prosecutor has utilized the power of discretion on the issue of not bringing a public claim, opposition against the decision of the public prosecutor is not admitted (Art. 173/5, CMK).

447. The same effect of dropping the prosecution is achieved under the delayed announcement of the judgment (Art. 231/2, CMK), if the accused cooperates with the court-ordered obligations (*infra*, para. 485).

448. After the investigation related to the crime of possessing narcotics for personal use (Art. 191, TCK; *supra*, para. 219) has been initiated, filing an indictment against the suspect shall be postponed for five years. A *controlled liberty measure* (Act No. 5402) shall be applied against the suspect at least for one year, which may be extended by the decision of the public prosecutor for a maximum of one year, each time for three months (Art. 191/3, TCK). The public prosecutor shall remind the suspect about the consequences of the violation of the obligations, explaining that the prosecution shall commence in case of insisting on refusing the treatment (Art. 191/2, TCK). In cases where the accused complies with treatment and measures, the prosecution shall be dropped at the end of the probation period (Art. 191/7, TCK).

449. H.T. Gökcan & S. Kaymaz, *Türk Ceza Kanunu ve Özel Yasalardaki Önödemeye Bağlı Suçlar*

Save for crimes that fall under the procedure of mediation (*infra,* paragraph 393), the public prosecutor must offer to the perpetrator of such crimes the pre-payment of a criminal fine by serving a friendly settlement order (Article 75/1, TCK).[450] The office of the public prosecutor notifies the perpetrator that he has to pay the (lower level) of a criminal fine within ten days and that no prosecution will ensue if it is promptly paid (Article 75/1-a, TCK). If the statutory penalty is imprisonment not exceeding six months, each day of imprisonment shall be calculated as 30 TL (Article 75/1-b, TCK). If the statute foresees imprisonment and a criminal fine, both shall be applied at the lower level (Article 75/1-c, TCK).

If the accused pays the proposed fine, the prosecution must be dismissed.[451] If the accused does not pay the fine, then the prosecutor shall prosecute.[452] If an offense subject to friendly settlement comes to the court by mistake, then the court shall offer the accused an opportunity to pay the fine before proceeding to trial.

In cases where the perpetrator commits another crime that falls under the scope of pre-payment of criminal fine within five years from the date of dropping the prosecution the amount of criminal fine to be paid shall be increased by half (Article 75/1-c, TCK). But for crimes listed in Article 75/6, reoffending within five years of the same crime prevents the application of pre-payment of criminal fine (Article 75/6, TCK).

There is a data bank for pre-payment of criminal fine. Decisions on dropping the prosecution or dismissal of pending cases shall be registered in this data bank, and such data shall only be utilized in connection with an investigation or prosecution by the prosecutor, judge or the court (Article 75/7, TCK).

392. Civil rights claims, recovery of property and confiscation shall not be affected in cases where the criminal proceedings are not initiated or are discontinued on the grounds of in-advance payment (Article 75/5, TCK).

(1998); T. Demirbaş, *Ceza Hukuku Genel Hükümler*, 15. Baskı, Seçkin, Ankara 2020, p. 735; A. Karagülmez, *Açıklamalı-Uygulamalı İçtihatlı Ceza Kararnamesi ve Ön Ödeme; Seçkin Yayınları* (2002). A. Karagülmez, *Suç Olmaktan çıkarma – İdari Para Cezaları – Açıklamalı Kabahatler Kanunu,* Seçkin Yayınları, 2005; H.Y. Sevük, *Çocuk Yargılamasında Ön Ödeme ve Sulh Hakiminin Ceza Kararnamesi*, Türkiye Barolar Birliği Dergisi, sayı 52, p. 66, Mayıs & Haziran 2004. Some legal experts are of the opinion that in-advance payment of a fine is no longer needed, as criminal fines are based on day-fine system in the Turkish Penal Code (İ. Özgenç, *Türk Ceza Hukuku Genel Hükümler, Gözden Geçirilmiş ve Güncellenmiş* 10. Bası, Ankara, Seçkin, 2014, p. 662).

450. N. Centel & H. Zafer, *Ceza Muhakemesi Hukuku*, 14. Bası, İstanbul, Beta, 2017, p. 524.

451. Unifying decision of Court of Cassation Apr. 11, 1983; 2/2, Savaş - Mollamahmutoğlu TCK Yorumu, p. 1677.

452. K. İçel et al., *İçel Yaptırım Teorisi,* 3. Kitap (İstanbul, Beta, 2000), p. 430.

4. Mediation in Criminal Matters

a. Introduction

393. The Penal Procedure Code[453] regulates mediation in criminal matters *(uzlaştırma)* as a form of ADR (Article 253, CMK).[454] In the field of complaint-crimes if the victim files a complaint, and in few crimes that are ex officio prosecuted, the public prosecutor asks both parties if they agree on mediation.[455]

The following crimes mentioned in Article 253, CMK, regulated in TCK are subject to mediation, although they are ex officio prosecuted and do not require the claim of the victim: Intentional wounding (except for subparagraph 3, Article 86 and Article 88, TCK), threat (Article 106/1, TCK), negligent wounding (Article 89, TCK), violation of the tranquility of domicile (Article 116, TCK), theft (Article 141, TCK), fraud (Article 157, TCK), kidnapping of a child and keeping him (Article 234, TCK), revealing the information or documents, that have the nature of commercial secrets, banking secrets or secrets of the customers (Article 239 except for subsection 4, TCK).

Mediation, introduced in criminal matters by the current Penal Procedure Code, was not well established in Turkey.[456] The amendment in 2006 by Act No. 5560 reflects the desire of practitioners to limit its application. In contrast, the Ministry of Justice tries to promote the application of mediation in Turkey by organizing training for prosecutors and judges.

In 2012, an act was enacted in order to extend mediation to civil matters *(Arabuluculuk Kanunu)*. This new act requires an intensive legal and practical training for lawyers, and candidates who are successful at the examinations shall be registered in a mediators list, and civil courts will inform parties to choose their mediators from that list.

In crimes against the sexual inviolability, mediation is excluded, even if their investigation and prosecution is dependent upon a complaint.

---

453. Mediation was regulated in the Penal Code, as one of the grounds for dismissal of a case (Art. 73, TCK). The amendment in 2006 repealed this provision. However, an agreement on mediation leads to dropping of a criminal investigation and bars prosecution, if the losses of the victim are compensated to the full extent (Art. 253, CMK).

454. F. Yenisey (ed.), *Uzlaşma Özel Sayı* (Bahçeşehir Üniversitesi Hukuk Fakültesi Hakemli Hukuk Dergisi, 2010, Özel Sayı: 1; H. Çolak, *Uyuşmazlıkların Alternatif çözüm Yolu Olarak, Uzlaşma*, Türkiye Barolar Birliği Dergisi sayı 63, Mart, Nisan 2006; S. Kaymaz & H.T. Gökçan, *Türk Ceza ve Ceza Muhakemesi Hukukunda Uzlaşma ve Önödeme, Yeni Türk Ceza Kanunu ve Özel Kanunlardaki Uzlaşmaya ve Önödemeye Bağlı Suçlar*, Ankara, Seçkin Yayınları, 2005; J. Starr, *Dispute and Settlement in Rural Turkey: An Ethnography of Law*, Netherlands, Leiden, 1978; E. Yurtcan CMK *Avukatının ve Uzlaşma Avukatının Başvuru Kitabı*, İstanbul, Beta, 2007; E. Gmurzynska, *Influence of Mediation on Transformation of Legal Representation*, in Prof. Dr. Feridun Yeniseye Armağan, Beta, İstanbul 2014, p. 835.

455. F. Yenisey (ed.), *Uzlaşma Özel Sayı*, Bahçeşehir Üniversitesi Hukuk Fakültesi Hakemli Hukuk Dergisi, 2010, Özel Sayı: 1; N. Centel & H. Zafer, *Ceza Muhakemesi Hukuku*, 14. Bası, İstanbul, Beta, 2017, p. 534.

456. E. Çetintürk, *Onarıcı Adalet ve Ceza Adalet Sisteminde Uzlaştırma*, Adalet, Ankara 2017; E.M.S. Özbek, O. Cüni & M. Özcan, *Ceza muhakemesi Hukukunda Uzlaştırma Eğitim Kitabı*, Alternatif Çözümler Daire Başkanlığı Yayını, Ankara 2018, M.R. Erdem, F. Eser & P.P. Özşahinli, *6763 Sayılı Kanuna ve Ceza Muhakemesinde Uzlaştırma Yönetmeliğine Göre Güncellenmiş 100 Soruda Uzlaştırma, Uzlaştırmacının El Kitabı*, 2. Baskı, Seçkin, Ankara 2017.

In crimes that are committed by more than one person, only the person who mediates shall draw benefit from the mediation, even if the other offenders have participated in the same offense (Article 255, CMK).

Where both of the parties agree, a mediator shall be appointed. If the parties agree on the compensation, then there is no criminal prosecution so long as the losses of the victim are fully recovered (Article 253/19, CMK).

b. Mediation Procedure

394. When a crime under investigation that is supported by sufficient evidence and ready for prosecution is subject to mediation, the file shall be referred to the mediation office, established at the prosecution office (Article 253/4, CMK). The Ministry of Justice has established a department for ADR in October 2016, which deals with all affairs related to mediators and mediation. At the same time mediation offices have been founded at local level (Article 253/24, CMK). The mediation office appoints a mediator for this case. The mediator in charge shall propose mediation to the suspect and to the victim or to the person who has suffered damage from the crime. In cases where the suspect, the victim or the person who has suffered damages from the crime is not an adult, the proposal of mediation shall be made to their legal representative. The mediator is entitled to make the proposal of mediation by a notification including the reasons for this proposal, or in case the suspect lives abroad, a rogatory letter. In cases where the suspect, the victim or the person who has suffered damages from the crime does not notify his decision about the mediation within three days after the proposal of mediation, it shall be considered that he has refused the mediation (Article 253/4, CMK).

In cases where a proposal for mediation has been made, the nature and legal consequences of accepting or refusing the mediation shall be explained to that person (Article 253/5, CMK).

If the victim, the person who has suffered damages from the crime, the suspect or their legal representatives cannot be reached because he is not present at the address that has been declared to the official authorities, or is outside the country or for any other ground, then the investigation shall be concluded in the usual way without mediation (Article 253/6, CMK).

In order to apply the mediation procedure in crimes where more than one person has been victimized or has been damaged, it is required that all of the victims or persons who have suffered damages from the crime accept the mediation (Article 253/7, CMK).

The proposal of mediation, or the acceptance of mediation, does not hinder the collection of evidence of the crime that is under investigation nor the application of the measures of protection (Article 253/8, CMK).

As mediation was not applied very frequently, the legislator made an amendment in 2006 in Article 253/9 CMK, by Act No. 5560, contrary to the spirit of mediation and empowered the public prosecutor to act as mediator. Thus, in cases where the suspect and the victim or the person who has suffered damages from the crime has accepted the proposal of mediation, the public prosecutor was entitled to conduct the mediation himself, or may ask the Bar Association to appoint a lawyer as mediator, or appoint a mediator from the list of persons who have obtained a law degree. Yet, in 2016, this provision was again abolished by Act No. 6763.

The same grounds that justify recusal of a judge in a case under Articles 22, 23 CMK, will also justify a motion for the recusal of the mediator (Article 253/10, CMK).

The appointed mediator shall be given a copy of each document included in the case file that is estimated as appropriate by the public prosecutor. The public prosecutor shall caution the mediator about the requirement of complying with the principles of confidentiality of the investigation (Article 253/11, CMK).

The mediator shall conclude the interactions of mediation within thirty days after he receives the copies of the documents included in the file of investigation. The public prosecutor may extend this period for a maximum of twenty days (Article 253/12, CMK).

The mediation conferences shall be conducted confidentially. The suspect, the victim or the person who has suffered damages from the crime, his legal representative, the defense counsel or the representative of the suspect may be present during the mediation conferences. In cases where the suspect, the victim or the person who has suffered damages from the crime does not attend the mediation conference personally, and his legal representative or representative also does not, that party shall be considered as having refused the mediation (Article 253/13, CMK).

The mediator is entitled to consult the public prosecutor about the procedure to follow during the mediation conferences; the public prosecutor may give orders to the mediator (Article 253/14, CMK).

c. Mediation Agreement

395. At the end of the mediation conferences, the mediator shall produce a report and submit it to the public prosecutor, together with the copies of the documents that have been handed over to him. If the mediation results in an agreement, the details of the terms of mediation agreement shall be clearly explained in the report that shall be furnished with the signatures of the parties (Article 253/15, CMK).

The suspect and the victim or the person who has suffered damages from the crime may apply to the public prosecutor at any time up until the indictment has been prepared, and produce the document that states that they have mediated their dispute, even if the proposal of mediation had been previously refused (Article 253/16, CMK).

If the public prosecutor establishes that the mediation has been achieved with the free will of the parties, and the subject of the contract is in conformity with law, then he shall put his seal and signature under the report or the document, and add it to the file of investigation (Article 253/17, CMK).

If the mediation ends without any positive result, the option of mediation shall not be applied again (Article 253/18, CMK).

If at the end of the mediation the suspect fulfills the subject of the contract at once, the decision on no prosecution shall be rendered. If fulfillment of the subject of the contract has been postponed to a future date, is subject to installments, or extends over a certain period of time, the public prosecutor will render a decision on *postponing the filing of public prosecution*, without checking the requirements that are listed in Article 171, CMK. During the postponement, the statute of limitations shall be interrupted. If the requirements of mediation are not fulfilled after the postponement period provided that decision has come to an end, the public prosecution shall be filed, without checking the requirements (not been convicted before, refraining from committing further crimes, favorableness; that are mentioned in Article 171/4 CMK (Article 253/19, CMK).

In cases, where the mediation is successful, no tort claim may be filed for the crime under prosecution; if there is a pending civil case, this case shall be considered as withdrawn. If the suspect does not fulfill the object of the contract, the report or the document of mediation shall be considered as a judgment of a civil court or a document that is listed in Article 38 of the Act on Enforcement and Bankruptcy, dated June 9, 1932, No. 2004 (Article 253/19, CMK) and shall be executed by bailiff.

The assertions made during the mediation conferences shall not be used as evidence in any investigation and prosecution or in any case (Article 253/20, CMK).

The statute of limitations for the prosecution and the duration of the case that is a requirement for prosecution shall not run from the date when the first mediation proposal has been made to the suspect, the victim or the person who has suffered damages from the crime, until the date when the initiative of mediation was unsuccessful, or until the date when the mediator prepares and submits his report to the public prosecutor (Article 253/21, CMK).

The fee of the mediator that is proportional to his work and expenses would be estimated and paid by the public prosecutor. This regulation was changed in 2016 by Act No. 6763; the fee of mediator is now determined by the Ministry of Justice according to a fee schedule (Article 253/22, CMK).

The fee of the mediator and other expenses of mediation shall be considered as court expenses. In cases where there is a successful mediation, these payments shall be compensated by the state treasury (Article 253/22, CMK).

Against the decisions rendered at the end of the mediation, the legal remedies that are foreseen in the Penal Procedure Code, are applicable (Article 253/23, CMK) (*infra*, paragraph 523).

d. Mediation at Prosecution Phase

396. In cases where it becomes evident after the public prosecution has been filed, that the crime under prosecution is within the scope of the mediation procedures, then the transactions of mediation shall be conducted by the mediation office upon referral by the court under the rules and procedures as specified in Article 253 (Article 254/1, CMK).

In cases where the mediation results in an agreement, the court shall decide to drop the prosecution if the accused has fulfilled the obligation in one single payment. If the fulfillment of the obligation is delayed for a later date, or if the payment is due on the installment plan, then the declaration of the judgment shall be postponed, without checking the requirements regarding the delayed announcement of the judgment in Article 231/5, CMK. During the period of postponement, the statute of limitations does not run. In cases where, after the decision on delaying the announcement of judgment has been rendered, the requirements of mediation are not fulfilled, the court shall announce the judgment, without checking the requirements that are mentioned in Article 231/11 (Article 254/2, CMK).

5. Speedy Adjudication

397. There is a new instrument introduced by Act No. 7188 in 2019, for speeding up the prosecution which comes as fourth in the ranking (Article 250, CMK): If postponing the filing of public prosecution does not work, the public prosecutor proposes to the suspect to apply speedy adjudication procedure at the end of the investigation phase. The scope of speedy adjudication is limited by the listed crimes: Trespass, endangering the safety of the road traffic, causing noise, forgery of money, breaking the seal, false declaration while preparing an official document, providing place and opportunity for gambling, utilizing the identity or identity information of another person, some crimes as in the Act on Guns and Knives and other Tools, Forest Act, the Act on Regulating the Playing Tools Such as Roulette or Table Football and the Act on Cooperatives.

398. The proposal shall be made in the presence of the defense lawyer, explaining that the final punishment will be reduced by half, and that its execution may be postponed under Article 51 of Penal Code. If this proposal is accepted. then the public prosecutor requests from the court in written, to make a ruling applying the speedy adjudication procedure. This request shall contain facts, law and determined sanction. The court interrogates the suspect in the presence of his defense lawyer and renders a judgment if it deems it appropriate. This judgment may be subject to opposition.

399. The court also may reject the request of speedy trial if the investigated crime is not listed in the court, or if the acceptance of the suspect is not voluntary and send the file back to the public prosecutor. After this decision, the investigation runs according to the general rules, and the public prosecutor shall write an indictment. Submissions of the suspect related to the acceptance of the speedy trial proposal shall not be used as evidence against him in later course of the trial.

6. Simplified Procedure

400. There is another alternative adjudication procedure in prosecution phase introduced by the Law No. 7188 in 2019, which will be implemented at the court of general jurisdiction for crimes carrying a maximum imprisonment term of two years or less as statutory sanction: the simple adjudication procedure (Articles 251 and 252, CMK). The simple adjudication procedure shall not be applicable to minors, the mentally ill, deaf and mute persons, and to crimes which are investigated or prosecuted upon an authorization or request. In cases where the crime has been committed in conjunction with another crime which is outside of the scope of simple adjudication procedure, this procedure shall not be applied either.

401. The court has discretion to apply this procedure after the approval of indictment for crimes carrying judicial fine and/or two years or less imprisonment of at the upper level as statutory sanction. If the court decides to apply the simple adjudication procedure, it notifies the indictment to the accused, to the victim and to the complaining party, and asks them to submit their submissions and defense within fifteen days. The notification shall include the note that the judgment may be rendered without conducting an oral hearing at trial. The court additionally requests concerned authorities and agencies to collect documents which are deemed necessary (Article 251/2, CMK). After the period of time allocated for submissions and defense has expired, and without collecting the view of the public prosecutor, the court renders one of the judgments as shown in Article 223, CMK, applying Article 61 of the TCK. Until rendering a judgment according to this article, at every stage of the procedure, the court is entitled to open a public main hearing and continue to adjudicate applying general rules of criminal procedure. In cases of rendering a conviction, the final punishment shall be reduced by one-fourth. The judgment rendered under the simplified adjudication procedure shall include an explanation about the procedure and consequences of an opposition.

402. Judgments not opposed timely shall become final. In case of opposition, the court that rendered the judgment shall open a public main hearing and continue to adjudicate applying general rules of criminal procedure. The hearing shall be conducted even if the parties are not present and a judgment according Article 223, CMK may be rendered. The court is not bound by the judgment which it rendered in the scope of simplified adjudication. However, if the opposition was filed by parties other than the accused, the reduction of the punishment by fourth shall be protected. This judgment may be subject to the legal remedies of general provisions of criminal procedure (Article 252, CMK).

C. The Dissolution of the Right to Prosecute

1. Abolition of Penal Provision

403. If the state has lost the right to prosecute, the public prosecutor may not proceed. Where a new law abolishes, or the Constitutional Court annuls an existing penal provision, there shall be no prosecution. According to Article 7/1, TCK, no one may be punished for an act that, although a felony or misdemeanor at the time of its commission, is no longer such under subsequent law. In this case, if a punishment has been already imposed, it shall not be executed.

2. Death of the Accused

404. The death of the accused shall terminate public prosecution. However, if the prosecution is related to confiscation, that part of the prosecution may continue, and the court may order confiscation (Article 64/1, TCK).

The death of a convicted person will set aside the imprisonment and the fine that has not been paid yet. However, if the judgment includes a confiscation and an order to pay court expenditures and has become final before the moment of death, this judgment must be executed upon the convict's family/legal successors (Article 64/2, TCK).

3. Grant of Amnesty or Pardon

405. Amnesty (*infra*, paragraph 631) terminates public prosecution and sets aside the punishment together with all its consequences (Article 65/1, TCK). A pardon sets aside, reduces or changes the punishment (Article 65/2, TCK).

4. Withdrawal of the Complaint and Pre-payment of Criminal Fine

406. Where initiation of legal prosecution for an offense is subject to the injured party filing a complaint, the public prosecution shall be discontinued if the injured party waives his complaint (Article 73, TCK). Such crimes are subject to mediation (Article 253, CMK), to suspension of prosecution (Article 171/2, CMK) and to delaying the announcement of the judgment (Article 231/6, CMK) as well. The first step is issuing of the claim (Article 73/1, TCK). If there is a claim, then mediation and other procedures can start. Crimes which carry only a criminal fine or imprisonment not exceeding six months, and some crimes explicitly listed are subject to pre-payment (Article 75, TCK) (*supra*, paragraph 391). Pre-payment of criminal fine is one of the reasons to drop the prosecution.

5. Limitation by Time

a. Statute of Limitations for Prosecution

407. Statute of limitations for prosecution implies that the duty (and even the right) of the state to prosecute a perpetrator expires after a certain lapse of time. This legal concept is also applicable for enforced punishments in the form of the statute of limitations for execution of punishment (*infra*, paragraph 633). According to rules of substantive criminal law (Articles 73–78, TCK), the state loses the right to punish a wrongdoer under such circumstances, and the case shall be dropped.

With the exception of some very serious crimes, all crimes are subject to the statute of limitations.[457] These serious crimes include: Crimes committed abroad

457. T. Demirbaş, *Ceza Hukuku Genel Hükümler*, 15. Baskı, Seçkin, Ankara 2020, p. 741.

against the Turkish nation and state (Articles 247–345, TCK) carrying aggravated life imprisonment, or life imprisonment or a prison term of more than ten years (only *statute of limitation for prosecution* is exempted; Article 66/7, TCK); genocide (Article 76/4, TCK); crimes against humanity (Article 77/4, TCK); organized crime of genocide and crimes against humanity (Article 78/3, TCK); and military high treason (Article 49/B, AsCK).

The time limits for the prosecution of crimes depend on the seriousness of the crime (Article 66/1, TCK), where the maximum imprisonment term shall be taken into account. The court takes them into consideration ex officio (Article 72/2, TCK).

The statute of limitations applies the following system (Article 68/1, TCK): Crimes for which the law imposes aggravated life imprisonment become statute-barred after forty years (Article 68/1-a, TCK); crimes for which the law imposes life imprisonment become statute-barred after thirty years (Article 68/1-b, TCK); crimes for which the law imposes twenty years or more of imprisonment become statute-barred after twenty-four years (Article 68/1-c, TCK); crimes for which the law imposes imprisonment of more than five but less than twenty years become statute-barred after twenty years (Article 68/1-d, TCK); crimes for which the law imposes up to five years imprisonment or criminal fine become statute-barred after ten years (Article 68/1-e, TCK).

There are special regulations for children who have been taught to commit crimes; if the child was in the age group of 12–15 when the crime was committed, time limits in the statute shall be discounted by half; if the child was in the age group of 15–18, it is discounted by two-thirds (Article 66/2, TCK).

b. Beginning, Suspension and Interruption Point of Time Limit for Prosecution

408. For completed crimes, time begins to run on the date of the commission of the crime; for attempted crimes, on the date of perpetration of the last criminal act; and for continuing and successive (continued) crimes, on the date when the last crime was committed (Article 66/6, TCK). If there are several crimes committed by the accused, the statute of limitations for prosecution shall be determined according to the existing evidence in the file regarding the reasons for aggravating the punishment (Article 66/3, TCK).

For crimes committed against children by their parents or by a person who oversees the child, the period indicated in the statute of limitations starts when the child attains 18 years of age (Article 66/6, TCK). There is a special regulation related to marriage: The time limit for prosecution shall start to run from the final judgment on the annulment of the wrongful marriage (Article 230/4, TCK).

The provision in the Penal Code applies to retrials: If there are grounds for re-opening a trial (Article 311, CMK), and the competent court gives a decision about giving leave to the request of re-opening (Article 318, CMK), then the time for prosecution for that particular crime starts to run *de novo* (Article 66/5, TCK).

In cases where initiating an investigation or prosecution depends on the permission or decision of another organ (e.g., in cases of discrediting Turkish Nation, etc., the investigation shall be suspended until the Minister of Justice renders a decision on permission; Article 301/4, TCK), or if the suspect is a fugitive and there is a decision about his status (Article 247, CMK), time limits for prosecution are suspended until this obstacle has been lifted (Article 67/1, TCK). There are other examples of suspension of the running of the statute of limitations, such as *prosecution of members of the Parliament* (Article 83/3, AY); *of soldiers* for alleged crimes carrying imprisonment up to two years (Article 20/1, 5, AsCK), until the end of the office. In cases of *delay of payment of mediated damages* (Article 253/19, CMK); *suspended prosecution* (Article 171/2, CMK) and delayed *announcement of the judgment* (Article 231/5, CMK), the statute of limitations shall be suspended.

The time period mentioned in the statute of limitations is interrupted (*zamanaşımının kesilmesi*) upon: The interview by the public prosecutor or questioning[458] by the judge of one of the suspects or accused (Article 67/2-a, TCK); the issuance of a pre-trial arrest warrant[459] against one of the suspects or accused (Article 67/2-b, TCK); the preparation of an indictment related to a crime (Article 67/2-c, TCK); and the judgment of conviction against at least one of the accused (Article 67/2-d, TCK).[460]

In cases where the statute of limitations period has been interrupted, the time for prosecution starts to run again but may be extended by one-half the amount of the time limit as foreseen in the law for this particular crime (Article 67/4, TCK). If there is more than one ground for interruption, the last one will be considered (Article 67/3, TCK).

c. Statute of Limitations for Misdemeanors

409. The Act for Misdemeanors (Articles 20–21, KK) sets time limits for prosecution: Five years for misdemeanors carrying an administrative fine of 100,000 TL and more (Article 20/2-a, KK); four years for misdemeanors carrying an administrative fine of 50,000 TL and more (Article 20/2-b, KK); three years for misdemeanors carrying an administrative fine of less than 50,000 TL (Article 20/2-c, KK); eight years for misdemeanors carrying an administrative fine depending on the seriousness of the conduct (Article 20/3, KK).

If the misdemeanor at the same time constitutes a crime, the statute of limitations for prosecution of crimes shall apply (Article 20/5, KK).

Time starts to run when the act defined as a misdemeanor has been committed or the result of this act had occurred (Article 20/4, KK).

458. The questioning by the judge after the judgment has been reversed by the Court of Cassation is not considered as a ground for interruption of the statute of limitation.

459. An arrest warrant issued by a foreign court based on Interpol request of Turkish authorities shall interrupt the statute of limitation (S. Tellenbach, *Begnadigung, Amnestie, Aufhebung der Strafbarkeit in der Türkei,* in *Nationales Strafrecht in rechtsvergleichender Darstellung, Teilband* 5, ed. Ulrich Sieber, Karin Cornils (Berlin, 2010), 709).

460. Time started to run on the date of the perpetration of the last criminal act, and for continuing and successive offenses on the date the situation ended or the series of successive offenses ended (Art. 103, repealed TCK).

d. Dismissing a Case as the Consequence of Expiration of Time Limits

410. According to Article 66 of TCK, the prosecution will be dismissed upon the lapse of the time periods provided by the Code.[461] If the punishment was set aside due to a lapse of time pursuant to the Code, the right to prosecute ends. According to Article 223/7 of the Turkish Code of Penal Procedure, a final judgment of a criminal court bars further prosecution for the same crime against the same person. A second case will not be admitted. Generally, the final decisions of the Turkish courts, as well as the final decisions of foreign courts, have the same effect. In cases of illegal drug exportation from Turkey, if the offender was tried by a foreign court, the Court of Cassation will not apply the ne bis in idem rule (*supra*, paragraph 91), and it will consider the crime as committed in Turkey through application of Article 8, TCK.[462]

6. *Non Bis in Idem*

411. In cases where there is a pending prosecution or a final judgment related to the same person on the same issue, there shall not be a second prosecution. In cases where there is a previously rendered judgement or a pending case against the same accused of the same conduct, the case will be dismissed (Article 223/8 CMK). The decision to drop the prosecution rendered at the end of preparatory investigation shall also prevent a second investigation or opening of a case, except if there is new evidence supporting sufficient suspicion to open the public prosecution and the criminal peace judge decides on this issue (Article 172/1, CMK). There are exceptions to the principle of *non bis in idem*, if the crime has been committed on Turkish territory, the perpetrator (a Turkish citizen or a foreigner) shall be tried in Turkey, even if he had been adjudicated in a foreign country (*supra*, paragraph 90).

IV. The Inquiry in Court

A. *General Characteristics*

412. The inquiry in court is open to the public (*infra*, paragraph 513). In cases where it is strictly necessary in respect to public morale or public security, the main hearing may be conducted closed to the public (Article 182, CMK). (The simple adjudication procedure, however shall be conducted in camera; *supra*, paragraph 400). Only legally obtained evidence shall be presented during the main hearing, and the judge shall only rely such evidence which has been discussed in his presence, evaluating it by exercise of his free and conscientious discretion (Article 217/1, CMK).

---

461. N. Kunter, *Ceza Davası Zamanaşımının Durması*, IBM (1948/IV), p. 178.
462. F. Yenisey, *Milletlerarası Ceza Hukuku, Ceza Yargılarının Milletlerarası Değeri ve Mevzuatı* (İstanbul: Beta, 1988), p. 245.

B. The Judge: An Active but Impartial Arbitrator

1. The Independent Status of the Judge

413. All judges are professionals;[463] there are no juries or laymen in the Turkish court organization.[464] Candidate judges and public prosecutors must complete a two-year training course (Act No. 3221, dated June 6, 1985). At the end of the training course, they must pass a written examination (Article 10, Act No. 3221).

The Turkish Judiciary is independent. Article 138/2 of the Constitution provides that "*no organ, office, agency or individual may give orders or instructions in connection with the discharge of the judicial power concerning a case on trial.*" The Council of Judges and Prosecutors (Article 159, AY) (*supra*, paragraph 22) provides for the independence of the judges. In its *Çıraklar and Incal* decisions, the ECtHR regarded the participation of a military judge on the panel and a military public prosecutor as a violation of the independence of judges. These judgments resulted in an amendment to the Constitution and to the Act on State Security Courts (DGMK), but did not prevent further judgments finding that Article 6, ECHR had been violated, such as the ECtHR decision in *Sadak and others v. Turkey* (July 17, 2001). Upon this decision, the Constitution and procedural laws have been amended as well (*supra*, paragraph 355).

Judges may not be dismissed but may resign. They need not retire until they reach the age of 65.

2. The Impartiality

414. The Turkish Penal Procedure Code provides some specific rules to safeguard the impartiality of judges.[465] The offices of prosecution and the trial are separate.[466] Article 22, CMK forbids the judge from judging his own case if he was injured by the accused or if he is a relative of the parties, as well as if he has been active in the same case as a prosecutor, an investigative police officer, a defender of the accused or of the victim; or if he was summoned as a witness or has delivered an opinion as an expert (Article 22, CMK).[467] If the judge was active during the trial at the first instance, he is barred from acting in the higher court's trial either during the opposition examination or during the appeal procedure at the Court of Cassation (Article 23, CMK). However, according to the case law of the Court of Cassation,

---

463. H. Hancı, *Hekimin Yasal Sorumlulukları ve Hakları*, Toprak Ofset Matbaacılık, 1999; M. Özen, *Hakimin Cezai Sorumluluğu*, Ankara, Seçkin Yayınları, 2004.
464. M. Kapani, *İcra Organı Karşısında Hakimlerin İstiklali* (Ankara, 1956), 7; N. Kunter, Türkiye'de Kaza Kuvveti, IHFM XXV (1960): sy 1-4; Ülkü Azrak, *Yargı ve İdare*, İHFM XXXIV (1969): Sy. 1-4.
465. E. Günay, *Yargısal Görevlerinden Dolayı Hakimlerin Tazminat Sorumluluğu ile Hakimlere, C. Savcılarına ve Avukatlara Karşı İşlenen Hakaret Suçları*, Ankara, Seçkin Yayınları, 2000.
466. N. Centel & H. Zafer, *Ceza Muhakemesi Hukuku*, 14. Bası, İstanbul, Beta, 2017, p. 625.
467. The exclusion of the Public Prosecutor is not regulated in Turkish Law (E. Yurtcan, *Ceza Yargılaması Hukuku*, 3. Bası, İstanbul, Beta, 1987, p. 109).

the judge who has decided to arrest the accused during the preliminary investigation is not considered as having made an opinion about the innocence or guilt of the accused.[468]

415. If the judge has previously participated in the decision-making of the first instance judgment of someone who is subsequently subject to a retrial (Article 311, CMK), he cannot be on the court panel deciding the merits of the case on retrial (Article 23/3, CMK).

The judge has an active role in the criminal proceedings. The aim of criminal proceedings is to reveal the factual truth. The judge takes the initiative in finding the factual truth and is not bound by the evidence submitted by the parties. The judge has the right to interrogate the accused and the civil party (claimant), appoint experts and call for witnesses if he considers it necessary.

C. The Beginning and Closing of the Inquiry in Court

1. The Beginning of the Inquiry

416. The presiding judge makes sure that the accused, his defence counsel, witnesses, as well as the summoned experts are present in the courtroom and declares the beginning of the main hearing by reading out the decision on the admissibility of the indictment (Article 191/1, CMK) (*infra,* paragraph 513).

2. The Closing of the Inquiry

417. The inquiry in court ends with the last word of the accused (Article 216/3, CMK). The presiding judge declares that the main hearing is concluded. Then the court makes a closed session in order to deliberate the judgement where only those judges shall be present who are eligible to vote. The outcome of this deliberation is the judgement of the court which shall be read out in the courtroom. The pronouncement of the judgement is the closing of the inquiry in the real sense (Article 231/1, CMK) (*infra*, paragraph 516).

§3. The Legal Position of the Accused and the Civil Party

I. Introductory Remarks

418. The rights of the suspect or the accused and the rights of the victim are the backbone of criminal procedure.[469] The focus on the rights of the suspect or accused

---

468. F. Yenisey, *Uygulanan ve Olması Gereken Ceza Muhakemesi Hukuku, Hazırlık Soruşturması ve Polis*, 3. Baskı, İstanbul, Beta, 1993, p. 62.
469. F. Yenisey & E. Cihan, *Menschenrechte im Strafverfahren*, Spain, AIDP National Report, 1993.

was reflected by the December 1992 amendment of the Turkish Code of Penal Procedure. This approach has been broadened by the legislature in 2004.

The victim may intervene in the public prosecution (*infra*, paragraph 429). The public criminal prosecution (Article 160, CMK) is a criminal claim; the *Private Rights Claim* (*supra*, paragraph 21) was an independent private claim but has not been copied into the current Code.

II. Legal Status of the Suspect, Accused and the Defense Counsel

A. The Provisions in the Code of Criminal Procedure

419. The present Turkish Code of Criminal Procedure regulates the suspect's rights during the preliminary investigation.[470]

For example, the owner of the place or the possessor of the movable thing has the right to be present at searches and seizures (Article 120, CMK), and the lawyer of the person to be searched may also be present during the search (Article 120/3, CMK). Suspects are entitled to have a defense lawyer present during the police interview (Article 147, CMK) as well as when interrogated by a judge and to have their lawyer present during the interrogation in cases of arrest (Article 91/6, CMK).[471]

The defense counsel has access to the file of the investigation with some exceptions. Limitations regarding protection of the confidentiality of investigations (Article 153/2, 3 and 4, CMK) were repealed in 2014 (Article 153, CMK); this provision was changed again in the same year by Act No. 6572, which introduced a list of crimes,[472] where access to the file may be limited by the judge.

---

470. N. Centel & H. Zafer, *Ceza Muhakemesi Hukuku*, 14. Bası, İstanbul, Beta, 2017, p. 161; Cüneyt Altıparmak, *AİHS ve İç Hukukumuz Çerçevesinde Müdafilik Kurumumuz*, İstanbul Barosu Dergisi cilt: 79, sayı: 2005/5; E. Doğan, *Sanık Hakları ve Müdafilik*, İstanbul: Beta, 2007; Fatih Selami Mahmutoğlu, Selman Dursun, *Türk Hukuku'nda Müdafiin Yasaklılık Halleri*, Ankara, Seçkin, 2004.

471. N. Centel, *Ceza Muhakemesi Hukukunda Müdafi*, İstanbul: Kazancı, 1984, p. 127; F. Erem & N. Toroslu, *Türk Ceza Hukuku, Özel Hükümler*, 3. Bası, Ankara, 1978, p. 573; F. Erem, *Adalet Onünde Eşitlik*, YD, 1981, p. 485.

472. This list includes the following crimes: (a) The following crimes in the Turkish Penal Code: (1) Killing with intent (Arts. 81, 82. 83 TCK), (2) Sexual assault (Art. 102 TCK, except for subs. (1), (3) Sexual abuse of children (Art. 103 TCK), (4) Producing and trading with narcotic or stimulating substances (Art. 188 TCK), (5) Forming an organization in order to commit crimes (Art. 220 TCK), (6) Crimes against the security of the state (Arts. 302, 303, 304, 307, 308 TCK), (7) Crimes against the Constitutional order of the state (Arts. 309, 310, 311, 312, 313, 314, 315, 316 TCK), (8) Crimes against the secrets of the state and spying (Arts. 328, 329, 330, 331, 333, 334, 335, 336, 337 TCK); (b) Smuggling with guns, as defined in Act on Guns and Knives and other Tools, dated Jul. 10, 1953, No. 6136 (Art. 12); (c) The crime of embezzlement as defined in Art. 160 of the Act No. 5411, dated Oct. 19, 2005, Act on Banks; (d) Crimes as defined in the Combating Smuggling Act.

420. The accused has a stronger position during the phase of inquiry in court. For example, he has the right to bring along witnesses, the right to have a non-public hearing and the right of having the last word at the end of the inquiry.[473] Also, the trial is public, and the impartiality of the judge is guaranteed by the Code (Articles 22/1, 23, CMK).

421. The statute of December 1992 (Act No. 3842) aimed to strengthen the accused's rights in light of Articles 5 and 6 of the ECHR.[474]

422. In order to facilitate the access to justice, the 4th Judicial Reform Package (*supra*, paragraph 50) loosened the conditions for granting legal aid. A party may be partially or fully exempted from payment if the court considers that court expenses could cause them to be victimized. On request, a hearing may be held to decide on the granting of such aid. The Ministry of Justice website provides information on legal matters and the Ministry also publishes brochures providing information on the applicable procedures. Civil society organizations and bar associations contribute to raising awareness of citizens' rights regarding access to justice.

423. According to Article 160 CMK, the public prosecutor has to conduct the investigations and give orders to the judicial police in order to search the factual truth as the basis of a fair trial. The police must report to the public prosecutor all arrests and interrogations of and interviews with the suspect (Article 90/5, CMK). The regulations concerning pre-trial detention and interrogation by the police are to be interpreted in the light of the provisions of Article 5 of the ECHR.

424. Attorneys[475] and some high state officials have the privilege of being tried in a higher court (*supra*, paragraph 97). While prosecuting a case, the public prosecutor must acknowledge this privilege.

B. Other Applicable Laws

425. Violation of the rights of suspects may amount a breach of a constitutional right. In such cases there is a possibility to apply with the ombudsman (*supra*, paragraph 12-f), to the civilian oversight authorities and as well as to file an individual complaint with the Constitutional Court (*supra*, paragraph 366).

According to the Article 24 of the "Ombudsman Institution Law" No. 6328, the Chief Ombudsman prepares a report about its recommendations based on citizen complaints at the end of every year and submits it to the Joint Committee at the

473. S. Donay, *İnsan Hakları Açısından Sanığın Hakları ve Türk Hukuku,* İstanbul: İstanbul Üniversitesi, 1982, p. 28.
474. B. Öztürk, *Ceza Muhakemesi Hukukunda Koğuşturma Mecburiyeti, Hazırlık Soruşturması,* 9. Bası, Ankara: Eylül Üniversitesi, 1991, p. 54.
475. N. Kunter, *Ceza Tatbikatında Amme Vazifesi ve Amme Hizmeti Tefriki ve Avukatın Durumu,* IHFM (1947): XIII/2, 755–772; F. Erem, *Avukatlar Hakkında Soruşturma İzni,* ABD (1977/2), pp. 264–265.

Grand National Assembly. The report shall be negotiated in a planary session. For example, the report for the year 2018 related to the quality of places where people were deprived of their liberty was debated on January 2, 2020.

Civilian oversight mechanisms of internal security forces are part of the new development in Turkey. The Law No. 6713, dated May 5, 2016 has created a "complaint information system" which receives the grievances of citizens against the members of internal security forces, submits such complaints to the related instances and gives back-up information to the citizen about the outcome of his complaint every two months.

III. Legal Status of the Victim and Injured Person as Civil Party

A. *General Observations*

426. The rights of the victim[476] as a civil party were not defined by the repealed Code. The victim of a criminal offense only had the right to intervene in the prosecution as a civil party during criminal proceedings. However, the civil party was entitled to claim damages during the criminal proceedings as well.

The current Penal Procedure Code includes a special subsection for the rights of the victim and person injured by the crime (Articles 233–236, CMK). However, the provision entailing the right to claim damages during the criminal proceedings is not included in the 2004 Code of Penal Procedure.

B. *Civil Party in the Preparatory Inquiry*

427. The civil party has the right to report the crime or to file a complaint about the committed crime (Article 158, CMK). Turkish Law differentiates between the informant (denouncer), who is reporting a criminal offense, and the civil party, who is the victim of or is injured by the crime. The victim and the person reporting the crime have the right to give testimony about the crime and shall be summoned by the prosecutor, the judge or the court (Article 233/1, CMK).

The victim and the person who filed a complaint have the right to ask the evidence of the crime be collected, to ask the public prosecutor to furnish them with copies of the documents included in the file of investigation (without violating the rule concerning secrets of the investigation) and to ask a lawyer appointed by the Bar Association to assist them if they do not have an attorney. This lawyer has access to the file under Article 153, CMK and the right to oppose the decision of the public prosecutor to drop the case (Article 234/1-a, TCK).

---

476. F.S. Akıncı, *Viktimoloji* (İstanbul: Beta, 2007); M. Açıkgözoğlu, *Ceza Hukuku Açısından Teori ve Uygulamada Mağdur Kavramı* (Ankara: Adil Yayınevi, 2000); S. Akdemir, *Ceza Hukukunda Mağdurun Korunması* (Izmir: Anadolu Matbaacılık, 1988). A.E. Akyazan, *Mağdurun Kovuşturma Evresindeki Hakları Kapsamında Soru Yöneltme Hakkı*, Ankara, 2009; V.Ö. Özbek, *Ceza Hukukunda Suçtan Doğan Mağduriyetin Giderilmesi*, Ankara, Seçkin Yayınvevi, 1999.

Child victims and victims who have suffered psychological damages in relation to the committed crime, are also protected by special measures. There are child monitoring centers (*Çocuk İzleme Merkezi;* ÇİM) in hospitals which are furnished with video recording facilities, social workers and experts. Child victims shall be interviewed by the experts in a private room and the public prosecutor observes this procedure, but the child does not see him (Ordinance issued by the Prime Minister's Office No. 2012/20; RG October 4, 2012). The video recording shall be played during the trial, and the victim shall not appear at court (Article 236/3, CMK).

There is an additional protection of the victim from *courtroom stress* during the investigation and prosecution phase (*Adli Görüşme Odaları Yönetmeliği*): An expert in a specially designed room outside the courtroom shall interview children and vulnerable victims. The expert shall ask questions posed by the parties, and this procedure shall be displayed in the courtroom. Parties are entitled to ask supplementary questions.

The victim of the crime has gained importance within the recent amendment in 2019, Act. No.7188, and the following regulations are incorporated in to the Penal Procedure Code:

The travel and accommodation expenses of the victim shall be covered by the state, if the victim has to travel outside of his home for the purpose of giving testimony or interactions related to forensic medicine (CMK 134/4). In cases where it is deemed needed by the public prosecutor or by the judge that the statement of a child is to be taken in a special environment, or in cases where they evaluate that the confrontation with the offender would be harmful, then the testimony of a child or a victim shall be taken in a special environment (Article 236/4, CMK). During the investigation phase, the testimony of a child who has been the victim of a sexual assault (Article 103/2, TCK) shall be taken by the intervention of an expert and under the supervision of the public prosecutor in a special center. The testimony of the child and the images shall be recorded. Unauthorized sharing of such recordings is a new crime (Article 136/2, TCK). During the prosecution phase, this procedure is applicable only if it is necessary in order to reveal the factual truth. In such cases, the procedure shall be conducted by a court-appointed judge in the above-mentioned center by the intervention of the expert: The child victim shall be brought to the nearest center (Article 136/5, CMK). Experts, assisting the hearing have to be married, have children and must have made an LLM in the field of family relations, or psychology or pedagogy.

428. Private Criminal Prosecution is a formal complaint filed by the victim or his legal representative against the commission of a crime. The current Penal Procedure Code has abolished this legal institution. There are other means of achieving compensation for the losses of the victim within the current Criminal Justice System, such as mediation in relatively small matters (Article 253, CMK) (*supra*, paragraph 393).

C. Civil Party in the Inquiry in Court

429. The intervention. The intervention in the public claim of an injured party is only possible during the inquiry in the court, and not during the preliminary investigation, as the intervention requires the existence of an official claim.[477]

Victims, whether individuals or a legal person, who have been damaged by the crime, as well as individuals who are liable due to their property, are entitled to intervene in the public prosecution during the prosecution phase at the court of the first instance at any stage, until the judgment has been rendered, announcing that they are putting forward their claim.

It is not permitted to put forward a request for intervening in the public prosecution during the proceedings of legal remedies. However, if the request that has been put forward during the proceedings at the court of the first instance has been rejected, or if there was no decision rendered at that stage, this issue shall be decided, if there is an explicit request at this point at the application for legal remedy (Article 237, CMK).

§4. Rules of Evidence

I. Principles of Evidentiary Law

430. The main principles of evidence[478] are based on the Continental European system.[479] The court must undertake a complete investigation to determine the factual truth.[480] The court is not dependent on the evidence of the prosecutor, the accused or the other parties. Witnesses can also be called on the court's own initiative.

The court is obliged to explain the means of proof included in the verdict, as well as provide the analysis used to include or exclude such proof (Article 230, CMK).

431. The accused is presumed innocent. As a consequence, there is no obligation for him to prove that he is innocent. In contrast, the judge has the obligation to search for the factual truth, and only if he is convinced that the accused is guilty may he convict him. Thus, neither the public prosecutor nor the accused has the burden of proof in Turkish Law. If the accused or the public prosecutor points out any factual aspect that is necessary for the decision during the course of criminal proceedings, the trial court has the obligation to determine the factual truth.

---

477. S. Onursal, *Kamu Davasına Müdahale* (İstanbul, 1968); I. Şahbaz, *Ceza Yargılamasında Katılanın Temyiz Duruşmasında Yer Almaması*, Türkiye Barolar Birliği Dergisi sayı 51 Mart & Nisan 2004.

478. A. Parlar, M. Hatipoğlu, Y.E. Güngör, *Açıklamalı: İçtihatlı Ceza Muhakemesi Hukukunda Deliller Çapraz Sorgu ve İspat* (2005).

479. S. Belgesay, *Kanuni ve Takdiri Deliller ve Temyiz Mahkemesinin Delilleri Takdiri* (Ankara, 1938), p. 11; S. Belgesay, *Hukuk ve Ceza Mahkemesinde Deliller* (İstanbul, 1960), p. 7. İ. Üzülmez, *Türk Hukukunda Suçsuzluk Karinesi ve Sonuçları*, Türkiye Barolar Birliği Dergisi, sayı 58, p. 41, Mayıs, Haziran 2005.

480. D. Gedik, *Ceza Muhakemesinde İspat ve Şüphenin Sanık Lehine Yorumlanması,* 3. Baskı, Adalet, Ankara 2018.

A defendant can never be under the obligation of self-incrimination; the right to remain silent is guaranteed (Article 147, CMK).

II. The Means of Proof

432. Law does not define the means of proof. Everything may be considered as evidence insofar as it is reasonable. The court considers the evidence freely in order to discover the factual truth. There is a freedom of evidence. However, that evidence should have been obtained lawfully (Article 38, AY; Article 217/2, CMK) (*infra*, paragraph 439).

433. The judges may use only the evidence, documents and statements presented and discussed at the open trial to reach their conclusions and form the judgment of the court (Article 217/1, CMK).[481]

Judicial presumptions are not accepted in Turkish Criminal Procedure.

434. Physical evidence. Official police report of the interrogation of the accused are not considered evidence in court. Only the written record during the hearing before the judge may be considered evidence (Article 209, CMK).[482] However, some special codes (e.g., Article 119, KTK) give the police the right to make some drawings of the scene of the crime. In such cases, the official police reports acquire the character of evidence.

435. The witness testimony. Testimony in court is considered evidence.[483] There is no age limit for a witness in Turkish Criminal Procedure Law. However, the accused is not entitled to give testimony as a witness on his own behalf.

Eyewitnesses to a crime have a duty to testify. However, the law provides that the family members of the accused may refuse to act as witnesses (Article 45, CMK).

The president of the court has the right to question witnesses (Article 59, CMK). The accused and the parties may also personally ask a specific question to the witness (Article 201, CMK). The president of the court has discretion over such requests. There is now a possibility of direct examination and cross-examination of witnesses by the defense lawyer and the public prosecutor; so far, however, this provision is rarely applied.[484]

Informers who give testimony about individuals attempting to endanger the constitutional order of the state will be rewarded, and their identity will be kept secret

481. M. Yayla, *Ceza Muhakemesi Hukukunda İspat ve Şüphe*, Seçkin, Ankara 2016, Metin Köse, *Ceza Kovuşturmasında Delillerin Ortaya Konulması ve Değerlendirilmesi,* Seçkin, Ankara 2017.

482. N. Kunter, F. Yenisey & A. Nuhoğlu, *Muhakeme Hukuku Dalı Olarak Ceza Muhakemesi Hukuku,* 18. Bası (İstanbul, Beta, 2010), p. 1392.

483. N. Kunter, F. Yenisey & A. Nuhoğlu, *Muhakeme Hukuku Dalı Olarak Ceza Muhakemesi Hukuku,* 18. Bası (İstanbul, Beta, 2010), p. 1346.

484. The European Court of Human Rights found in the *Sadak and Others* Judgment of Jul. 17, 2001, that the accused not having an opportunity to ask questions of a witness who made statements against them during the preliminary investigation was a violation of Art. 6.

during the trial (Article 58/2, CMK; Added Article 1 of Act No. 1481, dated August 15, 1971). Statements of anonymous witnesses are permitted in some cases, for example by Article 19/4 the Combating Smuggling Act 2007.[485]

A scientific expert[486] is not considered a witness; his scientific opinion is not a witness testimony, but an explanation of factual findings.

436. Witness protection. There is a Witness Protection Act since 2007, Act No. 5726.[487] Witnesses of crimes carrying punishment of more than ten years of imprisonment and more than two years imprisonment of organized crimes as well as all kind of terrorism crimes may be protected (Article 3, Act No. 2007-5726).

437. Confession. The confession of the accused is generally considered a ground for mitigated punishment. Some special legislations contain provisions about either not punishing or mitigating the punishment of the accused, if the confession is useful in solving the crime (Articles 93, 110, 168, etc. TCK).

438. Expert witness. Expert opinion is not considered evidence in Turkish Law.[488] According to the Code of Penal Procedure, the court must ask the opinion of the scientific expert if the matter relates to technical points or to special knowledge (Article 62, CMK). It is forbidden for the court to ask experts their opinion about matters related to law.[489]

III. Exclusion of Evidence

439. The exclusionary rule did not exist in Turkish Penal Procedure Code until 1992. This deficiency in Turkish Law was much criticized by scholars.[490] According to the repealed Code (Article 254/2, CMUK) illegally obtained evidence by investigating and prosecuting authorities would be disregarded when reaching a verdict, it was thus excluded.[491]

The concept of the exclusionary rule[492] was broadened in 2001 by adding a subparagraph to the Constitution: *Items obtained in violation of an Act, may not be used as evidence at court* (Article 38/7, AY).

---

485. S. Erman, *Kaçakçılık* (İstanbul, 1981), 616; S. Selçuk, *Kanıtların Toplanması* (YD 1977/3), p. 57.
486. Y. Deryal, *Türk Hukukunda Bilirkişilik* (2004). Gökçen, Balcı, Alşahin, Çakır, Ceza Munakemesi Hukuku - I -, 2. Baskı, Adalet Yayınevi, Ankara 2017, p. 366.
487. A.E. Akyazan, *Türk Hukukunda Tanıkların Korunması,* Ankara: Afşaroğlu Matbaası, 2010.
488. N. Kunter, F. Yenisey & A. Nuhoğlu, *Muhakeme Hukuku Dalı Olarak Ceza Muhakemesi Hukuku,* 18. Bası, İstanbul, Beta, 2010, 1397; N. Gürelli, *Türk Ceza Muhakemesi Hukukunda Bilirkişilik,* İstanbul, İstanbul Üniversitesi, 1967, p. 95.
489. N. Gürelli, *Ceza Muhakemesinde Bilirkişilik Kurumuna İlişkin Meseleler* (İstanbul: Doğanay Armağanı, İstanbul Üniversitesi, 1982), p. 65; S. Dönmezer, *Mecburi Ehlihibre*, IHFM. X, 1–2, p. 415.
490. Ö. Tosun, *Ceza ve Medeni Muhakeme Hukuku Açısından Hukuka Aykırı Yollarla Elde Edilen Delillerin İspat Kuvveti* (İstanbul, 1976), p. 12; H. Bıyıklı, *Ceza Muhakemesi Hukuku ve Kanıtların Toplanmasında Doğruluk Kuralı* (YD 1977/III), 85; F. Erem, *Usul Hiylesi* (YD 1977/III), p. 171; S. Selçuk, *Kanıtların Toplanmasında Yasallık, Dürüstlük ve Total Ceza Adaleti* (YD 1977/3), p. 113.
491. O. Gürakar, *Ses ve Görüntü Kayıtlarının Delil Değeri* (Prof. Dr. Çetin Özek Armağanı, Galatasaray

The current Penal Procedure Code also includes provisions in this respect, but the wording is slightly different: *The court may only use legally obtained evidence while deciding on the guilt* (Article 217/2, CMK). Illegally obtained evidence may not be put forward during the discussions at the main trial (Article 206/2-a CMK), and the court has to dismiss such evidence, furnishing reasoning for the exclusion (Article 230/1-b, CMK). If any illegally obtained evidence has been used to form the judgment, the Court of Cassation will overrule the verdict (Article 289, CMK).

As a result of these regulations, even the slightest breach of a *Law* or an *Act* will result in the exclusion of evidence.[493]

If forbidden interviewing methods (*infra*, paragraph 486) were used, the statement or confession obtained as a result of such methods is excluded by the Code. The consent of the interviewed person does not cure the illegality (Article 148, CMK).

Üniversitesi Yayını, 2004); V. Bıçak, *Improperly Obtained Evidence: A Comparison of Turkish and English Laws* (Ankara: Yardımcı, 1996).

492. B. Öztürk, *Yeni Yargıtay Kararları Işığında Delil Yasakları* (Ankara, 1995); V. Bıçak, *Improperly Obtained Evidence* (Ankara, 1996); S. Kaymaz, *Ceza Muhakemesinde Hukuka Aykırı (Yasak) Deliller* (Ankara, 1997); N. Kunter, F. Yenisey & A. Nuhoğlu, *Muhakeme Hukuku Dalı Olarak Ceza Muhakemesi Hukuku*, 18 (Bası, İstanbul, 2010), p. 1411.

493. E. Şen, *Türk Ceza Yargılaması Hukukunda Hukuka Aykırı Deliller Sorunu* (İstanbul, 1998).

Chapter 2. Powers, Rights and Duties in the Pre-trial Proceedings

§1. The Powers and Duties of the Public Prosecutor and the Police in the Preliminary Inquiry

I. Introductory Remarks

440. The public prosecutor has the duty to investigate crimes (Article 160, CMK). There is an obligation to investigate if the prosecution service obtains information supported by facts. If the results of the investigation show that there is sufficient evidence, he must prosecute (Article 170/2, CMK). However, the 2004 Code of Penal Procedure has introduced for exceptional cases the concept of prosecutorial discretion (Article 171, CMK).[494]

A police officer investigates cases only when the prosecutor has ordered him to do so (Article 161/1, CMK).

The duties and powers of the public prosecutor and the judicial police begin at the same time as the preliminary inquiry, and they end with its closing. When an arrest has been made, however, a judge must decide on the limitation of individual liberty. Although the public prosecutor is in charge during the preliminary investigation, all investigative powers revert to the court when he submits the indictment to the court.

Before the 2004 legislation, police and prosecution powers to investigate offenders caught in the *Act of in Flagrante Delicto* were broader. The current Penal Procedure Code does not include special powers for such crimes.

II. Covert Policing Methods

A. *Interception of Correspondence Through Telecommunication*

1. Listening and Recording of Correspondence and Evaluating the Information about the Signals

441. The Penal Procedure Code includes provisions for interception of correspondence through telecommunication, the use of undercover agents (*infra*, paragraph 447) and surveillance with technical means (*infra*, paragraph 448).[495]

The criminal peace judgeship[496] or, in cases of peril in delay, the public prosecutor, may decide to listen to or record the correspondence through telecommunication or to evaluate the information about the signals of the suspect or the accused,

494. N. Kunter, F. Yenisey & A. Nuhoğlu, *Muhakeme Hukuku Dalı Olarak Ceza Muhakemesi Hukuku,* 18. Bası, İstanbul, Beta, 2010, p. 724.

495. Covert policing methods and operations had been introduced to Turkey in 1999 by Act No. 4422, whereas the repealed Code on Criminal Procedure did not contain any rules on this subject.

496. This provision has been changed several times during the course of the turbulent political investigations and trials in 2013, by Acts No. 2014-6526, No. 2014-6572, and No. 2016-6763. Originally, the criminal peace judgeship was competent for rulings related to the interception of

if during an investigation or prosecution conducted in relation to a crime there are strong grounds of suspicion indicating that a crime, listed in subsection 8 has been committed and there is no other possibility to obtain evidence. The public prosecutor shall submit his decision immediately to the judge for his approval and the judge shall decide within twenty-four hours.[497] In cases where the duration expires or the judge decides the opposite way, the public prosecutor shall lift the measure immediately (Article 135/1, CMK).

No one may listen and record the communication through telecommunication of another person except under the principles and procedures as determined in this article (Article 135/9, CMK).[498]

When requesting the measure, the public prosecutor must prepare a document, or a report, indicating the identity of the owner, or the person who is utilizing this line (Article 135/2, CMK).

The communication of the suspect or the accused with individuals who enjoy the privilege of refraining from testimony, as a witness shall not be recorded. In cases where this circumstance is revealed after the recording has been conducted, the conducted recordings shall be destroyed immediately (Article 135/3, CMK).

The decision that shall be rendered according to the provisions of CMK 135/1 shall include the nature of the charged crime, the identity of the individual, upon whom the measure is going to be applied, the nature of the tool of communication, the number of the telephone, or the code that makes it possible to identify the connection of the communication, the nature of the measure, its extent and its duration. The decision on the measure may be given only for a maximum duration of two months; this period may be extended for one more month. In cases of organized crime, committed within the activities of such organization's extensions totaling up to a maximum three months may be added to the regular periods, not more than one month for each time (Article 135/4, CMK).

---

telecommunication, and the provision had the following wording: *The Judge of the Criminal peace judgeship or, in cases of peril in delay, the public prosecutor, may decide to locate, listen to or record the correspondence through telecommunication or to evaluate the information about the signals of the suspect or the accused, if during an investigation or prosecution conducted in relation to a crime there are strong grounds of suspicion indicating that the crime has been committed and there is no other possibility to obtain evidence.* The 2014-6526 amendment recognized the competence of the court of assizes, and required an unanimious voting by initial ruling and in case of any opposition against the decision, thus making it very difficult to apply this undercover power. The amendment by the Act No. 2014-6572 separated *metering* (*infra*, para. 391) from listening and recording of conversations; metering was under the competence of a single judge, and listening, recording still under the competence of the court of assizes. In 2016, however, by Act No. 6763, listening and recording was given under the authority of the criminal peace judgeship again. Later, during the period of state of emergency administration after the failed coup on Jul. 15, 2016, provisionally the public prosecutor had the power of decision in cases of urgency (Art. 3/1-k, KHK 668, dated Jul. 26, 2016; adopted as a Law by Act No. 2016-6755).

497. During the state of emergency administration in 2016, KHK 668 Art. 3/1-k had extended this period up to five days, and the public prosecutor was the only decision maker. Since the state of emergency is lifted, this regulation no longer applies.

498. N. Meran, *Adli ve Önleme Amaçlı İletişimin Denetlenmesi (Telefon Dinleme, SMS, MMS, e-mail İzleme), Gizli Sorusturmacı, Teknik Takip*, Ankara, Adalet Yayınevi, 2009; F. Yenisey & A. Nuhoğlu, *Ceza Muhakemesi Hukuku*, 3. Baskı, Seçkin, Ankara 2015, p. 438; Cumhur Şahin, *Ceza Muhakemesi Hukuku I*, 9. Bası, Seçkin, Ankara, 2018, p. 363; Y. Ünver & H. Hakeri, *Ceza Muhakemesi Hukuku*, 17. Baskı, Adalet, Ankara 2020, p. 466.

Decisions rendered and interceptions conducted according to the provisions of this Article shall be kept confidential while the measure is pending (Article 135/7, CMK).

The provisions contained in Article 135 CMK related to listening, recording and evaluating the information about the signals are only applicable for certain crimes which are listed[499] in Article 135/8, CMK and for few crimes named in related statutes.[500]

2. Metering

442. The legislator clearly distinguished between listening, recording and evaluating the information about signals (Article 135/1, CMK) and metering (Article 135/6, CMK). First methods of interception of telecommunication constitute a deeper intrusion into the private life. In contrast, metering includes only information about the connections, and is not limited by the list of crimes indicated in Article 135/8, CMK. This measure will be decided by the criminal peace judgeship during the investigation phase and by the court of the first instance during the prosecution phase. In cases of metering, the identity of both parties of the conversation and time, as well as the telephone numbers will be recorded and listed (Article 135/6, CMK).

3. Location of the Mobile Phone and Interception of Communications of a Lawyer

443. The location of a mobile phone may be established in order to be able to apprehend the suspect or the accused for every crime, not limited by the list of crimes indicated in Article 135/8, CMK. The decision of the judge is required. In

499. The listed crimes read as follows: (a) The following crimes in the Turkish Penal Code: (1) Smuggling with migrants and human trafficking (Arts. 79, 80, TCK), (2) Killing with intent (Arts. 81–83, TCK), (3) Torture (Arts. 94–95, TCK), (4) Sexual assault (Art. 102, TCK, except for sub. 1), (5) Sexual abuse of children (Art. 103, TCK), (6) Qualified theft (Art. 142, TCK), theft by using violence (Arts. 148, 149, TCK) and qualified theft by deceptions (Art. 158, TCK), (7) Producing and trading with narcotic or stimulating substances (Art. 188, TCK), (8) Forgery of money (Art. 197, TCK), (9) Forming an organization in order to commit crimes (Art. 220, TCK, except for subss. 2, 7 and 8), (10) Prostitution (Art. 227, TCK), (11) Cheating in bidding (Art. 235, TCK), (12) Unlawful money lending (Art. 241, TCK), (13) Bribery (Art. 252, TCK), (14) Laundering of proceeds stemming from crime (Art. 282, TCK), (15) Disrupting the state's unity and territorial integrity (Art. 302, TCK), (16) Crimes against the constitutional order (Ars. 309, 311, 312, 313, 314, 315, 316, TCK), (17) Crimes against the secrets of the State and spying (Arts. 328, 329, 330, 331, 333, 334, 335, 336, 337, TCK); (b) Smuggling with guns, as defined in Act on Guns and Knives and other Tools, dated Jul. 10, 1953, No. 6136 (Art. 12). (c) The crime of embezzlement as defined in Act on Banks, Art. 22, subsecs. (3) and (4); (d) Crimes as defined in the Combating Smuggling Act, which carry imprisonment as punishment; (e) Crimes as defined in Act on Protection of Cultural and Natural Resources, Arts. 68 and 74.

500. There has been three more groups of crimes added by Act No. 7078 dated Feb. 1, 2018: The crime of illegal planting of hemp, as regulated in Art. 23/5 of Act on Controlling Narcotic Substances, and crimes in Art. 5 of the Act on Regulations Related to Gambling, as well as Art. 228, TCK shall be subject to all kinds of secret investigation methods.

cases of peril in delay, the public prosecutor may give an order. The decision related to this matter shall include the number of the mobile phone and the duration of the interception. The interception shall be conducted for a maximum of two (previously it was three) months; this period may be extended for one month (Article 135/5, CMK).

444. Interception of communications in the office and domicile of a defense attorney. In connection with investigations related to the suspect or the accused, Article 135 shall not be applied for telecommunication devices in the office, dwelling and domicile of a defense counsel (Article 136, CMK).[501]

4. Procedure of Enforcement of Interception of Telecommunications

445. The decision rendered according to Article 135 shall be enforced immediately by the officials of the institutions which provide the telecommunications service, in cases where it is requested in writing by the public prosecutor or by the judicial police official who has been empowered by the public prosecutor to locate, listen to or record the correspondence through telecommunication and to implant the relevant devices; if this request is not fulfilled, the use of force is permitted. The beginning and ending date and time of the interaction and the identity of the individual who is enforcing the decision shall be put in the records (Article 137/1, CMK).

The recordings that are produced according to Article 135/1, CMK shall be decoded by individuals who are being appointed by the public prosecutor and shall be transcribed into written form. Recordings in a foreign language shall be translated by a translator into the Turkish language (Article 137/2, CMK).

In cases where there is a decision rendered about not prosecuting the suspect, or where the judge does not give his approval according to the first subsection of Article 135, the application shall be terminated immediately by the public prosecutor. In such cases, the recordings shall be destroyed within ten days under the supervision of the public prosecutor and this event shall be recorded in the files (Article 137/3, CMK).

In addition, if the interceptions have been destroyed, the office of the public prosecution shall inform the related individual in writing not more than fifteen days after the date of the end of the investigation phase, about the reasons, context, duration and the outcomes of the measure, that the recordings related to locating and listening have been destroyed (Article 137/4, CMK).

446. Coincidental evidence. If a search or seizure reveals a piece of evidence that is not connected to the current investigation or prosecution, but there are reasonable grounds of suspicion that another criminal offense was committed, those items shall be immediately secured and the public prosecutor shall be informed thereof (Article 138/1, CMK).

501. R. Çulha et al., *Ceza Muhakemesinin Soruşturma Evresindeki Süjeler için CMK Cep Kitabı*, Türkiye Barolar Birliği Yayınları, Ankara 2015.

If during the interception of correspondence through telecommunication, a piece of evidence has been obtained that is not related to the ongoing investigation or prosecution, but raises the suspicion that a crime that is listed in Article 135/8 has been committed, this evidence shall be secured and this circumstance shall be immediately notified to the office of the public prosecutor (Article 138/2, CMK).

B. Undercover Investigations

447. As long as it is not a provocation to crime, the Court of Cassation tolerates covert police methods (Article 139, CMK). Pseudo-buying of narcotics (a drug-sting operation), for example, is allowed if the seller has already committed such crimes before. If however, a person would be committing this crime for the first time upon the offer of the undercover agent, such a method is illegal because it amounts to entrapment.[502] In cases where there are strong indications of suspicion based on concrete evidence (included by Act No. 2014-6526) that the crime under investigation has been committed, and if there are no other available means of obtaining evidence, judge, and in cases of peril in delay, the public prosecutor, may decide to empower a public servant to act as an undercover investigator (Article 139/1, CMK).[503]

The identity of the investigator may be changed. He is entitled to engage in legal interactions and transactions with this identity. In cases where it is necessary to produce and maintain the identity, the needed documents may be prepared, altered and used.

The decision related to the appointment of the undercover investigator and other documents should be secured by the related office of the public prosecutor. Even after the end of his mission, the identity of the undercover investigator shall be kept secret.

---

502. F.S. Akıncı, *Polis, Toplumsal Bir Kurum Olarak Gelişmesi*, İstanbul, Polis Alt Kültürü veİnsan Hakları, 1990, p. 168; Since 1999, and even more so since 2005, the Turkish Police have legal tools to combat organized crime. These include wiretapping (Art. 135 CMK; Art. 2, repealed ÇASÖMK) and surveillance (Art. 140, CMK) and the use of undercover agents (Art. 139, CMK). Not included are the criminal investigation of registers and computer data, which was recognized by Art. 4, repealed ÇASÖMK, but was not included in the new CMK. If there are strong indications that assets belonging to individuals who are under suspicion of being involved in organized crime, have also been involved, then many kinds of movable and immovable goods may be seized (Art. 138 CMK).

503. Article 139/1, CMK, as amended by Act No. 2014-6526 recognized the competence of the court of assizes. Decisions according to this Article were delivered unanimously by the court of assizes, and in cases of opposition, the court dealing with the opposition had also to decide unanimously (Art. 139/1, CMK). In 2016 however, by Act No. 6763, undercover investigations were given under the authority of the criminal peace judgeship.

The undercover agent is entitled to conduct every kind of investigation related to the criminal organization, the activities for which he has been appointed, as well as investigations related to crimes committed within the activities of this criminal organization.[504]

The investigator shall not commit a crime while fulfilling his duty. He shall not be held responsible for crimes being committed by the criminal organization, which he has been appointed to investigate.

Personal information obtained through appointing an investigator shall not be used except during the criminal investigation or prosecution for which he has been appointed.

C. Surveillance with Technical Means

448. Decisions on surveillance with technical means shall be delivered by the public prosecutor, whose decision will be submitted to the judge for approval within twenty-four hours, and the judge makes his decision within twenty-four hours.[505] If there are strong indications of suspicion based on concrete evidence that crimes listed[506] in Article 140/1, CMK have been committed, and if there is no other available means of obtaining evidence, the activities of the suspect or the accused, conducted in fields open to the public and the suspect's working places, may be subject to surveillance by technical means, including voice and image recording.

Surveillance with technical means shall be ordered by the judge and in cases where there is peril in delay, by the public prosecutor.[507] The decisions rendered by

504. The provisions of this article shall only be applicable for the following crimes (Art. 139/7, CMK): The crimes of the Turkish Penal Code: Producing and trading with narcotic or stimulating substances (Art. 188, TCK), forming an organization in order to commit crimes (Art. 220, TCK except for subsecs. 2, 7 and 8), forming armed organizations (Art. 314, TCK) or supplying weapons for such organizations (Art. 315, TCK). Smuggling weapons as defined in the Act on Fire Arms and Knives as well as Other Tools (Art. 12). Crimes as defined in the Act on Protection of Cultural and Natural Resources, Arts. 68 and 74.

505. Decisions on surveillance with technical means were delivered unanimously by the court of assizes. In cases of opposition, the court dealing with the opposition also had to decide unanimously (Art. 140/2, CMK). In 2016, however, by Act No. 6763, the power to decide on surveillance with technical means were given under the authority of the public prosecutor, to be approved by the judge.

506. Crimes regulated in the Turkish Penal Code: Smuggling migrants and human trafficking (Arts. 79, 80, TCK), trading with organs and tissues (Art. 91, TCK), killing with intent (Arts. 81, 82, 83, TCK), qualified theft (Art. 142, TCK) and robbery (Arts. 148 and 149, TCK), qualified theft by deception (Art. 158, TCK), trading in narcotics or stimulating substances (Art. 188, TCK), forgery in money (Art. 197, TCK), forming an organization with the aim of committing crimes (Art. 220, subs. 3 TCK), prostitution (Art. 227, TCK) cheating in bidding (Art. 235, TCK), unlawful money lending (Art. 241, TCK), bribery (Art. 252, TCK), laundering of property proceeds stemming from crime (Art. 282, TCK), disrupting the unity and integrity of the state (Art. 302, TCK), offenses against the constitutional order and its functioning (Arts. 309, 311, 312, 313, 314, 315 and 316, TCK) and crimes against the secrets of the state and spying (Arts. 328, 329, 330, 331, 333, 334, 335, 336, 337, TCK). Smuggling weapons as defined in the Act on Fire Arms and Knives as well as Other Tools (Art. 12). Crimes as defined in Combating Smuggling Act that require the punishment of imprisonment. Crimes as defined in the Act on Protection of Cultural and Natural Resources, Arts. 68 and 74.

507. N. Centel & H. Zafer, *Ceza Muhakemesi Hukuku*, 14. Bası, İstanbul, Beta, 2017, p. 454.

the public prosecutor shall be submitted for the approval of the judge within twenty-four hours. The judge delivers his decision, within twenty-four hours. In cases where this time limit has expired or the judge does not approve of public prosecutor's move, registrations made shall be destroyed immediately (Article 140/3, CMK).

The decision related to the surveillances with technical means may be rendered for a maximum of three weeks (*previously it was 4*). This time limit may be extended for one week, if needed. The judge, however, in crimes related to the ones committed within the activities of an organization, is entitled to extend this period several times for not more than one week each, not exceeding an additional four weeks, if needed. The above-mentioned durations shall be doubled if the measures of surveillance by technical means and appointing an undercover investigator are applied simultaneously[508] during an investigation (Article 140/3, CMK).

The evidence obtained shall only be used for investigations or prosecutions of the crimes listed above, and shall not be used outside of this scope; and the evidence shall be immediately destroyed under the supervision of the public prosecutor, if it is not useful for the criminal prosecution (Article 140/4, CMK).

The provisions of this article shall not be applied inside the dwelling of an individual (Article 140/5, CMK).

III. The Powers to Check and Search

A. The Powers to Check

449. There is no special provision in the Code of Penal Procedure that gives the police the power to stop and check people.[509] However, there is a provision in the Police Act (Article 4A, PVSK) that permits the police to stop and ask someone for identification. If the person is without identification or there is suspicion that a false identity is being used, the police have the power to arrest this person until his identity is cleared up or to detain him for twenty-four hours (Article 40, KK).

The power to stop and ask for identification arises when there are reasons to believe that a crime has been committed or that a danger must be averted (administrative or judicial police function) (Article 4A/1, PVSK).

In cases of alleged breach of duty by the police, if they are acting in an administrative capacity, such as regulating traffic on a highway, they are subject to a special procedure (*supra*, paragraph 423) applied to state officials. However, if the police duty was related to a judicial police function, such as arresting a suspect, then the public prosecutor prosecutes them ex officio (Article 161/5, CMK).

---

508. There was a discussion, triggered by the Court of Cassation, ruling that extraordinary investigation techniques should be applied one after the other (first interception of telecommunications, second surveillance with technical means), and if both of them did not produce evidence, only then the appointment of an undercover investigator was permitted. The amendment of KHK 694, dated Aug. 25, 2017, approved by Act No 7078, dated Feb. 1, 2018, stating the extension of the time period, in cases of side-by-side application of secret investigation methods put an end to this discussion.

509. M.B. Eryılmaz, *Türk ve İngiliz Hukukunda ve Uygulamasında Durdurma ve Arama,* Ankara, Seçkin Yayınları, 2003.

B. The Power to Search after Stopping

450. 2015 Amendments by internal security package. The Act 2015–6638 introduced a new legal status for Turkish police law and penal procedure law. A police chief appointed by the governor is now entitled to give orders to conduct a search and to detain a suspect (Article 4A/6, PVSK). After a stop conducted under the provisions of Article 4A, PVSK, police were empowered to search the individual and his belongings, if there are any grounds to believe that the person is carrying weapons or dangerous substances. In such cases the police chief empowered by the governor[510] would issue a written order to search; the power of giving an oral order prior to search in urgent cases has been repealed by the Constitutional Court on May 4, 2017, K. 2017/98.

IV. The Powers of Entry, Search and Seizure

A. The Powers of Entry and Search

451. Protection of privacy and family life. Search and seizure law is closely related to the right to privacy and to family life.[511] Amendments to the Constitution by Act 4709 require a written court order, or in urgent cases a written order of the superior, authorized by an Act (Articles 20 and 21, AY as amended by Act No. 2001-4709). The grounds on which to issue a search warrant are listed in the Constitution.[512] A judge must approve the written order of the superior within twenty-four hours.

Preventive search. Preventive searches are governed by the Police Act (Article 9, PVSK).[513] Before conducting the preventive search the decision of the judge must be obtained; in case of emergency, the superior administrative authority has jurisdiction to give a written order for a preventive search. This does not include the chief of the police; only the governor of a city is entitled to give orders to take such steps.

---

510. *The police chief appointed by governor* is also empowered to issue a detention order in flagrant crimes listed in Art. 91/4 CMK (*infra*, para. 416).

511. S. Aksoy, *Önleme ve Koruma Tedbiri Olarak Arama*, Ankara, Seçkin, 2007; Veli Özer Özbek, *Ceza Muhakemesi Hukukunda Koruma Tedbiri Olarak Arama*, Ankara, Seçkin Yayınevi, 1999.

512. Unless there exists a decision duly given by a judge on one or several of the grounds of national security, public order, prevention of crime, protection of public health and public morals, or protection of the rights and freedoms of others, or unless there exists a written order of an agency authorized by law, in cases where the delay is prejudicial, again on the above-mentioned grounds, neither the person, nor the private papers, nor the belongings of an individual shall be searched nor shall they be seized (Art. 20/2, AY).

513. The governor was entitled to give orders to the police to conduct preventive searches in necessary cases when the public order or rights of individuals were at risk (Art. 9/1, PVSK). Since 1985, the police have had the power to search persons in order to prevent harm to others. According to an amendment to Art. 9 of the Police Act, a highly ranked police official may order a search of the person if there are facts that indicate that danger exists or that violent acts will be committed. However, after the 2001 amendment to Art. 20 of the Constitution by Act No. 4709, the Police Act is restricted. Today, any search without a court order or, in urgent cases, a written order of the provincial governor, is illegal (Art. 9, PVSK).

Preventive searches in military bases have been regulated in 2018 by amendments in several statutes by Act No. 7145.[514]

Searching individuals and their luggage in airports is an exception and is considered a preventive measure necessary to avert danger at airports and borders (Act No. 5442 dated 1949, added Article 2 on August 29, 1996, by Act No. 4178).

Search during an arrest is another exception. The police may conduct a search of the individual for the sake of his or her own protection.[515]

452. Judicial search. When there is reasonable suspicion indicating that the person is carrying or hiding evidence of an offense, or that he has committed a crime, he and his premises may be searched (Article 116, CMK). The 2014–6526 amendment had introduced the term "strong suspicion" based on concrete evidence in February, but soon after, Act No. 2014-6572 went back to the original term "reasonable suspicion" in December.

Consent search is forbidden. Even if an occupant grants permission, the police are not entitled to enter the house and conduct a search. On November 23, 2003, the 10th Chamber of the High Administrative Court held that the individual cannot waive the right to privacy, and consequently consent to a search is not valid.

453. Search conducted in a domicile. Only a court may order entry into a domicile. During the OHAL administration (2016–2018), the public prosecutor was empowered to issue written a search order in urgent cases for terrorism crimes (Article 3/1-d, KHK 668, approved by Act No. 6755 on November 8, 2016). After the end of the emergency administration, this power no longer exists. Entering the domicile of the suspect and conducting a search therein is regulated by two factors: First, to arrest the suspect, and second, to seize evidence (Article 116, CMK). Search at night is exceptional.

The Code provides a limited power of entry to search domiciles of persons who are not under suspicion (Article 117, CMK).

If there are reasonable grounds to believe that the person to be arrested or the evidence to be seized are in the domicile, then the police are entitled to enter, after obtaining a written order of the public prosecutor or judge. In this case, the order of the public prosecutor must be submitted for subsequent approval to the criminal peace judgeship. This limitation does not apply if the suspect is arrested in the domicile of a third party or if he enters it during hot pursuit (Article 118/2, CMK). However, if the offender is caught in the act of committing an offense, the police have a duty to enter the domicile (Articles 13 and 20, PVSK).

The owner or the tenant of the dwelling may be present during the search (Article 120, CMK). During a search conducted in domicile, or working place upon written

---

514. The Act No. 7145, dated Jul. 25, 2018 has been designed to substitute lifted powers of state of emergency administration, and has inserted into Military Internal Service Law (1961-211) new Art. 56A and 56B, which regulate preventive searches in and control of all individuals who enter military bases. Same powers have been recognized for coast guard personnel (Additional Art. 7 to the Act No. 2692) and gendermarie (added Art. 15A to Act No. 2803).

515. If offenders were caught in the act, the repealed Code No. 3005 allowed the police to carry out searches. This power to search during arrest is now regulated at the Search Regulations for the Police (Art. 6/3, *Arama Yönetmeliği*).

decision of the judge, the public prosecutor must be personally present at the location of search; if the presence of the public prosecutor is not possible, there must be two witnesses from the neighborhood (Article 119/4, CMK). In cases where this provision is violated, the Court of Cassation considers that products of such searches are illegally obtained evidence (Article 217/2, CMK). Provisionally, during the OHAL administration (2016–2018), if the public prosecutor was not present, it was sufficient to have just one witness (Article 3/1-e, KHK 668, approved by Act No. 6755 on November 8, 2016).

The police shall not inspect documents or the papers of the person subject to search; it is the public prosecutor and judge's authority to inspect. A complete book-list of the items put under protection shall be made, and the possessor of the papers may use his own signature. Before the inspection of papers by the public prosecutor or the judge, the possessor or his agent, or his representative or his defense council shall be summoned to be present at that time; in case they fail to appear, the inspection shall be implemented (Article 122/2, CMK). Provisionally, during the OHAL administration (2016–2018) judicial police agents were empowered to inspect documents belonging to the person subject to a search related to terrorism crimes (Article 3/1-g, KHK 668, approved by Act No. 6755 on November 8, 2016). After the end of the emergency administration this power no longer exists.

Search conducted in public buildings. Formerly, universities were considered immune from police entry. In 1973, however, there was an amendment to the Police Act that gave the police the right to enter university buildings if there was a report of crimes being committed there (Article 20, PVSK).

The power to enter public buildings and search therein is larger. However, at night this power is limited. There is an exception to the rule only if the offender is caught in the act, or if entry is necessary to recapture an escaped arrestee or prisoner (Article 118/2, CMK).

Reporting a search. A written report is to be made upon entry into a domicile or other premises. The report should provide the place and time of the entry if seizure was made and a detailed description of the seized items (Article 121, CMK).

B. Obtaining Scientific Evidence by Search of Computers

454. Search of computers, computer programs and transcripts, copying and provisional seizure. Upon the request of the public prosecutor during an investigation with respect to a crime, the judge (and in urgent cases the public prosecutor since the 2018–7145 Act) shall issue a decision authorizing the search of computers and computer programs and records used by the suspect, the copying, analyzing, and making transcripts of those records if it is not possible to obtain the evidence by other means, and if strong suspicion based on concrete evidence is existing (Article 134/1, CMK).

Provisionally, during the OHAL administration (2016–2018), the public prosecutor was empowered to issue a written order for computer search and seizure in urgent circumstances, only valid for terrorism crimes; his decision was subject to the approval of the judge within five days, and the judge makes his ruling within ten days. If the judge did not approve or make his decision within the required time, the seizure would be lifted. Seizure was also permitted, if the copying procedure lasts for a long time (Article 3/1-j, KHK 668, approved as a Law by Act No. 6755, dated November 8, 2017). After the end of the emergency administration, this power no longer exists.

Article 16 of the Act No. 7145, dated July 25, 2018, designed to substitute lifted powers of OHAL administration, incorporated the above-mentioned power of the public prosecutor into the Penal Procedure Code with some alterations. Previously, only the judge was competent for issuing a computer search order; now the public prosecutor is also empowered in urgent circumstances, to be submitted for approval to the judge within twenty-four hours, and the judge makes his decision in twenty-four hours. In cases where the time limits are exhausted, or the judge does not approve the public prosecutor's move, copies of computer programs and transcripts of their contents shall be destroyed immediately.

If computers, computer programs and computer records are inaccessible, as the passwords are not known, or if the hidden information is unreachable, or the copying procedure takes a long time (added clause by Act No. 2018-7145), then the computer and the equipment that are deemed necessary may be provisionally seized in order to retrieve and to make the necessary copies. Seized devices shall be returned without delay in cases where the password has been determined and the necessary copies are produced. However, the suspect is not obliged to give his password to the investigating authorities; he has to right to remain silent.

While enforcing the seizure of computers or computer records, all data included in the system shall be copied. A copy of this copied data (according to subsection 3) shall be produced and be given to the suspect; this exchange shall be recorded and signed (Article 134/4, CMK).

It is also permissible to produce a copy of the entire data or some of the data included in the system, without seizing the computer or the computer records. Copied data shall be printed on paper and this situation shall be recorded and signed by the related persons (Article 134/4, CMK).

C. The Powers of Seizure

455. Seizure of movable goods. Two kinds of goods may be seized: anything that can serve as evidence, and goods to be confiscated (e.g., weapons that were used in committing the offense, or goods that are prohibited, like illegal drugs). If the possessor consents to giving up such goods, they will be kept in custody. If there is no consent, the state has the power to seize them through use of adequate force (Article 123, CMK).

Some items are exempted from seizure. The state is not empowered to seize goods that are in possession of persons who have the right to withhold information about such goods and testimony according to Articles 45 and 46 of the Code of Penal Procedure (Article 126, CMK). Provisionally, during the OHAL administration (2016–2018), officials were empowered to confiscate letters or documents in possession of such individuals subsequent to a search related to terrorism crimes (Article 3/1-ğ, KHK 668, approved by Act No. 6755 on November 8, 2016). After the end of the emergency administration this power no longer exists.

Communications between defense counsel and client (Article 154, CMK) and printing machines used by the press (Article 30, AY) are also exempt from seizure.[516]

Only a judge, and if there is peril in delay, the public prosecutor (by a written order) is entitled to rule on the seizure of goods (Article 127/1, CMK). During the preliminary investigation, the criminal peace judgeship is entitled to give an order for the seizure of goods. After prosecution has begun (i.e., the approval of indictment according to Article 175, CMK), the trial court decides. If the public prosecutor or police have seized the items without a prior court order, the judicial approval must have been obtained within twenty-four hours (before 2001 it was three days). If the ruling of the judge cannot be obtained within forty-eight hours, the seizure becomes null and void (Articles 20, 21, AY, and Article 127/3, CMK).

456. Seizure of immovable property and on rights and accounts receivables. The items such as immovable goods, transport vehicles of land, sea or air, accounts in banks or in other financial institutions, contents of a rented safe as specified in Article 128/1, CMK, belonging to the suspect or the accused, may be seized in cases where there are strong grounds of suspicion tending to show (based on concrete evidence), that the crime under investigation or prosecution has been committed and that these items have been obtained from this crime which is included in the list in Article, 128/2 CMK. Even in cases where these immovable goods, rights, accounts receivables and other values or belongings are in possession of individuals other than the suspect or the accused, the seizure is permitted.

Prior to the decision on seizure of the specified items, a report must have been obtained from the Banking Supervision Authority (*Bankacılık Düzenleme Kurulu*), the Department for Investigation of Economic Crimes (*Mali Suçları Araştırma Kurulu*), the Treasury Department (*Hazine Müsteşarlığı*) or the Public Accounts Audit Standards Department (*Kamu Gözetimi, Muhasebe ve Denetim Standartları Kurumu*) that such property has been acquired by committing a crime. This report shall be prepared within three months; if special circumstances necessitate so, this time period may be extended, upon request for two more months (Article 128/1, sentence 3, CMK).

The decision on seizure according to Article 128, CMK shall be rendered only by the criminal peace judge (Article 128/9, CMK).[517] This means that the public prosecutor is not empowered to seize immovable goods. Provisionally, during the OHAL administration (2016–2018) the public prosecutor was empowered to seize immovable goods in urgent cases in investigations related to terrorism crimes. The move of the public prosecutor was subject to the approval of the judge. In such investigations, a report from the related authority, identifying the relations to a

516. A. Gökçen, M. Balcı, M.E. Alşahin, K. Çakır, *Ceza Muhakemesi Hukuku- I,* 2. Baskı, Adalet Yayınevi, Ankara 2017, p. 270.

517. Unanimous decision by the court of assizes, and in case of opposition, unanimous decision of the examining court had been introduced by Act No. 2014-6526 after the political tented investigations at that time. Such exceptional regulations had been introduced in all other secret investigation methods as well, and all have been abolished in 2016 by Act No. 6763.

crime was not required (Article 3/1-ı, KHK 668, approved by Act No. 6755 on November 8, 2016). After the end of the emergency administration this power no longer exists.

A decision on the seizure of an immovable shall be enforced by placing a note in the title (Article 128/3, CMK).[518] A decision on the seizure of vehicles operating on land, sea and air shall be enforced by placing a note in the title, where they are registered (Article 128/4, CMK). A decision on the seizure of accounts at banks and other financial institutions shall be enforced by immediately informing the bank or financial institution by means of technical communication. The related decision shall also be notified to the bank or financial institution separately. The interactions at the bank account, aimed to make the decision of seizure ineffective, which are conducted after the decision has been rendered, are void (Article 128/5, CMK).

A decision on the seizure of shares at a firm shall be enforced by notifying the administration of the related firm and the head of the commerce title by means of technical communication immediately. Notice of the related decision shall also be sent to the bank or financial institution separately (Article 128/6, CMK).

A decision on the seizure of rights and accounts receivables shall be enforced by immediately notifying the related real or legal person by means of technical communication. The related decision shall also be notified to the real or legal person separately (Article 128/7, CMK).

In cases where there are violations of the requirements set forth in the decision on seizure, Article 289 of the TCK on the *misusing of the power of protection* shall apply (Article 128/8, CMK).

A procurator may be appointed in order to govern the seized immovable property, if needed (Article 128/10, CMK; added by KHK 674, approved by Act No. 6758). This appointment shall be ordered only by a judge (Article 128/9, CMK).

---

518. Crimes listed in Art. 128/2, CMK are as follows: (a) The following crimes as defined in the Turkish Penal Code: (1) Genocide and crimes against humanity (Arts. 76, 77, 78, TCK), (2) Smuggling migrants and human trading (Arts. 79, 80, TCK) and Trading with organs and tissues (Art. 91, TCK), (3) Theft (Arts. 141, 142, TCK), (4) Aggravated theft (Arts. 148, 149, TCK), (5) Breach of trust (Art. 155, TCK), (6) Forgery (Arts. 157, 158, TCK), (7) Fraudulent bankruptcy (Art. 161, TCK), (8) Producing and trading of narcotic or stimulating substances (Art. 188, TCK), (9) Forgery of money (Art. 197, TCK), (10) Forming an organization in order to commit crimes (Art. 220, TCK), (11) Forgery in public bids (Art. 236, TCK), (12) Forgery in fulfilling of obligations (Art. 236, TCK), (13) Unlawful money lending (Art. 241, TCK), (14) Embezzlement (Art. 247, TCK), (15) Extortion (Art. 250, TCK), (16) Bribery (Art. 252, TCK), (17) Crimes against state security (Arts. 302, 303, 304, 305, 306, 307, 308, TCK), (18) Crimes against the constitutional order and its functioning (Arts. 309, 311, 312, 313, 314, 315, 316, TCK), (19) Crimes against state secrets and spying (Arts. 328, 329, 330, 331, 333, 334, 335, 336, 337, TCK); (b) Smuggling weapons as defined in the *Act on Firearms and Knives as well as Other Tools* (Art. 12); (c) Embezzlement as defined in the Banking Act (Art. 22/3 and 4); (d) Crimes as defined in the Combating Smuggling Act that carry imprisonment as punishment; (e) Crimes as defined in Arts. 68 and 74 of the Act on Protection of Cultural and Natural Resources.

V. The Powers of Arrest

457. An arrest deprives the suspect of his personal freedom when he is caught red-handed.[519] It can be made without a written order of a court.[520] Turkish law sharply distinguishes between arrest (*yakalama*) (Article 90, CMK), police custody (*gözaltı*) (Article 91, CMK) and pre-trial detention (*tutuklama*) (Article 100, CMK). Pre-trial detention always requires a written order of a magistrate.[521]

458. Regular arrest. The powers of arrest are regulated by Article 90, CMK, which contains detailed provisions. Any citizen may arrest an offender during the commission of the crime, or during hot pursuit, if in the meantime the offender might escape or not be identifiable (Article 90/1, CMK). The police have a broader power and the duty of arrest at flagrant crimes, and in cases where the requirements of issuing of a pre-trial detention order exists, but if there is no time for applying to the judge (Article 90/2, CMK). Additionally, if the public prosecutor had issued an arrest order *(yakalama emri),* which was provisionally applicable during the OHAL administration (2016–2018) for terrorism related crimes, the police were also empowered to arrest suspects (Article 3/1-a KHK 668, approved by Act No. 6755 on November 8, 2016).

The public prosecutor shall be immediately informed about the arrest, and the police shall act upon the orders of the public prosecutor (Article 90/5, CMK).

Prosecutor's order for police custody. The public prosecutor may issue an order for police custody, if there is *concrete evidence that indicates the suspicion of the committed crime* (Article 91/2, CMK).

Duration of police custody in ordinary crimes. If the arrest is related to a crime while the offender was committing it, the arrested person will be brought to a criminal peace judgeship within twenty-four hours for interrogation. He will be immediately taken to the appropriate court if a prosecution has already been instituted. The time necessary to bring him before the judge is not included in the twenty-four-hour requirement, but it may not exceed twelve hours (Article 91/1 CMK).

Turkish Law has a special regulation for collectively committed crimes: the twenty-four-hour period of deprivation of liberty for crimes committed by three or more persons may be prolonged up to four days by a written order of the public prosecutor, if the collection of evidence becomes difficult. However, in collective crimes, the prolongation shall be given one day each time and the total duration may not exceed four days altogether (Article 91/3, CMK).

The police must inform the suspect of his rights during the arrest, and if he requests so, he has the right to have his counsel present during the interrogation

---

519. M.B. Eryılmaz, *Arrest and Detention Powers in Turkish and English Law and Practice in the Light of the European Convention on Human Rights* (Boston: Martinus Nijhoff Publishing, 1999). A. Karagülmez, *Tutuklama Nedenleri ve Tutuklama İsteminin Reddi Kararına İtiraz Konusunda 5271 Sayılı CMK'nın İncelenmesi*, Türkiye Barolar Birliği Dergisi, sayı 58 sayfa 120, Mayıs, Haziran 2005; I. Şahbaz, *Avrupa İnsan Hakları Sözleşmesinde Kişi Özgürlüğü ve Güvenliği*, Türkiye Barolar Birliği Dergisi, sayı 58 sayfa 163, Mayıs & Haziran 2005.
520. N. Centel, *Ceza Muhakemesi Hukukunda Tutuklama ve Yakalama* (İstanbul: Beta, 1992), p. 17; O. Apaydın, *Kişi Güvenliğine İlişkin Sorunlar, Habeas Corpus*, İBD (1980/54): p. 12.
521. N. Centel & H. Zafer, *Ceza Muhakemesi Hukuku*, 14. Bası, İstanbul, Beta, 2017, p. 374.

(Article 150/1, CMK). For children and for suspects of crimes carrying imprisonment at the lower level of more than five years, there is an obligation to appoint a lawyer if the suspect does not already have one (Article 150/2 and 150/3, CMK).[522]

Arraignment before the judge. The criminal peace judgeship interrogates and may release the arrested person if he or she determines that pre-trial detention was not necessary or if the reasons for arrest no longer exist. There is a requirement that an appointed defense lawyer be present during this interrogation (Article 91/6, CMK).

459. Administrative police custody for crimes committed during social disturbances and arrest of terrorism suspects. The internal security package (Act No. 2015-6638) extended police powers for preservation of the public order (a). Police powers related to police custody, which are still applicable, have been extended in the period of the OHAL administration by Act No. 2016-2018 in governmental decrees (KHK), and in 2018, the Act 5175 made new regulations for terrorism related police custody, to be explained below (b).

(a) Police arrest during social disturbances. For preservation of the public order, the police chief appointed by the governor may issue a detention order in flagrant crimes listed in Article 91/4, CMK as amended by Act No. 6638. For crimes committed during social disturbances where violent acts, capable of disturbing public order have broadened, police custody is up to forty-eight hours; it applies for collectively committed crimes.

When the reason for taking into custody no longer exists, or immediately after the proceedings are completed, and in any case at the end of the twenty-four or respectively forty-eight hours period, the public prosecutor shall be informed about the arrest. Afterwards the police shall act in accordance with the orders of the public prosecutor.

If the individual is not released, proceeding shall be done according to provisions of first three paragraphs of Article 91, CMK.

---

522. The judgment for *Salduz v. Turkey*, of the Grand Chamber of the ECtHR announced on Nov. 27, 2008, is an important change in its case law with regards to interrogation during police custody entailing violations of the right to a fair trial because of inadequate pre-trial legal assistance. Articles 135, 136 and 138 of the former Code of Penal Procedure related to legal assistance were not applicable to persons accused of offenses falling within the jurisdiction of the former State Security Courts. Such restrictions on the right of access to a lawyer in proceedings before the former State Security Courts were lifted on Jul. 15, 2003 (Law No. 4928). Thus, the violations found against Turkey in *Salduz* are based on legal statutes that no longer exists. The basic outcome of *Salduz* case law is however, that the current Turkish law follows the Convention: Arts. 149 and 150 of the new Code of Penal Procedure provide that all detained persons have the right of access to a lawyer from the moment they are taken into police custody. The ECtHR on Feb. 23, 2010, ruled in *Yoldaş v. Turkey*, that there had been no violation of the applicant's right to a fair trial, since the applicant had in fact been entitled to legal assistance during police custody. The court found that the applicant had been adequately informed of his right to legal assistance and that he himself had declined to effectuate this right. Turkish law now complies with treaty obligations in this regard. In that regard the circular (*Genelge*) No. 24 of the Turkish Minister of Justice of Jan. 1, 2006, calls for care and diligence in the effectuation of the rights provided by Turkish law in this regard (Pınar Ölçer, *New Rules Regarding the Pre-Trial Right to Assistance in Article 6 ECHR: Salduz v. Turkey and 72 Further Decisions*, in *Criminal Law in the Global Risk Society*, ed. Feridun Yenisey, Ulrich Sieber (Series of the Max Planck Institute for Foreign and International Criminal Law and Bahçeşehir University Joint Research Group, Volume T 1, Istanbul 2011), p. 374).

The crimes enlisted in Article 91/4, CMK reads as follows: (a) Crimes that involve violence and ferocity which take place during social conflicts; (b) Following crimes regulated in the TCK, dated 26/9/2004, No. 4237: (1) Killing with intent (Articles 81, 82), negligent killing (Article 85), (2) Intended wounding (Articles 86, 87), (3) Sexual assault (Article 102), (4) Sexual abuse of children (Article 103) (5) Theft (Articles 141, 142), (6) Aggravated theft (Articles 148, 149), (7) Producing and trading with narcotic or stimulating substances (Article 188), (8) Violating the precautions relating to epidemics (Article 195), (9) Prostitution (Article 227), (10) Cruelty (Article 232); (c) Crimes listed in the Anti-Terrorism Act; (d) The crimes that are counted in Article 33/1-a of the Meetings and Demonstrations Act, dated 6/10/1983, No. 2911; (e) Violating the curfew order given according to the Provincial Administration Act, dated 10/06/1949. No. 5442; (f) Crimes that are counted in Article 3 of the Prevention of Smuggling Act, dated 21/3/2007, No. 5607.

(b) Terrorism related police arrest during the OHAL administration and regulations by Act No. 7145. During the OHAL administration in 2016–2018, duration of police custody was extended up to thirty days plus the time needed for arraignment for terrorism crimes, and for the duration of the OHAL administration (Article 6/1-a, KHK 667, dated July 23, 2016, approved by Act No. 6749, dated October 18, 2016). Since police custody of thirty days was too long to be justified according to the influence of the ECHR case law, Article 10, KHK 684, dated January 23, 2017 (approved by Act No. 7074 on February 1, 2017) reduced this period to seven days with an extension of another seven days by the public prosecutor.

Right after the OHAL administration was lifted in July 2018, Article 13 of the Act No. 7145, dated July 25, 2018 made provisional regulations regarding the duration of police custody, the interrogation of the suspect by the police and the inspection of pre-trial detention decisions (*infra*, paragraph 460) in terrorism crimes, by adding a provisional Article No. 19 to the Anti-Terrorism Act No. 3713, which will be in force for three years.

According to this amendment, police custody shall not exceed forty-eight hours (and in collectively committed crimes, the custody is for four days) from the moment of the arrest; time required for the arraignment to the nearest judge or court is not included to this time (Provisional Article 19/1-a, sentence 1, TMK).

Furthermore, there is an interesting regulation allowing for the extension of the police custody: In cases where the collection of evidence poses difficulties, or where the investigation is comprehensive, the public prosecutor shall ask for an extension. The judge shall inspect this request by interviewing the arrested suspect personally, and shall give a decision to extend the police custody, limited with forty-eight hours or four days respectively. As the extension may be repeated maximum twice, police custody may last for six days, or twelve days in collectively committed crimes, but with a judge's decision (Provisional Article 19/1-a, sentence 2, TMK). The same procedure is also applicable for suspects arrested upon an arrest order of the public prosecutor (Provisional Article 19/1-a, sentence 3, TMK).

This provisional regulation for terrorism crimes about the extension of police custody seems to bring more safeguards to suspect's rights, but incorporates some practical problems such as the role of the defense lawyer, where to keep the arrested suspect (in jail or under police custody), what to do, if the submissions made by the suspect during the interview by the judge contradict the submissions during the questioning by the judge during arraignment for a pre-trial decision and if this new provision is colliding with the Article 91/5, CMK application to the criminal peace judgeship, to be explained below.

460. Application to the criminal peace judgeship. There is a legal remedy against the arrest, physically conducted by the police and against the written order from the public prosecutor relating to the prolongation of the arrest period (Article 91/5, CMK): the arrested person or his lawyer, his legal representative, his first- or second-degree relatives or his spouse have the right to demand a decision from the criminal peace judgeship or on the legality of the arrest as such.

The criminal peace judgeship shall review the file and shall give his decision immediately or, at the latest, within twenty-four hours. He may reject the application if he considers the arrest or prolongation period to be justified, or he may order that the arrested person be brought to the public prosecutor together with the documents relating to his investigation (Article 91/5, CMK).

If the arrest (or the pre-trial detention) was unconstitutional, the arrested individual may claim damages under Article 141, CMK (*infra* paragraph 474).

461. Prohibition of repeated arrest. If the arrested person is to be released because the time limit on the arrest has run out or because the criminal peace judgeship has ordered his release, the same person may not be arrested for the same actions again, unless there is new and sufficient evidence against him. To arrest the suspect again, the public prosecutor must provide a written order (Article 91/6, CMK).

VI. Miscellaneous

A. The Police Powers at the Scene of the Offense

462. Crime scene investigations. The 2007 amendment by Act No. 5681 regulated judicial powers of the police, obligating the police to be active after a crime has been notified directly to the police, and taking all measures necessary in order to protect evidence at the crime scene, but wait for instructions of the public prosecutor for investigation. The police are not entitled to investigate the crime unless there is an order given by the public prosecutor (Additional Article 6/1-8, PVSK).

B. The Power to Call in Experts

463. Samples obtained from the crime scene shall be evaluated in crime labs of the police and gendarme and security forces without calling in experts. The court may appoint an expert in cases related to technical knowledge. Additionally, the public prosecutor, the intervening party, and the accused may ask an expert to produce a scientific opinion about the issue which is the subject matter of the adjudication to be used to evaluate the written opinion of the court-appointed expert (Article 67/6, CMK).

§2. Powers, Rights and Duties Within the Framework of the Pre-trial Detention

I. Introductory Remarks

464. Detention of a suspect in the course of preparatory inquiry constitutes a major restriction on liberty rights. Therefore, the appropriate application of provisions of pre-trial detention is very important both for conducting an effective crime investigation, and protecting the human rights of a suspect. There shall be no arrest warrant rendered if arrest is not proportionate to the importance of the case, expected punishment or security measure (Article 100/1, CMK). The incarceration of the suspect shall only be decided by the judge, if an alternative measure of judicial control (*infra,* paragraph 479) would not be sufficient in a given case, and he has to explain these legal and factual grounds in his pre-trial detention warrant (Article 101/1, CMK).

II. The Warrants of Attachment and of Arrest

A. The Warrants of Attachment

465. The suspect, the victim or the witness must be present in person during an interview by the judge, the prosecutor or the police. In the event the person invited does not appear and does not give testimony as requested, the court can issue a formal summons known as a warrant of attachment, which is to be served on the non-appearing person.

Furthermore, the judge has the power to issue a warrant of attachment a*gainst a suspect or accused*, if there are sufficient reasons to issue a warrant of pre-trial detention (Article 146/1, CMK). In addition, the public prosecutor may issue a written order to the police to bring the arrested person or the accused together with relevant documents, to the office of public prosecutor (Article 146/5, CMK).

B. Warrant of Pre-trial Arrest

466. The liberty of a suspect may only be restricted upon a warrant of pre-trial detention issued by a judge.[523] There is no mandatory detention in Turkish Law, and the public prosecutor has no authority to issue a decision about the pre-trial detention of the suspect or accused.

523. F. Yenisey, *Vorlaeufige Festnahme und Untersuchungshaft im türkischen Strafrecht*, Report submitted to the Symposium held Sep. 24–28, 1990, in Poland: Human Rights and Pre-Trial Detention, in F. Dünkel & J. Vagg, Untersuchungshaft und Untersuchungshaftvollzug, *Waiting for Trial, Freiburg i.Br.* (1994): pp. 729–748; 1. N. Centel & H. Zafer, *Ceza Muhakemesi Hukuku*, 14. Bası, İstanbul, Beta, 2017, 379; F. Gölcüklü, *Ceza Davasında Şahıs Hürriyeti*, Ankara, 1958, p. 27; A.K. Yıldız, *Ceza Muhakemesi Hukukunda Tutuklama ve Adli Kontrol,* in *Criminal Law in the Global Risk Society,* ed. Feridun Yenisey, Ulrich Sieber, Series of the Max Planck Institute for Foreign and International Criminal Law and Bahçeşehir University Joint Research Group, Volume T 1, İstanbul

The criminal peace judgeship during the preliminary investigation (Article 94, CMK) or the court of competent jurisdiction during the trial stage (Article 101, CMK) is entitled to issue a warrant of pre-trial detention if there is concrete evidence that shows the existence of a strong suspicion of a crime (Article 100/1, CMK) and sufficient facts indicating that he will escape,[524] or facts regarding prior behavior sufficient to conclude that he will try to destroy evidence, influence witnesses to give false testimony, or unjustifiably influence or bribe experts (Article 100/2, CMK).[525]

However, in crimes listed[526] in Article 100/3, CMK, the Code allows the judge to issue a warrant of pre-trial detention on a strong suspicion of guilt and presumption that the other requirements are self-evident. This is only possible if the investigated crime is one of the crimes as listed in the Code. This method of listing only very severe crimes in this provision aimed to reduce the incarceration rates. However, the application of this *catalogue crimes* went the other direction and in cases of a suspicion of such a crime, judges started to rule only on the strong suspicion without considering the danger of fleeing or obscuring evidence.

As regards to the *Demirel v. Turkey*[527] group of cases, the committee welcomed the efforts made by the Turkish authorities in the context of the third and fourth

---

2011, p. 631; V. Gültaş, *5271 sayılı Ceza Muhakemesi Kanununun Işığı Altında Tutuklama*, 2006.

524. This legal obligation foreseen by the Code is not being fulfilled in general by judges while deciding the pre-trial arrest. As explained by many judges, the reason for this neglect is preserving impartiality. If a judge writes detailed motives of his pre-trial decision, furnished with accompanying facts, they fear they will be rejected as a judge who has formed an opinion against the suspect, if they act in the trial as well. However, we do not agree with this explanation, as it is a constitutional provision that all decisions of the judiciary must be furnished with motives based on facts (Art. 141/3 AY).

525. M. Albayrak, *Tutuklu ve Hükümlü El Kitabı*, Ankara, Adalet Yayınevi, 2007; V. Gültaş, *5271 Sayılı Ceza Muhakemesi Kanununun Işığı Altına Tutuklama ve Kanun Yolları* (2008). A.S. Sürücü, *İnsan Hakları Avrupa Mahkemesi Kararlarında ve Türkiye'de Tutuklama* (2010), N. Centel, *Ceza Muhakemesi Hukukunda Tutuklama ve Yakalama*, İstanbul, Beta, 1992, p. 38.

526. For the below-mentioned crimes, if strong grounds for suspicion are present, "the ground for arrest" may be deemed as existing: (a) The following crimes as defined in the Turkish Penal Code: (1) Genocide and crimes against humanity (Arts. 76, 77, 78, TCK), (2) Intentional killing (Arts. 81, 82, 83, TCK), (3) Intentional wounding committed with a gun (Art. 86/3-e, TCK) and intentional wounding which has been aggravated by its result Art. 87, TCK) (4) Torture (Arts. 94, 95, TCK), (5) Sexual assault (Art. 102, except for subs. 1, TCK), (6) Sexual abuse of children (Art. 103, TCK), (7) Theft (Arts. 141,142, TCK), and aggravated theft (Arts. 148,149, TCK) (8) Producing and trading in narcotic or stimulating substances (Art. 188, TCK), (9) Forming an organization in order to commit crimes (Art. 220, except for subss. 2, 7 and 8, TCK), (10) Crimes against the security of the state (Arts. 302, 303, 304, 307, 308, TCK), (11) Crimes against the Constitutional order and crimes against the functioning of this system (Arts. 309, 310, 311, 312, 313, 314, 315, TCK), (b) Smuggling weapons, as defined in Act on Guns and Knifes and other Tools, dated 10.7.1953, No. 6136, (Art. 12), (c) The crime of embezzlement as defined in Act on Banks, dated 18.6.1999, No. 4389, Art. 22, subss. (3) and (4). (d) Crimes as defined in Combating Smuggling Act, dated 10.7.2003, No. 4926, and carry imprisonment as punishment. (e) Crimes as defined in Act on Protection of Cultural and Natural Substances, dated 21.7.1983, No. 2863, Arts. 68 and 74. (f) Crime of intentionally starting a fire in forests, as defined in Act on Forests, dated 31.8.1956, No. 6831, Art. 110, subss. 4 and 5. (g) Crimes listed in Art. 33 of the Act on Meetings and Demonstrations dated 6/10/1983, and number 2911. (h) Crimes listed in Art. 7 of the Anti-Terror Act dated 12/4/1991 and number 3713.

527. ECtHR, Application No. 18623/03. The applicant complained of the length of the criminal proceedings brought against him. With regard to the systemic situation which it has identified, the court

Reform Packages to align Turkish legislation and practice with the Convention requirements, noted with satisfaction statistical information demonstrating that there is a significant decrease in the period of detention on remand and an increase in the use of preventive measures as an alternative to detention, and invited the Turkish authorities to continue providing information on the developments in judicial practice. Unfortunately, after the failed coup in July 15, 2016, during the application of the OHAL administration, the number of detainees increased and the quality of pre-trial detention decisions dropped.

467. Limitations of pre-trial detention order. Pre-trial arrest regulations and application of the pre-trial detention in Turkey have been one of the major legal disputes in the last few years.[528] In order to reduce the number of incarcerations, the minimum length of imprisonment punishment that carries a pre-trial detention was extended to up to two years again in 2012 (Article 100/4, CMK). According to a recent amendment, if a crime carries only a criminal fine, or imprisonment term up to two years, pre-trial detention shall not be applied except crimes committed against badly integrity (Article 100/4, CMK).

There is another exception to the limitation of pre-trial detention for crimes committed against medical personnel in hospitals to address the problem of physical assaults mainly against doctors in emergency services. The additional Article 12 to the Act About Medical Services No. 3359, added in 2014 by Act No. 6514 exempts intentional injury of medical personnel from the rule in Article 100/4 CMK.

Children under the age of 15 may not be arrested for crimes carrying imprisonment up to five years at the upper level (Article 21, ÇKK).[529]

468. Rights of the detained suspect. The requirement of proportionality of the pre-trial detention to the probable punishment is one of requirements of pre-trial arrest: In cases where the pre-trial-arrest is not proportional to the punishment or security measure, the judge may not render a decision in this respect (Article 100/1, sentence 2, CMK).

Before the criminal peace judgeship issues a warrant for pre-trial detention, the defense attorney may consult the file (under the restrictions of Article 153/2, CMK; *supra*, paragraph 419)[530] and the criminal peace judgeship has to interview the suspect, who must be present. A pre-trial detention warrant *in absentia* has been excluded by the current Code.

---

is of the opinion that general measures at national level must be taken in the execution of the present judgment in order to ensure the effective protection of the right to liberty and security.

528. Before and during the 2011, and later in 2018 elections, some candidates in custody were elected as members of Parliament, but the courts did not release them. Additionally, there was a political crisis between Turkey and the United States of America because of the incarceration of a pastor charged with espionage and some terrorism crimes. Therefore, there are ongoing discussions to reform the regulations related to the pre-trial detention.

529. According to the repealed Penal Procedure Code, crimes involving punishment up to six months imprisonment was prohibited in this age group. However, if the crime provoked public anger or if the accused had no domicile or no home or could not identify himself, he was arrested and placed in pre-trial detention (Art. 104/3, repealed CMUK).

530. M.R. Erdem, *AİHM Kararları Işığında Tutuklu Sanık Bakımından Hazırlık Soruşturması Dosyasını İnceleme Hakkı*, Dokuz Eylül Hukuk Fakültesi Dergisi Cilt 6 sayı: 1, sayfa 67.

If the suspect requests it, his counsel may be present during this interview without the need for a prior written power of attorney (Article 150/1, CMK). But even if the suspect did not ask for a lawyer, a mandatory defense lawyer is appointed on his behalf (Article 101/3, CMK).[531] The public prosecutor and the defense lawyer have the right to make arguments before the decision.

As pre-trial detention is a restriction of personal freedom before a final judgment of the trial court about the guilt of the accused, it requires a written decision of a judge, furnished with motives. Detailed motives of most of the decisions have, however, not been satisfactory in the past. For this reason, the legislature made an amendment to Article 101 CMK by Act No. 6352 in 2012. According to this amendment, a judge must clearly write in any decision about pre-trial detention, extension of detention or any decision related to pre-trial detention, facts and related evidence which indicate strong suspicion that the suspect has committed the crime, and reasons of pre-trial arrest, such as likelihood of escape or obscuring of evidence, and that in that particular case, pre-trial detention is in proportion to the gravity of the allegedly committed crime (Article 101/2, CMK).

The police must inform the relatives of the person in detention about the fact that he was placed in police custody (Article 13, PVSK).[532] Before doing so, the police must consult with the public prosecutor (Article 95, CMK). If the accused has been taken before the judge, he can immediately inform his relatives or *any other individual* and talk to them in person, if the judge orders so (Article 107/2, CMK).

469. Arrest order. Since the pre-trial arrest decision in the absence of the suspect has been abolished by the current Penal Procedure Code, there is a substitute decision: the arrest order (Article 98, CMK).[533]

Suspects who have been arrested upon an arrest order, shall be brought in front of the competent judge or court within twenty-four hours at the latest (Article 94/1, CMK). When the suspect has been arrested in another location, in such cases he shall be brought to the nearest justice building, and the competent judge or court shall interrogate the suspect by means of voice and image transfer (Article 94/2, CMK).

531. According to the repealed Code, if the accused was not present, the judge decided upon the request for pre-trial detention submitted by the prosecutor in a closed session, after a review of the report in the absence of the accused (Art. 106, repealed CMUK). In such cases, the public prosecutor issued a warrant of arrest on the decision of pre-trial detention of the magistrate (Art. 131, repealed CMUK) and the police would arrest the accused when executing the court decision. The new Code does not include a court decision in order to arrest the suspect if he is not present. At the moment of arrest, the decision of the judge would be handed to the accused (Art. 106/3, repealed CMUK) and he would be informed that he has the right to contest the court decision (Art. 106/4, repealed CMUK).

532. The exception of danger to the investigation if relatives are informed was abolished in 2002.

533. If the accused had been taken into custody pursuant to the warrant of pre-trial detention of the judge, he was brought immediately, or at the latest, within twenty-four hours, before a competent judge. This judge interviewed him and determined whether to continue the detention (Art. 108/1, repealed CMUK). The time required to bring the accused to the nearest court was not included in this twenty-four-hour period (Art. 108/2, repealed CMUK).

III. The Continuation of Pre-trial Detention

470. (a) Upper time limits of detention. Upper time limits[534] of detention during the preparatory investigation and thereafter differs in Turkey: *The duration of the detention during the investigation* phase shall not exceed six months in cases of courts of general jurisdiction and one year in cases of the court of assizes. This period may be extended in cases of terrorism, organized crime and collectively committed crime (Article 102/4, CMK).

The overall duration of detention, including both the investigation and prosecution phases is one year for crimes outside of the jurisdiction of the court of assizes, but it may be extended for another six months, if necessary (Article 102/1, CMK). In cases where the crime is under the jurisdiction of the court of assizes, the maximum period of detention is two years, but it may be extended up to a maximum of three years; if the crime is committed against the state or is a crime under Anti-Terrorism Law, it may be extended for not more than five additional years (Article 102/2, CMK).[535]

There are also special rules for children: The period of maximum duration of detention shall be reduced by half for children who have not attained 15 years of age, and by four third for children who have not attained 18 years of age (Article 102/5, CMK).

The decision regarding the extension shall be rendered after taking the opinions of the public prosecutor, the suspect or the accused, and of the defense counsel (Article 102/3, CMK).

The above-mentioned time limits start with the moment of the arrest. There is a legal dispute however, about the day when it is terminated: According the "definition of the accused" in Penal Procedure Code, the duration must be calculated until

534. Since 1992, there has been a time limit for pre-trial detention. The maximum period for pre-trial detention was originally six months. According to the repealed legislation, if the official claim had been put forward, the time limit was two years or until the decision of the court (Art. 110/1, repealed CMUK). According to this regulation, the decision of pre-trial detention lost its legal value when the requisite time had run out. However, for crimes carrying penalties of imprisonment of more than seven years or of the death penalty, if the official claim was not put forward or the final judgment was not given within the time limitations, the accused could be further kept in pre-trial detention, or he could be released on bail (Art. 110/2, repealed CMUK).

535. If the crime was under the provision of the Anti-Terrorism Act, it was possible to double this period, up to ten years (repealed Art. 10/5, TMK). The Constitutional Court had abolished this provision related to extension in 2013, and in 2014, Art. 10, TMK was repealed. Stating a maximum duration of the pre-trial arrest in the Penal Procedure Code caused problems for crimes against the state or against the constitutional order of the state. Due to the difficulties in conducting the trial within a reasonable time, the judgments could not be rendered for many years, or in many cases, after the judgment of the court of the first instance has been rendered, the case is still pending at the Court of Cassation for several years because of the heavy caseload of this court. In order not to release dangerous accused, the maximum duration of pre-trial arrest as regulated in Art. 102, CMK, was be applied double for such crimes. For practical reasons, the application of this provision on maximum duration of pre-trial arrest (Art. 102 CMK) had been suspended until Dec. 31, 2010. In beginning of Jan. 2011, the time limitation for pre-trial arrest was in force and some one-hundred very dangerous persons convicted at the trial level and waiting for the decision of the Court of Cassation upon an appeal for more than ten years, have been released under judicial control. In March 2014, however, the limitation on the duration of pre-trial arrest was dropped to maximum five years and more people were released.

the verdict gets final, at the end of appeal procedures (Article 2/1-b, CMK). The Court of Cassation has taken another view and considered the day of the announcement of the judgment at the end of the main hearing as the upper limit of detention. This approach does not include the time spent in jail while the case is pending at the appeal, which usually takes years.

(b) Examination of the continuation of detention. During the preliminary investigation, the continuation of pre-trial detention will be examined every thirty days by the criminal peace judgeship at the request of the public prosecutor (Article 108/1, CMK). During the trial, the court must make this examination during each session on its own initiative (Article 108/3, CMK). This examination is aimed at determining whether the circumstances related to pre-trial detention have changed or not.

During this periodical control of pre-trial detention, the suspect and his defense attorney must be present; the control cannot be conducted on examination of the file (Article 108/1, CMK). The judge must hear the suspect and/or his lawyer when reviewing, on a monthly basis as provided for by the law, whether the conditions for continued detention are met. Prior to amendment by Act No. 2013–6459, the judge based his decision on the opinion of the prosecutor, of which neither the suspect nor his lawyer was informed. Since the duration of pre-trial detention is usually very long in Turkey due to intervals between the days when trial is conducted, this inspection for determining the continuation of the pre-trial detention in specific cases is very important for the defense. Therefore, the defense frequently asks for such inspection, which is an additional workload for the first instance courts. The legislator tried to welcome the problems of practitioners, and during the OHAL the administration permitted to conduct such inspections *in camera*, in absence of the suspect and his lawyer (Article 6/1-ı, KHK 667; Article 3/1-c, ç, KHK 668).

The Act No. 7145 dated July 25, 2018, introduced a regulation in the Anti-Terrorism Act, as a Provisional Article 19, applicable for three years which reads as follows: "*Motions for opposition to the pre-trial detention orders and motions for release from detention may be examined on case file in absence of the parties. Motions for the release from detention may be ruled on case file together with the examination of continuation of detention the latest within 30 days of duration. The examination of continuation of detention according to Article 108 CMK shall be conducted the latest within 30 days of durations on case file, with 90 days durations however, by listening to the individual or his lawyer; without the requirement of a motion*" (Provisional Article 19, TMK, added by Act No. 7145, dated July 25, 2018).

471. Enforcement of detention. The obligations of pre-trial detainees or unconvicted prisoners were regulated in Penal Procedure Code prior to the 2005 reform. The legislator however regulated the enforcement of pre-trial detention by the Code of Enforcement of Punishments (Articles 111–116, CGIK). The provisions of this Code, which are contained in Articles 9, 16, 21, 22, 26–38, 34–53, 55–62, 66–76,

78–88 (amended by KHK No. 650 in 2011), are applicable to the unconvicted prisoners on remand. The provisions related to convicted prisoners are also applicable for the suspects and accused under the pre-trial detention.[536]

In cases where one of his kin, including a person of the second-degree consanguinity or affinity relationship by marriage, or spouse dies, the unconvict prisoner may be given permission up to two days, travel time excluded, to participate in the funeral ceremony, accompanied by an external security force official.

Permission to leave prison shall be granted during the investigation phase by the public prosecutor who leads the investigation, and during the prosecution phase by the judge or the court in charge of the prosecution if there is no concern with respect of the well-being of the investigation or the prosecution and with respect to security (Article 116/2, CGIK, added paragraph by Act No. 2011-6217; amended by KHK/650 in 2011; regulated in 2013 by Act No. 6492, and amended again by KHK 696 in 2017, approved by Act No. 7079 on February 1, 2018).

IV. The Lifting of the Warrant of Arrest

472. Legal remedies and human rights issues. The decision of the criminal peace judgeship related to the pre-trial decision may be challenged by the way of opposition, and unlawful arrest or unlawful pre-trial arrest may cause compensation (*infra*, paragraph 474).

473. Opposition. The accused person and the public prosecutor may put forward an opposition before a higher court against the judge's order or the court's decisions related to detention or maintenance of pre-trial detention (Article 267, CMK). The

536. Unconvicted prisoners in High Security Closed Penal Enforcement Institutions will be subject to the following limitation: Suspension of execution of imprisonment term because of an illness; entrance and registration into a prison facility; instruction of convicted prisoners and their relatives and concerned; following the rules of security programs and health maintenance; protection of establishments and furniture; keeping the doors closed and preventing contacts; keeping personal goods in rooms and outlying areas; search; the quality and application conditions of disciplinary measures; disciplinary measures except postponement of conditional release; condemnation; depriving from participation of some activities; denying the fee-paid work; hindering or restricting of correspondence or communication tools; secluding; disciplinary measures applicable to child convicted prisoners; disciplinary inquiry; repetition of activities requiring disciplinary measures; enforcement and abolition of disciplinary measures; measures applicable by the directorate; using of compulsory tools; earning rewards; grievance and objection; transfers; transfer depending on disciplinary reason; transfer depending on necessary grounds; transfer depending on disease reason; measures applicable during transfers; the right to meet an attorney-at-law and a notary; participating in cultural and artistic activities; freedom of speech; utilizing the library; rights of utilizing the periodical or transitory publications; rights of communication through phone; utilizing radio, television broadcasting and internet; rights of receiving and sending letters, fax and telegraph messages; right to accept gifts sent from outside at certain dates as mentioned in this Code; freedom of religion and right of conscience; requests of examination and treatment; nutrition of convicted prisoners; determining the improvement regime; number of convicted prisoners and security measures to be taken; educational programs; benefiting from education; examination and treatment; health inspection; forwarding to hospital; disease hindering enforcement; rejection of nutriment and drinks served; visit; visits to foreign inmates; essentials of visits and meetings; gymnastics; library and participating in courses.

decisions rendered on opposition are not subject to further appeal (but may be subject to an extraordinary appeal by way of cassation; *infra*, paragraph 559). However, if the higher court decides to place the accused in pre-trial detention in the opposition, there is a further remedy of opposition (*infra*, paragraph 528) against this decision (Article 271/4, CMK).

The judge or court renders the decision *in camera*, referring the case file, but may ask the opinion of the public prosecutor or of the other party prior rendering a decision in the course of the opposition procedure (Article 270/1, CMK). In cases related to pre-trial arrest decision in connection with Articles 101 and 105 CMK, however, it is mandatory to notify this opinion to the suspect, accused or their defender. Suspect, accused or defender may submit their views within three days (Article 270/2, CMK), The decision related to the opposition and other motions related to release from custody (*supra,* paragraph 470) shall be rendered in adversarial proceedings (in contrast to regular opposition hearings, which are conducted *in camera*).

474. Compensation for illegal investigation measures such as arrest and detention. Unlawful detention may lead to claim for compensation (Article 141 CMK).[537] The state is responsible for compensation, but it may recover the cost from the officer who had conducted the illegal arrest according the rules of a civil claim (Article 19, AY).[538] In cases where a judge or prosecutor causes damages of an arrestee by personal fault, unjust deed or by other forms of responsibility, the claim of damages may only be addressed to the State. The state shall pay damages and shall ask later the individual judge or prosecutor to pay back (Article 141, CMK).

KHK No. 694 in 2017, approved by Act No. 7078 in 2018 incorporated two new subsections to Article 142, CMK, regulating the fee of the lawyer representing the plaintiff in the compensation case, and obliged the state to pay the compensation within thirty days the latest into a bank account of the plaintiff (Article 142/9, 10, CMK).

475. Population of non-convicted prisoners. As of June 10, 2013, detainees constituted around one-fifth of the prison population (as compared with one-half at the end of 2006), the vast majority of those who were detained for up to a year and a very small proportion for more than three years. The number of detainees accused of crimes falling under Article 100/3 of the Penal Procedure Code dropped significantly in the first half of 2013, as compared with both 2011 and 2012. This Article covers the so-called catalogue crimes (*supra*, paragraph 466) which include those tried in the context of high-profile cases. There was a significant decrease in detention-on-remand periods and an increase in the use of preventive measures as an alternative to detention, both overall and for crimes falling under Article 100 of the Penal Procedure Code.

537. S. Baytar, *Koruma Tedbirlerinden Doğan Zararın Karşılanması* (Türkiye Barolar Birliği Dergisi, sayı 61, Kasım, Aralık, 2005).

538. A. Parlar & F. Yıldırım, *Açıklamalı - İçtihatlı Silahlı Çeteler ve Terör Suçları ile Haksız Yakalama ve Tutuklamaya İlişkin Tazminat Davaları* (2001).

As of the date January 4, 2012, there were 246.416 suspects or accused detained in pre-trial detention facilities. As of the date of December 31, 2019 there were 291.546 convicted prisoners (*hükümlü*) and prisoners in remand custody (*tutuklu*).[539]

V. Opposition and Appeal to the Court of Cassation

A. *Opposition Against the Pre-trial Detention Warrant*

476. Procedure of opposition against pre-trial detention. Decisions related to the pre-trial detention may be rendered by the criminal peace judgeship in criminal matters during the investigation phase, and by the competent court in the prosecution phase. As a rule, there is no opposition against the rulings of the court (*infra*, paragraph 528). The statute made an exception for court-ruled detentions: The decisions of the court ordering to the pre-trial detention are subject to opposition (Article 271/4, CMK).

There are other special rules related to the opposition against pre-trial detention decisions: If there is an opposition to a pre-trial detention warrant which is given by the criminal peace judgeship in criminal matters after an opposition, who rejected the first pre-trial detention request cannot be the opposition resort (Article 268/3-b, CMK).

In cases where the legal opinion of the public prosecutor has been obtained according to Articles 101 and 105, CMK, this opinion shall be submitted to the suspect or accused or to his defense attorney. The suspect, accused or his defense attorney may notify their view within three days (Article 270/2, CMK).

B. *Extraordinary Way of Appeal to the Court of Cassation*

477. Rulings of judges and courts which had been finalized without an inspection of the court of regional appeal or the Court of Cassation may be subject to the extraordinary way of "reversal in the interest of justice" (*infra,* paragraph 559). Under the wording of the statute (Article 309, CMK), the final decision of the magistrate in opposition procedure should have been eligible for the way of "reversal in the interest of justice." The Court of Cassation, however does not hear such applications on the basis that the main case is pending. This jurisprudence blocks the way to a higher court. As a consequence, there is no case-law of the Court of Cassation related to the application of pre-trial arrest. In contrast, the Constitutional Court inspects human rights violations in regard of application of pre-trial arrest while the case is pending at the first instance courts.

539. https://data.tuik.gov.tr/Kategori/GetKategori?p=adalet-ve-secim-110&dil=1.

VI. The Need of the Adjustment of the Procedure on the Detention

478. The application of pre-trial arrest in daily life is one of most important issues under discussion in Turkey.[540] Existing regulation in the Penal Procedure Code needs to be adjusted to the protection of human rights in line of decisions of the Constitutional Court, as well as ECtHR and efficient criminal justice system. The procedure of the required oral hearing of rendering a pre-trial detention is not regulated in detail in the Code. As the pre-trial detention restricts the right on liberty, the provisions of the Penal Procedure Code should be adjusted to the needs of such necessities.

VII. An Alternative to the Pre-trial Detention: Judicial Control

A. Judicial Control Measures

479. The Turkish Penal Procedure Code has initiated a legal barrier to the deprivation of liberty through pre-trial arrest in the form of judicial control and security deposit.[541]

In cases where the grounds as regulated in Article 100, CMK are present, which would have resulted in arrest, a decision to put the suspect under judicial control may be rendered, instead of arresting him (Article 109/1, CMK).[542]

Even in cases where the Code prohibits pre-trial arrest, the provisions of judicial control may still be applicable (Article 109/2, CMK).

Judicial control in Article 109, CMK is designed for reducing the number of pre-trial detentions in Turkey,[543] and therefore provides for the possibility for the suspect to remain under controlled liberty, in which case he has to obey some restrictions on his life style imposed by the judge. Judicial control includes one or more obligations imposed on the suspect as stated below (Article 109/3, CMK):

(a) To not travel outside of the country.
(b) To regularly appear in person at places for periods that will be specified by the judge.
(c) To obey the calls of authorities or persons specified by the judge and, if necessary, fulfill the measures of control with respect to professional activities or issues of continuing education.
(d) Not to be able to drive any or some vehicles and, if necessary, to leave his driving license in the office of the registry in return for a receipt.

540. A survey conducted by BAU, MPI and HKS showed that decisions rendered between 2005 and 2013 related to pre-trial detention are not furnished with notice and reasoning as required by law. F. Yenisey & A. Nuhoğlu, *Tutuklama Kurumunun Uygulanması Hakkında Görüşler,* in Bahçeşehir University Law Review Volume 10, pp. 125–126.
541. İ. Yılmaz, *5271 sayılı Ceza Muhakemesi Kanunu'nda Adli Kontrol,* Adalet, Ankara 2016.
542. N. Centel & H. Zafer, *Ceza Muhakemesi Hukuku*, 14. Bası, İstanbul, Beta, 2017, p. 417.
543. Previously, crimes carrying a penalty of more than three years of imprisonment were not included in the scope of judicial control. However, this limitation was abolished; since 2012, judicial control is thus applicable to all sorts of crimes (Art. 109, CMK).

(e) To obey and accept the measures of medical diligence, treatment or examination, including being hospitalized for withdrawal from dependency on narcotics, stimulating or evaporating substances and alcohol.
(f) To deposit an amount of money as a safeguard, which shall be determined by the judge upon the request of the public prosecutor, after taking into account the financial conditions of the suspect, and whether it shall be paid by more than one installment and the period of payment.
(g) Not to be permitted to have or to carry weapons and, if necessary, to leave the guns to the judicial depositary in return for a receipt.
(h) To provide real and personal guarantees for the availability of money to assure rights of the injured party; the judge upon the request of the public prosecutor shall specify the amount and the payment period of the money.
(i) To provide assurance that he shall pay alimony regularly, pursuant to the judicial decisions, and that he shall fulfill the obligations towards his family.
(j) To not leave his home.
(k) To not leave a district.
(l) To prohibit him from entering certain places or districts.

In the application of the obligation of driving restrictions mentioned in subsection (d), the judge or the prosecutor may permanently or temporarily allow the suspect to drive vehicles in his professional activities (Article 109/5, CMK).

Time periods that are spent under judicial control are not considered as restriction of freedom and shall not be subtracted from the punishment. This provision shall not apply to inpatient treatment time spent in hospitals mentioned in subparagraph 3, subsection (e) (Article 109/6, CMK).

In cases where the arrested individual has been released because the upper limits of pre-trial detention have been exceeded, provisions about judicial control may be applied (Article 109/7, CMK).

480. Judicial control decision and the competent authorities to issue the decision. The suspect may be taken under judicial control in every phase of investigation upon the request of the public prosecutor and with the decision of the criminal peace judge (Article 110/1, CMK).

During the application of judicial control, upon the request of the public prosecutor, the judge may put the suspect under one or more new obligations, may partly or completely revoke the obligations that constitute the content of the control, or may alter the obligations or temporarily exempt the suspect from obeying some of them (Article 110/2, CMK).[544]

The provisions of this article and Article 109, CMK are applicable at every stage of the prosecution phase by the judicial authorities with subject matter jurisdiction and venue, when it is deemed necessary (Article 110/3, CMK).

---

544. F. Yenisey & A. Nuhoğlu, *Ceza Muhakemesi Hukuku,* 3. Baskı, Seçkin, Ankara 2015, p. 346; C. Şahin, *Ceza Muhakemesi Hukuku I,* 9. Bası, Seçkin 2018, p. 318; B. Öztürk, D. Tezcan & M.R. Erdem et al., *Ceza Muhakemesi Hukuku,* 9. Baskı, Seçkin, Ankara 2015, p. 483; Y. Ünver & H. Hakeri, *Ceza Muhakemesi Hukuku,* 17. Baskı, Adalet, Ankara 2020, p. 366; N. Centel & H. Zafer, *Ceza Muhakemesi Hukuku,* 14. Bası, Beta, İstanbul 2017, p. 386.

Upon the request of the suspect or the accused, the judge or the court may render a decision under the second paragraph of Article 110 within five days, after obtaining the opinion of the public prosecutor (Article 111/1, CMK). The decision on judicial control may be subject to a motion of opposition.

The judicial authority having proper venue may immediately issue a pre-trial arrest warrant with respect to the suspect or the accused who voluntarily fails to comply with the conditions of judicial control, regardless of the duration of the custodial penalty that may be inflicted upon him (Article 112/1, CMK). In cases where judicial control is applied after the maximum duration of pre-trial detention is expired, the suspect may also be detained if he violates his obligations; the duration of this detention shall not exceed nine months in crimes subject to the court of assizes, and two months in other crimes (Article 112/2, CMK).

B. Security Deposit

481. Security deposit for assuring the appearance. The concept of "bail" as money paid for the release of the accused as security is existing within the alternatives of judicial control measures (Article 109/3-f, CMK), but in daily practice utilized very rarely. The security that shall be deposited by the suspect or accused shall guarantee the following points: First, it shall ensure the presence of the suspect or accused during all the procedural interactions, during the execution of the judgment and during the fulfillment of other obligations he may be required to fulfill. Second, the security shall be used to make the following payments in the following order: The expenditures that any intervening party has made, security for compensating the damages that occurred through the offense and for restitution, in cases where the suspect or the accused is prosecuted because he did not pay the alimony, public expenses or criminal fines (Article 113, CMK).[545]

The decision that obliges the suspect or the accused to deposit a security shall include each portion separately covered by the security.

In cases where the suspect or the accused consents, the court or public prosecutor may issue an order upon the request of the victim or recipient of the alimony, the portion of the security to be paid to them in advance that would cover the losses of the victim or the sum that constitutes the alimony (Article 114/1, CMK). If there is a final court judgment in favor of the victim or the alimony recipient, related to the events that constitute the substance of the investigation or prosecution, then the payment may be ordered even if there is no consent of the suspect or the accused (Article 114/2, CMK).

In cases where a convict had fulfilled all the requirements as laid down in paragraph 1 of Article 113, then the security deposit that would guarantee the obligations listed in said Article 113 paragraph 1, subsection (a) and the portion of the security that is specified in the decision, which is to be rendered according to the second paragraph of the same Article, shall be returned to him (Article 115/1, CMK); the second portion of the remaining security that was not paid to the victim of the crime or alimony recipient shall be returned to the suspect or accused, as well

545. F. Yenisey, Ayşe Nuhoğlu, *Ceza Muhakemesi Hukuku,* 6. Baskı, Seçkin, Ankara, 2018, p. 350.

as in cases where a decision of non-prosecution or acquittal had been rendered. Otherwise, except in the absence of a good reason, the security shall be transferred to the state treasury as income.

In cases of a conviction, the security shall be used to cover such as the expenditures of the intervening party, public expenses and criminal fines in accordance with the first paragraph of the subsection (b) of Article 113, CMK. The remainder shall be returned.

§3. The Powers and Duties of the Judge and the Rights of the Suspect in the Preparatory Inquiry

I. Introductory Remarks

482. The judge acting within the preparatory inquiry has a constitutional obligation in protecting the rights of the suspect. The legislator has empowered the criminal peace judge (*supra,* 372) for this purpose.

II. The Power to Intercept Telecommunication

483. In order to trace correspondence through telecommunication of a suspect, the police need to have warrant of a judge, and in exigent cases a written order of the public prosecutor (Article 135, CMK) (*supra,* paragraph 441). If the written order of the public prosecutor is not approved by the judge, all recordings must be deleted (Article 137, CMK).

III. The Powers of Entry, Search and Seizure

484. In order to conduct a search in relation with a suspect, the police need to have warrant of a judge, and in exigent cases a written order of the public prosecutor (Article 119/1, CMK) (*supra,* paragraph 451). If the seized evidence upon the written order of the public prosecutor is not approved by the judge, seizure ends automatically (Article 127/3, CMK).

IV. Powers to Interview the Accused and Witnesses

A. Interviewing the Accused

485. According to the 1992 regulations, special provisions apply during the interview of the accused by the police and the public prosecutor, as well as during the interrogation by the judge (Article 147, CMK).[546]

546. E. Cihan, *Ellinci Yılda Ceza Muhakemesi Süjesi Olarak Sanığın Sorgusu,* IHFM (1984/ 1-4): 139–146; F. Gölcüklü, Sanık Gerçeği Söylemeye Mecbur mudur? AUSBFD (1954/4): No. IX,

The procedure of interviewing the suspect shall follow certain rules: At the beginning the interviewer shall ask for and write down the person's identity; the interviewed person must give correct answers regarding his identity; then the suspect or the accused shall be advised of the offense he is suspected of; afterwards the suspect's right to counsel will be acknowledged: he has the right to engage counsel on his behalf. If he cannot afford to retain counsel, he may demand a lawyer appointed by the bar association of that district.

If the suspect demands a lawyer appointed by the bar association, that lawyer may be present during the interview on the condition that this causes no delay in the investigation. There is no requirement for a written power of attorney for the requested lawyer. Furthermore, the interviewed person is entitled to inform his or her relatives about the arrest if he wishes to do so. He must also be advised of this right (*infra*, paragraph 468).

The interviewed person must be advised that he has the legal right to remain silent. He will be given notice that he may demand collection of exculpatory evidence that would favor him. Questions about his personal status will be asked (Article 147/1-a, CMK).

An official report of the interview will be prepared. This report must contain the following: (a) the place and date where the interview took place; (b) the names and positions of the persons who were present during the interview, including the identity of the interviewed person; (c) a statement about carrying out the above-mentioned requirements of the interview and whether any were not completed along with the reasons for that; (d) a statement of the facts and a statement that the official report has been read by the interviewed person and by his defense lawyer, if he was present, and that they have signed the report; and (e) if they did not sign the report, the reasons for their refusal (Article 147/1-i, CMK).

The police may interrogate a suspect only if the public prosecutor orders to.[547] In ordinary cases, the police are not entitled to have any contact with the detainee. Therefore, if the suspect is detained by the judge's order, the police may not conduct an interview.

486. Illegal methods of interviewing. The testimony during the interview must be given freely. The Turkish Code of Penal Procedure lists the prohibited methods of interviewing suspects (Article 148, CMK). The use of torture, drugs given by force, stress or pressure tactics, fraud, physical violence or force, and devices that

121–146; C. Şahin, *Hazırlık Soruşturmasında Sanığın Kolluk Tarafından Sorgulanması,* Konya: Doktora Tezi, 1993; T. Demirbaş, *Sanığın Hazırlık Soruşturmasında İfadesinin Alınması,* İzmir, 1996.

547. During the state of emergency administration after the failed coup in Jul. 15, 2016, Art. 6/1-c, f of the Decree in Power of Act (KHK) No. 667 in 2016, approved by Act No. 6747 dated Oct. 18, 2016 gave the judicial police (provisional and valid for terrorism crimes only) the power of interrogation of all suspects on their own initiative. Additionally, it empowered the judicial police to interrogate detained suspects who are in correctional facilities waiting for the trial.

influence free will are forbidden (Article 148/1, CMK).[548] The person being interviewed may not be offered illegal promises (Article 148/2, CMK).

Evidence that has been obtained through illegal means is excluded, even if the individual gives his consent (Article 148/3, CMK) (*supra*, paragraph 439).

If, during the police questioning, there is no defense counsel present, and the accused denies his testimony later at court, such testimony cannot be considered as evidence for forming the judgment (Article 148/4, CMK). This provision is an innovation of the Turkish Legislature, which was enacted prior to the *Salduz v. Turkey*[549] decision of the ECtHR. Unfortunately, in cases where the defense attorney is not experienced, or did not provide the suspect with sufficient legal advice, a confession in the presence of the lawyer at the police station may still be used as very strong evidence against the accused later at the trial.

If the police have interviewed a suspect once, and later there is a need for further questioning, the police are not empowered to re-interview the same person for the same investigation (Article 148/5, CMK).[550]

B. *The Interviewing of Witnesses*

487. The public prosecutor may interview a witness in the investigation phase. In cases where a witness is not able to appear at the trial, then the court may rule that this shall be heard by letter rogatory (Article 180/1, CMK)- Individuals have a public duty to testify if they have been summoned.[551] Witnesses served with a summons are obliged to comply (Article 146/7, CMK). They must appear and give testimony. An individual who refuses to do so without reason has to pay the costs as estimated by the judge (Article 44/1, CMK).[552] The police have no power to interview individuals as "witnesses" during the preparatory inquiry; the police interview must be repeated in the course of the main hearing.

548. O. Tosun & N. Gürelli, *Heyecan Göstergesiyle Yalanın Bulunması ve Ceza Hukuku,* IHFM, No. XXX (1964): 3; S. Kaymaz, *Yasak Sorgu Yöntemi Olarak Aldatma* (Yargıtay Dergisi, Cilt 24, 1998), p. 73.

549. Case of Salduz v. Turkey, Application No. 36391/02, 27 November 2008.

550. Act No. 7145 dated Jul. 25, 2018 introduced a provisional regulation, valid for 3 years and applicable for terrorism crimes only, by inserting the Provisional Art. 13 to the Anti-Terrorism Act No. 3713 which reads as follows: *In situations where the need to interview the terrorism suspect in relation with the same case arises again, this interview may be conducted by the public prosecutor, or by the security forces upon a written order of the public prosecutor.* This regulation can result in delays of cases due to requirements of *Salduz v. Turkey* decision of ECtHR, if the defense lawyer is not present at the second police interview, the submissions of the suspect may not be used as evidence at the judgment. Furthermore, allegations against police regarding the unlawful interrogation techniques may increase.

551. N. Şensoy, *Cezada ve Hukukta Şahitlik* (İstanbul, 1952), p. 8.

552. A. Önder, *Ceza Muhakemeleri Usulü Hukukunda Şahitlikten Çekinme Hakkı,* IHFM XXIX, No. 4 (1963): 4, 876–932; T.T. Yüce, *Meslek Adamının Tanıklıktan Çekinme Hakkı* (YD 1980/ VI, 1–2), 51–62; K. İçel, *Gazetecilerin Tanıklıktan Çekinme Hakları* (Ceza Hukuku ve Kriminoloji Mecmuası, Cilt 1, sayı 1), p. 37.

V. Miscellaneous

A. The Powers of Inquiry "On the Spot"

488. The criminal peace judge is empowered to investigate a case exceptionally, if the public prosecutor is out of reach, or if the event is broad and complicated and therefore beyond the scope of the duties of the public prosecutor and where the offense is detected in the act, as well as where there is peril in delay (Article 163, CMK).

B. Preventive or Repressive Measures in Internet

1. Preventive Measures in General

489. There are some preventive measures regulated in the Penal Procedure Code, such as some of the judicial control obligations (*supra,* paragraph 479), and there are some preventive measures regulated in various statutes outside[553] of Penal Procedure Code, such as preventive police search (*supra,* paragraph 451) or the blocking of the Internet access, which have some impact on criminal investigations and collecting of evidence.

Regulating various activities on the Internet has been a priority of the executive. In this regard, the Act No. 5651 on "Regulation of Broadcasts via the Internet and Combating Crimes Committed by Means of Such Publications" was put into force on May 4, 2007. This statute defines judicial (*infra*, paragraph 491) as well as administrative (*infra*, paragraph 492) measures such as blocking access *(erişimin engellenmesi;* blocking content via blocking access to a domain name or from IP address or URL blocking or other similar methods), and content removal *(içeriğin yayından çıkarılması;* removing the content from the servers or from the hosted content) by content or hosting providers. Such limitations on the freedom of expression has been subject to some decisions of the Constitutional Court in the way of individual constitutional complaint (*supra*, paragraph 366), and resulted by decisions finding violation of basic rights.[554] As a consequence, the legislator has enacted the Act No. 7252, dated July 23, 2020 and established a *"Committee on Digital Media at the National Grand Assembly,"* comprising of 17 members from various political parties that has the power to oversight of the Internet related issues and making suggestions for legal developments. A week later, the next numbered statute, *"Act on Amendment of the Act No. 5651 on Regulation of Broadcasts via Internet and Combating Crimes Committed by Means of Such Publications,"* dated July 29, 2020

553. As of Apr. 7 2021, there is a new law regulating security clearances for employment of civil servants (Act No. 7315, Güvenlik Soruşturması ve Arşiv Araştırması Kanunu). Intelligence services, police authorities and local executive administrations are entitled to conduct an investigation while collecting personnel data and submit the outcomes to the evaluation commission which makes the final decision about the employment of the individual.

554. Wikimedia Foundation Inc. ve Diğerleri Başvurusu, § 73-77; Birgün İletişim ve Yayıncılık Başvurusu, § 63-72; Ali Ergin Demirhan Başvurusu, RG May 2, 2020, § 41.

introduced further limitations and required the foreign service providers to appoint an agent in Turkey who is entitled for receiving notifications issued by Turkish authorities. The ordinance of this appointment is in force since October 2, 2020. Details of preventive or repressive measures on Internet are explained below.

2. Measures in Cyber Media: Blocking of Internet Access and Access to Data

a. Responsibilities of Providers

490. Responsibility of disclosure. Content, hosting and access providers are responsible for providing their identification information on the Internet in a manner by which the users have access to such information, pursuant to the principles and procedures set forth in the regulation; and keep such information up-to-date (Article 3/1, Act No. 5651).

The content, hosting or access provider who fails to fulfill the above-mentioned responsibility shall be imposed an administrative fine of TRY 2,000 to TRY 50,000 by the presidency (Article 3/2, Act No. 5651).

Notification to those who conduct operations within the scope of this law within or outside the boundaries of Turkey can be made via various communication channels including tools on their websites, e-mailing to an address that can be found through research of domain name, IP address etc. or other communication tools (Article 3/3, Act No. 5651). In cases where the related person is located outside of Turkey, the same procedure applies, and the notification shall be considered as effective after the fifth day of the interaction (Article 3/5, Act No. 5651, inserted in 2020, by Act No. 7253).

Responsibility of the content provider. The content provider is responsible for any kind of content it presents on the Internet (Article 4/1, Act No. 5651).

Content provider shall not be responsible for the content belonging to a third party to which it gives a link. However, if it is clear from the content provider's way of presenting such third-party content, to which the link leads, that it adopts the content and aims to provide access to that specific content, it may be held liable pursuant to general provisions (Article 4/2, Act No. 5651).

Content provider shall submit the relevant information requested by the presidency within the scope of the duties given to the presidency by this law and other laws, and take measures requested by the presidency (Article 4/3, Act No. 5651).

Responsibilities of the hosting provider. Hosting providers are not responsible to check the hosted content or make a research on whether the content constitutes an unlawful activity (Article 5/1, Act No. 5651).

The hosting provider shall, remove the illegal content from broadcast, provided that it has been informed about the illegal content pursuant to Articles 8 and 9 of this Law (Article 5/2, Act No. 5651).

The hosting provider shall be obliged to store the traffic information in relation to the provided hosting services for a period of not less than a year and not more than two years which will be regulated by bylaw, and to provide the accuracy, confidentiality and integrity of these information (Article 5/3, Act No. 5651).

Hosting providers, within the scope of the principles and procedures to be determined with bylaws, may be categorized based on the nature of their businesses and be differentiated in respect of rights and liabilities (Article 5/4, Act No. 5651).

The hosting provider shall be obliged to submit the information requested by the presidency in the requested form, and take measures requested by the presidency (Article 5/5, Act No. 5651).

Hosting providers who do not notify the hosting provider or fulfill the obligations determined by this law shall be imposed an administrative fine from 100,000 TL to 1.000,000 TL by the presidency (Article 5/6, Act No. 5651, as amended in 2020, by Act No. 7253).

Responsibilities of the access provider. Access providers are responsible for blocking access to illegal content broadcast by its user, provided that it has been informed about the illegal content pursuant to this law. Access providers shall save the traffic information indicated in the regulation, for a period that will be determined by the regulation, which may not be less than six months and more than two years. Access providers are required to notify the authority, content providers and its customers at least three months prior to termination, if it decides to terminate its operations and deliver the saved traffic information to the authority pursuant to the principles and procedures set forth in the regulation. Access providers shall take measures to prevent alternative access methods to the content subject to blocking access decisions. Access provider shall submit the information requested by the presidency in the requested form, and take measures requested by the presidency (Article 6/1, Act No. 5651).

The access provider shall not be responsible to check whether the content accessed is illegal or raises any responsibilities (Article 6/2, Act No. 5651).

The access provider that fails to comply with the responsibilities set forth under subsections (b), (c), (ç) and (d) of paragraph 1 shall be imposed an administrative fine of TL 10,000 up to TL 50,000 (Article 6/3, Act No. 5651).

Responsibilities of mass use providers. Mass use providers who provide mass use in a commercial manner shall obtain permission from the local district official. Information regarding such permission shall be forwarded to the authority by the local district official within thirty days. The local district official supervises these. Procedures and principles regarding granting the permission license and supervision are provided by the regulation (Article 7/1, Act No. 5651).

All Internet mass use providers, regardless of acting in a commercial manner or not, shall take measures to be designated by bylaw for blocking access to illegal content and storing access records concerning the usage (Article 7/2, Act No. 5651).

Internet mass use providers having commercial purposes are obliged to take measures regarding the protection of family and minors, prevention of crime and detection of criminals where the procedures and grounds are set in bylaws (Article 7/3, Act No. 5651).

Internet mass use providers having commercial purposes who violate the liabilities specified in this article shall be sanctioned one of the penalties of a warning, an administrative fine from 1,000 TL to 15,000 TL, or a suspending of their commercial activities for up to three days, by the local district official according to the degree of the violation and within the scope of the procedures and grounds set by the bylaws (Article 7/4, Act No. 5651).

b. Removing Content and Access Blocking Decisions and Enforcement of Such Decisions

491. There are two options for removing content or blocking access: by a judicial decision, or by an administrative order (*infra,* paragraph 492). Access to broadcasted data on the Internet shall be blocked or it will be removed by a judicial decision if there is sufficient suspicion that the content constitutes provocation to commit suicide (Article 84, TCK), sexual harassment of children (Article 103, paragraph 1, TCK), to ease the usage of drugs (Article 190, TCK), to supply material constituting a health hazard (Article 194, TCK), obscenity (Article 226, TCK), prostitution (Article 227, TCK), to provide place and opportunity for gambling (Article 228, TCK), crimes mentioned in the *Law on Crimes Against Atatuörk* dated July 25, 1951 and numbered 5,816 (Article 8/1, Act No. 5651).

A judge shall hand down an access-blocking or data removing decision during the investigation phase and by a court during the prosecution period (for the distinction between the term “court” and “judge,” please refer to *supra,* paragraph 372). A public prosecutor may also take access-blocking or content removal decisions during the investigation period, if failure to do so might result in delay and cause irreparable damages. In such a case, the public prosecutor shall submit his decision to a judge for approval within twenty-four hours, and the judge shall grant a decision within the following twenty-four hours. If the access blocking or content removal decision is not approved in this timeframe, the precaution decision shall immediately be eliminated by the public prosecutor. Blocking access or content removal decisions may be granted temporarily for a limited period of time if the purpose seems to be achievable. An access blocking or content removal decision granted as a protective precaution may be objected to pursuant to provisions of Penal Procedural Code (Article 8/2, Act No. 5651). A copy of the access blocking decision taken by a judge, a court or a public prosecutor shall be sent to the executing authority (Article 8/3, Act No. 5651, as amended in 2020, by Act No. 7253).

In cases where the content of the broadcasted data constitutes a crime under subsection 1 of Article 8, Act No. 5651, and the content provider or hosting provider is outside of Turkey, the access blocking decision shall be rendered ex officio by the president; even if the contents provider or hosting provider is located in Turkey, the president shall render access blocking decision ex officio, if the content of broadcasted data constitutes one of the crimes listed in subsection 1, (a), (2), (5) and (6) (Article 8/14, Act No. 5651).

Access blocking decision shall be rendered immediately, and at the most within four hours as of the notification of the decision executive (Article 8/5, Act No. 5651).

The president shall file a criminal complaint with the public prosecution office in cases where he identifies the individuals who broadcasted data, content of access blocking decision (Article 8/6, Act No. 5651).

If at the end of the investigation the prosecution is dropped, the access blocking or data removal decision shall be void per se. In such cases, the public prosecutor shall send a copy of the decision for dropping the prosecution to the authority (Article 8/7, Act No. 5651).

If the court reaches a verdict of acquittal during the prosecution phase, the access blocking or data removal decision shall be void per se. In such a case, the court sends a copy of the decision of acquittal to the authority (Article 8/8, Act No. 5651).

In case where the content of the broadcasts that constitute the crimes mentioned in paragraph 1 are removed from the broadcast, the public prosecutor shall eliminate the decision regarding blocking the access or removing the content during the investigation phase and by the court during the prosecution phase (Article 8/9, Act No. 5651).

As the access blocking or data removal decision has been rendered as a procedural measure, the responsible persons working at the hosting provider or access provider, who fail to comply with that decision shall be punished with criminal fine from 500 days to 3,000 days, if their conduct does not carry a heavier penalty (Article 8/10, Act No. 5651).

In cases where the access blocking decision has been rendered as an administrative measure (*infra,* paragraph 492) and the access provider fails to comply with the decision, the President shall rule on an administrative fine for the access provider at the amount of 10,000 TL to 100,000 TL. If the access blocking decision is not executed within twenty-four hours after the time the administrative fine has been ruled on, the authority may cancel the respected authorization (Article 8/11, Act No. 5651).

Where the authority renders administrative fines in relation to the misdemeanors in this Act, the parties may apply to legal remedies according to the Administrative Procedure Code (Article 8/12, Act No. 5651).

Decisions rendered by judges or courts and send to the authority in order to fulfill required interactions may be oppose by the authority according to the rules set by Penal Procedure Code (Article 8/13, Act No. 5651).

A decision for blocking access to the broadcastings on the Internet may be rendered by the institutions and organizations defined in Article 3 (1/ç) of the Act on Regulating Taxes, Funds and Shares Received from the Games of Chance Revenues, dated March 14, 2007, No. 5602, if they detect that crimes within the scope of their duties are being committed in the Internet medium. Such decisions shall be sent to the Authority for their implementation (Article 8/14, Act No. 5651).

Decisions based on Article 8, 9 and 9/A of this law, to be rendered in due course of the investigation, shall be rendered by the criminal peace judge, authorized by The Board of Judges and Prosecutors, if there are more than one criminal peace judge in that location (Article 8/15, Act No. 5651).

c. Removal of Content and/or Blocking Access in Non-delayable Cases

492. In cases related to the protection of the right to life and property, the protection of national security and public order, the prevention of crimes being committed, or the protection of general health the judge may decide on the removal of content of and/or blocking access to broadcast. In such non-delayable cases however, the presidency may also decide on the removal of content of and/or blocking access to broadcast decisions which shall be carried out immediately and four hours after the notification of the decision in the latest (Article 8A/1, Act No. 5651). The decision shall be notified to the access providers and the relevant content and hosting providers immediately by the president. Content removal and/or blocking access content removal and/or blocking access decisions given by the president upon the request of the presidency or the related ministries, shall be presented by the president to the approval of the criminal peace judgeship within twenty-four hours. The judge shall take his decision in twenty-four hours, otherwise the decision is invalidated automatically (Article 8A/2, Act No. 5651).

The blocking access decisions given in scope of this article shall be given in terms of content blocking of the broadcasting, section, and part (URL, etc.) that the violation happens in. However, in cases where technically the violation cannot be prevented through blocking access of the content regarding the violation or where by preventing access to the content regarding the violation, the whole of the website may be blocked (Article 8A/3, Act No. 5651).

A criminal complaint shall be filed against those who make and disseminate Internet content that constitutes a crime in scope of this article by the office of chief public prosecutor. The information needed to contact the perpetrators of these offenses, shall be given to judicial authorities by the decision of the judge by content, hosting, and access providers. Those providers responsible for content, hosting, and access providers, who do not supply this information, when the action does not constitute another crime necessitating a heavier punishment, shall be subjected to a criminal fine from 3,000 days to 10,000 days (Article 8A/4, Act No. 5651).

Access providers and related content and hosting providers who do not execute the content removal and/or blocking access decision within the scope of this article shall be subjected by the President to a fine from 50,000 TL to 500,000 TL (Article 8A/5, Act No. 5651).

d. Removal of Content from Broadcast and Access Blocking

493. Any real person or legal entity or institution or entities, who claim that their personal rights are violated due to a content on the Internet, may apply with the warning method to that content provider, or to the hosting provider if the content provider cannot be reached, and may request the removal of such content from the broadcast; they also may request the blocking of access to the content by directly applying to the criminal peace judgeship (Article 9/1, Act No. 5651).

Such requests shall be responded to within twenty-four hours at the latest by content and/or hosting providers (Article 9/2, Act No. 5651).

The judge may decide to block access within the scope of this article in accordance with the requests of those who claim that their personal rights are violated by the content of the broadcast on the Internet (Article 9/3, Act No. 5651).

Blocking access decisions within the scope of this Article shall as a rule is only against the specific broadcast, section, or part under which the content violating the personal rights appears (i.e., URL blocking). It is, however, not possible to block access to the entire website. That said, if the judge decides that the violation cannot be prevented by URL blocking, he also may order to block access to the entire website by specifically stating his justification (Article 9/4, Act No. 5651).

The blocking access orders granted by the judge within the scope of this Article shall be sent directly to the Union (Article 9/5, Act No. 5651).

The judge shall render his decision regarding applications based on this Article within twenty-four hours the latest without conducting an open hearing. Objections may be raised against these decisions pursuant to the Penal Procedure Code (Article 9/6, Act No. 5651).

The decision of judge shall be invalidated automatically in the event that the content subject to blocking access order is removed (Article 9/7, Act No. 5651).

The blocking access decision delivered to the access provider by the union shall be implemented within four hours at the latest by the access provider (Article 9/8, Act No. 5651).

If a content that is the same with or similar to the content which is the subject of the blocking access order within the scope of this Article is broadcasted on other Internet addresses, the decision shall be applied against those other Internet addresses as well if the related person applies to the union in this respect (Article 9/9, Act No. 5651).

The judge may rule upon the demand of the person who has been the victim of the violation of his personal rights that his name shall be disconnected from the Internet address subject to the decision (Article 9/10, Act No. 5651, as amended by Act No. 7253).

The responsible person who fails to comply with the order of the criminal peace judgeship in a timely manner and by fulfilling conditions set forth in this Article shall be sentenced to a punitive fine from 500 days to 3,000 days (Article 9/11, Act No. 5651).

e. Blocking Access to Content Due to the Right to Privacy of Personal Life

494. Those who claim that their rights to privacy of personal life are violated by the content of the broadcast on the Internet may apply directly to the authority and request blocking access to the relevant content (Article 9A/1, Act No. 5651).

The complete address of the broadcast in violation URL containing the violation, the explanation regarding the reasons of violation and identity of the information shall be submitted together with the application. The request shall not be put to process if the data submitted lacks some of the information (Article 9A/2, Act No. 5651).

The President shall deliver the request to the Union of Service Providers at once for the implementation of the request; access providers shall implement the request within four hours at the latest (Article 9A/3, Act No. 5651).

The decision to block access to the Internet shall be implemented by blocking access to content (i.e., URL blocking) that relates to broadcast, section, part, and image, video that violates the privacy of personal life (Article 9A/4, Act No. 5651).

Those who request blocking access shall submit their request to the criminal peace judgeship in twenty-four hours starting from the application for blocking access due to violation of their rights to privacy of personal life on the Internet. The judge shall decide whether the content on the Internet violates the applicants' right to privacy of personal life, and grant their decision in forty-eight hours at the latest, and send it directly to the Presidency; otherwise, the measure of blocking access shall be reversed automatically (Article 9A/5, Act No. 5651).

The presidency may raise objections against to the order given by the judge in accordance with the provisions of the Penal Procedure Code (Article 9A/6, Act No. 5651).

The decision of the judge shall be invalidated automatically in the event that the content subject to blocking access order is removed from being broadcast (Article 9A/7, Act No. 5651).

The blocking access may be realized by The Information and Communication Technologies Authority via the order of the President in non-delayable cases based on the protection of privacy of personal life (Article 9A/8, Act No. 5651).

The blocking access decision which is given based on paragraph (8) of this Article shall be submitted to the criminal peace judgeship by the president for their approval within twenty-four hours. The judge shall announce his decision within forty-eight hours (Article 9A/9, Act No. 5651).

C. The Power to Call in Experts

495. Expert witness. Expert opinion is not considered evidence in Turkish Law.[555] According to the Code of Penal Procedure, the court must ask the opinion of the scientific expert if the matter relates to technical points or to special knowledge (Article 62, CMK). It is forbidden for the court to ask experts their opinion about matters related to law.[556]

D. Mental and Bodily Examination and Inspection of the Crime Scene

496. Mental examination of the suspect. When an expert has recommended that the accused be given a mental examination during the preliminary investigation, the Criminal Peace Judgeship (and, where the proceedings are more advanced, the competent court) may order the accused to be placed under examination in an official institution. A warrant against drug and alcohol addicts can be issued at any stage of the proceedings.

Where the accused has no legal representation, legal representation shall be appointed for him by the court (Article 74/2, CMK).

497. Physical bodily examination of the suspect or the accused, and taking samples. In order to obtain evidence of a committed crime, the judge or the trial court by its own motion, or upon the request of the public prosecutor or the victim and in cases where there is peril in delay, the public prosecutor may issue an order

555. N. Kunter, F. Yenisey & A. Nuhoğlu, *Muhakeme Hukuku Dalı Olarak Ceza Muhakemesi Hukuku*, 18. Bası, İstanbul, Beta, 2010, 1397; N. Gürelli, *Türk Ceza Muhakemesi Hukukunda Bilirkişilik*, İstanbul, İstanbul Üniversitesi, 1967, p. 95.

556. N. Gürelli, *Ceza Muhakemesinde Bilirkişilik Kurumuna İlişkin Meseleler* (İstanbul: Doğanay Armağanı, İstanbul Üniversitesi, 1982), p. 65; S. Dönmezer, *Mecburi Ehlihibre*, IHFM. X, 1–2, p. 415.

to conduct an internal physical bodily examination[557] on the suspect or the accused, or to take samples from his body, such as blood or like biological samples, as well as hair, saliva or nail samples.[558] It is also possible to utilize these provisions after the suspect has been officially accused and has the legal status of an accused. The decision of the public prosecutor shall be submitted for the approval of the judge or the court within twenty-four hours. The judge or the court shall issue its decision within twenty-four hours. Unapproved decisions shall be invalid, and evidence so obtained shall not be used (Article 75/1, CMK).

The internal physical bodily examination or an intervention in order to take blood or similar biological samples from the body may only be conducted if it does not harm the subject's health.

The internal physical bodily examination or taking blood or similar biological samples from the body shall only be undertaken by a medical doctor or by another member of the medical profession.

Any examination of the genital organs or anus shall be deemed as internal physical bodily examination.

There shall be no internal physical bodily examination undertaken related to crimes that carry imprisonment of less than two years; in these instances, it is also forbidden to take blood or similar biological samples from the body, as well as hair, saliva and nail samples.

The decisions ruled according to this article by a judge or the court may be subject to a motion of opposition.

Alcohol tests and taking blood samples according to special provisions in the Police Act shall not be prevented by this regulation.

498. The physical bodily examination on, and taking samples from, third parties. The judge or the court upon the request of the public prosecutor or on their own motion or, in cases of peril in delay, the public prosecutor, may decide to conduct external or internal physical bodily examination on the victim or take blood or similar biological samples from the body of the victim, as well as hair, saliva and nail samples in order to obtain evidence of a crime, so long as this shall not create a danger to the subject's health and there is no surgical intervention. The decision of the public prosecutor shall be forwarded to the judge or the court for approval within twenty-four hours. The judge or the court shall give their decision within twenty-four hours after it has been submitted to him. This period is not applicable for other investigative measures that are submitted for approval. Unapproved decisions shall be invalid, and evidence so obtained shall not be used (Article 76/1, CMK).

In cases where there is the consent of the victim, obtaining a decision according to the rules as mentioned above is not required.

Where there is a need to determine the parentage of a child, a decision according to the rules in Article 76/1, CMK is required in order to conduct this research.

---

557. N. Kunter, F. Yenisey & A. Nuhoğlu, *Muhakeme Hukuku Dalı Olarak Ceza Muhakemesi Hukuku*, 18. Bası, İstanbul, Beta, 2010, p. 1569.

558. F. Selami Mahmutoğlu, Beden Muayenesi ve Vücuttan Örnek Alınması, in *Criminal Law in the Global Risk Society*, eds. F. Yenisey & U. Sieber (Series of the Max Planck Institute for Foreign and International Criminal Law and Bahçeşehir University Joint Research Group, Volume T 1, Istanbul 2011), p. 393.

The witness may refrain from bodily examination or giving body samples upon the grounds of their right to refrain from testimony. If the individual is a child or mentally ill, the decision to refrain shall be made by his legal representative. In cases where the child or the mentally ill person is capable of understanding the legal meaning and consequences of taking the witness stand, his view on the subject shall also be asked. In cases where the legal representative is the suspect or the accused, then the judge must make the decision. However, evidence of the crime obtained in this way shall not be used as evidence in the further stages of the lawsuit unless the legal representative who is not under criminal charges as a suspect or an accused gives his consent.

Judge or court decisions rendered under this provision may be subject to opposition.

The physical bodily examination of a female shall be conducted by a female medical doctor upon her request and if it is possible. (Article 77, CMK)

499. Molecular-genetic tests shall be conducted on the material obtained through interactions described in Articles 75 and 76, CMK, only if it is necessary to determine the family connections or to determine if those body samples are related to the suspect or to the accused or to the victim. Tests that are outside of the scope of these aims are forbidden (Article 78/1, CMK).

Such permitted tests may also be conducted on other body parts, that have been found and seized, and their owner's identity is not known. Tests outside the scope of determining the identity are prohibited (Article 78/2, CMK).

Molecular-genetic tests[559] according to Article 78 shall only be conducted upon a judge's order. The ruling shall also contain the name of the expert appointed to conduct the test (Article 79, CMK).

An expert may be selected from the officially appointed experts or from the individuals who are required to act as an expert or from officials who are not attached to the investigating or prosecuting authorities, or from officials belonging to an objectively separate structural branch of the investigating or prosecuting authority. These individuals are obliged to take all suitable organizational and technical precautions in order to prevent illegal conduct of molecular-genetic tests and so that unauthorized third parties may not obtain knowledge about the outcomes. The items subject to test shall be delivered to the experts without labeling them with the name, family name, address and date of birth of the person from whom the items originate.

The outcome of the analysis of samples obtained according to Articles 75, 76, and 78, CMK are considered as personal data and shall not be used for another purpose. The individuals who have access to the files shall not disclose the information to unauthorized persons (Article 80/1, CMK).

As soon as the prosecution ends (or, the time limit for opposing the decision to drop the prosecution is exhausted, or the opposition has been overturned, or the

559. F. Yenisey, *Genetics Related Regulations in Turkish Criminal Law and Criminal Procedure*, in Genetics, Robotics, Law, Punishment, D. Provolo & S. Riondato & F. Yenisey (eds.), Padova University Press, 2014, p. 253.

court gives a final judgment on acquittal, or a judgment is rendered on not punishing the accused and those judgments are made final), the samples and information shall be destroyed immediately in the presence of the public prosecutor. This destruction shall be documented and its documentation shall be kept in the file (Article 80/2, CMK).

500. Fixing the identity in a physical way. If the committed crime requires a maximum prison term of two years or a more severe punishment, upon the order of the public prosecutor, a picture shall be taken, measurement of the body shall be made, fingerprints or palm prints shall be taken, special marks on the body, that would enable the recognition of the suspect, shall be made and the accused shall be registered. A voice sample and a video film shall be produced as well, and inserted into the file where the interactions related to the investigation and prosecution are kept (Article 81, CMK).

In cases where the prosecution ends, all related records shall be removed from the files and be destroyed in the presence of the public prosecutor. This action shall be documented.

E. Other Investigation Methods

501. Judicial inspection of the crime scene. Judicial inspection of the crime scene shall be conducted by the trial court or by a member of the court who was delegated to perform that task, or by the court that has been asked to perform a specific legal duty by a rogatory letter, and if there is peril in delay, by the public prosecutor (Article 83, CMK).

The minutes of the judicial inspection shall contain information about the existing facts and the absence of the evidence of the crime that might to be expected to exist according to the special circumstances of the situation.

The suspect, the accused and the victim and their defense counsel and representatives may be present during the judicial inspection (Article 84, CMK).

In the event that a witness or expert is unable to be present at the trial, or it would be difficult for him to appear because he is living far away, the provisions of Article 180, CMK, first paragraph about delegating another court shall apply during his hearing. If the presence of the suspect or the accused may prevent one of the witnesses from testifying truthfully, it may be ruled that the suspect or the accused shall be removed from the courtroom during this interaction.

The individuals who have the right to be present during this interaction shall be informed of the date of the scheduled interaction in advance of the due day (Article 181/1, CMK). If the suspect or the accused is in custody, the trial court may decide that he may be present during the judicial inspection only if it is necessary (Article 181/2, CMK).

502. Showing the crime scene. The public prosecutor is entitled to conduct a crime scene visit with the suspect, if the suspect has already given some information about the crime of which he is suspected (Article 85, CMK).[560] The chief of the judicial police is also empowered to conduct a crime scene visit with the suspect, if the crime is related to terrorism or organized crime (Article 85/1, CMK).

The defense counsel may also be present during the crime scene visit by the suspect, if this does not delay the investigation (Article 85/2, CMK). Crime scene visit by the suspect shall be documented as regulated in Article 169, CMK.

503. Line-ups. Identification of suspects by the eyewitnesses is regulated in Police Code in Turkey. The 2007-5681 Act regulated line-ups: Upon the written order of the public prosecutor, the police shall prepare a line-up for identification of the suspect by the eye witness. Before starting a line-up, the person who is going to identify the suspect shall write a description of the perpetrator he or she observed. Similar looking individuals will be placed in a room, where the eyewitness can see them, but the suspect and the others cannot. The line-up shall be repeated at least two times and shall be recorded (Additional Article 6/9-17, PVSK).

In order to find out the competent public prosecution office, the police had been given the authority to investigate in cyber space by searching for identities of Internet users. Service providers were obliged to provide the police with the requested information (Additional Article 6/9, PVSK, as amended by Article 27 KHK 680, approved by Act No. 7072 on February 1, 2018). Since the Constitutional Court has annulled the power of investigation in cyber space in 2020, the police no longer have this authority.

560. A. Karagülmez, *Yer Gösterme İşlemi ve 5271 Sayılı Ceza Muhakemesi Kanunu'nun 85. Maddesinin İncelenmesi*, Türkiye Barolar Birliği Dergisi, sayfa 62, Mart & Nisan 2005.

Chapter 3. The Inquiry in Court

§1. The Trial in the Court of General Jurisdiction

I. General Characteristics

504. Except for the "simplified adjudication procedure" (*supra,* paragraph 400), the inquiry in the court of general jurisdiction is public and adversarial. According to the length of imprisonment term as determined in the Penal Code, there are two options in the course of a main hearing at the court of general jurisdiction: If the upper level of the imprisonment term is below two years, the court has a discretion to apply the "simplified adjudication procedure" (Article 251, CMK). The court may also decide to conduct a regular hearing, the same procedure applicable in the court of assizes as explained below (*infra,* paragraph 513).

During the trial, all procedural transactions are submitted orally, and the court examines the accused, witnesses and experts.[561] The judge has an active role in the inquiry in court, and he must have direct access to all evidence. The trial is held without interruption in the presence of the judges who will formulate the judgment of the court, but it may be interrupted for a reasonable time (Article 190/1, CMK). The trial is conducted in the presence of the accused (Article 193/1, CMK). There are some exceptions to this rule if the crime is punishable by criminal fine or confiscation (Article 195, CMK).

505. The court must give its opinion on the facts directly and immediately. All the proceedings conducted in the preliminary investigation should be repeated in court and are open to the parties' criticism. A confession from the accused to the police where his lawyer was not present is not considered evidence if the accused does not approve (in the trial) his submission to the police (Article 148/4, CMK). In reality, however, courts rely to a great extent on the file prepared during the preliminary investigation, and they only make further investigation if there are some discrepancies in the testimony or offered evidence.

506. The inquiry in court is public. However, in cases involving public morals or public security, the whole trial or a part thereof may be held in closed session. The court has discretion to decide whether the inquiry shall be public or not, and this decision will be declared in a public session (Article 182/2, CMK). The decision on a closed inquiry and the final judgment of the court shall always be declared in a public session (Article 182/3, CMK). In such cases, the verdict shall be pronounced in an open session (Article 182/3, CMK).

There is an obligation to hold a closed session if the case involves a child under 18 years of age. In such cases, the verdict will be pronounced in a closed session (Article 185, CMK).

Publication of trials conducted in closed sessions is forbidden (Article 187/2, CMK; Article 19 BasK). Publication of the contents of an open trial may also be

561. N. Centel & H. Zafer, *Ceza Muhakemesi Hukuku*, 14. Bası, İstanbul, Beta, 2017, p. 573.

forbidden by a decision of the court, if it is against national interests, or if it is of a nature that may provoke the committing of crimes, etc. (Article 187/3, CMK).

There is a restriction on voice and image recordings at the court buildings and within the courtroom (Article 183, CMK).

507. The rules that govern the procedures of different criminal courts are generally the same. Repealed Military Courts, however, applied a special Code of Penal Procedure (Act No. 353). There are slight differences between the procedures in the courts of assizes dealing with terrorism crimes and the procedures in the courts of general jurisdiction. In addition, the structures of the courts are different. According to the provisional Article 19 TMK, added by Act No. 7145 dated July 25, 2018, terrorism courts shall apply special procedural rules for arrest and pre-trial detention for three years, until July 25, 2021 (*supra*, paragraph 470).

II. The Course of the Trial

508. In cases where the simplified procedure is applied, there is no main hearing, and the court renders its decision *in camera*, based on the case file. This method of adjudication is similar to the penal order of the repealed Penal Procedure Code which is applicable in some other jurisdictions in Europe.[562] The current Penal Procedure Code does not include the penal order.

There are other legal concepts in the field of minor crimes, such as *mediation* (Article 253 CMK; *supra*, paragraph 393), *suspension of prosecution* (Article 171/2 CMK; *supra*, paragraph 390), *delayed announcement of the judgment* (Article 231/2, CMK; *infra*, paragraph 519) and *suspension of the imprisonment* (Article 51, TCK; *supra*, paragraph 339).

III. Inquiry in the Absence of the Accused and Fugitives

509. Inquiry in the absence of the accused. Book 5, section 1 of the Turkish Code of Penal Procedure deals with the Inquiry in the Absence of the Accused and Fugitives, (Articles 244–248, CMK). These provisions do not allow the court to render a judgment against the absent accused or fugitive, but only to force him to appear before the court. If the court has questioned the accused once, however, the court may come to a judgment even if the accused does not appear at the later phases of the trial (Article 194/2, CMK).

Inquiry in the absence of the accused has been criticized by academics and is now restricted, but is also extended to *fugitives* (*infra*, paragraph 510) by the subsequent

562. Formerly the criminal peace court was entitled to order a sanction directly if the crime was within its jurisdiction (Art. 386, repealed CMUK). This power of the penal order of the peace court was limited to fines, light imprisonment up to three months, prohibition from exercising a profession and confiscation of goods, whether as single sanctions or all at once.

legislation.[563] In criminal procedure, the word *absence* (*gaip*) has a technical meaning. The accused is considered absent if his whereabouts are not known or if he is in a foreign country and summoning him to a competent jurisdiction appears not possible or inappropriate (Article 244/1, CMK). In such cases, the Turkish criminal law no longer allows an inquiry in the absence of the accused,[564] and the court only may conduct investigation in order to collect and preserve evidence (Article 244/2, CMK). The defense counsel or the spouse of the accused has the right of presence during such an investigation.

In such cases, the court publicly announces the accused's obligation to appear (Article 245, CMK) and may grant him immunity from pre-trial arrest (Article 246/1, CMK). There is no immunity if the accused is convicted, or imprisoned, or tries to escape (Article 246/2, CMK).

510. Inquiry in absence of the fugitives. The current law has introduced a new legal concept: An individual who hides himself in Turkey or abroad in order to escape a prosecution pending against him is called fugitive (Article 247/1, CMK).

There are some crimes, listed in Article 248, CMK, where the court serves a summons to the known address of the accused against whom there is a prosecution pending. If the accused does not comply with the summons, the court may order his arrest. If this does not help, then the court may decide to publish in a newspaper that if he does not appear within fifteen days, his belongings and rights within Turkey shall be seized temporarily (Article 246/2, CMK).

The court may render a pre-trial arrest warrant *in absentia*[565] against the fugitive accused (Article 248/5, CMK), but may also grant him immunity from pre-trial arrest (Article 246/1, CMK). Of course, such immunity loses its effect if the accused is convicted of a crime and sentenced to imprisonment or tries to escape (Article 246/2, CMK).

§2. The Trial in the Court of Assizes

511. The general Code of Penal Procedure is valid for all types of courts. Only a few exceptions are applied relating to the type of crime or the status of the accused.[566]

---

563. N. Kunter, F. Yenisey & A. Nuhoğlu, *Muhakeme Hukuku Dalı Olarak Ceza Muhakemesi Hukuku*, 18. Bası (İstanbul, Beta, 2010), p. 1275; B. Öztürk, *Suç Muhakemesi Hukukunda Gaiplik ve Gaiplerin Muhakemesi*, İstanbul, 1984, p. 137; E. Yurtcan, *Tutuk Sanığın Vareste Tutulmuş Olması Durumunda Gıyabında Hüküm Verilmesi Yasaya Aykırı Değildir* (Yasa Hukuk Dergisi, 1978), 1185.
564. In the past it was possible to make a trial inquiry if the subject of the litigation was a crime that might be punished with a fine, confiscation of goods or both (Art. 270/1, repealed CMUK).
565. This is an exception to the new rule, that the suspect or the accused must be present if the decision on pre-trial arrest is rendered (Art. 101, CMK).
566. Different procedural rules to be applied at the courts dealing with organized crime were abolished in 2014 by Act No. 6526 (repealed Art. 10, TMK); the Act No. 7145 dated Jul. 25, 2018, however, introduced provisional procedural rules for terrorism crimes again, applicable for three years (*supra*, para. 470).

The inquiry in court is divided into three phases: preparation of trial session (*infra*, paragraph 512), the trial itself (*infra*, paragraph 513) and the conclusion of the trial with a judgment (*infra*, paragraph 516).

I. Preparation of Trial Session

512. For the preparation of the trial session, the president of the court schedules a date for the inquiry (Article 175/2, CMK). There must be at least one week between the day on which the summons was served and the day on which the accused must appear (Article 176/4, CMK). The court (no longer the public prosecutor) sends the summons to the accused (Articles 36, 176/1, CMK) and to his counsel (Article 176/3, CMK) to appear on the given date.

An indictment, together with the summons, shall be served on the accused (Article 176/1, CMK).

If the accused is not under arrest, there must be a notice of the trial date in the served summons. In this notice, the court mentions that the accused will be brought by force or be arrested if he does not appear at the trial (Article 176/2, CMK).

If the accused is in pre-trial detention, he will be summoned to the trial according to Article 35/3 of the Penal Procedure Code. If the accused is arrested, he will be brought to the court clerk's room, where the clerk has the duty to ask him if he requires defense counsel during the trial (Article 176/3, CMK).

The president of the court has the right to subpoena witnesses, call experts or make further investigation of facts of the case at this stage (Article 180/2, CMK).

II. The Course of the Trial

513. The inquiry begins with checking whether the witnesses and experts are present.[567] After that, the identity and personal status of the accused are verified (Article 191/3-a, CMK). Then the indictment as well as his conducts and evidence which constitute the subject of the allegations and the legal nature of the accusations against him shall be explained (Article 191/3-b, CMK). The wording in this provision was amended by Act No. 6763 in 2016. Previously, there was an obligation of reading the indictment, but as the procedure of reading indictments of about thousands of pages in political cases was time consuming, the legislator substituted this word "reading" with the word "*explain.*" Same amendment has been made with respect to the trial at the second instance by the regional Court of Appeal (*infra*, paragraph 530).

After establishing his identity, explaining the accusations against him, the accused is questioned according to Article 147 of the Turkish Code of Penal Procedure (Article 191/3-c, CMK), and asked if he is ready to give explanations (Article 191/3-d, CMK).

---

567. F.Yenisey & A. Nuhoğlu, *Ceza Muhakemesi Hukuku*, 6. Baskı, Seçkin, Ankara, 2018, p. 748; N. Centel & H. Zafer, *Ceza Muhakemesi Hukuku*, 14. Bası, İstanbul, Beta, 2017, p. 712.

During the above-mentioned procedure the witnesses are not allowed to be present in the courtroom (Article 191/2, CMK).

514. There is an obligation for the prosecution to be present in the trial procedure at the court of general jurisdiction and at the court of assizes (Article 188, CMK). In order to utilize the public prosecutors sitting in the courtroom for accelerating investigations, public prosecutors have been removed from trial session until 2020.

All phases of the final investigation (trial) are conducted in the presence of the defendant (Article 193/1, CMK), including all formalities of procedure, especially the proof of guilt (Article 216, CMK), but there are some exceptions to this rule: In cases where light sentences are involved, that is, where the offense is punishable by confiscation alone or in combination with some other sanctions (Article 195, CMK), the trial may proceed even if the defendant does not appear in court.

A defendant may be excused from attending trial, except where the crime carries a serious punishment (five years of imprisonment at the lower level) (Article 196/2, CMK). If such motion is granted, and the defendant has not been questioned as to the principal facts of the case, then he must be questioned by rogatory letters (Article 196, CMK). If the punishment provided in the Penal Code for this crime is more than five years of imprisonment at the lower level, the accused must be present in the courtroom.[568]

In addition, the defense counsel is entitled to be present in the courtroom, in cases where the defendant himself is absent (Article 197, CMK).

There are developments in Turkish Law regarding the application of video-conference technology during criminal procedure, both in investigation and in trial stage. In this respect Article 196/4, CMK reads as follows: "*The accused, who is present in Turkey, may be interrogated by live video-conferencing, if the judge or the court deems it necessary*" (SEGBİS: simultaneous image and voice transfer system). Such SEGBİS application is also permitted during the witness' testimony.

515. After the accused has been questioned, evidence is presented to the court. If the accused was not present, and he was not questioned, the presentation of the evidence is nevertheless not postponed.[569] The presented evidence will be explained to the accused when he returns (Article 200, CMK).

After each presentation of evidence or after hearing a witness, the public prosecutor, defense counsel and the *lawyer representing the victim* may personally ask questions to the accused, to any intervener, to the witness and to the expert (Article 201, CMK). This is a new approach of the new Penal Procedure Code, to give leave to ask questions personally. The repealed legislation allowed only those questions suggested to, and posed by, the presiding judge. When those questions have been

---

568. CGK Mar. 23, 2010 (2009/10–245–2010/62).
569. A. Önder, *HUMK 150 ve CMUK 378, 379 ve 380. Maddeleri Muvacehesinde Tarafların, Avukatın ve Mudafiin Söz Söyleme ve Savunma Serbestliği, AdD* (1948), IXL, pp. 1034–1051; Ş. Alpaslan, *Anglo-Amerikan Hukukunda Mahkemeye Saygısızlık Suçu ve Türk Hukukundaki Durum*, IHFM I974/XL, 1–4, pp. 243–287.

asked to each witness personally, the president of the court asks the accused whether he has anything to say (Article 215, CMK).[570] This type of questioning is a kind of *cross-examination.*[571]

The Penal Procedure Code was amended in January 2013, to allow defendants to conduct their defense in a language of their preference other than Turkish at certain stages of the judicial process, even if they can express themselves adequately in Turkish. In the past, some accused Turkish citizens with Kurdish origin refused to talk Turkish during pending trials for political reasons, even though they were very fluent in the Turkish language and had studied at Turkish educational institutions. Such political trials caused an amendment of Article 202, CMK by Act No. 6411 in 2013.

The paragraphs added to Article 202 give to the accused an option to choose the language in which they can express themselves best. If the accused selects for his oral arguments any language other than Turkish, he must choose an interpreter from the list of certified translators. It is important to note that the cost of translation shall *not* be paid by the state.

When the presentation and discussion of evidence is complete, the public prosecutor, the injured (civil) party and the accused have the right to be heard. The public prosecutor has the right to respond to the accused and the accused and his attorney have the right to reply to the public prosecutor.

The accused always has the right of the last word (Article 216/3, CMK). Even if the accused has a defense attorney, he personally has the right to the last word.

The trial ends with the issuing of the judgment.

III. Conclusion of Trial and Judgement of the Court

516. After conducting the inquiry according to regulations as prescribed by the Code, the president of the court announces that the inquiry is completed and concludes the session (Article 223/1, CMK). Afterwards, the court holds a closed session in private chambers to discuss the outcome of the inquiry.

There is no jury in Turkish Criminal Law, not even in the court of assizes. Therefore, there is no distinction between the verdict and the sentence. Before reaching the judgment, the court must decide whether the proven facts constitute a criminal offense. If not, the accused will be acquitted. If the court decides that it has been proven that the accused has committed a crime, and there are no grounds to justify the acts, the accused is pronounced guilty and convicted. Afterwards, the court determines the punishment (*supra*, paragraph 312).

570. T.T. Yüce, *Alman ve Türk Ceza Muhakemeleri Usulünde Savunma Hakkı, AdD* (1960/11), pp. 1017–1028.

571. A.E. Akyazan, *Karşılaştırmalı Hukukta ve Türk Hukukunda Doğrudan Soru Yöneltme (Çapraz Sorgu)* (Ankara, 2009). G. Arıkan, *Çapraz Sorgu İçin Hazır mıyız?* (Ankara Barosu Dergisi sayı, 2005/4).

517. The categories of the judgments of the trial court. The trial court may issue the following categories of judgments[572] at the end of the trial: Acquittal (Article 223/2, CMK); no ground for punishing on the grounds of lacking culpability (Article 223/3, CMK); no ground for punishing (Article 223/4, CMK); conviction, in cases in which the facts are proven (Article 223/5, CMK); conviction in cases where the facts are proven and the accused is mentally ill, security measure instead of punishment, or a security measure and punishment (Article 223/6, CMK); rejection of the case,[573] (Article 223/7, CMK); and dismissal or dropping of the case (Article 223/8, CMK).

If there is a ground for dismissing the case or setting the punishments aside pursuant to the Penal Code, or if it is obvious that the conditions of criminal prosecution will not be realized, the court dismisses the case. *Suspension of proceedings* is no longer considered a *judgment.*

518. Conviction, and reasons for the decision. A conviction is comprised of two parts: The decision of the court and the reasons for this decision. Normally, the decision of the court and its reasons will be read aloud and explained at the same time and written into the minutes of the proceedings.[574] However, sometimes the reasons may be read afterwards. The law permits the court to prepare it within fifteen days after the pronouncement of the judgment (Article 232/3, CMK).

The judgment must contain the category of the decision, the numbers of the articles of the Penal Code that were applied, the duration or extent of the sanction and notice about the possible legal remedies provided by law against the judgment (Article 232/1, CMK).

Reasons for the decision. According to Article 230 of the Code of Penal Procedure and Article 61 of the Penal Code, the reasons for the decision must be laid down accurately. Here, the proven facts should be discussed. The mere mentioning of the related article of the Penal Code is not considered a valid reason.

519. Delayed announcement of the judgment. The delayed announcement of the judgment (Article 231/5-14 CMK) is regulated in Turkish Criminal Procedure Code since 2006. Act No. 2006-5560 added new subsections to Article 231, which were amended in 2008 by the Act No. 5728, in 2010 by the Act No. 6008 and in 2014 by the Act No. 6545.[575]

In cases where at the end of the trial, the accused is sentenced by imprisonment of two years or less, or a fine, the court may decide to delay the pronouncement of

---

572. E. Günay, *Uygulamalı Ceza Davalarında Hüküm Kurma Esasları ve Hükmün Bozdurulması,* 2006.

573. N. Kunter, F. Yenisey & A. Nuhoğlu, *Muhakeme Hukuku Dalı Olarak Ceza Muhakemesi Hukuku,* 18. Bası, İstanbul, Beta, 2010, p. 1489.

574. N. Kunter, *Yargılama Makamlarında Dağılan Oyların Toplanması Sorunu* (YD 1983/ Temmuz, p. 354); F. Yenisey & A. Nuhoğlu, *Ceza Muhakemesi Hukuku,* 6. Baskı, Seçkin, Ankara, 2018, p. 754; Y. Ünver & H. Hakeri, *Ceza Muhakemesi Hukuku,* 17. Baskı, Adalet, Ankara, 2020, p. 664; B. Öztürk et al., *Ceza Muhakemesi Hukuku,* 9. Baskı, Seçkin, Ankara, 2015, p. 630.

575. A. Yıldırım, *Hükmün Açıklanmasının Geri Bırakılması,* Seçkin, Ankara 2018.

the judgment. The provisions related to mediation are preserved. Delaying the pronouncement of the judgment has the effect that the judgment that has been rendered shall not be enforced and shall not create any legal effect against the accused (Article 231/5, CMK).

In order to be able to render *the decision on delaying the pronouncement of the judgment,* the following requirements must have been fulfilled: The accused must not have been convicted for a crime of intent previously, the court must consider the special qualities of the personality of the accused and his behavior during the main trial and the court has to reach the belief that the accused shall not commit further crimes.

In addition, the damage to the victim or the public, due to the committed crime must have been repaired to the fullest extent by giving back the same object, by restoring the circumstances as they were before the crime had been committed or by paying the damages (Article 231, CMK).

In cases where the accused does not consent, there shall be no decision on delaying the pronouncement of the judgment rendered (Article 231/6, CMK).

If the court decides to delay the pronouncement of the judgment, the judgment cannot include a suspension of the execution of an imprisonment term of less than one year, or conversion of a short-term imprisonment into alternative sanctions (Article 231/7, CMK).

In cases where a decision on delaying the pronouncement of the judgment has been rendered, the accused shall be subject to a probation term for five years. In cases where the accused commits another intentional crime within the probation period, he shall not enjoy the privilege of delayed pronouncement of the judgment (Article 231/8, CMK). The court may decide that the accused shall be subject to an obligation of probation, not exceeding one year: (a) In cases where he has no profession or skill, the court may decide that he shall take part in an education program in order for him to obtain a profession or a skill. (b) In cases where he has a profession or a skill, the court may decide that he shall work for a fee in a public institution or in a private place, under the supervision of another person who performs the same profession or skill.

The court may decide that he shall be prohibited from going to certain places, or that he shall be obliged to visit certain places or to fulfill another obligation which shall be determined by the discretion of the court.

During the period of probation, the statute of limitations for prosecution shall be interrupted by the probation measure (Article 231/8, CMK).

In cases, where the accused is not able to fulfill the requirement that is mentioned in subsection (c) of subparagraph 6 immediately, the court may decide as well that the pronouncement of the judgment shall be delayed under the requirement that the accused pays the damages of the public or of the victim to the full in monthly installments (Article 231/9, CMK).

In cases where there has been no intentional crime committed during the period of probation and the obligations related to the measures of controlled liberty (probation), the judgment, of which the pronouncement had been delayed, shall be annulled, and the court shall render the decision on dismissing the case (Article 231/10, CMK).

In cases where the accused has committed a new intentional crime during the period of controlled liberty (probation), or has violated the obligations related to the controlled liberty, the court shall pronounce the judgment. However, the court may evaluate the circumstances related to the accused who was not able to fulfill the obligations imposed on him and may decide that the portion of the punishment (which may be determined up to one-half of the original one) shall not be executed, or if the requirements are present, to suspend the imprisonment, or to convert the punishments in the judgment into alternative sanctions, thus forming a new judgment (Article 231/11, CMK).

The decision on delaying the pronouncement of the judgment may be subject to opposition.

Decision related to *the delaying the pronouncement of the judgment* shall be recorded in a specified data bank for this purpose. These recordings may only be utilized for the purpose mentioned in this article, if it has been requested by the public prosecutor, the judge, or the court, in relation to an investigation or prosecution (Article 231/13, CMK).

The provisions of this article related to *delaying the pronouncement of the judgment* shall not be applied for crimes that are mentioned in the *reform laws*, (*supra*, paragraph 13) protected by the provisions of Article 174 of the Constitution (Article 231/14, CMK).

The amendment in 2008 done by Act No. 5728 extended the one-year imprisonment term up to two years (Article 231/5, CMK). This amendment had an unexpected consequence on the whole criminal justice system, because courts have understood this as a *substantive criminal law provision*, not as a purely *procedural clause*. For this reason, they applied the *ex post facto law principle* of the Penal Code to all finalized cases carrying less than two years imprisonment, and these cases have all been reopened in subsequent years. This is one of the causes of delays in Turkish Criminal Justice System.

IV. Enforcement of Final Criminal Judgments

520. The enforcement of criminal judgments was regulated in Book Eight of the repealed Penal Procedure Code. These provisions have been transferred into the Code on Enforcement of Punishments and Security Measures (CGIK) (*infra*, paragraph 564).

Only final convictions (res judicata) may be enforced (Article 20, CGIK). The public prosecutor enforces final judgments. The president of the court or the judge who handed down the conviction approves the final judgment by his signature.

Enforcement of foreign judgments was regulated by Act No. 3002. This act has been repealed by Act on International Legal Cooperation in Criminal Matters (Act No. 2016-6706) (*supra*, paragraph 95).

521. Postponing the enforcement of the judgment. The enforcement of custodial punishments will be postponed if the convicted person is mentally ill (Article 16,

CGIK). Other illnesses constitute a ground for postponing the execution of the custodial punishment if they are likely to place the sentenced person in a life-threatening situation (Article 16/2, CGIK).

Except for imprisonment longer than three years, the execution of custodial punishments may be postponed at the request of the sentenced person if its immediate execution would harm him or his family, as this is outside the purpose of the punishment (Article 17/1, CGIK).

522. Arrest warrant. If the convicted person does not appear at the request of the public prosecutor, or if there is suspicion that he will flee, then the public prosecutor will issue an arrest warrant (Article 20/1, CGIK).

§3. The Legal Remedies

I. Introductory Remarks

523. According to Turkish doctrine, legal remedies in Turkish criminal procedure are divided into two categories: Ordinary legal remedies and extraordinary legal remedies.[576]

Ordinary legal remedies are based on court judgments that are not final (not res judicata). Extraordinary legal remedies apply against court judgments that are final and enforceable (res judicata).[577]

524. Legal remedies can be divided according to the categories of judicial decisions. There are no legal remedies against measures taken by the public prosecutor and police.[578] The only exception to this rule is petitioning the criminal peace judgeship (*supra*, paragraph 460) to overturn or check an arrest or rule against the prolongation of police custody. This was introduced into Turkish Law in 1992 (Article 128, repealed CMUK; now Article 91/5, CMK).

With respect to decisions of magistrates, there is the legal remedy of *opposition*. With respect to judgments of the trial courts, one can seek relief from the Court of Cassation. If the Code provides no exceptions, there is no legal remedy against court orders rendered during the course of the trial.

525. Some general requirements apply to all legal remedies. The first one is interest. Only the party who has interest in the review of the decision may apply for a remedy: The acquitted person has no interest in a legal remedy if the acquittal is based on the facts of the case.

Ordinary legal remedies have devolutive effect. A different court must try the action when a legal remedy has been invoked.

576. N. Centel, H. Zafer, *Ceza Muhakemesi Hukuku*, 14. Bası, İstanbul, Beta, 2017, 813. C. Şahin & N. Göktürk, *Ceza Muhakemesi Hukuku – II* -, 7. Bası, Seçkin, Ankara 2018, p. 245.

577. E. Yurtcan, *Kesin Hüküm*, İstanbul, 1987, p. 25.

578. Ç. Özek, *Yargının İdari Denetimi,* in *Atatürk'ün 100* Doğum Yılını Kutlama Kolokyumu, İstanbul Üniversitesi, İstanbul 1981, p. 115.

The petition for a legal remedy has a suspensive effect and the original judgment of the trial court does not become final or res judicata.

There are requirements for applications for legal remedies. The appropriate court may only judge the case on the request of parties. Exceptionally, in the Court of Appeal, there is an automatic review if the court has ordered imprisonment exceeding fifteen years (Article 272, CMK).

526. If a party does not apply for a legal remedy (review), the judgment becomes final. However, in cases where final decisions rendered by the regional Court of Appeal are in favor of the accused, other accused at the same case who did not file a petition appeal shall benefit from such decisions if they are applicable to them (Article 280/3, CMK added by Act No. 7035 in 2017). It applies if the Court of Cassation quashes the judgment of the trial court because of a mistake in punishment, then the non-appealing party benefits from the decision (Article 306, CMK).

527. If the accused alone had requested the petition of appeal by the Court of Appeal, or a petition of revision by the Court of Cassation, or if the public prosecutor put one forward on his behalf, and the judgment of the trial court is renewed by the by the Court of Appeal, or quashed by the Court of Cassation, then the trial court is not empowered to increase the sentence in the new trial (Articles 283, and 307/4, CMK).

II. Ordinary Legal Remedies

A. Opposition

528. Competent authority to hear the opposition. Opposition is generally applicable against magistrates' decisions if it is not excluded by regulation. Opposition is not available against the judgments of the court, however. Challenging decisions of the court is only possible in instances where they are explicitly provided by the Code.[579]

The magistrate who hears the opposition has the power to examine both the facts and the applicable law and will give his opinion in the form of a new decision on the case. Act No. 2014-6545 has recently amended provisions related to opposition.

Opposition against the decision of a judge (or in exceptional cases against the decision of a court) shall be filed by rendering a petition with the authority that rendered the decision within seven days after the interested parties had learned about the decision, as ruled in Article 35, CMK. It can also be submitted orally while the

579. N. Gürelli, *Itiraz Kanunyolu*, İstanbul, Ceza Adaleti İlkeleri Sempozyumu, İstanbul Üniversitesi, 1973, p. 63; F. Yenisey & A. Nuhoğlu, *Ceza Muhakemesi Hukuku*, 6. Baskı, Seçkin, Ankara 2018, p. 836; B. Öztürk et al., *Ceza Muhakemesi Hukuku*, 9. Baskı, Seçkin, Ankara 2015; Y. Ünver & H. Hakeri, *Ceza Muhakemesi Hukuku*, 14. Baskı, Adalet, Ankara 2018; N. Centel & H. Zafer, *Ceza Muhakemesi Hukuku*, 14. Bası, Beta, İstanbul 2017.

oral submission must be taken into records. The president of the court or the judge shall approve the submission or the signature, which had been taken into the records (Article 268/1, CMK).

The judge or the court, whose decision had been subject to opposition, shall correct the decision, if he determines that the opposition is justified; otherwise, the judge or court shall send the application in at most three days to the authority that has jurisdiction to make the inspection on the opposition (Article 268/2, CMK).[580]

Competent authorities to rule on an opposition. Oppositions against the decisions of the *office of the criminal peace judgeship in criminal matters* shall be examined by the *office of the criminal peace judgeship*, which has the following number in its district of jurisdiction. If the decision belongs to the last numbered office of the criminal peace judgeship, then the oppositions shall be addressed to the first office of the criminal peace judgeship. In the jurisdictions where no court of assizes is valid and there is only one office of the criminal peace judgeship, the oppositions shall be addressed to the office of the criminal peace judgeship in the jurisdiction of the court of assizes. If there is only one office of the criminal peace judgeship in the jurisdiction of the court of assizes, then the oppositions shall be addressed to the office of the criminal peace judgeship, which is attached to the closest court of assizes (Article 268/3-a, CMK).

Opposition to the decisions against the judge of general jurisdiction in criminal matters shall be inspected by the court of assizes in his district of jurisdiction. Oppositions to the decisions rendered by the court of assizes and its president, shall be inspected by the subsequent numbered chamber of the court of assizes, and for the last numbered chamber, by the first chamber; if there is only one chamber of the court of assizes at that location, by the nearest court of assizes (Article 268/3-c, CMK).

Oppositions to the decision of the member of the court, who was delegated to accomplish a certain interaction, shall be inspected by the president of the court of assizes, in the district of jurisdiction; oppositions to the decisions of the court that had been asked to perform an interaction by a letter of rogatory shall be inspected by the provisions in above mentioned numbers by the president or the court of their local jurisdiction (Article 268/3-d, CMK).

The oppositions to the decisions of the criminal chambers of the Regional Court of Appeal on Facts and Law and to decisions of the chambers of Court of Cassation, where the Court of Cassation has ruled as a Court of First Instance, shall be inspected as follows: Decisions of the member shall be inspected by the president of the chamber to which he is attached; the decisions of the president of the chamber and the decisions of the chamber shall be inspected by the subsequent numbered chamber; the decisions of the last numbered chamber shall be inspected by the first criminal chamber (Article 268/3-d, CMK).

580. C. Şahin & N. Göktürk, *Ceza Muhakemesi Hukuku - II -*, 7. Bası, Seçkin, Ankara 2018, p. 261.

529. Procedure of opposition in general. In case of an opposition, the magistrate may change his previous decision within three days (Article 268/2, CMK).[581] Filing a motion of opposition does not suspend the execution of the decision (Article 269/1, CMK). However, the authority whose decision was subject to opposition, or the authority that is going to inspect the decision, may make a ruling on suspension (Article 269/2, CMK).

The authority that is going to inspect the opposition may notify the opposition to the public prosecutor and to the opposing party in order to give an opportunity of a written argument. The authority may conduct inspection and exploration and may give orders to those to be conducted, if it deems necessary (Article 270/1, CMK).

Except for decisions related to pre-trial arrest (which shall be rendered adversarial; *supra,* paragraph 473) and other cases laid down in the Code, a decision upon the motion of opposition shall be rendered without conducting a main trial. However, if deemed necessary, the public prosecutor, and subsequently the defense counsel or the representative shall be heard. If the opposition is deemed justified, the authority shall also rule on the subject matter of the opposition. The decision shall be rendered within the shortest possible period of time (Article 271/3, CMK).

Except for decisions related to the pre-trial arrest, decisions of the court upon the motion of opposition are final, and not subject to a further opposition, or revision by the Court of Cassation (Article 271/4, CMK).

B. Appeal

530. Appeal (istinaf). The motion of appeal has come into force on July 20, 2016.[582] All judgments rendered by the courts of the first instance are subject to appeal on fact and law, except for those mentioned in Article 272/3, CMK, to be explained below.

Judgments related to a custodial penalty of fifteen years and more should be inspected by the Regional Court of Appeal by its own motion (Article 272/1, sentence 2, CMK).[583]

---

581. According to the repealed legislation, if the remedy provided is so-called urgent opposition (within a week), the judge who rendered the opposed decision did not have the power to give a new decision on the related case (Art. 304/4, repealed CMUK). In such cases, only the high magistrate could give a new decision if the former decision was illegal.

582. RG Nov. 27, 2015, 29545.

583. F. Yenisey, *Ceza Muhakemesi Hukukunda İstinaf ve Tekrar Kabulü Sorunu*, İstanbul 1979; C. Ünsal, *Ceza Muhakemesinde İstinafın Gelişimi ve Bölge Adliye Mahkemelerinde Muhakemenin Yapılması*, Seçkin, Ankara 2014; A.T. Sarıgül, *Ceza Muhakemesi Hukukunda İstinaf*, Seçkin, Ankara 2012; A.R. Çınar, *Türk ve Alman Ceza Yargılama Hukukunda İstinaf*, Adalet, Ankara 2010; M.R. Erdem, *Ceza Muhakemesinde Yeni Bir Denetim Muhakamesi Yolu Olarak İstinaf*, Seçkin, Ankara 2010, A. Parlar & O. Sekmen, *Ceza ve Hukuk Muhakemesinde İstinaf ve Temyiz*, 2. Baskı, Bilge Yayınevi, Ankara 2017, A. Parlar, R. Yaman & E. Şensoy, *Ceza Yargılamasında İstinaf Sistemine Göre İspat Gerekçe ve Hüküm*, Aristo, İstanbul 2017, C. Ünsal, *Ceza Muhakemesinde İstinaf*, 2. Baskı, Seçkin, Ankara 2016, N. Meran, *Ceza Yargılamasında İstinaf ve Temyiz*, Adalet, Ankara 2016, E. Yurtcan, *Ceza Yargılaması Hukuku:* İstinaf yargılamasını, Yargıtay'ın yeniden yapılandırılmasını, OHAL ceza yargılaması kurallarını ve yorumunu içeren 13. Bası, Adalet, Ankara 2016, S. Kaymaz, *Ceza Muhakemesinde İstinaf*, Seçkin, Ankara 2017, D. Güngör, *Ceza*

Decisions of the court rendered prior to the judgment and constituting a basis for the judgment, or decisions against which no other legal remedy has been foreseen by the Code, may be attacked in connection with the appealed judgment (Article 272/2, CMK).[584]

For judgments recognizing criminal fines up to 3,000 TRY (3,000 included), the way of the appeals of law and facts is not open. For convictions to fines which have been converted from imprisonment, however, if the original conviction was a prison term, and it has been converted into a criminal fine, such a fine shall be open to appeal (Article 272/3-a CMK).

Additionally, judgments of acquittal rendered for crimes that require a criminal fine not above 500 days as the upper level of the punishment, the law does not provide a legal remedy (Article 272/3-b, CMK).

531. Motion of appeal and its time limit. A motion of appeal shall be lodged within seven days after the pronouncement of the judgment by a petition submitted to the court that rendered the judgment, or by making a declaration to the clerk of the court. This declaration shall be taken into the records, and the judge shall approve the record. With respect to the accused that is under arrest, the provisions of Article 263 shall apply (Article 273/1, CMK).

If the judgment has been pronounced in the absence of the individuals who have standing according to the law to appeal on fact and law, the period starts running on the date of notification (Article 273/2, CMK).

Public prosecutors attached to the courts of assizes may appeal against judgments of criminal courts of general jurisdiction in their district of jurisdiction. The above-mentioned public prosecutors may file a motion of appeal within seven days after the judgment arrives at the office of the public prosecution in that judicial district (Article 273/3, CMK).

Submitting the motives for the application. Failure to submit the grounds for the application in the petition or declaration shall not prevent the admissibility of the application of the following parties: The accused, the intervening parties, the individuals who had filed a petition of intervention and their request was not ruled upon or was denied, or, finally, of the individuals who had suffered damages that would entitle them to intervening party status (Article 273/4, CMK). The public prosecutor shall submit the motives for filing a motion of appeal together with the written petition, writing them clearly, together with the reasoned justification.[585] The petition of the public prosecutor shall be notified to the parties. The parties may submit their responses in this respect within seven days after the date of the notification (Article 273/5, CMK).

Muhakemesinde İstinaf, Yetkin, Ankara 2016, M. Artuç & M.T. Elmas, *Ceza Yargılamasında Duruşma Yönetimi ve İstinaf,* 2. Baskı, Adalet, Ankara 2017.

584. C. Şahin & N. Göktürk, *Ceza Muhakemesi Hukuku – II -*, 7. Bası, Seçkin, Ankara 2018, p. 266.

585. The regulation of motion for the way of cassation in this respect is opposite: All parties have to submit the motives of application at the beginning, if not, the case shall not be heard by the Court of Cassation (*infra,* para. 537).

Effects of an application. In cases where the application for the motion of appeal is timely, the judgment shall not be final (Article 275/1, CMK), and the court shall serve the motives of the judgment to the parties within seven days (Article 275/2, CMK).

532. Running of the period of appeal during the period of restitution. The accused is entitled to ask restitution against judgments rendered against him in his absence. During the period of restitution, the period of appeal runs as well. If the accused files a motion on restitution, he must file a separate motion of appeal on fact and law. In such cases, interactions related to the petition of appeal shall be suspended until a decision about the request of restitution has been rendered (Article 274, CMK).

533. Inspection of the motion by the court that rendered the judgment. The court that has rendered the attacked judgment is entitled to inspect the petition and may deny the motion with a decision for the following reasons: If the petition was submitted after the expiry of the legal period, if the judgment is not open to appeal or if the party that had filed the motion lacks standing (Article 276/1, CMK).

The public prosecutor or the parties who filed a motion of appeal may ask the regional Court of Appeal to rule on this issue within seven days after the notification of the decision on denial. In such cases, the file shall be sent to the regional Court of Appeal. This shall not be a ground to suspend the execution of the judgment (Article 276/2, CMK).

If the court that rendered the judgment does not reject the petition of appeal then the petition of appeal or a copy of the record about the application will be served to the other party. The opposite party is entitled to give its response within seven days after the date of notification (Article 277/1, CMK).

If the opposite party is the accused, then he may give his response with a declaration, which shall be included in the record by the court recorder. The provisions of Articles 262 and 263 related to the applications of legal representatives and arrested suspects are reserved.

After the response has been handed over or the fixed time limit for this purpose has expired, the file of the lawsuit shall be sent to the regional Court of Appeal (Article 277/2, CMK).[586]

534. Duties of the public prosecutor at the regional Court of Appeal. There are public prosecution offices attached to the regional courts of appeal. Originally the public prosecutor at the Court of Appeal was empowered to conduct additional investigation and produce a legal opinion about the factual side of the case. When the file arrived at the Office of the Public Prosecution of the Regional Court of Appeal, it was inspected, a legal opinion of that office was prepared and the entire file, together with the legal opinion was handed over to the criminal chamber of that

586. Prior to the amendment by Art. 15, KHK No. 674, approved by Act No. 6758 dated on Nov. 10, 2016, the file of the lawsuit would be sent to the Office of the Chief Public Prosecution of the Regional Court of Appeal. Originally, the role of the public prosecutor at the regional court was more significant, as stated below.

court. Also handed over were attached documents and evidence required to be given if there were any. The legal opinion, which had been prepared by the Office of the Chief Public Prosecution of the Regional Court of Appeal, would also be given to the parties (Article 278, CMK, original wording before amendment).

As this type of regulation created additional work for the public prosecutor, and dealing with facts in legal remedies was not a habit for Turkish practitioners, the law has been changed. The investigative powers of the public prosecutor, as well as the production of a legal opinion have been removed.

In 2017, however, Article 23 of the Act No. 7035 provided the Office of the Chief Public Prosecution of the Regional Court of Appeal with a new extraordinary power of opposition (Article 308/A, CMK; *infra*, paragraph 558).

535. Procedures at the regional Court of Appeal and prosecution: the pre-inspection on the file. When the case-file arrives at the Court of Appeal, it will be distributed to the competent chamber. The chamber shall conduct the missing parts of the notification, if there are any (Article 278 CMK).

Thereafter the regional Court of Appeal makes a pre-inspection of the case, considering the venue first, and if it lacks jurisdiction, it makes a formal decision to submit the file to the competent court (Article 279/1-a, CMK). If it considers that the petition was not timely or the decision could not be appealed, or if the petitioner does not have the right to file this motion, the court denies the petition of the appeal (Article 279/1-b, CMK). This court decision may be subject to an opposition (Article 279/1, sentence 2, CMK).[587]

In cases where an application overcomes all the above-mentioned inspections successfully, the Regional Court of Appeal goes into the merits of the case *in camera* (Article 280, CMK). This inspection of the substance of the application is called prosecution at the Court of Appeal, which consists of reading the case file and the evidence submitted together with the file and is closed to the parties.

At the end of this inspection, the chamber may rule to deny the petition of appeal on the merits, if it establishes that the judgment bears no illegality in respect to procedure or to substantive law, that there is no missing evidence or the interactions were complete, and that the evaluation in respect to the proof is adequate (Article 280/1-a, first half sentence CMK).

The second option would be to correct the errors of the application of law, which can be corrected on the basis of the file, without hearing the facts of the case (Article 280/1-a, second half sentence CMK). This method is very similar to the way of cassation; therefore the statute mentions Article 303/1, CMK, subsections (a), (c), (d), (e), (f), (g) and (h), a regulation applicable for revision.

In cases where the Court of Appeal deems it appropriate to apply the lower level of punishment for the committed crime, in the same line as in the opinion of the public prosecutor of the court of the first instance, then it may correct the error in application of the law and rule to deny the petition of the appeal on the merits (Article 280/1-b, CMK).

In cases where grounds for dropping the case exist, and where there is no need for further investigation of facts, or where the court of the first instance had made

587. S. Kaymaz, *Ceza Muhakemesinde İstinaf,* Seçkin, Ankara 2017, p. 104.

a legal error in ruling to a security measure the Court of Appeal may correct the error in application of the law and rule to deny the petition of the appeal on the merits (Article 280/1-c, CMK).

The next option of ruling is quashing the judgment of the first instance court if the court made an error in ruling that is very grave, the so-called errors that constitute absolute violation of law (*infra*, paragraph 538; Article 289, CMK, except for subsections g, and h). In such cases the Court of Appeal sets aside the judgment, if it establishes that there is a ground of such illegality in the judgment of the court of the first instance and sends the file to the court of the first instance whose judgment has been set aside, or to a different court of the first instance within its district of jurisdiction, which the court deems appropriate (Article 280/1-d, CMK).

Quashing a judgment is a very special decision reserved for the way of cassation (*infra,* paragraph 550), and does not fit into the system of appeal on fact and law. Existence of this option of decision-making is an evidence of the assertion that the Turkish way of appeal is in reality an "extended way of cassation" that may inspect facts included in the case file. The judges at the Court of Appeal utilized this form of decision very frequently during the first two years of application, quashing the judgment as it was not furnished with good reasons, therefore the legislator has exempted subsections (g) and (h) of Article 289, CMK, related to the failure of the motives of the judgment and to illegal restrictions of defense.

As mentioned above (*supra*, paragraph 525), final decisions rendered by the regional Court of Appeal according to Article 280, CMK are in favor of the accused; other accused that did not appeal shall benefit from them also (Article 280/3, CMK, added by Act No. 7035 in 2017).[588]

The last option for the Court of Appeal is to rule on conducting a new trial, if there are factual or legal errors at the judgment of the court of the first instance (Article 280/1-e, CMK). This decision is the most important ruling during the procedure of appeal, as it brings the pending case back to the prosecution phase; this means that an inspection of an existing judgment has ended and the Court of Appeal is going to form its own judgment based on the indictment submitted to the court of the first instance.

At the end of this renewed trial, the Court of Appeal shall either rule to deny the petition of appeal on the merits, or set aside the judgment of the court of the first instance and make a new ruling on the merits (Article 280/2, CMK).

In such cases the court shall start with the preparations of the main hearing and the president of the regional Court of Appeal, or a member of the court appointed by him, shall determine the day of the main hearing according to the Article 175, CMK and make the necessary calls (Article 281, CMK).

The summons to the accused shall include the warning that failure to appear at the main hearing of the lawsuit opened upon his petition will lead to inadmissibility.

The court decides on hearing the witnesses and experts that are deemed necessary and conducts judicial inspection (Article 281, CMK).

---

588. S. Kaymaz, *Ceza Muhakemesinde İstinaf,* Seçkin, Ankara 2017, p. 134. U. Aşkın, *Ceza Muhakemesinde İstinaf Kanun Yolu,* Adalet, Ankara 2018, p. 190.

536. The main hearing at the Court of Appeal. If the main trial is opened, general provisions related to the main hearing and judgment apply: The inspection report of the member who has been appointed previously to review the whole written file and produce a report shall be explained,[589] as well as the final judgment of the court of the first instance, which is provided with reasons. The transcripts of the witnesses, the transcripts of the preparatory works by the Regional Court of Appeal itself, if it has conducted such investigation, the transcripts of the judicial inspection, and submissions and reports of experts shall also be explained (Article 282/1-a, b, c, d, CMK).

Witnesses and experts whose hearing at the main trial at the Regional Court of Appeal are deemed necessary shall be summoned (Article 282, CMK).

At the end of this renewed trial, the Court of Appeal shall either rule to deny the petition of appeal on the merits or set aside the judgment of the court of the first instance and make a new ruling on merits (Article 280/2, CMK).

If the petition of appeal was submitted only by the accused, or in favor of him, the newly rendered judgment shall not contain a heavier sanction than that determined by the former judgment (Article 283, CMK).

Decisions in favor of the accused may be also beneficial for other accused of the same case, who did not appeal (Article 280/3, CMK) (*supra,* paragraph 526).

Against the decisions and judgments rendered by the regional Court of Appeal, there is no right to *insist*, which is given against decisions of the Court of Cassation (*infra*, paragraph 555).

According to Article 284, CMK, provisions opening the way of opposition (Article 268 CMK) and the way of cassation[590] (Article 286, CMK), as well as the recently introduced extraordinary opposition against final decisions (Article 308/A, CMK; *infra*, paragraph 558) are reserved.

C. *Way of Cassation*

537. The nature of the way of cassation. The way of cassation *(temyiz)* regulates the party's petition to the Court of Cassation for quashing the judgments of the regional courts of appeal rendered in the second instance. Only violation of the law can be argued in this legal remedy (Article 288, CMK). The aim of this legal remedy is to achieve a unified application of legal provisions throughout all parts of Turkey, and secure a development of law, resolving difficult legal problems by decisions of the Court of Cassation.[591]

---

589. The wording of Art. 282/1-a, b, c, d was *reading* of the related documents before amendment done by the KHK 696, dated Nov. 20, 2017; it has been changed to *explanation*.

590. C. Şahin, *Ceza Muhakemesi Hukuku II-*, Seçkin, Ankara 2015, p. 248.

591. S. Keskin, *Ceza Muhakemesi Hukukunda Temyiz Nedeni Olarak Hukuka Aykırılık,* Istanbul: Alfa Basım Yayım Dağıtım, 1997.

At the request of any party involved in a case, the way of cassation is awarded against the judgment of criminal chambers of regional Court of Appeal, as listed in Article 286 CMK (*infra*, paragraph 539).[592]

Violation of the rules in favor of the accused does not give the public prosecutor the right to have the judgment reversed (Article 290 CMK).[593]

538. *Regular and absolute grounds for the way of cassation.* An appeal on cassation may be filed only on the regular ground that the judgment has violated the law. The failure to apply a legal rule, or its erroneous application, is a violation of the law (Article 288 CMK).

Absolute violations of the law: The following points are considered absolute violations of the law and will be invoked ex officio, even if they have not been mentioned in the petition or declaration of cassation (Article 289/1, CMK):

(a) The court did not convene in the way prescribed by law.
(b) A judge who is by law prohibited from participation in judicial functions participated in the decision-making process.
(c) A judge concurred in passing judgment, although he had been challenged because of substantial doubt concerning his impartiality, and the challenge was accepted or unlawfully rejected.
(d) The court established its jurisdiction to hear a prosecution case in violation of the law.
(e) Court hearings occurred in the absence of the public prosecutor or of individuals whose presence is required by law.
(f) There occurred a violation of the principles of an open trial by failure to pronounce the judgment openly.
(g) The judgment did not include good reasons (Article 230 CMK).
(h) The decision of the court restricted the right of the defense on points that were relevant to the judgment.
(i) The judgment was based on illegally obtained evidence (Article 289, CMK).

539. *Judgments which may be brought to the way of cassation and prohibitions.* Only a limited number of judgments rendered by criminal chambers of the Regional Court of Appeal are open to the way of cassation (Article 286/1, CMK). Prohibitions of appeal cassation are listed in Article 286/2 CMK below.

This is a very important change in Turkish penal procedure law, as prior to July 20, 2016, judgments of the first instance courts were subject to the way of cassation only.

Decisions given before the judgment, which form the basis for the judgment, or the decisions against which no other legal remedy had been foreseen, may be appealed together with the judgment as well (Article 287, CMK).

---

592. If the conviction was related to deprivation of liberty for fifteen years or more, however, then the Court of Cassation examines the case automatically (Art. 305/1 repealed CMUK). This provision is now transferred to the appeal (Art. 272/1, sentence 2 CMK).

593. C. Şahin & N. Göktürk, *Ceza Muhakemesi Hukuku - II -*, 7. Bası, Seçkin, Ankara 2018, p. 278.

Prohibition of the way of cassation: Reversal judgments rendered by criminal chambers of the regional Court of Appeal may not be appealed on cassation (Article 286/1, CMK).

Other judgments, against which the way of cassation is closed are listed in Article 286/2, CMK, as follows:

(a) Judgments rendered by criminal chambers of the Regional Court of Appeal denying appeal on the merits against the judgments of the Court of the First Instance, related to imprisonment of up to five years, and decisions related to any kind of fines.
(b) Judgments rendered by criminal chambers of the Regional Court of Appeal related to punishments of up to five years custodial penalty, that do not alter the characteristics of the offense and the final punishment as described in the judgment of the Court of the First Instance.
(c) All kinds of decisions of the Regional Court of Appeal related to the decisions of the Court of First Instance concerning alternative measures, converted from imprisonment; and decisions on denying appeal on the merits.
(d) All kinds of decisions of the regional Court of Appeal, related to the decisions about crimes, that are under the competence of the court of the first instance, and impose a custodial penalty of up to two years.
(e) All kinds of decisions of the regional Court of Appeal, related to the judgments rendered by the courts of the first instance in crimes that carry criminal fine only.
(f) Decisions rendered by the regional Court of Appeal on denying appeal on the merits about applications against decisions of the courts of the first instance, that rule on confiscation of goods or rights only or in relation to a judgment that deems it not necessary to rule so.
(g) Where the judgment of the regional Court of Appeal was an acquittal on appeal on fact related to offenses that require custodial penalty for ten years (including the tenth year), or that require various fines in connection with the decisions of acquittal rendered by the court of the first instance and decisions of denial of motions for appeals of fact.
(h) Decisions of the court of the first instance reversed by the regional Court of Appeal, in relation to striking a lawsuit, or dismissal of a lawsuit, or a decision not to punish or a postponement of the prosecution or sentencing because of marriage.
(i) Decisions of the regional Court of Appeal, which contain more than one sentencing decision, as long as they stay within the limits of the above-mentioned rules.

The casuistic method of such regulation is very complex and excludes the way of cassation for many crimes thus the unified application of law is limited.

540. Motion on cassation and the time limit. A motion on cassation must be filed within fifteen days (it was 7 before 2017-7035 amendment) of the pronouncement of judgment. The declaration will be included in the records and approved by the judge. The provision of Article 293 CMK related to the accused under arrest takes precedence (Article 291/2, CMK).

If the judgment has been pronounced in the absence of the individuals who have the right to apply for cassation, the period for appeal begins to run from the date of the notification (Article 291/2, CMK).

For judgments not in favor of the accused, pronounced in his absence, in connection with the motion for restitution, the provisions of Article 274 related to running of the period of appeal during the period of restitution shall apply (Article 292, CMK).

541. Formal requirements of an application. The petition should be directed to the registrar of the Regional Court of Appeal in writing or orally, upon which a record shall be made and signed by the petitioner (Article 291/1, CMK).

542. Legal consequences of an application. A petition on cassation, filed within the foreseen period, prevents the judgment from becoming final (Article 293/1, CMK). If the judgment and its motives have not been explained to the appealing public prosecutor or the parties, the motives shall be communicated within seven days after the regional Court of Appeal has knowledge of the request on cassation (Article 293/2, CMK).

543. Contents of an application for cassation: motives. The public prosecutor or the parties filing a motion on cassation must indicate in their petition or declaration the legal aspects (Article 294/1, CMK) on which they base their request for the judgment to be reversed.

According to the repealed Penal Procedure Code (Article 305), however, there was no obligation until June 2016 to state the grounds for the petition. Two words were sufficient: I appeal. Now, there is an obligation to submit the application setting forth detailed grounds of appeal on law.

If the petition for appeal on cassation or the declaration does not contain the grounds, the appealing party shall submit an additional petition to the regional Court of Appeal within seven days. This seven-day period starts with the expiry of the period set for submission of a petition or with the notification of the decision of the judgment. The public prosecutor shall openly state in his petition of appeal whether the appeal had been put forward in favor or against the accused (Article 295/1, CMK).

If the appeal is filed by the accused, the additional petition must be signed by the accused or by his lawyer before submission (Article 295/2, CMK).

If the accused does not have a defense lawyer, he may declare his motives for appeal on cassation to the registration clerk, who will take them on record. The record must be approved by the judge (Article 295/3, CMK).

544. Inspection of a motion of appeal on grounds of admissibility by the regional Court of Appeal that rendered the decision. The regional Court of Appeal whose judgment has been appealed on cassation shall inspect the petition of appeal and rule on denial if it was submitted after the legal time limit expired, if the judgment was not subject to appeal on law, or if the person had no standing (Article 296/1, CMK).

If the court rejects the application, the public prosecutor or the parties who make the appeal may request from the Court of Cassation within seven days after the notification of the order, a ruling on this issue, and the file shall be sent to the Court of Cassation. However, the execution of the judgment shall not be postponed on this ground (Article 296/2, CMK).

A copy of the petition of appeal on cassation or the appellate brief regarding the appellate request, which the regional Court of Appeal has not rejected under the provisions of Article 296 CMK, shall be issued to the opposing party. The opposing party shall submit the written answer within seven days (Article 297/1, CMK).

If the opposing party is the accused, he may also submit his answer of declaration to the court registrar who prepares the record accordingly. After the answer has been submitted, or the time limit for an answer has expired, files pertaining to the case shall be forwarded by the office of public prosecution at the regional Court of Appeal to the office of the chief public prosecution at the Court of Cassation (Article 297/2, CMK).

545. Legal opinion of the Attorney General. It is the duty of the Attorney General at the Court of Cassation to produce an independent report about the legal status of the case, considering parties' submissions. If the legal opinion of the Chief Public Prosecution at the Court of Cassation (Attorney General) contains views that may be unfavorable, or if the parties file a motion of appeal on law, the related chamber will notify the accused or his defense lawyer, as well as the intervening parties or their representatives. The related party may respond in writing within one week after the notification (Article 297/3, CMK). The notifications will be valid (according to the rule in Article 35 of the Act on Notifications) if they are sent to the address that is included in the file (Article 297/4, CMK).

546. Inspection of the petition of appeal on cassation by the Court of Cassation. If the Court of Cassation determines that the petition of appeal has not been submitted in time, a declaration has not been made, the judgment cannot be appealed, the individual appealing does not have standing, or the appellate petition or the appellate declaration does not contain grounds for appeal, then the request for appeal shall be rejected (Article 298, CMK).

547. The Court of Cassation will only examine the file. Only if the crime is an offense that imposes custodial punishment for ten years or more, an adversary session will be allowed upon demand of the parties or on its own motion if it deems that adequate (Article 299/1, CMK). Prior to 2017 amendment by KHK No. 696, parties were also empowered to make a petition for oral hearing.

The day of the main hearing shall be notified to the accused and to his lawyer, if he so requests. The accused has the right to be present at the main hearing or may be represented by his lawyer (Article 299/1, CMK). If the accused is under arrest, he cannot request to be present at the main hearing (Article 299/2, CMK).

Before the main hearing, the report prepared by the member of the court appointed for this mission or by the examination judge shall be explained to the members. If necessary, the members may also examine the files. The hearing shall start after these issues have been resolved (Article 300/1, CMK).

During the main hearing, the Chief Public Prosecutor at the Court of Cassation or the public prosecutor from the Court of Cassation in charge on his behalf, the accused, the intervening party and their counsels will present their claims and defenses. The party who made the request for appeal speaks first. In any case, the accused has the last word (Article 300/2, CMK).

548. The scope of the examination by the Court of Cassation. The first limitation to examination is critical: Only the mistakes in the application of the law are reviewed. The factual findings are excluded from examination.

The Court of Cassation inspects only the points indicated in the appellate petition or in the appellate brief, and the facts declared in the appellate petition or appellate brief, if the appellate request is based on procedural matters (Article 301, CMK). This new regulation is the opposite of the previous one: The examination by the Court of Cassation was not limited to the issues raised by the appellant. The court had the power to examine the whole file and may quash the judgment because of a fundamental error in law made by the trial court that could have changed the outcome of the judgment and that was not known to the parties (Article 320, repealed CMUK).

The problem of *partly* res judicata (*kısmi kesinleşme*) of those matters not objected to in the final petition and being excluded from review by way of cassation, does not exist in Turkish Law.

There are four modalities of decisions of the Court of Cassation: Rejecting the petition (*infra,* paragraph 549), quashing the judgment of the trial court (*infra,* paragraph 550), rendering a new judgment while correcting minor legal errors (*infra,* paragraph 551) and dismissing the case (*infra,* paragraph 552).

549. Rejection of the appellate request upon merits by the Court of Cassation. The Court of Cassation can reject a petition if it does not meet the necessary legal requirements. If the findings of the Court of Cassation about the judgment of the regional Court of Appeal are in accordance with the law, the petition of appeal shall be rejected (Article 302/1, CMK).

In this case, the judgment of the trial court becomes final and res judicata. However, the public prosecutor of the Court of Cassation, the Attorney General, has the power of an extraordinary opposition (*infra*, paragraph 559) against this decision of the Court of Cassation.

550. Quashing the judgment. The Court of Cassation has the power to quash the judgment of the regional Court of Appeal (Article 302/2, CMK).

The Court of Cassation may quash the contested judgment on the basis of violations of the law *affecting the judgment* that are pointed out in the appellate petition and the appellate brief. Reasons for reversal shall be shown separately in the written judgment (Article 302/2 CMK). Provisions of Article 289 about absolute violations of the law shall have precedence (Article 302/5, CMK).

If the judgment is quashed because of the reasons shown in the appellate petition or the appellate brief, also all other legal errors discovered by the Court of Cassation shall be shown in the written judgment, even if they were not expressly declared one by one in the appellate petition or the appellate brief (Article 302/3, CMK).

If the violations of law causing the judgment to be quashed stems from legal transactions that have been the foundation of the judgment, they shall also be quashed (Article 302/4, CMK).

551. Correcting minor legal errors. The Court of Cassation does not have the power to deal with factual findings of the case, and for this reason it may not interfere with the judgment itself. The Court of Cassation may only quash the judgment of the trial court if it determines that there are mistakes of law. However, in exceptional cases, as provided by the Code, where the mistake can be set aside without considering the facts, the Court of Cassation can correct the judgment on its own initiative without quashing the decision (Article 303 CMK). This occurs in the following cases:

(a) A decision for an acquittal or dismissal of the case, or for a fixed punishment with no certain minimum or maximum limits, is necessary.
(b) The Court of Cassation concurs with the view of the Office of the Chief Prosecution at the Court of Cassation to apply the minimum degree of punishment prescribed by law.
(c) The number of the article of the provision was written incorrectly, even though the nature, characteristics and punishment of the crime determined in court was correct.
(d) In situations where a law that went into effect after the judgment reduces the punishment, and in the determination of the court's punishment of the accused, the reason for the decrease was not accepted at the trial court, then a reduced sentence of the crime shall be required. In situations where according to a new law the act is no longer considered a crime, no punishment at all shall be imposed.
(e) No deduction, or a wrong deduction, was made in determining the punishment, which is to be given according to the suspect's date of birth and the date of the crime, which were established openly.
(f) A material error was made in determining the duration or the amount of the punishment, which is to be given at the end of maximizing and minimizing.
(g) The sentencing was for less or more because of non-consideration of the provisions of Article 61, TCK.
(h) Legal errors in court expenses and errors in determining the fee of the lawyer.

552. Dismissing the case. If the grounds for dismissal and setting aside of punishments (*infra*, paragraph 630) are present, the Court of Cassation is entitled to dismiss the case.

553. Pronouncement of judgment by the Court of Cassation. The judgment shall be pronounced in accordance with the provisions of Article 243. If there is no possibility to do so, the ruling shall be made within seven days from the ending of the hearing (Article 305, CMUK).

554. Where to send the decided case file. The file regarding the decisions given according to the first paragraph of Article 333 or Article 334 shall be forwarded by the Court of Cassation to the Office of Court of Cassation Chief Prosecutor, in order to be sending to the Regional Court of Appeal that rendered the judgment.

If the judgment was quashed because the court, in violation of the law, considered itself in charge or having authority, then the Court of Cassation forwards the file to the court that effectively is in charge and having authority (Article 304, CMK).

The Regional Court of Appeal shall give the file, within seven days from the date of the file's arrival from the Court of Cassation, to the Office of Chief Prosecutor of the regional Court of Appeal, in order to be forwarded to the court of the first instance in charge of necessary interactions.

Except in cases of Article 334, the Court of Cassation shall forward the file to the regional Court of Appeal whose judgment had been quashed, or to another regional Court of Appeal, to be reviewed and decided again.

555. Procedures after reversal: (a) Initial hearing. The Regional Court of Appeal that is to retry the case upon the decision of reversal of the Court of Cassation shall ask the related individuals for their responses regarding the reversal (Article 307/1, CMK).

Once the record is sent back, the trial court must seek the opinion of the parties concerned about the quashed decision (Article 307/1, CMK). It then has two options: The first is to accept the error and begin a new trial, the second option is to insist on the initial judgement.

Since the first judgment is invalid, at the end of the second trial, a new judgment shall be rendered by the trial court that is subject to ordinary review in the Court of Cassation. The authorized chamber of the Court of Cassation will examine this decision.

If notification to the addresses shown in the file of the accused or of the intervening party and their lawyers was not possible, or even if the notification was achieved but their arguments against the reversal could not be taken because they did not show up to the main hearing, then the main hearing will continue, and the case will be concluded in their absence. However, if the punishment to be inflicted on the accused is more severe than it was in the quashed judgment, then the accused must be heard in any case (Article 307/2, CMK).

(b) Insist: The Regional Court of Appeal has the right to insist on its former judgment if the Court of Cassation decides to quash.[594] This *insisting decision* on the first judgment may be appealed again. If not appealed, the first judgment rendered by the trial court becomes final and res judicata. However, the decisions rendered

594. N. Kunter, *Türk Muhakeme Hukukunda İsrar Hakkı,* IHFM, No. 455–447 (1981), p. 173.

by the General Assembly of the Criminal Chambers of the Court of Cassation are not subject to such insistence and shall be final.

If the parties appeal the *insisting* decision to the Court of Cassation, the General Criminal Assembly of the Court of Cassation will examine this case. The decisions of the General Criminal Assembly are final and the trial court has no further right of *insisting* upon the original judgment (Article 307/3, CMK).

(c) Effect of reversal for other accused who did not appeal the case. If the judgment was quashed in favor of the accused, because of a violation of sentencing law, and this is applicable to the other defendants who have not put forward a request for appeal, they also shall benefit from the reversal of judgment, as if they themselves had filed the motion for appeal (Article, 306 CMK).

(d) Reformatio in peius. If the motion of appeal on cassation was filed only by the accused, or by the Office of Public Prosecution on his behalf or by individuals mentioned in Article 262, then the punishment included in the new judgment cannot be more severe than the previous judgment (Article 307/4, CMK).

556. Individual complaint against final judgments. Anyone who claims that his or her fundamental rights have been violated can apply to the Constitutional Court if other domestic remedies have been exhausted. The 2010 constitutional amendment introduced a new legal remedy of individual petition to the Constitutional Court. Relevant legislation entered into force in September 2012, and the Constitutional Court started receiving individual applications (*supra*, paragraph 366).

Another option is to file a complaint with the ombudsman. The Ombudsman Institution became operational following a period of intensive work and began receiving applications in April 2013, including cases related to the *Gezi Park* protests.

The next step is an individual application with the ECtHR.

III. Extraordinary Legal Remedies

557. The Penal Procedure Code includes four extraordinary legal remedies: (1) opposition of the public prosecutor at the regional Court of Appeal and (2) opposition by the Attorney General (*infra*, paragraph 558), (3) reversal in the interest of the administration of justice (*infra*, paragraph 559) and (4) re-opening of a trial in form of "revision of sentences" (*infra*, paragraph 640).[595]

A. *Extraordinary Oppositions by the Public Prosecutor's Office at the Court of Appeal and by the Attorney General*

558. (a) Extraordinary opposition by the public prosecutor's office at the Court of Appeal. There is a new extraordinary legal remedy against the final decisions rendered by the regional courts of appeal, since July 20, 2017, added to CMK as Article 308/A by Act No. 7035: The office of public prosecution at the regional Court of

595. E. Günay, *Ceza Muhakemesi Hukukunda Olağanüstü Kanun Yolları* 2. Baskı, Seçkin, Ankara 2015.

Appeal, by its own initiative, or upon request of the parties may oppose against final decisions of criminal chambers of the regional Court of Appeal, within thirty days after the decision was served to the office, but there is no time limit for motions in favor of the accused. The motion of opposition is directed to the same chamber that rendered the final decision. The chamber shall inspect the motion within the shortest time possible, and may correct its own decision, if it deems necessary, or reject the motion of the extraordinary opposition. The decision on rejection is final (Article 308/A, CMK, added by Act No. 7035 in 2017).

(b) Extraordinary opposition by the Attorney General at the Court of Cassation. The Chief Public Prosecutor at the Court of Cassation is entitled to file a motion of opposition with the CGK in Criminal Matters within thirty days after the date when the final judgment was rendered. He may also do so if he had filed a request on the correction of the judgment after the related decision of the chamber had been handed over to him (Article 308, CMK).[596]

The extraordinary way of legal remedy has been amended in 2012 by Act No. 6352, which added two more paragraphs to Article 308 CMK: In case of a petition, the file shall be sent to the Chamber of the Court of Cassation, which has rendered that decision. The Chamber is entitled to change its original decision, if it deems the opposition is well founded; otherwise, the Chamber shall send the file to the CGK (Article 308/2 and 3 CMK added by Act No. 6352, in 2012).

B. Extraordinary Way of Cassation

559. Reversal in the interest of justice. The Ministry of Justice has the power to give a written order to the Attorney General to seek review of a final judgment of the Court of First Instance, or any decision of a magistrate that is res judicata, if this judgment of the court or judicial decision was not previously reviewed in any way by the regional Court of Appeal or by the Court of Cassation (Article 309/1, CMK). The wording in Article 310/2, CMK has been amended from Minister of Justice to the Ministry of Justice in 2006 by Act No. 5560. This review is designed to improve the law and unify the application of the law in the country.[597] This extraordinary legal remedy is accepted as in the best interest of the law and cannot affect the interests of the accused.[598]

If the Ministry of Justice finds out there has been an illegality in a decision or a judgment that had been final without being inspected by an appeal or an appeal on cassation only, it will request a reversal by the Court of Cassation. The request shall be submitted to the Chief Public Prosecutor's Office at the Court of Cassation and shall mention the legal grounds (Article 309/2, CMK).

596. U. Alacakaptan, *Temyiz Mahkemesi Başsavcılığının Ceza Genel Kuruluna Yaptığı İtiraz Hükmün Kesinleşmesine Engel Olur mu,* AUHFD (1967/47), 1–4, pp. 287–292.

597. N. Centel & H. Zafer, *Ceza Muhakemesi Hukuku,* 14. Bası, İstanbul, Beta, 2017, p. 871.

598. N. Kunter, Olağanüstü Kanunyolunda Reform, in *Ceza Adaleti Reformu İlkeleri Sempozyumu,* İstanbul, İstanbul Üniversitesi, 1973, 110; O. Tosun, Temyiz Kararlarına Karşı Kanunyolları, in *Ceza Adaleti Reformu İlkeleri Sempozyumu,* İstanbul, İstanbul Üniversitesi, 1973, pp. 123–151.

The Chief Public Prosecutor at the Court of Cassation will write down these grounds without altering them. He shall submit his writing, which includes a reversal petition, to the related penal chamber of the Court of Cassation. The penal chamber of the Court of Cassation shall reverse the decision or judgment in benefit of the administration of the justice if the submitted grounds are founded (Article 309/4, CMK).

Consequences of this reversal are as follows:[599]

- If the judgment is one decision as described in Article 223, CMK, which does not solve the essence of the dispute, the judge or the court that had rendered the decision shall do the required inspection and exploration and consequently render the adequate decision (Article 309/4-a, CMK).
- In cases where a conviction has been reversed, and the grounds of reversal are not related to the essence of the dispute or are related to the procedural interactions, eliminating or limiting the rights of the defense, then the judge or the court shall conduct new trial and shall render a new judgment. This judgment shall not impose a penalty, which is heavier than the one in the original judgment (Article 309/4-b, CMK).
- If the reversed judgment is not a conviction and the grounds of reversal are related to the points that resolve the essence of the dispute, this shall not have an unfavorable outcome for the accused and does not require new adjudication (Article 309/4-c, CMK).
- If the grounds of reversal require the setting aside of the punishment or require a lighter penalty, then the Chamber of the Court of Cassation directly rules on either lifting the punishment or on the more lenient punishment (Article 309/4-d, CMK).

In cases where a judgment of reversal has been rendered under the provisions of this Article, there shall be no right to insist (*supra,* paragraph 555-c) (Article 309/5, CMK).

560. Motion by the Chief Public Prosecutor at the Court of Cassation in favor of the criminal justice system. The Chief Public Prosecutor at the Court of Cassation is entitled to file a motion of appeal in favor of the criminal justice system by his own motion only in cases as shown in Article 309. If the Ministry of Justice appealed in accordance with Article 309, the Chief Public Prosecutor at the Court of Cassation may not subsequently exercise this power repeatedly (Article 310, CMK).

599. C. Akkaya, *Kanun Yararına Bozma ve Yargıtay C. Başsavcısının İtiraz Yetkisi*, Ankara, Kartal Yayınevi, 2007.

Part III. Execution and Extinction of Sanctions

Chapter 1. Sources of Penitentiary Law and Nature of Regulations

561. Although the Penitentiary Law is related to the enforcement of criminal judgments, it is nevertheless a separate branch of law. It regulates the relationship between the convicted individual and the state, from the beginning of the custodial penalty until the end of the execution of a final judgment.[600]

There are special rights and powers resulting from this unique relationship.[601] Only a judge is entitled to decide under which conditions a person may be punished. Therefore, the individual rights of the convicted person are to be considered. If the enforcement agencies violate these rights, civil, penal and disciplinary consequences will result.[602]

562. Sources of Penitentiary Law in Turkish Law were mainly derived from administrative regulations. There was no Act in the strict sense of the word. Though the procedure for enforcement of punishments was regulated in the repealed Turkish Code of Penal Procedure and in the repealed Code of Enforcement of Punishments, the execution of custodial penalties was not regulated by a law, but only by ordinances.

This has been remedied by a new Code on *Execution of Punishments and Security Measures* (*Ceza ve Güvenlik Tedbirlerinin İnfazı Hakkında Kanun: CGIK; 2004–5275: RG December 29, 2004*), in force since June 1, 2005.

600. V.Ö. Özbek, *İnfaz Hukuku, İnfaz Hukukunun Temel Kavramları*, Ankara, Orion, 2007; T. Demirbaş, *İnfaz Hukuku,* Seçkin, Genişletilmiş ve Gözden Geçirilmiş 4. Baskı, Ankara 2015.

601. O. Tosun, *Suçluların Cezaevinde İyileştirilmesinde Yeni Yöntemler*, İstanbul, 1967; R. Erkilet & S. Coşarcan, *Tatbikatımızda C. Müddeiumumileriyle Münferit Sulh Hakimlerinin Vazifeleri,* Ankara, 1955; M.A. Sebük, *Ceza Evlerinde İşlenen Cürümler ve Firar Hadiseleri*, İstanbul, 1945.

602. F. Erem, *Diyalektik Açısından Ceza Yargılaması Hukuku*, Ankara, Altıncı Bası, 1986.

Chapter 2. General Principles Concerning the Execution of Sentences and Orders

§1. General Principles

563. The main aim of the execution of custodial punishments is the rehabilitation of the offender and his reintegration into society.

The following principles govern the execution of custodial sentences. The main rule is that human rights must be respected. Certain rights of the convicted individual, however, are limited by the judgment, and this limitation will also influence other rights to a certain degree. It cannot be argued that the convicted person has lost all his civil rights. A minimum standard of humane treatment is guaranteed: the protection against abuse, the right to medical treatment and education, to get information from newspapers, and to contact close relatives, as well as other fundamental rights.

Confidentiality is an important aspect of the execution of the judgments. The execution of punishment is not made public, in order to protect the convicted person from harmful public exposure, which might lead to mistreatment of his family by others.

§2. Entering the Facility

564. Issuing an arrest order for convicts of imprisonment terms. If the convict does not comply with the summons issued for serving the punishment or security measure and fails to appear within ten days after the notification of the summons, or flees or makes an impression that he is about to flee, the public prosecutor shall issue an arrest order (Article 19/1, CGIK).

In order to enforce an imprisonment term of three years for a crime committed with intent (or if the crime has been committed by negligence, more than five years imprisonment), an arrest order shall be issued directly (Article 19/2, CGIK).

In cases where the imprisonment term is the result of a converted criminal fine, the convict shall first be summoned before any arrest warrant may be issued (Article 19/3, CGIK). This arrest warrant does not empower the police to conduct a search in the domicile; the criminal peace judge is authorized to issue a search warrant pursuant to Article 119, CMK (Article 19/4, CGIK).

565. Suspension of execution of the imprisonment punishments on grounds of illness. The execution of the punishment of convicts who are suffering from a mental disease shall be suspended, and the convicted prisoner shall be put under treatment and protection in a health institution as mentioned in Article 57 TCK, until he has recovered (Article 16/1, CGIK).

In cases of other illnesses, the execution of the punishment shall continue in specified sections for prisoners within the official health institutions. However, in cases, where the execution of imprisonment would pose a certain danger to the life of the convict, the execution of his term shall be suspended until he has recovered (Article 16/2, CGIK).

The office of the public prosecution, where the execution has taken place, shall render the decision on the suspension of execution as mentioned in above paragraphs, on the basis of a medical report that has been given by the Legal Medical Institute, or by the medical council of a fully equipped hospital approved by the Legal Medicine Institute and designated by the Ministry of Justice.

The convict and his legal representative shall be notified of the decision on the suspension of the execution of imprisonment and the obligations to be imposed on him. The convict or his legal representative shall give notice to the related office of public prosecution of the location where the convict during the period of suspension shall be accommodated and/or stay.

The health conditions of the convict shall be inspected by the office of the public prosecution which rendered the decision of suspension, or upon his request by the office of the public prosecution, where the convict is present or where his treatment is conducted, within the periods as laid down in the medical report. If there is no period stated in the report, such inspections shall be conducted within periodical intervals of one year. According to the outcomes of the inspection, the public prosecution office, which rendered the decision on suspension, shall decide on the continuation of the suspension or not. Upon the request of the office of the public prosecution, which rendered the decision of suspension, the office of the security forces and the officers where the notification had been done shall fulfill the measures related to observation of the convict. If there is a violation of the obligations mentioned in this paragraph, the decision of suspension shall be lifted by the office of the public prosecution, which rendered it. Against this decision there may be a motion filed with the justice of executions (Article 16/3, CGIK).

Execution of a custodial punishment of a pregnant woman or for a woman who is not yet one year and six months post-delivery shall be postponed. If the child dies or is given to another individual other than the mother, the punishment shall be executed commencing two months post-delivery (Article 16/4, CGIK).

Paragraph 4 of Article 16, CGIK is not applicable to inmates who get pregnant after they have entered the closed correctional facility and have more than six months to serve, nor to inmates who are deemed dangerous on the basis of their conduct and behavior.

The portion of the sanction, which is foreseen in paragraph four for such persons, shall be executed in a suitable location within the correctional facility (Article 16/5, CGIK).

If an inmate is not capable to live alone within the circumstances of the correctional facility, without support of another person, because of a severe illness, or an injury, the execution of punishment shall be suspended under the procedure as regulated in paragraph 3 of this article (Article 16/6, CGIK).

566. Suspension of the execution of the judgment upon the request of the convict. The office of chief public prosecution may suspend the execution of an imprisonment term of less than three years for crimes committed by intent and less than five years for crimes committed by negligence, if the convict appears upon the summons (Article 17/1, CGIK). The suspension may be granted a maximum of two times, and each suspension may not be longer than one year (Article 17/2, CGIK). In cases where a new prosecution is initiated against the convict on the basis of a new intended crime, the suspension shall be lifted and the execution of the prior sentence starts immediately (Article 17/3, CGIK).

Execution of an imprisonment term as defined in paragraph 1 of Article 17 may be interrupted for a term, not exceeding six months, by the decision of the office of chief public prosecution, in necessary and very urgent cases, such as, the case where the convict should have the opportunity to conclude his/her higher education, the death of the convict's mother, father, spouse or children, or because the continuous illness or disability of the mentioned individuals in the family made them unable to work in the agricultural fields of the family, or because the illness of the convict requires a continuous treatment. This interruption shall not be applied more than two times (Article 17/4, CGIK). Approval of the request may be subject to security or any other condition.

The provisions of this article are not applicable to the convicts of terrorism crimes, crimes committed within the activities of a criminal organization and crimes against sexual inviolability; those inmates against whom execution of punishment specified for repeated offenders are decided; persons who are subject to disciplinary incarceration or to a restriction of liberty (Article 17/6, CGIK).

Chapter 3. The Prison System

§1. Organisational Structure

I. Prison Administration and Classification of Penitentiaries

A. Closed Penal Enforcement Institutions

567. There are different categories of Penal Enforcement Institutions: Closed penal enforcement institutions (Article 8, CGIK), high-security closed penal enforcement institutions (Article 9, CGIK), closed penal enforcement institutions particularly for women (Article 10, CGIK), closed penal enforcement institutions for children (Article 11, CGIK), closed penal enforcement institutions for young females and males (Article 12, CGIK), observation and classification centers (Article 13, CGIK), open penal enforcement institutions (Article 14, CGIK), child education institutions (Article 15, CGIK).

The closed penal enforcement institutions have interior and exterior security officers and are set up with technical, mechanical, electronic and physical prevention tools against escape. The doors of rooms and of all corridors are closed. The Code stipulates, however, those situations in which contact with prisoners in other rooms and with the outside environment is possible, so long as sufficient security is provided to work on individual and collective rehabilitation procedure. Inmates who break the rules can be sent to strictly secure penal enforcement institutions (Article 8, CGIK).

568. High security closed penal enforcement institutions. High security closed penal enforcement institutions are establishments that have interior and exterior security officers, and that are set up with technical, mechanical, electronic and physical prevention tools against escape. The doors of the rooms and all corridors are closed. In the situations, however, where the Code mentions, contact between the convicted prisoners in other rooms and the exterior environment is possible (Article 9/1, CGIK).

The high security closed penal enforcement institutions have security measures similar to closed penal enforcement institutions, but the prisoners are accommodated in cells for one to three persons. Individual or group treatment procedures will be applied (Article 9, CGIK).

569. Closed penal enforcement institutions for women. Closed penal enforcement institutions for women are the establishments in which the women prisoners serve their custodial penalties. The interior security officers are women.

If no special women's prison is available, women prisoners will serve their term in a special section of another penitentiary, separated from the rest, with different doors, windows, corridors, rooms, entrances and exits (Article 10, CGIK).

570. Closed enforcement institutions for children. Children between ages 12 and 18 years are scrutinized according to their gender and physical body status and sheltered in separated sections of these institutions (Article 11/2, CGIK). They can shelter the children and minors transferred from educational institutions on disciplinary and other matters. They have special measures to prevent escapes, with interior and exterior security officers, but the main focus remains on education and instruction (Article 11/1, CGIK). Closed enforcement institutions for children are where they are kept during pre-trial detention.

The lack of sufficient purpose-specific institutions for children force the authorities to accommodate the children and minors in closed penal enforcement institutions for adults. However, if there is no section for minors, girls will be sheltered in the women's section of closed penal enforcement institutions, and boys will be accommodated in the special section of other closed penal enforcement institutions. All institutions shall provide education and instruction to the children and minors (Article 11/4, CGIK).

There are establishments for young convicted prisoners who have attained the age of between 18 and 21 by the beginning of the enforcement of the sentence. The regime is oriented around education and instruction, but outside and inside security personnel prevent escape (Article 12/1, CGIK).

571. Child and minor educational institutions. Child and minor educational institutions are establishments where the penalty is enforced with the aim of educating the children, teaching them professional skills and reintegrating them into society. There are no specific measures for the prevention of escape in these institutions beyond those provided under the supervision and responsibility of the interior security staff (Article 15/1, CGIK).

Minors who are attending an educational or learning program when reaching the age of 18 can stay in these institutions until they have attained the age of 21 in order to complete the program.

Children who are detained in these institutions may not be transferred to the closed penal enforcement institutions (Article 15/3, CGIK).

B. Open Penal Enforcement Institutions

572. Open penal enforcement institutions. In open penal enforcement institutions, priority is given to the rehabilitation of the convicted prisoners and teaching them a profession. There are no specific prevention measures against escape and no exterior security staff. The supervision of the personnel in the institution is deemed to provide sufficient security (Article 14/1, CGIK).

According to need, open penal enforcement institutions for young women offenders may be established. The basic principles and the procedure of allocation of convicted prisoners into the open penal enforcement institutions are laid down in a directive (Article 14/6, CGIK).

Offenders serving a term of three years or less (five years for crimes committed by negligent) may be allocated directly to an open penal enforcement institution, after an evaluation conducted according to Article 89, CGIK. Terrorism, organized crimes and crimes against sexual inviolability are exempted from this rule (Article 14/2, CGIK). Inmates convicted by these crimes or to an imprisonment term of ten years or more, may be allocated to an open penal enforcement institution upon the decision of the observation board which must be approved by the judge of enforcement of penalties (Article 14/4, CGIK).

Prisoners in open penal enforcement institutions can be sent back to a closed penal enforcement institution upon the decision of the board of the related institution. This will happen if the prisoner escapes or has been punished with a discipline action higher than caution, if there is an arrest warrant beyond the crime for which the prisoner is serving the sentence and if the prisoner's age, health status, bodily and mental abilities make him or her unsuitable for work. This resolution shall be submitted to the approval of the judge of the enforcement of penalties (Article 14/5, CGIK).

573. Early release for inmates in open penal enforcement institutions. To be allocated to the open penal enforcement institution has an important consequence for the inmate as he or she will be early released from prison. Ordinance on leaving for open penal enforcement institutions has been changed in August 2015 and necessary time period was halved in order to transferring from closed penal enforcement institutions to open penal enforcement institutions for convicted persons. Before this change convicts had to spent 1/5 of their punishment but now this percentage reduced to 1/10. This change is likened as an implicit amnesty and criticized.

II. Classification of Prisoners

A. Observation of a New Prisoner

574. Observation. A new prisoner shall be observed and classified in the *observation and classification center* (Article 23, CGIK) prior to assigning him/her to a particular facility.[603]

First, the individual characteristics of the convicted prisoners, their body, mental and health circumstances, their prior life before committing the crime, their social environment and relationships, their artistic and professional activities, moral tendencies, their concept of crime, the duration of their sentence and the crimes they have committed shall be established. Subsequently, they will be assigned to an appropriate facility and the enforcement and rehabilitation regime will be established. This will happen either in the *observation and classification centers*, which work with the observation, inspection and evaluation method, or in the special departments of the closed penal enforcement institutions, which are reserved for this

603. The internal regulation published in the Official Gazette of Dec. 29, 2020 regulates details of observation of inmates and establishes centers for "observation and classification" (Art. 4), as well as "observation and administration boards" (Art. 13). This internal regulation also includes guidelines for risk assessment (Art. 30) and evaluation improvement (Art. 31). The outcomes of these assessments play an important role for early release of the inmates.

purpose. The prisoners shall be sent to the high security enforcement penal institutions, to regular enforcement penal institutions, or open enforcement penal institutions, depending on the type of the crime they have committed, their tendencies and their behavior.

Prisoners will be sent to strictly secure penal enforcement institutions or to normally secured penal enforcement institutions according to the type of crime committed and whether they have to be strictly observed and supervised because of their attitudes and behavior. In these institutions, if possible, there must be present specialized personnel with expertise and experience in the field of criminology, penology or criminal law, along with medical doctors, experts in the field of legal medicine, social workers, experts in the field of guidance, and other personnel.

Women, children and young convicted prisoners shall be observed and classified in a separate Observation and Classification Center, which shall be established in places deemed necessary. If no such institution exists, they shall be established in the special departments of enforcement penal institutions reserved for women, children and young convicted prisoners.

The observation committee, in observation rooms reserved for single persons, must conduct the observation of the convicted prisoners. The duration of the observation of convicts deserving of a prison term of more than two years shall not exceed sixty days. This shall be determined according to the qualification of the crime and to the type and duration of the punishment (Article 23, CGIK).

B. Classification of Prisoners

575. Convicted prisoners shall be classified into the below-mentioned groups (Article 24, CGIK): Prisoners who are first-time offenders, recidivists, habitual offenders or professional criminals; prisoners who need to have a special enforcement regime because of their mental and bodily conditions or age; dangerous prisoners; terrorist offenders; and members of a profit-oriented criminal organization. Furthermore, the convicted prisoners are classified according to their ages, the duration of their sentence and the type of the crime.

Inmates convicted for anarchistic acts and acts of terrorism or disturbing public order, or robbery or killing with the purpose of political separatism, are put together in special closed prisons (Article 9, CGIK) with special penal measures and special security devices.

Enforcement of *strict (or aggravated) life imprisonment* (*supra,* paragraph 279) happens along the following guidelines (Article 25, CGIK): The prisoner is placed in an individual cell. He has the right to stay at least one hour in the open air and to practice sports, subject to approval. Depending on the risk the prisoner poses; these time limits may be extended. During this period, the prisoner may perform an art or a professional activity if the conditions of the institution allow it. The prisoner is entitled to receive a visit by his spouse, those in lineal consanguinity, his brothers and sisters and his tutor. They may visit the convicted prisoner one by one, with an interval of fifteen days, at most for one hour. The governor of the institution determines the day, hour and conditions. The prisoner may talk on the telephone to these people once in fifteen days for a ten-minute period of time under conditions that the governor of the institution deems appropriate.

576. Organized crime convict and dangerous convicts. A second group is composed of convicted prisoners who have been punished by aggravated life imprisonment, and those who have been convicted of the crime of forming or leading a criminal organization, regardless of the duration of their prison sentence, or one of the below mentioned crimes, which are committed within the activities of such an organization, shall be sent to such high-security closed penal enforcement institutions (Article 9/2, CGIK): Crimes against humanity (Articles 77 and 78, TCK), intentional killing (Articles 81 and 82, TCK), producing and trading with narcotic or stimulating substances (Article 188, TCK), crimes against the security of the state (Articles 302, 303, 304, 307 and 308, TCK), and crimes against the constitutional order or crimes against the well-functioning of this order (Articles 309, 310, 311, 312, 313, 314, and 315, TCK).

Furthermore, those convicts shall also be sent to these facilities who are dangerous because of their conduct and behavior, those that need to be under special supervision and surveillance, those who disturb the discipline and order in another correctional facility, and those who persistently oppose the means or procedures of rehabilitation (Article 9/3, CGIK).

577. If the high-security penal enforcement institutions do not have sufficient possibilities, then the high-security sections of other closed penal enforcement institutions, which are available for the convicted prisoners, who need to be under private custody and control, shall be used (Article 9/4, CGIK); In particular, the convicted prisoners who have been convicted to lifelong imprisonment, who serve half of the term as indicated in Article 107, CGIK in good conduct, those who have been convicted to a specified term, one-third of their term in good conduct, and those who are mentioned in subparagraph 3 of Article 9.

Convicted prisoners, who served one-third of the rest of their total imprisonment terms in good conduct, may be selected to be sent to other penal enforcement institutions in accordance with their manner and personality (Article 9/1 CGIK).

§2. The Penitentiary Regime

I. Enforcement of Short-Term Imprisonment

578. Short-term custodial punishments and special kinds of enforcement. There are regulations about the execution of the short-term custodial punishments through commutation to other measures (*supra*, paragraph 281), and special forms of execution, as well as nighttime execution and the recovery of the damages suffered by the victim are foreseen.

The following special forms of execution may be ordered by the judge of enforcement of penalties, upon the request of the inmate: (a) weekend and nighttime execution (Article 110/1, CGIK), (b) execution of penalty in the home of the convicted female, the convicted person who attained the age of 65 (Article 110/2-a, CGIK), and execution of penalty in the home of the convicted person who attained the age of 70 (Article 110/2-b, CGIK) and those who attained the age of 75 (Article 110/2-c, CGIK).

II. Rules of Enforcement of Long-Term Custodial Punishments

579. The Penal Code has divided long-term custodial punishments (more than one-year imprisonment) into two categories: lifelong imprisonment and imprisonment of limited duration (Article 49, TCK) (*supra*, paragraph 280).

580. The individualized *final punishment* (*supra*, paragraph 326) is the penalty to be served in the correction facility. The Penal Code does not include privileges[604] for adults, but only for children less than 15 years of age who serve only the half of their term (Article 107/5, CGIK).

III. Aspects of Living Conditions

A. *Visits, Correspondence and Telephone*

581. Right to have visitors. The convicted prisoner may be visited during working hours for a minimum of one-half an hour and a maximum of one hour, once a week (under the condition of being documented) by the following persons: By the spouse, by the relatives of third-degree kinship as well as by the guardian and administrator, and by up to a maximum of three other individuals, whose names and addresses are provided during the admission to the institution and which cannot be changed except in exceptional circumstances.

The duration of visits with juvenile inmates shall be fixed not less than one hour and not longer than three hours (Article 83/1, CGIK).

Other individuals (except those mentioned in the first paragraph of Article 83) may conduct visits according to the written permission of the Office of the Chief Public Prosecutor. The visit shall be done in accordance with regulations of the Ministry of Justice determining the provisions and durations (Article 83/3, CGIK).

Foundations, commissions and organizations must seek permission from the Ministry of Justice in order to visit the correctional facilities and to meet the convicted prisoners. This provision is also applicable for those who are doing scientific research and for members of audio and visual media. The Ministry of Justice is also entitled to give permission to those individuals who demand to visit with the convicted prisoners (Article 85, CGIK).

604. Prior to 2005 Criminal Law Reform, penalties for prisoners who are to serve their sentence in open and half-open prisons were reduced by six days per month (added Art. 2, repealed CIK). Escaped prisoners (added Art. 2/6, repealed CIK) and convicted persons for whom the Grand National Assembly had decided that the death penalty would not be executed (added Art. 2/8, repealed CIK) were excluded from this privilege.

The convicted prisoner may be visited for purposes of audit by designated representatives of the international foundations and organizations regulated in international agreements to which Turkey is a party, when the grounds of the visit is furnished and the permission of the Ministry of Justice is granted.

The measures required for the security of visits and meetings shall be taken by the management of the institution. The visits and meetings will occur under the supervision of the institution's personnel except as otherwise prohibited by law.

Collective meetings amongst the convicted prisoners cannot occur if the individuals cannot be brought together due to security reasons. The visits and meetings may be postponed in extraordinary circumstances like natural disaster, fire and disorder, even if they were permitted before (Article 85/4, CGIK).

582. Right to interview with attorney. The convicted prisoner has the right to interview attorneys practicing the profession of lawyering without submitting a power of attorney to a maximum of three times (Article 59/1, CGIK).

Any interview with an attorney or notary shall take place, upon the presentation of proof of professional identities, during the work hours, except for holidays, in designated interview areas and in a manner that the interview can be watched for security reasons. The conversations cannot be listened to (Article 59/2 CGIK).

Attorneys, even if they have a power of attorney, shall not interview more than one convicted prisoner at the same time (Article 59/3, CGIK).

583. Attorney-client privilege. Documents or copies of documents, files which an inmate gives to his lawyer during the interview, or the lawyer to the inmate, and notes taken by them relating to the consultation amongst them shall not be subjected to examination; the consultation of the lawyer with the inmate shall not be listened to and shall not recorded (Article 59/4, CGIK).

The following provisions have been inserted to Article 59 CGIK by KHK No. 676 in 2016, and approved by Act No. 7070, dated February 1, 2018: In cases where there are indications or documents that reveal that during the lawyer-inmate consultation of inmates convicted of crimes as listed in Article 220 TCK and crimes listed in second book, fourth section and fifth section of TCK, public security or security of the institution is endangered, a terrorism organization or other criminal organization is being steered, orders or directives to such organizations are submitted, or through comments open or covered messages forwarded, consultation of the lawyer with the inmate voice and image may be recorded, an official may be appointed to be present during the interview, documents or copies of documents, files which an inmate gives to his lawyer during the interview, or the lawyer to the inmate, and notes taken by them related to the consultation may be seized, or days and hours of the interview may be restricted upon the request of the public prosecutor, by the decision of the judge of corrections for a duration of three months (Article 59/5, CGIK).

The judge of enforcement may subsequently extend the duration of the restriction several times, not exceeding three months, or limit its application, or lift it, considering the inmates' compliance with regulations, the danger posed by the inmate for the public and for the correctional institution, and the development in rehabilitation activities (Article 59/6, CGIK).

In cases where the authorities find out that the interview of the inmate is being misused in direction of forbidden purposes stated in the subsection five, the interview shall be interrupted immediately, and a record shall be produced furnished with the motives. The inmate and the lawyer shall be informed about this regulation before the interview starts (Article 59/7, CGIK).

In cases where such a record has been produced about an inmate, he may be banned from interviewing his lawyers for six months by the judge of corrections upon the request of the public prosecutor. The decision related to the lawyer-ban shall be notified to the related presidents' office of the bar association. The public prosecutors' office may ask the presidents' office of the bar association for changing the named lawyer. The appointed lawyer shall be compensated according the rules set by Article 13 of the Act on Application of Penal Procedure Code, No. 5320, dated March 23, 2005 (Article 59/8, CGIK).

These provisions are also applicable for inmates, who are at the same time suspect or accused of terrorism crimes mentioned in subsection five, interviewing their lawyers (Article 59/10, CGIK).

Decisions rendered by the judge of enforcement may be subject to opposition (Article 59/8). Decisions rendered in relation with the pre-trial detainees is under the authority of criminal peace judgeship during the preliminary investigation, and of the court during the prosecution phase (Article 59/11, CGIK).

584. Convicted foreigners. Under the international conventions to which Turkey is a party and under the principle of reciprocity, the convicted prisoners of Turkish nationality or foreign citizens, who are subjected to an investigation or a prosecution in foreign countries, who desire to bring suit in foreign countries or before international judicial authorities, or who are involved in a lawsuit, may have interviews with their foreign citizen attorneys, on the conditions that the interview is restricted to these investigations, prosecutions, and lawsuits that are brought or to be brought and that the power of attorney is presented. Foreign lawyers who do not have a power of attorney may interview the convicted prisoner in the presence of a lawyer who is licensed in a bar association in Turkey (Article 59/12, CGIK).

A foreign inmate may be visited by the representatives of his citizenship (Article 84, CGIK).

585. Convicted prisoner's right to communicate through the phone: Convicted prisoners, in Closed Penal Enforcement Institutions, may make phone calls through public and pay phones in accordance with the principles and procedures determined in the Regulation. The conversation over the phone shall be monitored by the administration and may be recorded when deemed necessary. This right may be restricted for convicts (*hükümlü*), who pose danger and are members of an organization. In open penal enforcement institutions, in education houses for children, the convicted prisoners may communicate through the above stated telephones without any restriction. All the convicted prisoners in the closed and open penal enforcement institutions may use the institution's telephone and fax devices in case of serious sickness or death of their mothers, fathers, wives and children. The conversations shall be determined by a transcript and the transcripts shall be kept in a special file. The convicted prisoners shall not keep or use mobile phones, wireless phones or cell phones and similar communication devices in open and close penal enforcement institutions and in education houses for children (Article 66, CGIK).

586. Convicted prisoner's right to receive and send letters, fax and telegrams. The convicted prisoner, except for the restrictions stated in this Article, has the right to receive letters, fax and telegrams sent to him and to send them on the condition that he pays the expenses. In institutions that have a commission of reading letters, the letters, fax and in institutions that do not have a commission shall control telegrams sent and received by the convicted prisoner, they shall be controlled by the highest superior of the institution. The letters, fax and telegrams, which endanger the security and order of the institution, show the charged personnel as a target, cause communication between the members of acts of terrorism, organization of crimes for beneficiary purpose or other organizations of crime, involve threats, insults, wrong and lie news that will cause panic among persons or institutions shall not be given to the convicted prisoner. If written by the convicted prisoner, they shall not be sent. The letters, fax and telegrams, written by the convicted prisoner to official authorities or to his attorneys for his defense, are not subjected to any control (Article 68, CGIK).

B. Information and Media

587. Convicted prisoner's right to benefit from radio, television broadcasts and Internet opportunities. On the grounds that there is central broadcasting system, the convicted prisoner depending on this system, have the right to watch and listen to the radio and television broadcasts. In institutions, where there is no central broadcasting system, watching television and listening to the radio shall be allowed by taking necessary measures in order to hinder those broadcasts that are not useful to be watched and listened to by using an independent antenna. These devices shall be purchased by the institution in the name of the convicted prisoner on the condition that he pays their price. No matter how; radios, televisions, and computers brought by people coming from outside shall not be let into the institution. In close and open penal enforcement institutions and in education houses for children, the use of computers shall be allowed merely within education and amelioration programs. It is possible to benefit from the Internet under supervision if education and the amelioration programs deem it necessary. The convicted prisoner may not have a computer in his room. However, in cases where the Ministry of Justice deems appropriate, computers used for educational or cultural purposes may be admitted into the correctional facility. These rights may be restricted for convicts (*hükümlü*), who pose danger and are members of an organization (Article 67, CGIK).

C. Prison Labor

588. Convicts are not allowed to work outside of the institution and cannot obtain temporary release or leave. They may not participate in any sport activities unless the governor of the institution gives specific permission (Article 31/1, CGIK).

The administration of the institution may employ convicted prisoners, who have served at least one year of their sentence and are of good behavior in the suitable internal services of the institution. Convicted child prisoners shall not work outside of their living areas, or outside of the aim of education. The convicted prisoner shall not be employed at the personal business of the governors and officers (Article 31/2, CGIK).

D. Disciplinary Measures and Awards

589. Disciplinary inquiry. Caution, admonition and deprivation of various activities shall be ordered and applied by the highest superior of the institution (Article 47 CGIK).

Constitutional Court repealed the provision of Article 48/1, CGIK in October 3, 2013, which made an analogy for not regulated wrongdoings for disciplinary sanctions.

590. Awards. Article 51, CGIK; dealing with awards provided for inmates has been totally changed by Act No. 6411 in 2013.

Convicts may be given the opportunity to earn support-based awards according to their general situation within or outside of correctional facilities, their participation in educational and rehabilitation activities, their attitude towards the order within the facility and their efforts to accomplish works assigned to them (Article 51, CGIK). The provisions of this article are applicable to juvenile convicts as well.

Awards provided for convicts are the following (Article 51/3 CGIK):

(a) Convicts who are inmates in closed correctional facilities and who are married may have a confidential visit with their spouses within the facility or its attachments without correctional personnel being present, one time every three months for a period of three hours up to twenty-four hours.
(b) Juvenile convicts may enjoy a family visit with their mother and father or their custodian once each two months from three hours up to twenty-four hours in the correctional facilities or its attachments without correctional personnel being present.
(c) Weekly visiting time may be extended up to two hours.
(d) Instead of a closed visit, an open visit may be awarded.
(e) The weekly visiting time, which has not been utilized for three weeks, may be combined and used collectively.
(f) Weekly telephone conversation periods and the number of conversations may be doubled.

(g) The inmate may be given priority for social, cultural and sports events or he may be awarded with an extended period of time for these activities.
(h) If the convict did not use the entire amount of the previous week, one-half may increase weekly expenditure amounts.
(i) He may be permitted to have a TV in a single room.
(j) A gift may be given to the inmate.
(k) A certificate of appreciation or letter of recommendation may be issued.

The procedure and principles of the awards system and the scope and conditions of such opportunities for awards shall be determined by an internal regulation, while taking into consideration the category of crime which has been committed (Article 51/4, CGIK).

E. Leave from Prison

1. Cases of Leaving the Closed Institutions

591. The enforcement of the sentence shall not be interrupted by any means, except in cases of mental illness or for reasons of medical necessity.

The convicted prisoner shall not be moved out of a closed institution, except for purposes of a leave, a forwarding to hospital or to a public prosecution office or to court, or for education, attendance at a workplace, or due to an adjournment of the punishment, release, a transfer, a natural disaster like an earthquake or a flood or a fire; a written order from a competent authority must exist (Article 92/sentence 1, CGIK). This privilege may be limited by the decision of the public prosecutor's office for inmates serving aggravated life imprisonment according to Article 9, CGIK, if there is a danger of using this opportunity for terroristic or other illegal purposes (Article 92/sentence 2, CGIK, added by KHK 674 in 2016, approved by Act No. 6758, dated October 11, 2016).

In cases where it is deemed necessary to verify the correctness of the obtained information about terrorism and organized crimes, a convicted prisoner or an *unconvicted prisoner* (i.e., a pre-trial detainee, or a person in trial, or convicted by the court of the first instance and awaiting appeal) may, upon the request of the competent authority or the office of the public prosecution, and with the ruling of the criminal peace judge, be taken from the correctional facility for a limited period of time. The criminal peace judge shall determine this period of time after he interviews the prisoner, according to the nature of the case. The total time period shall never exceed fifteen days, and each trip away from the facility shall not exceed four days. Time away from the facility shall be considered as a time period served in imprisonment or in pre-trial detention.

The health situation of the prisoner shall be documented by the report of the doctor when he is leaving the correctional facility and when he returns. A copy of documents about the interactions conducted during any visit at crime scene shall be sent to the Office of the Public Prosecution in order to be kept in the file of the concerned individual (Article 92/2, CGIK). This legal instrument has been utilized very frequently during the OHAL administration after July 15, 2016.

592. Some reasons for temporary leave. Those convicted prisoners who have served one-fifth of their sentence with good behavior, upon request, may be given a temporary leave of up to ten days, not including the travel days, in the following cases (Article 94/1, CGIK): (a) In case of death of the mother, father, spouse, fellow or child, on the request of the convicted prisoner and with both the proposal of the governor of the institution and the approval of the public prosecution office; (b) In case of a documented important and serious illness forming a threat to the life of one of the relatives mentioned above or in case of the damage caused by a natural disaster like an earthquake, a flood, a fire, on the request of the convicted prisoner and with the opinion of the governor of the institution, proposal of the public prosecution office and approval of the Ministry of Justice.

Except for convicted prisoners of aggravated life imprisonment, mentioned at Article 25 CGIK, a visit permit under the supervision of an external security official may be granted to a not dangerous convict, including inmates in the high-security correctional facilities, upon the request of the inmate and with the approval of the Chief Public Prosecutor, in cases where one of his relatives or his spouse has passed away in order to attend the funeral ceremony, up to two days (except for the travelling time), or when his mother, father, spouse, brother or sister, child or mother or father of his spouse has an important or severe illness, which has been reported as life-threatening by the Council of Health, in order to visit each of the listed ill persons and this only once for a period of up to one day, exclusive of the travel time (Article 94/1, CGIK).

The governor of the province where the visited place is located shall, after considering the security issues and after taking necessary security measures, determine, whether the convicted prisoner shall stay overnight either in his own house, or in the house of one of the relatives listed at subsection (a) of Article 94/2, CGIK, or in another secure place, or in the closed correctional facility at the visited place, if during the visiting permit overnight stay is necessary. This permission may be granted maximum two times with an interval of minimum one month (CGIK Article 94/2-b).

2. Special Leave

593. To those in open institutions and those who are qualified to be transferred from closed institutions into the open institutions, a special leave may be given up to three days, exclusive of travel days, once every three months (as amended by Act No. 2011-6411; previously it was three days for three times each during one year), upon the proposal of the governor and approval of the office of the public prosecution, in order to maintain their relations with families or strengthen them and provide compatibility with the public. Such terms of permissions may be added together in cases of necessity such as disasters and illness (Article 95, CGIK).

3. Transfer to Another Institution

594. In order to grant a request for transfer of convicted prisoners to another institution, the following conditions must be fulfilled (Article 54, CGIK):

(a) They shall present a petition specifying at least three places which are suited for their situation and they want to go.
(b) They shall agree to pay transfer expenses in advance.
(c) There shall not be less than five months to their probation.
(d) They shall show good behavior and shall not have disciplinary punishment, or if they did, it should have been waived.
(e) The location, ability of inclusion and category shall be convenient to the institution to which they want to go, and it shall not be a jail.
(f) The institution shall be an institution that accommodates convicted prisoners suitable to the duration of their sentence.
(g) The institution shall not be one the convicted prisoner had to leave previously for disciplinary reasons.

The convicted prisoners transferred to another institution shall not ask for another transfer unless they have spent two years in their new institution. This period shall be six months for children.

Subparagraph (b) of Article 54/1 is not applicable for juvenile convicts (Article 54 CGIK).

595. Security measures to be taken in transfers. During transfer of convicted prisoners to the institution or to somewhere else, necessary measures shall be taken in order to prevent them from associating with other people and from being observed by others (Article 58/1, CGIK).

The convicted prisoner shall not be transferred by vehicles in which the aeration and light is inadequate and in a torturous and degrading manner. The measures to be taken during transfers shall not go beyond what is necessary to prevent the escape of the prisoner and realize the above-stated prevention or go beyond the aim of preventing them from arguing amongst each other and with the officials.

Transfers to the *child educational institution* shall be conducted under the supervision of the personnel of the Enforcement Institute. Transfers to the open penal enforcement institutions shall be achieved without presence of the personnel of the enforcement institute.

In such cases, the inmate must enter the enforcement facility to which he/she has been transferred on the same day, if both facilities are in the same province. If both facilities are in two different provinces, the director of the correctional facility must accomplish the entry within the time limits as set. For those inmates who do not enter within the specified time limits, provisions of Article 97, CGIK shall be applicable.

The convicted prisoner shall be given food and his comfort shall be provided for during the transfer under the supervision of the assigned person (Article 58, CGIK).

596. Transfer of convicts of other nationalities and commutation of sanctions of a foreign judgment. The foreign prisoner will only be transferred to his country if that country guarantees the execution of the Turkish judgment or executes an equivalent of those penalties (*supra*, paragraph 96).

IV. Forms of Alternative Execution of the Prison Sentence

A. Weekend, Nighttime and Home Enforcement

597. Weekend and nighttime execution for imprisonment of one year and six months or less. Custodial punishments of one year and six months or less may be enforced in a special way, according to the discretion of the judge of enforcement of penalties (Article 110/1, CGIK).

The decision of *enforcement during the weekend* will be enforced by entering the enforcement institution by 7 p.m. of every Friday and leaving at the same hour of every Sunday. The decision of *enforcement at night* shall be enforced by entering the enforcement institution by 7 p.m. every day and leaving at 7 a.m. in the morning (Article 110/1, CGIK). This kind of sentence allows the convicted individual to serve a prison term without losing work and helps prisoners and their families financially.

598. Execution of penalty in the home of the convicted person. This privileged form of execution differs according to duration of imprisonment term, gender and age (Article 110/2, CGIK): The decision of enforcement at the residence may be rendered for a custodial penalty of one year or less imprisonment for women, child and convicts aged over 65. An enforcement at the residence decision may be rendered for a custodial punishment of two years or less if the convicted person has attained the age of 70 (Article 110/2-b, CGIK). Enforcement at the residence is possible for a custodial penalty of up to four years if the convicted person has attained the age of 75 (Article 110/2-c, CGIK). In cases where the convicted person who has to serve five years or less imprisonment is ill and is not capable of supporting his living alone in the conditions of prison, or is a woman who has to serve three years or less imprisonment and has given birth to a child within past one year, the judge of the enforcement of penalties may decide that the enforcement continues at the residence (Article 110/3 and 4 CGIK). Except for subsections 3 and 4 of this provision, special kinds of execution shall not be applicable for inmates who are convicted for organized terrorism crimes, for crimes against sexual inviolability, for inmates who serve an imprisonment term converted from criminal fine, and for those who serve a full imprisonment term as they have violated the conditions of bail (Article 110/9, CGIK).

If there has been any damage related to the crime of conviction, for all forms of home execution alternatives, it is additionally required to compensate this damage to the full by returning the object (i.e., *in integrum restitutio*), or by paying the damages (Article 110/2, CGIK).

599. Specified procedure. The judge of enforcement of penalties may rule on special forms of execution (Article 110/1 and 110/2, CGIK). Prior to the amendment in 2020 by Act No. 7242, the court, which has rendered the judgment and if the convicted prisoner is at another location, the local court of the same degree was empowered to rule.

A decision on a special kind of enforcement may also be rendered after the execution of the punishment has started (Article 110/6, CGIK). Parole is also applicable for those who are under the special kind of enforcement; execution of punishment through the application of a controlled liberty measure which is regulated in Article 105A, CGIK (*infra,* paragraph 601) shall be applied (Article 110/5, CGIK).

The judge of the enforcement of penalties may terminate the application of such specified execution if demanded so. In cases where the requirements of special enforcement procedures are violated without a valid excuse, it shall also be terminated, and the execution continues in the closed facility. The duration spent in the open institution shall be deducted from the total imprisonment term. In cases where the provision of this subsection is applied, Article 105/A, CGIK shall not apply (Article 110/5, CGIK).

Decisions rendered in this scope may be opposed before the court (Article 110/8, CGIK).

B. Enforcement of Imprisonment as a Controlled Liberty Measure

600. The overcrowding of correctional facilities has led the legislature to introduce a new approach in 2012 by Law No. 6462: the "execution of punishment through application of a controlled liberty measure" (Article 105A/1). The legislator extended its application by further Laws in 2013-6462, 2014-6545, 2016-KHK 671 and lastly by Law No. 7242 in 2020.

The 2012-6462 law has been very helpful to the set purpose: 35,337 prisoners were released between April 11, 2012 and December 31, 2012; 105,126 in the year 2013, and between January 1, 2014 and February 28, 2014, 16,126 prisoners. The total number of non-convicted prisoners is 24,020, and the total number of convicted prisoners is 127,505 (altogether 151,525) as of March 14, 2014. Without the application of Article 105/A, CGIK, the total number of inmates would be more than 156,559.

In order to achieve an adjustment of inmates to the outside life and to maintain and strengthen their family ties, and taking into consideration the evaluation report prepared by the administration of the correctional institute, upon the request of a well-behaving inmate who has spent one fifth of the duration to become eligible for conditional release, and who is allocated to an open correctional facility, or to a juvenile educational facility, the judge of corrections, located where the inmate is serving his sentence may decide that the execution of his imprisonment term until he will be eligible to enjoy conditional release shall be executed through the application of a controlled liberty measure (Article 105A/1). The duration of controlled liberty measure shall not exceed three years.

Good behavior inmates, who have satisfied the conditions in order to be separated into an open correctional facility, but who have not been, or who have been sent back to closed correctional facility on a ground outside of their control, shall benefit from as set forth in paragraph one, if the inmate meets the other requirements (Article 105A/2, CGIK).

The following inmates, who meet the other requirements, may benefit from the punishment procedure set forth in the above paragraphs (Article 105A/3, CGIK): (a) Female inmates, who have a child between 0-6 years of age; (b) Inmates, who have spent four-fifth of the duration to become eligible for conditional release, cannot support their living without the assistance of another person, because of a severe mental illness they suffer, or due to impairment, or loss of their mental capacities. The status of severe illness, impairments or loss of mental abilities shall be documented by a report, issued by the Forensic Medicine Institute or by a hospital furnished with full medical branches, as designated by the Ministry of Justice. The duration of controlled liberty measure applied according to this subsection shall not exceed four years.

In cases where the imprisonment term is a prison term based on a criminal fine that has not been paid, the date of entitlement to parole shall be taken into consideration (Article 105A/4 CGIK).

The office of Controlled Liberty Directorate shall select amongst one or more the following: (a) making him/her work in a public benefit work without receiving a compensation, (b) putting him under control and supervision in a house or in a district, (c) prohibiting him from visiting designated places or districts, (d) participating in the designated activities. The selected obligations will be applicable for the convicted prisoner for whom controlled liberty has been ordered as a modality of execution of imprisonment term during the period until his conditional release is earned. Taking into consideration the risks and needs the convicted prisoner is confronting; the obligations may be altered (Article 105A/5, CGIK).

In cases where the convicted prisoner, (a) does not apply in person to the specific office of Controlled Liberty Directorate which he had mentioned in his petition within three days after he has left the correctional facility, (b) refuses to comply with the obligations imposed on him, or to fulfill the control and rehabilitation program prepared by the Controlled Liberty Directorate, or the considerations and suggestions and control plan offered by the officials of that directorate, or (c) asks to be sent back to the correctional facility, the execution judge renders a decision upon the request of the Directorate of Controlled Liberty about sending the inmate back to the closed correctional facility in order to serve the remaining imprisonment term until the date of his eligibility for conditional release (Article 105A/6, CGIK).

In 2013 and 2014, the Constitutional Court repealed some provisions regulated in Article 105A/7, CGIK. The legislator introduced a new regulation in 2020 by Law No. 7242: In cases where the released convicted prisoner is prosecuted for a crime he allegedly committed with intent after he was released, and its punishment is two years or less at the lower level, upon the request of the Directorate of Controlled Liberty the enforcement judge shall rule on sending the convicted prisoner back to the open enforcement facility. The enforcement judge shall decide on resuming of the execution of punishment through application of a controlled liberty measure, if the suspect is acquitted at the end of the prosecution.

Convicted prisoners who are obliged to apply to the Directorate of Controlled Liberty, but do not apply although two days have passed, and those prisoners subject to an order to return back to the closed correctional facilities who do not comply with this decision within two days and do not surrender to the closest chief public prosecution office, are subject to Articles 292 and 293 of TCK (Article 105A/8, CGIK).

The report about conditional release furnished with motives, prepared by the Directorate of Controlled Liberty about a convicted prisoner, who has complied with the obligations and to the controlled plan, shall be sent to the relevant court in order to make the interactions according Articles 107 and 108 CGIK (Article 105A/9, CGIK).

Principles and procedures related to the form of execution of imprisonment term through applying controlled liberty measure shall be regulated in an internal regulation.

§3. Prisoners' Rights, Complaint Procedure and Judicial Control

601. Principles and procedures related to the form of execution of imprisonment term through applying controlled liberty measure shall be regulated in an internal regulation.

I. Prisoners' Rights

A. Participating in Activities of Art and Culture, Freedom of Expression

602. Participating in cultural activities. In penal enforcement institutions, programs representing various branches of culture and art shall be organized as long as there are convenient circumstances and procedure regarding the participation of convicted prisoners in these activities shall be regulated. The fundamental goal of these programs is to help the convicted prisoners to improve their expression skills and to increase their knowledge. Institution's culture and art programs shall be regulated by the governor of the institution in accordance with the principles determined by Ministry of Justice. Governmental institutions that are in charge of culture and art affairs shall give necessary support, for this purpose. The publishing activities carried out by convicted prisoners within the freedom of expression are dependent on the provisions regulating the principles of work in institution and the related conditions (Article 60, CGIK).

603. Benefiting from the library. A library or a bookcase shall be formed in the Penal Enforcement Institutions depending on the size of the institution. In the libraries or the bookcases, as far as the circumstances are convenient, other than the books being used as source for the classes, there shall also be books, which will help the convicted prisoners to spent their spare times, to gain reading habit and to enlarge their visions. The convicted prisoner shall be given the opportunity to go to the institution's library and to check and to choose books at least once a week. Itinerant libraries may also render this service (Article 61, CGIK).

604. Right to benefit from continuous or transient publications. The convicted prisoner, on the condition that he pays the price, has the right to benefit from continuous and transient publications (such as newspapers and books), that are not seized. More publications than necessary shall not be present in the rooms. Thus, publications that are seized shall be put in a depot of objects in the name of the convicted prisoner. All sorts of publications, which endangers the institutions' security and involves obscene news, articles, photographs and comments, shall not be given to the convicted prisoner. However, the lesson books of convicted prisoners attending their education and training at every stage, shall not be subjected to any control (Article 62, CGIK). Publications, which would tamper with the security of the correctional institution, or contain indecent news, writings, pictures and explanations shall not be given to the inmates.

B. Rights and Obligations in Daily Life

605. Accommodation of convicted prisoner. The convicted prisoner, who is considered dangerous shall be accommodated in a single room or a room for three persons, other convicted prisoners shall be accommodated in rooms for number of people, which shall be determined by the administration, according to the physical construction of the facility, its capacity and security concerns. One type of bed and sufficient bedding sets that are proper for the regional climate shall be given to each convicted prisoner. To associate and make a connection shall not be allowed for the men and women, the convicted prisoners and the prisoners, the children with each other and with adults, the people who are convicted prisoner for organized crimes and organized crimes for beneficiary purpose and the people who are convicted prisoner for acts of terrorism. Taking the climate circumstances into account, sufficient place, light, heat and aeration shall be provided in the rooms. (Article 63, CGIK).

606. Clothing of the convicted prisoner. In cases where an indigent convicted prisoner requests, the administration shall provide him with an outfit, which is suitable for the climate and the health. Outfits of convicted prisoners shall not be in the shape and the color of uniforms of interior and exterior security personnel. (Article 64, CGIK).

607. Accommodation of the convicted prisoner's children indigent for care. Children of 0-6 (0-3) year of age, whose mothers are convicted prisoners and who have no relatives outside to take care of them shall stay with their mothers. These children, at daytime, shall be accommodated in Social Services under the institution or in the Society for the Protection of Children or other institutions. Children, who stay with their mothers, shall be given food and drinks depending on their age, situations and needs. Children, older than 3 years old, shall be placed in a kindergarten or a public nursery upon the order of judge. Contact with their mothers shall be provided for these children in accordance with a program and a procedure to be determined (Article 65, CGIK).

608. The convicted prisoner's right to accept a present sent from outside. The convicted prisoner has the right to accept a present which is not forbidden to enter the institution and is sent from outside on religious festival days, new year and on his/her birthday. The principles and procedure of this shall be regulated in the institution rules (Article 69, CGIK).

609. Freedom of religion and belief. The convicted prisoner may practice his religious beliefs without any restriction, in a manner that will not disturb the order and hinder work and may obtain and keep the things necessary for practicing his religion and books and written works that are essential for his religious life. The convicted prisoner shall be allowed to be visited by ministers of his religion and to contact with them on the condition that it will not endanger the institution's security (Article 70, CGIK).

610. The convicted prisoner's demands of medical examination and treatment. The convicted prisoner has the right to benefit from examination and treatment opportunities, medical tools in order to protect his mental and physical health and the diagnosis of his illnesses. For this purpose, the convicted prisoner shall be priorly treated in the health station of the correctional facility, and if this is not possible, in the prisoners' section within the hospitals, run by the state or Universities (Article 71, CGIK).

611. The nutrition of the convicted prisoner. The convicted prisoner, in order to stay healthy and strong, shall be given meals that are nutritious both in quantity and quality, in compliance with health circumstances, and reasonably varied, according to the age, health, the properties of his work and religious and cultural specialties, in accordance with the principal calorie to be determined together by Ministry of Justice and Ministry of Health; drinking water shall also be provided. The convicted prisoner, except for the provided daily meals and materials of necessity, may satisfy his needs from the institution's canteen. In institutions where there is no canteen, these materials may be acquired from outside with the permission and under the supervision of administration. The sick convicted prisoner shall be given food, which will be determined by the institution's doctor. Children, who are staying in the institution with their mothers and mothers, who are breast feeding their child shall be given adequate food, fitting to their needs (Article 72, CGIK).

II. Complaint Procedures and Judicial Control

A. Complaint Procedures

612. The Code on Execution of Punishments and Security Measures lays down provisions on prison discipline and lists the punishable acts, the penalties relating to them and the procedure to be followed. The European Committee for Prevention of Torture and Inhuman or Degrading Treatment or Punishment examined this legislation (CPT/inf (2008) 13) and established that these provisions are in line with the standards. Caution, admonition and deprivation of various activities shall be ordered and applied by the governor of the institution. Other disciplinary sanctions may only be imposed after an inquiry by the officer appointed by the governor of the institution.

613. The inquiry must be initiated promptly or within maximum of five days as from learning of the act requiring other disciplinary punishments. The inquiry shall be completed within maximum of fifteen days and the issued report and its joints shall be exposed to the discipline commission. The time of inquiry may be extended with the written approval of the enforcement judge depending on the qualification of the act and the inquiry.

614. Disciplinary punishment shall not be applied without receiving a defense. The convicted prisoner, with respect to whom a disciplinary inquiry is conducted, shall be informed in writing of the character of the act he is accused of and its results, and the fact that he shall present his defense in three days, otherwise he will be assumed to have abandoned these rights. The defense may be presented in writing or orally. The oral defense shall be recorded by a transcript. The defense of those, who do not know Turkish, or who are deaf or dumb shall be received with the help of a translator. Disciplinary punishments shall be decided by the discipline commission within a maximum of three days by an examination over documents. Discipline commission may decide to apply a disciplinary punishment stated by statute, or to drop the prosecution that there is no ground for application of a disciplinary punishment. The decisions of discipline commission shall be written and be furnished with a rationale and shall clearly specify the competent authority, where to appeal and the time of complaint. The ones with respect to whom an inquiry is conducted shall be promptly informed by the administration of the discipline commission's decision. In situations, where it is compulsive to take security measures because the interior order of the institution and the convicted prisoners' rights to their life and body are subject to danger, the governor of the institution shall initiate the inquiry in addition to the application of security measures stated in Article 49. In such cases the enforcement judge (Judge of Enforcement of Punishments) shall be informed thereof (Article 47, CGIK).

B. Judicial Control by the Enforcement Judge

615. The Law on Enforcement Judges, No. 4675, dated May 16, 2001 lays down the competence of "enforcement judges," provides that objections filed against disciplinary sanctions shall be dealt with by such a judge. The prisoner concerned, his close relatives or legal representative can file an objection against a disciplinary sanction (Article 4, Law No. 4675). Sections 1–7 of the Law No. 7242, dated April

14, 2020 have extended the competences of enforcement judges to include rendering all decisions related to the period of enforcement of final sentences, such as revocation of conditional release; prior to this amendment, the court which rendered that decision had the jurisdiction.

616. In cases of complaints submitted by the prisoner, the enforcement judge shall decide on the basis of the case file, without holding a hearing, but may conduct an examination ex officio or request further information from the parties if the interest of justice so require (Article 6/2, Law No. 4675). Objections against disciplinary sanctions however, shall be rendered after collecting the requested evidence and obtaining the defence of the prisoner where the prisoner can present his submissions in person and in the presence of his lawyer, or through a lawyer only (Law No. 6008, dated July 22, 2010 amended Article 6 of Law No. 4675).

§4. Early Release

I. Conditional Release

617. The conditional release of a prisoner[605] who is serving a custodial penalty is now governed by Article 107 of the Code of Enforcement of Punishments and Security Measures (CGIK) with some exceptions, such as in crimes against the constitutional order, crimes against national defense, and for convictions of life imprisonment related to organized crimes (Article 107/16, CGIK).[606]

Originally, this provision was the subject of Articles 16 and 17 of the repealed TCK, but the Code of Enforcement of Punishments, Article 19 abolished those provisions.

The duration of minimum custodial punishment that is compulsory before conditional release may be granted varies according to the type of punishment or crime.[607]

618. The duration of custodial punishment to be served in case of conviction and sentenced to an aggravated life imprisonment is thirty years; in case of a conviction and sentenced to life imprisonment, it is twenty years (Article 107/2, CGIK).

The time to be served in prison in case of *conviction of more than one aggravated life imprisonment* or conviction of an *aggravated life imprisonment and life imprisonment* is thirty-six years (Article 107/3-a, CGIK).

---

605. Veli Kafes TCK *Öntasarıları ve İçtihatlar Işığında Hukukumuzda şartla Salıverilme, Uygulamadaki Sorunlar* (1998); E. Günay, *Uygulamada Tutukluğun Ceza Mahkumiyetinden Mahsubu, şartla Tahliye ile Müddetname Tanzimi* (2001); K. İçel et al., *İçel Yaptırım Teorisi*, 3. Kitap, İstanbul, Beta, 2000, p. 415.

606. A.C. Yenidünya, *Mukayeseli Hukukta ve Türk hukukunda Şartla Salıverme* (2002); S. Donay, *Türk Ceza İnfaz Hukuku*, Beta Yayınları, İstanbul 2014, 170, E. Şen & B. Başer, *Koşullu Salıverilme, Denetimli Serbestlik ve Ceza İnfaz Sorunları*, Seçkin, Ankara, 2016.

607. N. Gürelli, Introduction, in *Turkish Criminal Code*, London: Sweet and Maxwell, 1965, p. 4; B. Öztürk, M.R. Erdem, *Uygulamalı Ceza Hukuku ve Güvenlik Tedbirleri Hukuku*, TCK Değişikliklerine Göre Yenilenmiş, 14. Baskı, Ankara 2014, Seçkin Yayınları, p. 501.

619. The part of the custodial penalty to be served in prison in case of conviction and sentence of more than one life imprisonment is thirty years (Article 107/3-b, CGIK).

If the convict has been sentenced to *one aggravated life imprisonment term and to an imprisonment of limited duration*, the maximum time to be spent in the correctional facility is thirty-six years (Article 107/1-c, CGIK).

If the convict has been sentenced to *one life imprisonment term and to an imprisonment of limited duration*, the maximum time to be spent in the correctional facility is thirty years (Article 107/1-d, CGIK).

If the convict has been sentenced to *more than one imprisonment term of limited duration*, the maximum time to be spent in the correctional facility is twenty-eight years (Article 107/1-e, CGIK).

The duration of custody in case of conviction to other kinds of custodial penalties is half (was two-third before the 2020-7242 amendment) of the prison term. The duration of custody remained two-third for the inmates convicted for intentional killing under Articles 81 and 82, TCK (Article 107/2, CGIK). The prisoner has to be on good behavior during this time (Article 107/1, CGIK).

620. Special rules of conditional release for prisoners convicted of organized crime. There are special rules on the minimum duration of imprisonment in organized crime cases, the special regulation for terrorist crimes and the decision on conditional release in these cases. In cases of imprisonment for forming an organization to commit crimes or leading such an organization, or in cases of a crime committed within the activities of such a crime organization (Article 107/4, CGIK), the duration of minimum imprisonment term for eligibility to be conditionally released differs according to the number or type of convictions.

621. Death penalty convicts. When the death penalty was abolished, Act No. 2002-4771 commuted death penalties against those convicted of terrorism to aggravated life imprisonment. The Act No. 2004-5218 later amended this Act. Terrorists convicted and sentenced to aggravated life imprisonment directly or by commutation of a death penalty are not eligible for conditional release, and they stay in prison until they die (Provisional Article 2 of the Code on the Execution of Punishments and Security Measures).

622. Recidivists. Recidivism is no longer a ground for aggravating the punishment. Conditional release for recidivists, however, requires a longer stay in the correctional facility if convicted and sentenced to aggravated life imprisonment, they have to spend thirty-nine years in prison before being eligible for parole; if convicted and sentenced to life imprisonment, thirty-three years; if convicted to more than one specific term of imprisonment, thirty-two years and if convicted and sentenced to one specific term of imprisonment only, they have to spend 2/3 of the prison term (Article 108/1, CGIK).

Recidivists remain under supervision after the completion of the prison term. The duration of the supervision is determined by the judge and shall not be less than one year (Article 108/4, CGIK). This period may be extended up to five years (Article 108/6, CGIK).

Provisional Article 5 of CGIK (added by Act No. 2013-6459) introduced an exception in 2013: "Whoever has been convicted and sentenced to a punishment that restricts the personal freedom because of a crime committed before 7 November 1982 and has been released under parole during the execution of the punishment; the parole shall not be revoked for such individuals, if they commit a new crime during the period of supervision."

623. The decision on conditional release. When an inmate is eligible for conditional release, the administration of the correctional facility prepares a detailed report for the enforcement judge at the place where the enforcement of imprisonment term is conducted. The enforcement judge has discretion in this respect and decides to release the convict if it deems appropriate. This decision is rendered on the basis of the file, and there is no open trial. If the court does not find it suitable to release the inmate at that point, it has to make its reasons explicit. The judge's decision on denial of release may be subject to opposition (Article 107/11, CGIK).

The enforcement judge may decide to impose a measure of controlled liberty on the released person, which shall be effective during the period of conditional release (Article 107/10, CGIK).

624. Obligations of the conditionally released inmate. Controlled liberty was a new concept when the new Penal Code introduced it for conditional release and suspended imprisonment as well as for similar legal concepts.[608]

The conditionally released inmate must not commit any intentional crime during the period of controlled liberty.

If the conditionally released person is of good behavior during this period, *the inflicted punishment shall be considered as served* (Article 107/14, CGIK).[609]

625. The duration of controlled liberty in cases of conditional release. The duration of controlled liberty the period of the sentence to be served in the CGIK facility, but it shall not last longer than the date of earned parole for imprisonment terms of specified time (Article 107/6, CGIK).

The judge may appoint an expert who will accompany the conditionally released person during the period of controlled liberty. The expert reports to the judge about the released prisoner's social development every three months.

626. Revocation of conditional release. If the conditionally released inmate commits a new intentional crime, or does not consistently fulfill the obligations imposed on him in spite of warning by the enforcement judge, the conditional release can be revoked (Article 107/12, CGIK).

---

608. H.A. Yavuz, *Ceza İnfaz Sistemi ve Denetimli Serbestlik*, Şeçkin, Ankara, 2018.

609. Under the repealed law, *the conviction was regarded as if not imposed at all*; under the new regime the legal consequences of the completed sentence will apply.

The decision on revocation of conditional release may be rendered by different authorities according to the conduct of the convict: If the conditionally released person commits a new intentional crime within the probation period or did not fulfill the imposed obligations, the enforcement judge has jurisdiction for the decision on revocation (Article 107/15).[610]

In cases where several imprisonment terms against the same convict had been summed up, or where the judgment had been rendered by a criminal chamber of the Regional Court of Appeal or by the Court of Cassation, the decision on revocation of conditional release shall be rendered by the enforcement judge according to the rules set forth in Article 101/2, CGIK, which is common for all judicial decisions, rendered during the execution of punishments. Article 101/2, CGIK reads now as follows: "In cases where imprisonment terms are to be summed up according to Article 99, CGIK, the enforcement judge where the court which imposed the heaviest punishment is located has jurisdiction; if the punishments are equal, the enforcement judge where the court which rendered the last decision is located has standing. In cases where the Court of Cassation had rendered the heaviest punishment in its capacity as a first instance court, the jurisdiction rests with the Ankara enforcement judge. If the Regional Court of Appeal had rendered the decision in its capacity as a first instance court, the enforcement judge in the city in the same region is empowered. In cases where the criminal chamber of the Regional Court of Appeal had rendered the judgment in trial, then the enforcement judge of the court of the first instance that rendered the initial judgment has standing."

The decision on the revocation of conditional release shall be rendered based on the case file. The way of opposition is open for such decisions (Article 107/15).

Upon the revocation of conditional release, the court also decides on the execution of the remaining part of the imprisonment term, beginning from the date when the new crime was committed and for a duration of twice the imprisonment term for each crime that he has committed (Article 107/13-a, CGIK). If the revocation is based on the convicted person not having fulfilled the obligations, the court may render a new decision regarding the imprisonment term, according to the qualification of the violation (Article 107/13-b, CGIK).

If the decision on conditional release has been revoked once, the inmate is no longer eligible for conditional release with respect to that particular sentence (Article 107/13, sentence 2 CGIK).

II. Forms of Provisional Release

627. The recent criminal law system foresees controlled liberty in some other instances, such as suspended imprisonment (Article 51/3, TCK), judicial control (Article 109, CMK) (*supra,* paragraph 479), suspension of prosecution (Article 171/

610. Prior to the amend, the regulation was as follows: The court that tries the newly committed intentional crime makes the decision on revocation, if it gives a conviction and sentence to imprisonment (Art. 107/15-a, CGIK). If the conditionally released person did not fulfil the imposed obligations, it will be the court that rendered the initial conviction (Art. 107/15-b, CGIK) that decides on revocation. It will be rendered on the file and is subject to opposition.

2, CMK) (*supra,* paragraph 390) and delayed announcement of the judgment (Article 231/2 CMK) (*supra,* paragraph 519) as well as for children who were dragged to commit crimes (Articles 5, 11, ÇKK).

The *execution of punishment through application of a controlled liberty measure* (Article 105A, CGIK) is also a special form of controlled liberty (*supra,* paragraph 601).

§5. Enforcement of Community Service and Criminal fines

628. Enforcement of community service. Penalties and security measures are the sanctions in the criminal justice system. The Turkish judicial system includes imprisonment and other penalties (community service and criminal fines).

Community service, formally called *public beneficiary work*, is one of the alternative sanctions regulated by Article 50/1-f TCK, as a substitute for short-term imprisonment. It cannot be used if the same individual has been convicted to another prison term (Article 105/3, CGIK).

The convict has to work for a public institution or a private institution that provides public services without receiving any compensation for his work where two hours of work equals one day of served imprisonment term. The amount of daily working hours shall be determined as minimum two, and maximum eight hours by the Controlled Liberty Authority (Article 105/1, CGIK). The Controlled Liberty Authority collects information about available work places and produces lists of certain type of work (Article 105/2, CGIK).

Community service may also be applied during the execution of the imprisonment term for conviction up to two years. In such cases, the inmate must have served half of his term on good behavior and apply for community service. The request may also be put forward by his legal representative or by the office of public prosecution.

629. Execution of criminal fine. The criminal fine is an amount of money determined according to the rules set forth in Article 52 of TCK (Article 106/1, CGIK).

After a fine is set, the court delivers the judgment, which includes the fine, to the office of the public prosecution. The office of public prosecution serves a payment order to the convict and sets a time limit for payment. The rules about notification in Article 20/3, CGIK apply.

If the convicted person fails to pay the fine within the time limit set in the payment order, the public prosecutor can decide to imprison that individual for the equivalent in days of his fine (Article 106/4, CGIK). This conversion into a prison term is automatic; there is no need for renewed judicial intervention (Article 106/5, CGIK). The conversion shall not result in a term of imprisonment exceeding three years. In cases of conversion of several convictions with sentences of fines, the conversion shall not exceed five years (Article 106/7, CGIK).

This imprisonment cannot be suspended, and the inmate cannot be conditionally released, except in cases indicated in Article 50/1-c TCK (Article 106/9, CGIK). If the imprisoned convict who was originally sentenced to a fine pays the equivalent days of his fine, with the exception of the days he has spent in prison, he will be freed (Article 106/8, CGIK). However, this imprisonment term, converted from fine is not considered as *short-term imprisonment* in the technical meaning and therefore it is not possible to apply the *special forms of execution of short-term imprisonment* as regulated in Article 110, CGIK.

It is forbidden to convert a criminal fine against a child into imprisonment (Article 106/4, CGIK).

Criminal fines may be paid by installments if the judgment of the court so provides (Article 106/5, CGIK). If there is no such decision, the convicted person who has paid one-third of the fine may file a request to pay the rest in installments. The public prosecutor can allow him to pay the rest in two installments: Two equal payments with a one-month interval (Article 106/6, CGIK). If the first installment is not paid, the right to make the second one shall be void and the unpaid portion of the fine shall be converted into the equivalent days of imprisonment.

Chapter 4. Extinction of Sanctions or Sentences

§1. Introduction

630. Grounds for dismissing actions and setting aside of punishments. Part I of Chapter 4 of TCK contains provisions regarding dismissing actions and setting aside punishments, where the legal link between the state and the accused person no longer exists.[611]

The grounds for the dismissal are: Death of the accused or the sentenced person (Article 64, TCK), amnesty and pardon (Article 65, TCK), statute of limitations for prosecution (Articles 66–67, TCK), statute of limitations for punishments (Articles 68–71, TCK), withdrawal of the claim by the injured party (Article 73, TCK) and pre-payment of the fine (Article 75, TCK).

Mediation (Article 253, CMK) (*supra*, paragraph 393), *suspended prosecution* (Article 171/2, CMK) and *delayed announcement of the judgment* (Article 231, CMK) (*supra,* paragraph 519), have the effect of dismissing the public prosecution, if the suspect or the accused complies with the legal obligations. The Court of Cassation regards the *delayed announcement of the judgment* as a *suspended dismissal decision.* There are some crimes, such as giving information about an illegal organization (Article 221, TCK), where the effective remorse results in a *no grounds for punishing* judgment of the trial court (Article 223/3, CMK).

§2. Amnesty and Pardon

631. Amnesty. Amnesty terminates public prosecutions and sets aside punishments together with all their penal consequences (Article 65/1, TCK).[612] Pardon (*özel af*) only sets aside or reduces the imprisonment term, or commutes it into a fine. It will not affect the consequences of the conviction or those suspended civil rights mentioned in the judgment (Article 65/2 and 3, TCK).[613]

According to Article 87 of the Constitution, the Grand National Assembly has the power to grant amnesty or pardon. This power of the Grand National Assembly was limited to ordinary crimes. Political crimes as defined in Article 14 of the Constitution were exempted.[614] The 2001 Act No. 4709 abolished this restriction, valid for crimes committed in the future. The Grand National Assembly has now to vote for amnesty or pardon with a three-fifths majority of the full members.

611. İ. Özgenç, *Türk Ceza Hukuku Genel Hükümler, Gözden Geçirilmiş ve Güncellenmiş* 10. Bası, Ankara, Seçkin, 2014, p. 675.
612. İ. Özgenç, *Türk Ceza Hukuku Genel Hükümler, Gözden Geçirilmiş ve Güncellenmiş* 10. Bası, Ankara, Seçkin, 2014, p. 869.
613. S. Keyman, *Türk Hukukunda Af*, Ankara, Ankara Üniversitesi Basımevi, 1965; V.Ö. Özbek, *İnfaz Hukuku*; Geliştirilmiş ve Güncellenmiş 5. Baskı, Seçkin, Ankara 2014, p. 337.
614. The 1991 Anti-Terrorism Act has implemented a tacit amnesty for political offenses by extending the application of conditional release. A. Sözüer, *Amnestien in der Türkei*, ZAR (2002), p. 100.

632. *Pardon.* The Constitution (Article 104/2-b, AY) grants the president the right to grant pardon and reduce the penalty, or even to lift it under certain circumstances.[615]

§3. The Limitation of the Penalty by Time

633. *Statute of limitations for execution of punishments.* There are two kinds of statute of limitations:[616] for prosecution (*supra*, paragraph 407) and for execution of punishment.[617] With the lapse of time, the consequences of a crime shall be forgotten and the probative value of the evidence shall be less. The majority of Turkish legal experts consider the statute of limitations as an issue belonging to substantive criminal law; some experts however, regard this concept as a procedural obstacle to prosecution.[618] The accused or the convicted person cannot waive the application of the statute of limitations; the court has to consider both types of statute of limitations by its own motion (Article 72/2, TCK).[619]

There is a new regulation with regard to the setting aside of penalties: Article 68, TCK. The period of time mentioned in the statute of limitations begins to run when the sentence becomes final or the execution of the penalty is interrupted for any reason such as when the execution of the penalty lapses according to reasons mentioned in CGIK. In such cases, the remaining term of punishment shall be the basis for determining the period of statute of limitations (Article 68/5, TCK). The court has to act ex officio, and the suspect, the accused or the convicted person cannot waive this right (Article 72/2, TCK).

634. *Time limits for punishments.* The statute of limitations shall not apply for torture (Art 94/6, TCK).

Punishments are set aside with the lapse of: Forty years for the aggravated life imprisonment (Article 68/1-a, TCK), thirty years for life imprisonment (Article 68/1-b, TCK), twenty-four years for imprisonment of twenty years or more (Article 68/1-c, TCK), twenty years for imprisonment of more than five years (Article 68/1-d, TCK), ten years for imprisonment of up to five years (Article 68/1-e, TCK) and twenty years from the date of finalization of the judgment for confiscation (Article 70, TCK).

---

615. A fifteen-year lengthy imprisonment of a convicted terrorist inmate was lifted on the expert evidence of the Legal Medicine Institute, upon diagnosis of an *incurable disease* (RG. Jan. 8, 2003). There are some hundred examples of such *pardon decisions* in the last years.
616. F.G. Taner, *Ceza Hukukunda Zamanaşımı* (2008).
617. İ. Özgenç, *Türk Ceza Hukuku Genel Hükümler, Gözden Geçirilmiş ve Güncellenmiş* 10. Bası, Ankara, Seçkin, 2014, p. 861.
618. S. Tellenbach, Verjährung in der Türkei, in Nationales Strafrecht in rechtsvergleichender Darstellung, Teilband 5, ed. Sieber & Cornils (Berlin, 2010), p. 705.
619. I. Döner, *Ceza Zamanaşımı*, Erzincan Hukuk Fakültesi Dergisi, Cilt 9, sayı 3-4, p. 35, Erzincan 2005; E. Günay, *Dava ve Ceza Zamanaşımı, Memnu Hakları İadesi, Adli Sicil Kayıtlarının Silinmesi*, Ankara, Seçkin Yayınları, 2003; T. Soysal, *5237 Sayılı TCK'nın 104/2 Maddesinin Anayasaya Aykırılığı Savıyla Anayasa Mahkemesi'ne Başvuru ve Bir Değerlendirme*, Legal Hukuk Dergisi, sayı 36 sayfa 4235, Aralık 2005.

Deprivation of rights is either a consequence of the punishment or is based on additional decision of the court. It has effect until the end of the period mentioned in the statute of limitations (Article 69, TCK).

635. Suspension and interruption of time limit for punishment. The execution of final judgments against a Member of Parliament shall rest until the end of his term (Article 83/3, AY). In cases where a convicted inmate commits a crime with intent that is punishable with a maximum imprisonment term of more than two years, the statute of limitation for execution of punishments shall be suspended (Article 71/2, TCK). The execution of final punishments of an inmate shall be suspended as long as he is serving an imprisonment term inflicted for another crime (Article 15, Act No. 2005-5320). Soldiers shall serve a short-term imprisonment for crimes committed prior to their drafting after completion of their military service; during this period the statute of limitations for execution of punishments is suspended (Article 118/1, CGIK).

Running of the time period for limitation is interrupted by a notification by a competent authority to the convicted person for enforcement of the sentence (Article 20/2, CGIK), or by an arrest for this purpose (Article 71/1, TCK). It is interrupted as well if the convicted individual commits another intentional crime that is punishable with a maximum of more than two years imprisonment (Article 71/2, TCK).

636. Special regulation for children. Punishment may not be executed upon lapse of half of the above-mentioned periods if the convict has completed the age of 12 but not yet attained the age of 15 at the commission date of the offense; as for the convicts who completed the age of 15 but not attained the age of 18, the statutory period is determined as two thirds of the above-mentioned periods (Article 68/2, TCK).

637. Statute of limitations for execution of administrative sanctions. In cases where time limits for execution have expired, a decision that includes an administrative fine or administrative confiscation will no longer have to be fulfilled.[620]

Time starts to run when the decision becomes final (Article 21/4, KK). However, time does not run if the execution of the administrative sanction did not start because of some legal requirements, or if it was impossible to execute it (Article 21/5, KK).

Administrative sanctions are set aside with the lapse of the following periods: seven years for the administrative fine of TRY 50,000 and upwards (Article 21/2-a, KK), five years for the administrative fine of TRY 20,000 and upwards (Article 21/2-b, KK), four years for the administrative fine of TRY 10,000 or more (Article 21/2-c, KK), three years for administrative fine of less than TRY 10,000 (Article 21/2-d, KK) and ten years for administrative confiscation (Article 21/3, KK).

620. According to the repealed Penal Code, in cases of misdemeanors, the time limit was four years for light imprisonment of more than one month or light fine up to TRY 5,400, eighteen months for all the other punishments (Art. 112, repealed TCK).

§4. Deletion of Conviction and Rehabilitation of Offenders

638. For details about the deletion of conviction *see* (*supra,* paragraph 299).

639. When the military took power in May 27, 1960 (*supra,* paragraph 39), the existing Constitution in power since 1924 was abolished by the Act No. 1, dated June 6, 1969, and a special court had been established under the name of "Supreme Court" *(Yüce Divan).* This court had rendered several decisions, including death penalties against former leaders and additionally on prohibition of rights. In order to demonstrate the condemnation of the military intervention in 1960, the recent government enacted the Law No. 7248 on June 23, 2020, and abolished the "Supreme Court" which no longer existed. The aim of this legislation is to recover damages and losses of individuals convicted by this extraordinary court by annulling all decisions rendered by the "Supreme Court" and all court registers have been ordered to be deleted. Whoever has been victim at that given time, or their heirs may apply to the Recovery Commission established at the Presidency and their losses will be recovered by the state.

§5. Revision of Sentences

I. Conditions Relating to the Nature of the Sanction Imposed

640. In cases of major miscarriages of justice, the Code provides for the possibility of commencing a new trial in order to revise the sentence.[621] If there is new evidence or a substantial error in fact, then a trial that had ended with a final judgment may be re-opened (Article 311/1, CMK).[622]

641. There are three categories of reasons for a new trial. The first is related to the re-opening of the trial in favor of the sentenced person (Article 311, CMK). The second is related to the grounds for a re-opening against the interest of the convicted (Article 314, CMK). The third ground is related to human rights issues.

642. The petition to reopen the trial must be filed with the court that has rendered the final decision. This court investigates the petition and re-opens the trial if it determines that there are sufficient grounds for suspecting factual mistakes were made. A motion for a new trial does not hinder the execution of the judgment. However, the court may rule on the postponement or stay of execution of the judgment (Article 312, CMK).

At the end of the new trial, the court is empowered to cancel the first judgment (Article 323/1, CMK).

---

621. A. Önder, *Muhakemenin Yenilenmesi ve Dirilmesi*, in *Ceza Adaleti Reformu İlkeleri Sempozyumu,* İstanbul Üniversitesi, 1973, pp. 7–62; A. Önder, *Muhakemenin İadesinde Yeni Olay*, IHFM, XXXI, ss. 1–4; E. Özgen, *Ceza Muhakemesinin Yenilenmesi,* Ankara, 1968.

622. C. Şahin & N. Göktürk, *Ceza Muhakemesi Hukuku - II -,* 7. Bası, Seçkin, Ankara 2018, p. 315.

The new sanction may be more severe than the first one. However, if the convicted person alone submitted the petition, the penalties cannot be increased (Article 323/2, CMK).

The execution of the judgment or the death of the convicted individual does not bar a motion for a new trial. The spouse of the deceased, his ascendants, descendants and siblings are entitled to file a motion for a new trial. If there are no such individuals, the Minister of Justice is also entitled to file a motion for a new trial (Article 313, CMK). Thus, the reputation of the convict who had passed away shall be reinstalled.

II. Circumstances Justifying Revision of the Sentence

643. Grounds for a new trial in favor of the convicted individual. A lawsuit concluded with a final judgment must be tried again in favor of the convicted individual, by granting him a new trial, in the following situations (Article 311/1, CMK): (a) If any document used at the main hearing that had an effect on the judgment was false; (b) If it is discovered that any witness or expert heard under oath testified or used his vote deliberately or negligently against the convicted individual, contrary to the facts, in a way that affected the judgment; (c) Save for fault caused by the convicted individual personally, if any of the judges who participated in the judgment had been in fault in executing his duties. This shall require a misuse of office that could lead to a criminal prosecution or conviction; (d) If the judgment of the criminal court was based upon a judgment given by a civil court, and this judgment was reversed by another judgment which became final; (e) If new facts or new evidence have been produced, which when taken into consideration solely or together with the evidence previously submitted, are of the nature that that would lead to the acquittal of the accused or lead to a conviction by application of a legal provision that carries a lighter penalty. (f) If a final judgment of the ECtHR has established that the criminal judgment violated the Convention on Protecting the Human Rights or its Protocols. Act No. 7145 dated July 25, 2018, inserted two new grounds into this subsection: In cases where an application with the ECtHR ended by a friendly settlement, or the motion was dropped by a one-sided declaration. Act No. 2013-6459 extended the time limit for individual applications to the ECtHR. Where the ECtHR has rendered a final decision related to a criminal court decision finding a violation of human rights, and this final judgment is pending before the Committee of Ministers of Council of Europe as of June 15, 2012, the re-opening of the trial is not permitted. Those who fall into this category have been given a provisional right for three months to file a motion of re-opening of trial (Provisional Art 2 to CMK, added by Article 21, of Act No. 6459, in 2013).

The same Act has introduced a new concept of *re-opening of investigation* for cases where the ECtHR rendered a final judgment establishing a violation of the Convention because the investigation had been dropped without conducting an efficient investigation, if there is a request within three months after the judgment is made final. In such cases, a new investigation shall be initiated (Article 172/3, CMK). As mentioned above, Article 172/3 was amended by Article 17 of the Act No. 7145, dated July 25, 2018 and the following wording was inserted: *in cases where an application with the ECtHR ended by a friendly settlement, or the motion was dropped by a one-sided declaration.* Thus, two new grounds were inserted in Articles 172/3 and 311/1-f, CMK.

644. The grounds for a new trial against the interests of the accused or the convict. A lawsuit that has concluded with a final judgment may be retried against the interests of the accused or convicted person by way of a new trial in the following situations (Article 314, CMK): (a) If a document submitted in favor of the accused during the main hearing that had affected the outcome of the judgment was false; (b) If any of the judges who had participated in the decision-making had been in (criminal) fault in favor of the accused or convict person while performing his judicial duties; or (c) If the accused, after being acquitted, has made a reliable confession in front of a judge.

III. Procedure of the Revision of the Sentence

645. Motion for a new trial inadmissible. A new trial for the changing of the penalty is inadmissible in order to achieve a change within the limits of the penalty of the same article of the Penal Code (Article 315/1, CMK). Additionally, if there is any other possibility to cure an error; the new trial will not be admitted (Article 315/2, CMK). A motion for a new trial, supported by an allegation of a crime, committed by a witness or by a judge etc. is only admissible if there has been a finalized conviction. Exceptionally, a motion is admissible when strong evidence supporting a conviction existed, but because of other reasons a conviction was not obtained as criminal investigation did not start or continue (Article 316, sentence 1, CMK). This provision does not apply in cases where new facts or new evidence have been produced, as regulated in Article 311/1-e, CMK (Article 316, sentence 2, CMK). The general provisions applicable to motions for legal remedies are also applicable on the motion for a new trial. Decisions on the admissibility of the petition for a new trial are rendered without opening a main hearing (Article 318, CMK). The petition for a new trial is denied as inadmissible if it is not made in accordance with the procedures set forth by the statute, or if no legal ground to justify a new trial has been submitted, or if no supporting evidence had been produced (Article 319/1, CMK). Admissible petitions for a new trial are notified to the public prosecutor and the other interested parties. They can submit their answers, if they have any, within seven days (Article 319/2, CMK). The decisions rendered on the basis of this article may be subject to a motion of opposition (Article 319/3, CMK).

646. Collection of evidence. If the court declares that the petition for a new trial is admissible, it may delegate a member of the court to collect evidence. He may interact with courts or use rogatory letters. The court is also entitled to do this on its own (Article 320/1, CMK). During the collection of evidence by the court or by a member of the court delegated to accomplish a certain mission or when a court has been asked to perform an action by a rogatory letter, rules related to investigation apply (Article 320/2, CMK). When the collection of the evidence is complete, the public prosecutor and the individuals against whom there is a pending judgment are invited to submit their opinions and considerations within seven days (Article 320/3, CMK).

647. Denial of the petition for a new trial on the basis of having no ground, otherwise declaring admissible. If the grounds for a new trial are not sufficiently justified, or if it turns out that in the specific case, they had no influence on the outcome of the judgment, the motion for a new trial is denied without opening a main hearing. In the other event, the court grants a new trial and opens a main hearing (Article 321/1, CMK). Decisions given according to this article may be subject to a motion of opposition (Article 321/3, CMK).

648. Inspection of the motion for a new trial without opening a main hearing. If the convicted individual is dead, the court does not open a new main trial. It decides after collecting all the necessary evidence on the acquittal of the convicted, or rejects the petition for a new trial. In other cases, the court also acquits immediately, without opening a main hearing, upon positive advice of the public prosecutor (Article 322/1, CMK). When it acquits, the court at the same time annuls the previous judgments (Article 322/2, CMK). If the individual who filed the motion for a new trial so requests, the decision on the annulment of the previous judgment may be published in the Official Gazette, as well as in other newspapers under the court's discretion, and the costs of the publication may be borne by the state treasury (Article 322/3, CMK).

649. Judgment to be rendered at the end of the renewed main hearing. At the conclusion of the main hearings, the court either approves the previous judgment, or it annuls the judgment and renders a new decision about the lawsuit. If the motion for a new trial had been filed in favor of the convict, the new judgment cannot impose a heavier penalty than the previous judgment (Article 323/2, CMK). In case of acquittal at the end of the proceedings, damages will be recovered according to the provisions in Articles 141–144 CMK (Article 323/3, CMK).

General Conclusion

650. Turkey places great effort in order to apply penal procedural rules in conformity with European Human Rights standards. The decisions of the Constitutional Court, the ECtHR, and the Court of Cassation have heavily contributed in this respect. The Constitutional Court delivered a number of important decisions aligning itself with the approach of the ECtHR. Implementation of judicial reform packages started to produce results in the matters of pre-trial detention and the use of preventive measures as an alternative to detention. There has been progress in the area of justice, freedom, and security, the terrorism courts and related legislation repealed. The terrorist attacks after the general elections in June 2015, and subsequent failed coup in 2016, however, forced the authorities to take efficient measures to combat terrorism.

The main problem of the Turkish criminal justice system is delayed adjudication. There are concerns in the practice of criminal justice system, such as prosecutors' ability to lead criminal investigations of the police. Ineffective investigation at the preparatory phase causes delays in court proceedings. Other causes of delay are: Bringing cases to the court which are not supported with sufficient evidence, sometimes two- or three-months of interval between the main hearing sessions in the prosecution phase, frequent application of pre-trial detention, waiting time for pending cases at the Court of Cassation and existence of extraordinary legal remedies.

Such problems have a negative impact on the growing population of convicted prisoners and prisoners in remand (in 2005 it was 55,966, in 2010 120,194 and in 2019 291,546).[623] In the 2020 COVID-19 pandemic time the recent amendment to the Law on Execution of Punishment and Measurement by Act No.7242 resulted in release of some 90,000 thousand inmates.

In order to improve the criminal justice system as a whole, there are efforts to reform. Amendments in 2019, created special procedures such as simplified procedure and speedy adjudication, in addition to the mediation in criminal matters. The aim of the legislator has been diminishing the case load pending at the courts of first instance which was successfully achieved. Such ADR systems took a significant number of cases from the docked.

The priority of the reform efforts undertaken in 2020, is that of *"time management"* within the public prosecution offices and courts, thus reducing unnecessary delays in the criminal justice system. Strengthening the relationship with EU, application of better human rights standards and improving fair trial principles in Turkey are the other aims. The legal framework needs to be revised in order to achieve an

623. https://data.tuik.gov.tr/Kategori/GetKategori?p=adalet-ve-secim-110&dil=1.

efficient criminal justice system that prevents human rights violations, both by criminals, as well as by state officials claiming to exercise their duties.

"Action Plan on Human Rights"[624] announced by the President on March 3, 2021, sets forth the main principles, aims, budget, monitoring, reporting and evaluation for strengthening the conception of the Rule of Law based on human rights in Turkey. Protecting the rights of the victim, strengthening judicial independence and the right to fair trial, strengthening the standards as regards the application of the presumption of innocence and strengthening the right to a reasonable time, as well as strengthening the access to justice are priority rights.

624. Ministry of Justice, "Action Plan on Human Rights, Free Individual, Strong Society; More Democratic Turkey," Ankara, 2021.

Selected Bibliography

Legislation

Edward Grieves, Vahit Bıçak, *Turkish Penal Code,* Translation realized with funding from the Foreign and Commonwealth Office Global Opportunities Fund, Re-Uniting Europe Programme. Ankara, September 2007.

Feridun Yenisey, *Turkish Penal Procedure Code*: *Ceza Muhakemesi Kanunu (2004–5271).* İstanbul 2021.

Mehmet Arslan, *Die tuörkische Strafprozessordnung; Ceza Muhakemesi Kanunu: vom 4. Dezember 2004 nach dem Stand vom 6. Januar 2017, Deutsche Übersetzung und Einführung,* Duncker & Humblot, Berlin 2017.

Silvia Tellenbach, *Das türkische Strafgesetzbuch: Türk Ceza Kanunu*, Deutsche Übersetzung und Einführung, Sammlung ausländischer Strafgesetzbücher in Deutscher Übersetzung, 2. Aufl.edition iuscrim, Freiburg.i. Br. 2001. *(Repealed Penal Code).*

Silvia Tellenbach, *Das türkische Strafgesetzbuch: Türk Ceza Kanunu*, Gesetz Nr. 5237 vom 26.9.2004 nach dem Stand vom 15.11.2008, Sammlung ausländischer Strafgesetzbücher in deutscher Übersetzung, Herausgegeben von Ulrich Sieber und Hans-Jörg Albrecht, Redaktion: Barbara Huber, Berlin 2008.

Journals

Annales de la Faculte de Droit d'Istanbul.

Ankara Barosu Dergisi (Law Review of Ankara Bar Association).

Ankara Hukuk (*Fakültesi*) (*Mecmuası*) (Law Review of College of Law, Ankara University).

Bahçeşehir Üniversitesi Hukuk Fakültesi Dergisi (Law Review of Bahçeşehir University, School of Law).

Hukuk Araştırmaları (Law Review of Marmara University, School of Law).

İlmi ve Kazai İçtihatlar Dergisi. İstanbul Üniversitesi Hukuk Fakültesi Dergisi (Law Review of the Istanbul University's College of Law).

Yargıtay Kararları Dergisi (Journal of Decisions of the Court of Cassation).

Yeditepe Üniversitesi Hukuk Fakültesi Dergisi (Law Review of Yeditepe University).

Books

Abdulkadir Akın, *İnfaz Hukuku,* Seçkin, 3. Baskı, Ankara, 2016.

Adem Sözüer, *Suça Teşebbüs*, 1994.

Selected Bibliography

Ahmet Adil Kubat, *Denetimli Serbestlik ve Cezaların İnfazı,* 9. Baskı, Seçkin, Ankara 2019.

Ahmet Cemal Ruhi, *Türk Ceza Kanunu'nda Uyuşturucu ve Uyarıcı Madde Suçları: En Son Yargıtay İçtihatları İle,* 2. Baskı, On İki Levha, İstanbul 2020.

Ahmet Cemal Ruhi, *Türk Ceza Kanununda Kasten Öldürme Suçları,* On İki Levha, İstanbul 2017.

Ahmet Emrah Akyazan, *Karşılaştırmalı Hukukta ve Türk Hukukunda Doğrudan Soru Yöneltme (Çapraz Sorgu)*, Ankara, 2009.

Ahmet Gökçen, *Tanzimat Dönemi Osmanlı Ceza Kanunları ve Bu Kanunlardaki Ceza Mueyyideleri*, İstanbul, 1989.

Ahmet Gökçen, *Halkı Kin ve Düşmanlığa Açıkça Tahrik Cürmü*, 2001.

Ahmet Gökçen et al., *Ceza Muhakemesi Hukuku,* 4. Baskı, Adalet Yayınevi, Ankara 2020.

Ahmet Gündel, *Atatürk'e ve Cumhurbaşkanına, Cumhuriyete, Hükümete Hakaret Suçları Yasadışı Yakalanan ve Tutuklananlara Tazminat Verilmesi Davaları*, Ankara, Seçkin Yayınları, 1997.

Ahmet Gündel, *Açıklamalı İçtihatlı 765 ve 5237 Sayılı Türk Ceza Kanunlarındaki Hırsızlık ve Dolandırıcılık Suçları*, Ankara, Seçkin Yayınları, 2005.

Ahmet Hulusi Akkaş, *Ceza Muhakemesi Bağlamında Yargı Mercileri Kararlarının Birbirleri Üzerindeki Etkisi,* Adalet, Ankara 2016.

Ahmet Polat, Serdar Kenan Gül, *Suçun Ölçümü*, Ankara, Adalet, 2010.

Ahmet Selçuk Sönmez, *Türk Ceza Kanunu'nda İftira Suçu,* Hâkim Yayınları, Ankara 2016.

Ahmet Sezer, *Ceza Usul Hukukunda Uzlaşma.* Adalet, Ankara 2010.

Akif Yıldırım, *Bireysel Başvuruda Ceza Yargılamasını İlgilendiren Kararlar,* Ankara, Anayasa Mahkemesi, 2017.

Akif Yıldırım, *Hükmün Açıklanmasının Geri Bırakılması,* Seçkin, Ankara 2018.

Ali Erdem Sevdim, *Türk Ceza Hukukunda Uyuşturucu veya Uyarıcı Madde Suçları.* Seçkin, Ankara 2014.

Ali Karagülmez, *Adli İdari Para Cezaları*, Seçkin Yayınları, 2001.

Ali Karagülmez, *Bilişim Suçları ve Soruşturma Kovuşturma Evreleri*, Seçkin Yayınları, 2005.

Ali Osman Onar, *Türk Ceza Hukukunda Hakaret Suçu,* Adalet, Ankara 2016.

Ali Parlar, *Türk Ceza Hukukunda Bilişim Suçları*, Ankara, 3. Baskı, Bilge Yayınevi, 2015.

Ali Parlar, *Türk Ceza Hukukunda Dolandırıcılık Suçları.* Bilge, Ankara 2015.

Ali Parlar, *Ceza Hukukunda Meşru Savunma ve Haksız Tahrik.* Bilge, Ankara 2015.

Ali Parlar, Orhan Sekmen, *Ceza ve Hukuk Muhakemesinde İstinaf ve Temyiz,* 2. Baskı, Bilge Yayınevi, Ankara 2017.

Ali Parlar, Reyhan Yaman, Erdal Şensoy, *Ceza Yargılamasında İstinaf Sistemine Göre İspat Gerekçe ve Hüküm,* Aristo, İstanbul 2017.

Ali Pehlivan, Kabahatler Hukukunun Genel Esasları, Beta, İstanbul, 2020.

Ali Rıza Çınar, *Konut Dokunulmazlığını İhlal Suçları*, 1999.

Ali Rıza Çınar, *Hukuka Aykırı Kanıtlar.* Türkiye Barolar Birliği Dergisi, sayı 55 Kasım-Aralık 2004.

Ali Rıza Çınar, *Türk Ceza Hukukunda Cezalar*, Ankara, 2005.

Ali Rıza Çınar, *Ceza Yargılamasında Temyiz Yolu.* Turhan Kitabevi, Ankara 2006.

Ali Rıza Çınar, *Türk ve Alman Ceza Yargılama Hukukunda İstinaf*, Adalet, Ankara 2010.
Ali Rıza Çınar, *Çocuk Ceza Hukuku,* Yetkin, Ankara 2020.
Ali Tanju Sarıgül, *Ceza Muhakemesi Hukukunda İstinaf*, 3. Baskı, TBB Yayınları, Ankara 2017.
Aslan Gündüz, *Eroding Concept of National Sovereignty: The Turkish Example, Marmara Journal of European Studies* 1, nos 1–2 (1991): 99-154.
Aslan Gündüz, *Security and Human Rights in Europe, European Community Institute,* Istanbul: University of Marmara, 1994.
Asuman İnce Tunçer, *Yalan Tanıklık Suçu,* Seçkin, Ankara 2020.
Aydın Kuyucu, *Kanun Yararına Bozma.* 2. Baskı, Adalet, Ankara 2012.
Ayhan Bozlak, *Türk Ceza Hukukunda Özel Hayatın Korunması.* Adalet, Ankara 2013.
Ayhan Döner, *Şeffaf Devlette Bilgi Edinme Hakkı ve Sınırları*, İstanbul: Vedat Kitapçılık, 2010.
Ayhan Önder, *Ceza Hukuku Genel Hükümler*, Cilt 1, İstanbul, Beta, 1991.
Ayhan Önder, *Ceza Hukukunda Tecil ve Benzeri Müesseseler*, İstanbul, 1963.
Ayhan Önder, *Şahıslara ve Mala Karşı Cürümler ve Bilişim Alanında Suçlar*, İstanbul, Filiz Kitabevi, 1994.
Ayşe Nuhoğlu, *Ceza Hukukunda Emniyet Tedbirleri.* Ankara, Adil Yayınevi, 1997.
Ayşe Nuhoğlu, *Aile Düzenine Karşı Suçlar*, İstanbul, Beta, 2009.
Ayşe Nuhoğlu (ed.), *Sanktionen gegen juristische Personen (Tüzel Kişiler Hakkında Uygulanan Yaptırımlar),* Series of the Max-Planck-Institute for Foreign and International Criminal Law and Bahçeşehir University Joint Research Group, Volume T2, Bahçeşehir Üniversitesi Yayınları, Istanbul 2013.
Ayşe Nur Tütüncü, *İnsancıl Hukuka Giriş*, 4. Baskı, İstanbul, Beta, 2020.
Ayşe Özge Atalay, *Türk Ceza Hukukunda Fuhuş Suçu,* XII Levha, İstanbul 2013.
Ayşe Özge Atalay, *Ceza Hukukunda Actiones Liberae in Causa Kuramı,* XII Levha, İstanbul 2019.
Aysun Dalkılıç, *Türk Ceza Hukukunda Müsadere.* Seçkin, Ankara 2013.
Bahri Öztürk, *Ceza Muhakemesi Hukukunda Koğuşturma Mecburiyeti, Hazırlık Soruşturması*, 9. Bası, Ankara, 9 Eylül Üniversitesi, 1991.
Bahri Öztürk, Mustafa Ruhan Erdem, *Uygulamalı Ceza Hukuku ve Güvenlik Tedbirleri Hukuku*, TCK Değişikliklerine Göre Yenilenmiş 20. Baskı, Ankara 2020, Seçkin Yayınları.
Barış Erman, *Tıbbi Müdahalelerin Hukuka Uygunluğu*, Ankara, Seçkin Yayınları, 2003.
Bekir Aksay, *Ceza Hukukunda Yaş Küçüklüğü, Kusur Yeteneğine ve Sorumluluğa Etkisi*, İstanbul, 1990.
Berrin Akbulut, *Türk Ceza Kanunu ile Kabahatler Kanununun Genel Hükümlerinin Yaptırım Hükümleri Dışında Karşılaştırmalı Olarak İncelenmesi*, 2. Baskı, Adalet, Ankara 2014.
Berrin Akbulut, *Ceza Hukuku Genel Hükümler,* 7. Baskı, Adalet, Ankara 2020.
Burcu Demren-Dönmez, *Ceza Muhakemesi Hukukunda Çapraz Sorgu.* 2. Baskı, Seçkin, Ankara 2019.
Çağatay Çınar, *Usulsüz Halka Arz ve İzinsiz Faaliyette Bulunma Suçları,* Seçkin, Ankara 2020.

Selected Bibliography

Çağla Erdoğan, *İşverenin İş ve Sosyal Güvenlik Hukukundan Kaynaklanan Cezai Sorumluluğu,* Adalet, Ankara 2016.

Canan Ateş Ekşi, *Uluslararası Ceza Mahkemesinin İnsanlığa Karşı Suçlar Üzerindeki Yargı Yetkisi*, Ankara, Seçkin Yayınları, 2004.

Cankat Taşkın, 5236 *Sayılı Kabahatler Yasası'nın Anayasa'ya ve Hukuka Aykırılık Yönünden İncelenmesi*, Türkiye Barolar Birliği Dergisi, sayı 61, Kasım, Aralık 2005.

Cemal Öztürkler, *Ölüm ve Bedeni Zarar Hallerinde Maddi Tazminatın Hesaplanması Teknikleri,* Ankara, Seçkin Yayınları, 2003.

Cengiz Apaydın, *Bilişim Suçları ve Bilişim Ceza Hukuku*, Yazarın Kendi Yayını, İstanbul 2017.

Cengiz Kütük, *Türk Ceza Hukukunda Zimmet Suçu,* Seçkin, Ankara 2016.

Cengiz Otacı, İbrahim Keskin, *Türk Kabahatler Hukuku*, 3. Baskı, HUKAB Yayınları, 2014.

Cengiz Otacı, *Genel Adap ve Aile Düzenine Karşı Suçlar*, Ankara, Seçkin Yayınları, 2000.

Cengiz Ünsal, *Ceza Muhakemesinde İstinafın Gelişimi ve Bölge Adliye Mahkemelerinde Muhakemenin Yapılması,* Seçkin, Ankara 2014.

Cengiz Ünsal, *Ceza Muhakemesinde İstinaf,* 2. Baskı, Seçkin, Ankara 2016.

Çetin Akkaya, *Cezaların Belirlenmesi ve Ceza ve Güvenlik Tedbirlerinin İnfazı ve İnfaz Hukuku;* 2. Baskı, Ankara, Kartal Yayınevi, 2007.

Çetin Akkaya, *Kanun Yararına Bozma ve Yargıtay C. Başsavcısının İtiraz Yetkisi*, Ankara, Kartal Yayınevi, 2007.

Çetin Akkaya, *Terör Suçları ve Cezalarının İnfazı*, Ankara, Adalet, 2009.

Çetin Arslan, Murat Kayançiçek, *Suçta Tekerrür*, Ankara, Seçkin, 2009.

Cumhur Şahin, *Hazırlık Soruşturmasında Sanığın Kolluk Tarafından Sorgulanması,* Konya: Doktora Tezi, 1993.

Cumhur Şahin, Nesihan Göktürk, *Ceza Muhakemesi Hukuku -I-*. 11. Bası, Seçkin, Ankara 2020.

Cumhur Şahin, Nesihan Göktürk, *Ceza Muhakemesi Hukuku -II-*, 11. Bası, Seçkin, Ankara 2021.

Dennis Howitt (Çev. Ed. Didem Yücel Elitez & Fulya Giray Sözen), Adli Psikoloji ve Suç Psikolojisine Giriş, Nobel, Ankara, 2021.

Derya Ormanoğlu, *Ceza Muhakemesi Hukukunda Aleyhe Değiştirme Yasağı,* On İki Levha Yayıncılık, İstanbul 2016.

Devrim Güngör, *Ceza Muhakemesinde İstinaf,* Yetkin, Ankara 2016.

Dilek Cengiz, *Türk Rekabet Hukukundaki Uyumlu Eylem ve Bu Eylemin Hukuki Sonuçları*, İstanbul, Beta, 2006.

Doğan Bülent Belli, *Basın Yoluyla Kişilik Hakkına Saldırıdan Doğan Hukuki Sorumluluk*, 2008.

Doğan Gedik, *5237 sayılı Türk Ceza Kanunu ve 5271 sayılı Ceza Muhakemesi Kanunu'na Göre Müsadere,* 2. Bası, Adalet, Ankara 2016.

Doğan Gedik, *Ceza Muhakemesinde İspat ve Şüphenin Sanık Lehine Yorumlanması,* 4. Baskı, Adalet, Ankara 2020.

Doğan Şenyüz, *Vergi Ceza Hukuku*, 10. Basım Ekin Yayınevi, Bursa 2020.

Doğan Soyaslan, *Teşebbüs Suçu*, 1994.

Doğan Soyaslan, *Ceza Hukuku Genel Hükümler*, 9. Baskı, Yetkin Yayınları, Ankara, 2020.
Doğan Soyaslan, *Kriminoloji (Suç ve Ceza Bilimleri),* 4. Baskı, Yetkin, Ankara 2020.
Doğan Soyaslan, *Ceza Hukuku Özel Hükümler*, Yetkin Yayınları, Güncelleştirilmiş 13. Baskı, Ankara 2020.
Doğan Soyaslan, *Ceza Muhakemesi Hukuku,* 8. Baskı, Yetkin, Ankara 2020.
Durmuş Tezcan, Mustafa Ruhan Erdem, Oğuz Sancaktar, Murat Önok, *İnsan Hakları El Kitabı,* 5. Baskı, Seçkin, Ankara 2014.
Durmuş Tezcan, *Ceza Özel Hukuku Seti,* Seçkin, Ankara 2020.
Durmuş Tezcan, Mustafa Ruhan Erdem, Murat Önok, *Teorik ve Pratik Ceza Özel Hukuku,* 18. Baskı, Seçkin, Ankara 2020.
Durmuş Tezcan, Mustafa Ruhan Erdem, Murat Önok, *Uluslararası Ceza Hukuku,* 6. Baskı Seçkin Ankara 2021.
Ekrem Çetintürk, *Onarıcı Adalet ve Ceza Adalet Sisteminde Uzlaştırma,* Adalet, Ankara 2017.
Emin Artuk, Ahmet Gökçen, Caner Yenidünya, *Türk Ceza Kanunu Şerhi, 1. Cilt*, 2. Baskı, Adalet Yayınevi, Ankara 2014.
Emin Artuk, Ahmet Gökçen, Mehmet Emin Alşahin, Kerim Çakır, *Ceza Hukuku Genel Hükümler* Ankara, Yenilenmiş Gözden Geçirilmiş 14. Baskı Adalet, 2020.
Engin Akın, *Terör ve Terörün Finansmanı Suçu*, Ankara, Adalet, 2009.
Eralp Özgen, *Suçluların Geri Verilmesi*, Ankara, 1962.
Erdal Doğan, *Sanık Hakları ve Müdafilik*, İstanbul, Beta, 2. Baskı, 2008.
Erdem İzzet Külçür, *Ceza Hukukunda Yer Bakımından Uygulama,* On İki Levha, İstanbul 2017.
Erdem İzzet Külçür, *Çevreci Terörizm,* Hukuk Akademisi, İstanbul 2020.
Erdener Yurtcan, *Ceza Muhakemesi Kanunu Şerhi*. Güncellenmiş. 9. Baskı, Seçkin, Ankara 2019.
Erdener Yurtcan, *Ceza Yargılaması Hukuku,* 16. Bası, Ankara 2019.
Eric Hilgendorf, Brian Valerius, (Çev. Salih Oktar), *Alman Ceza Hukuku Genel Kısım*, Yetkin, Ankara, 2021.
Eric Hilgendorf, (Çev. Salih Oktar), Alman Tıp Ceza Hukukuna Giriş, Yetkin, Ankara, 2021.
Ergin Ergül, *Hukuki, Mali, Ekonomik, Aktüel Boyutları ve İlgili Mevzuatıyla Karaparanın Aklanması ve Suçları*, 1998.
Ergin Ergül, *Karapara Endüstrisi ve Aklama Suçu*, 2001.
Ergin Ergül, *Kara Ekonomi ve Aklama Suçları*, Ankara, Yetkin Yayınları, 2005.
Ergun Özbudun, *Constitutional Law*, in Introduction to Turkish Law, ed. *Tuğrul Ansay, Don Wallance Jr., Işık Önay,* Seventh Edition, Ch. 2, Kluwer, Deventer 2020.
Erhan Günay, *Öğreti ve Uygulamada Yeni Türk Ceza Kanunundaki Etkin Pişmanlık ve Gönüllü Vazgeçme*, Yetkin Yayınları, Ankara 2005.
Erhan Günay, *Teori ve Uygulamada Olası Kast Bilinçli Taksir, Öldürme ve Yaralama Kastı*, Seçkin Yayınları, 2007.
Erhan Günay, *Ceza Muhakemesi Hukukunda Olağanüstü Kanun Yolları, 2. Baskı, Seçkin, Ankara 2016.*

Erkam Yılmaz, *Yardım veya Bildirim Yükümlülüğünün Yerine Getirilmemesi Suçu,* Seçkin, Ankara 2020.
Erkan Canak, *Çapraz Sorgu.* İstanbul 2005.
Erol Çetin, *Yeni Türk Ceza Yasasındaki Hakaret Suçları*, Ankara, Seçkin Yayınları, 2008.
Erol Cihan, Feridun Yenisey, *Ceza Muhakemesi Hukuku.* 2. Bası Istanbul, Beta, 1996.
Ersan Şen, *Devlet ve Kitle İletişim Araçları Karşısında Özel Hayatın Gizliliği ve Korunması*, 1996.
Ersan Şen, *Türk Ceza Yargılaması Hukukunda Hukuka Aykırı Deliller Sorunu*, İstanbul, 1998.
Ersan Şen, *Türk Hukukunda Telefon Dinleme, Gizli Soruşturmacı X Muhbir.* 5. Bası, Ankara 2011.
Ersan Şen, *Karşılıksız Çek Suçu.* 4. Bası, Seçkin, Ankara 2013.
Ersan Şen, *Şike*. Yargın Hukuk Yayınları, İstanbul 2012.
Esma Nur Turhan, *Vorsatz und Fahrlässigkeit im deutschen und türkischen Strafrecht,* Verlag Dr. Kovac, Hamburg 2020.
Fahrettin Demirağ, *Ceza Muhakemesi Hukuku İşlemleri ve Adli Yazışmalar,* 2. Baskı Seçkin, Ankara 2020.
Fahrettin Demirağ, *Türk Ceza Kanununun Genel Hükümleri Işığında Askeri Ceza Kanunu,* Üçüncü Baskı, Seçkin, Ankara 2020.
Fahri Gökçen Taner, *Türk Ceza Hukuku'nda Cinsel Özgürlüğe Karşı Suçlar,* 2. Baskı, Seçkin, Ankara 2017.
Faruk Erem, *Diyalektik Açıdan Ceza Yargılaması Hukuku,* 6. Bası, Ankara 1986.
Faruk Erem, Nevzat Toroslu, *Türk Ceza Hukuku, Özel Hükümler,* 3. Bası, Ankara, 1978.
Faruk Turhan, *Ceza Muhakemesi Hukuku,* Asil Yayın, Isparta 2006.
Faruk Turinay, *Suçta ve Cezada Kanunilik İlkesinin Anayasal Temelleri.* XII Levha, İstanbul, 2013.
Fatih Birtek, *AİHM, Anayasa Mahkemesi ve Yargıtay Kararları Işığında Ceza Muhakemesinde Delil ve İspat,* 2. Baskı, Adalet, Ankara 2017.
Fatih Birtek, *Türk Ceza Hukuku Genel Hükümler,* 6. baskı, Adalet, Ankara 2018.
Fatih Selami Mahmutoğlu, Selman Dursun, *Türk Hukuku'nda Müdafiin Yasaklılık Halleri*, Ankara, Seçkin, 2004.
Fatih Selami Mahmutoğlu, Serra Karadeniz; Burak Akın, Arzu Buşra Bayrakdar, Engin Turhan, Damla Kuz, Mesut Seçkin, Elif Arayan, *Türk Ceza Kanunu Genel Hükümler Şerhi*, Beta, İstanbul 2017.
Fazlı Doğan, *Berufung im Strafprozess unter besonderer Würdigung der geschichtlicher Entwicklung, der Reformvorschläge und der Wiedereinführungsfrage in der Türkei.* Marburg 2005.
Feridun Yenisey, *Ceza Muhakemesi Hukukunda İstinaf ve Tekrar Kabulü Sorunu,* İstanbul 1979.
Feridun Yenisey, *Juvenile Delinquency in Turkey*, Messmer & Otto; *Restorative Justice on Trial*, Dordrecht, Boston, London: Kluwer Academic Publishers, 1992.
Feridun Yenisey, *Milletlerarası Ceza Hukuku, Ceza Yargılarının Milletlerarası Değeri ve Mevzuatı*, İstanbul 1988.

Feridun Yenisey, *Uygulanan ve Olması Gereken Ceza Muhakemesi Hukuku, Hazırlık Soruşturması ve Polis*, 3. Baskı, İstanbul, Beta, 1993.
Feridun Yenisey (ed.), *Uluslararası Ceza Divanı*, İstanbul, Arıkan Yayınları, 2007.
Feridun Yenisey (ed), *21. Yüzyılda Hukuk Eğitimi* (Legal Education in the Twenty-First Century), the book of the international conference, Bahçeşehir University/ The Union of Turkish Bar Associations/ Atlanta's John Marshall School of Law.
Feridun Yenisey, Ulrich Sieber (eds.). *Criminal Law in the Global Risk Society.* Series of the Max Planck Institute for Foreign and International Criminal Law and Bahçeşehir University Joint Research Group, Volume T 1, Istanbul 2011.
Feridun Yenisey, *Genetics Related Regulations in Turkish Criminal Law and Criminal Procedure*, in Genetics, Robotics, Law, Punishment, D. Provolo & S. Riondato & F. Yenisey (ed.), Padova University Press, 2014, p. 253.
Feridun Yenisey, Gottfried Plagemann, *Alman Ceza Kanunu (StGB).* Gözden Geçirilmiş ve Genişletilmiş 2. Baskı, Beta, İstanbul 2015.
Feridun Yenisey, *Kolluk Hukuku*, İstanbul, Beta, 2. Baskı, 2015.
Feridun Yenisey, Ayşe Nuhoğlu, Ulrich Sieber, Silvia Tellenbach (eds.), *Alman ve Türk Ceza Hukukunun Güncel Sorunları: 20-22 Kasım 2014 Tarihlerinde Düzenlenen Uluslararası Kolokyum Kitabı = Aktuelle Probleme im deutschen und türkischen Strafrecht: Internationales Kolloquium 20.-22 November 2014,* Ankara, Türkiye Adalet Akademisi Yayınları, T3, Ankara 2016.
Feridun Yenisey, Ayşe Nuhoğlu (eds.), *Ceza Muhakemesi Hukuku Başvuru Kitabı,* 6. Baskı, Bilge, Ankara, 2021.
Feridun Yenisey, Ayşe Nuhoğlu (eds.), *Yargıtay Ceza Genel Kurulu Kararlarının Değerlendirilmesi,* Seçkin, Ankara 2020.
Feridun Yenisey, Ayşe Nuhoğlu, *Ceza Muhakemesi Hukuku,* 8. Baskı, Seçkin, Ankara 2020.
Feridun Yenisey, Salih Oktar, Ayla Oktar, *Alman Ceza Muhakemesi Kanunu (StPO).* 3. Baskı, Beta, İstanbul 2020.
Feridun Yenisey, (Yayın Kurulu: H. Çınar, S. Kaymaz, S. Oktar, C. Ünsal) Ceza Muhakemesinde İstinafın Beş Yılı, Seçkin, Ankara, 2021.
Feridun Yenisey, Translation of the Turkish Penal Procedure Code, 4. Bası, Beta, İstanbul 2021.
Friedrich-Christian Schroeder, Torsten Verrel, (Çev. Salih Oktar), *Ceza Muhakemesi Hukuku*, Yetkin, 2019.
Fusun Sokullu Akıncı, *Polis, Toplumsal Bir Kurum Olarak Gelişmesi*, İstanbul, Polis Alt Kültürü ve İnsan Hakları, 1990.
Füsun Sokullu Akıncı, *Viktimoloji* İstanbul, 3. Baskı, Beta, 2016.
Gottfried Plagemann, *Von Allahs Gesetz zur Modernisierung per Gesezt, Gesetz und Gesetzgebungen im Osmanischen Reich und der Republik Türkei*, Berlin: Lit Verlag, 2009.
Gözde Güder, *Türk Ceza Kanununda Sahte ve Taklit Suçları,* İstanbul Medipol Üniversitesi İstanbul 2016.
Güçlü Akyürek, *Yargılamanın Yenilenmesi,* Seçkin, 2. Baskı, Ankara 2018.
Gülşah Bostancı Bozbayındır, *Ceza Hukukunda Haksız Tahrik.* Beta, İstanbul 2013.
Günal Kurşun, *Ceza Muhakemesinde Hüküm,* Seçkin, Ankara 2016.
Güneş Okuyucu Ergün, *Ceza Muhakemesi İşlemleri*, Yetkin, Ankara 2015.
Gunnar Duttge, Yener Ünver (eds.), *Aktuelle Grundlagenprobleme des Materiellen*

Strafrechts. Özyeğin Üniversitesi, İstanbul 2012.
Gunnar Duttge, Yener Ünver (eds.). *Das Schuldprinzip des Türkischen StGB im Spiegel des Deutschen Strafrechts.* Seçkin, Ankara 2013.
Hakan Hakeri, *İhmal Kavramı ve İhmali Suçların Çeşitleri*, Ankara, Seçkin Yayınları, 2003.
Hakan Hakeri, *Kasten Öldürme Suçları*, Gözden Geçirilmiş İkinci Baskı, Seçkin, Ankara 2007.
Hakan Hakeri, *Ceza Hukuku Genel Hükümler;* 24. Baskı, Adalet, Ankara 2021.
Hakan Karakehya, *Ceza Muhakemesi Hukuku,* 2. Baskı, Savaş Yayınevi, Ankara 2016.
Hakan Karakehya, *Ceza Muhakemesinde Maddi Gerçeğin Tespiti*, Savaş Yayınevi, Ankara 2016.
Hakan Yavuz, *Ceza İnfaz Sistemi ve Denetimli Serbestlik,* Şeçkin, Ankara 2018.
Haluk Çolak, *Ceza Yargılaması Hukukunda Çapraz Sorgu.* Bilge yayınları, Ankara 2005.
Haluk Çolak, Mustafa Taşkın, *Ceza Muhakemesi Kanunu Şerhi. 2.* Baskı, Seçkin Yayınevi, Ankara 2007.
Hande Ulutürk. *Türk Hukukunda Akıl Hastalığı ve Akıl Hastalığının Kusur Yeteneneğine Etkisi*, Seçkin, Ankara 2014.
Hamide Zafer, *Ceza Hukuku Genel Hükümler*, 7. Baskı, Beta, İstanbul, 2019.
Harun Bulut, *Kişilik Hakları ve Kişilik Haklarına Saldırıdan Kaynaklanan Hukuk Davaları*, Beta, İstanbul, 2006.
Hasan Sınar, *İnternet ve Ceza Hukuku*, 2001.
Hasan Sınar, *Bir Koruma Tedbiri Olarak Türk Ceza Muhakemesi Hukukunda Tutuklama,* On İki Levha Yayıncılık, İstanbul 2016.
Hasan Tahsin Gökcan, *Mühür Bozma, Yedieminlik Yükümlülüğüne Uymama, İhtiyati Tedbir Kararına Aykırılık Suçları ve Zarara Yol Açan Yediemin ile Haksız Tedbir Uygulatana Karşı Tazminat Davaları*, Ankara, Seçkin Yayınları, 2001.
Hasan Tahsin Keçeligil, Türk Ceza Hukukunda Taksirin Esasları, Yetkin, Ankara 2016.
Hüseyin Ertuğrul, Uluslararası Ceza Hukukunda Hükümlülerin Nakli, Adalet, Ankara 2016.
Hüseyin Karaahmetoğlu, *Sporda Şiddet Şike ve Teşvik Primi,* İstanbul 2015.
Hüsnü Aldemir, *Seri Muhakeme ve Basit Yargılama Usullleri,* Adalet, Ankara 2020.
İbrahim Korkmaz, *Kişisel Verilerin Ceza Hukuku Kapsamında Korunması,* Seçkin, 2. Baskı, Ankara 2019.
İlhan Akbulut, *Kan Gütme Saiki ile Adam Öldürme*, İstanbul, Kazancı Hukuk Yayınevi, 2006.
İlhan Üzülmez, *Türk Hukukunda Tekerrür*, Ankara: Turhan, 2003.
İlyas Şahin, *Teknik Araçlarla İzleme.* 2. Bası, Adalet, Ankara 2015.
İnan Yılmaz, *5271 sayılı Ceza Muhakemesi Kanunu'nda Adli Kontrol,* Adalet, Ankara 2016.
İzzet Özgenç, *Suça İştirakin Hukuki Esası ve Faillik*, 1996.
İzzet Özgenç, *Ekonomik Çıkar Nedeniyle İşlenen Suçlar.* Ankara: Seçkin, 2002.
İzzet Özgenç, *Suç Örgütleri,* 13. Bası, Seçkin, Ankara 2020.
İzzet Özgenç, *Türk Ceza Hukuku Genel Hükümler,* Gözden Geçirilmiş ve Güncellenmiş 16. Bası Ankara, Seçkin, 2020.

İzzet Özgenç, *Zimmet Suçu*, Seçkin, 2. Baskı, Ankara, 2012.
Kadri Keskin, *Para Cezaları, Ön Ödeme Ceza Tabloları, Erteleme, Paraya çevirme, Harçlar*, Desen Ofset, Ankara 1996.
Kayıhan İçel et al., *İçel Suç Teorisi,* Beta, İkinci Bası, İstanbul 2000.
Kayıhan İçel Yener Ünver (ed.), *Malvarlığına Karşı Suçlar ve Ekonomik Suçluluk*, Ankara, Seçkin, 2009.
Kayıhan İçel, Yener Ünver, *Kitle Haberleşme Hukuku*, 8. Baskı, İstanbul, Beta, 2009.
Kayıhan İçel, *Ceza Hukuku Genel Hükümler,* 6. Baskı Beta, İstanbul 2021.
Kemal Karanfil, *Sulh Ceza Hakimliği*, Adalet, Ankara 2016.
Kemal Şimşek, *Yabancıların Türkiye'de Yargılanması ve Uluslararası Adli Yardımlaşma.* Adalet, Ankara 2014.
Kısmet Erkiner, *Uluslararası Spor Tahkim Mahkemesi C.A.S.*, İstanbul, 2. Baskı, On İki Levha, 2010.
Klaus Tiedemann, çeviri Ayşe Nuhoğlu, *Ekonomi Ceza Hukuku*, Seçkin Yayıncılık, Ankara 2017.
Köksal Bayraktar, *Hekimin Tedavi Nedeniyle Cezai Sorumluluğu*, İstanbul, 1971.
Köksal Bayraktar, *Siyasal Suç*, İstanbul, 1982.
Köksal Bayraktar, Vesile Sonay Evik, Gülşah Kurt, *Özel Ceza Hukuku: Uluslararası Suçlar,* 2. Bası, On İki Levha Yayıncılık, İstanbul 2017.
Köksal Kocaağa, Ceza koşulu (sözleşme cezası), Yetkin Yayınları, Ankara 2018.
Koray Doğan, *Ceza Muhakemesinde Belirsizlik, Kuşkudan Sanık Yararlanır İlkesi "in dubio pro reo,"* Seçkin, Ankara 2016.
Kudret Güven, *General Principles of Turkish Law.* Third Edition, Ankara: Bilge Kitabevi, 2007.
Levent Kurt, *Açıklamalı İçtihatlı Tüm Yönleriyle Bilişim Suçları ve Türk Ceza Kanunundaki Uygulaması*, Ankara, Seçkin Yayınları, 2005.
Mahmut Koca, İlhan Üzülmez İlhan. *Türk Ceza Hukuku Özel Hükümler, 7. Baskı,* Adalet, Ankara 2020.
Mahmut Koca, İlhan Üzülmez, *Türk Ceza Hukuku Genel Hükümler,* 13. Baskı, Seçkin, Ankara 2020.
Mehmet Emin Alşahin, *Yargıtay Kararları Işığında Mala Zarar Verme Suçları (5237 Sayılı TCK. m. 151 vd.)*, Ankara, Turhan Kitabevi, 2010.
Mehmet Gönlübol, Türkkaya Ataöv, *Turkey in the United Nations, a Legal and Political Appraisal*, Ankara: Ajans Turk Press, 1960.
Mehmet Sinan Altunç, Ceza Hukukunda Tekerrür, İstanbul, Yayınlanmamış Doktora Tezi, 2010.
Mehmet Yayla, *Ceza Muhakemesi Hukukunda İspat ve Şüphe*, Seçkin, Ankara 2016.
Melda Sur, *Uluslararası Hukukun Esasları*, İstanbul, 14. Baskı, Beta, 2020.
Meral Ekici Şahin, *Ceza Hukukunda Rıza.* XII Levha, İstanbul 2012.
Mesut Bedri Eryılmaz, *Arrest and Detention Powers in Turkish and English Law and Practice in the Light of the European Convention on Human Rights*, Martinus Nijhoff Publishing, Boston 1999.
Mesut Bedri Eryılmaz, *Türk ve İngiliz Hukukunda ve Uygulamasında Durdurma ve Arama,* Seçkin Yayınları, Ankara 2003.
Metin Köse, *Ceza Kovuşturmasında Delillerin Ortaya Konulması ve Değerlendirilmesi,* Seçkin, Ankara 2017.

Metin Tokel, *Ceza İnfaz Kurumlarında Açlık Grevleri,* Adalet, Ankara 2016.
Mithat Arman Karasu, *Kente Karşı Suç: İmar Uygulamaları Bağlamında Kente Karşı İşlenen Suçlar*, 2009.
Mualla Buket Soygüt Arslan, *Türk Ceza ve Ceza Usul Hukukunda Uzlaşma Kurumu.* Galatasaray Üniversitesi Yayınları, İstanbul 2008.
Muhammet Açıkgözoğlu, *Ceza Hukuku Açısından Teori ve Uygulamada Mağdur Kavramı*, Adil Yayınevi, Ankara 2000.
Muhammet Celal Kul, *Uluslararası Ceza Mahkemesi ve Uluslararası Tecâvüz (saldırı) Suçu = International criminal court and the crime of aggression = Cour penale internationale et le crime d'agression,* On İki Levha Yayıncılık, İstanbul 2016.
Muhammet Emre Tulay, *Kriminelle Vereinigungen im deutschen Strafrecht im Vergleich zum türkischen Strafrecht unter besonderer Berücksichtigung der Beteiligungsdogmatik*, Holzkirchen, 2018.
Muharrem Özen, *Meşru Müdafaa*, Ankara, Seçkin Yayınları, 1995.
Muharrem Özen, *Ceza Hukukunda Objektif Sorumluluk*, 1998.
Muharrem Özen, *Hakimin Cezai Sorumluluğu*, Ankara, Seçkin Yayınları, 2004.
Murat Aydın, *Ceza Muhakemesi Hukukunda Kendini İtham Etmeme Hakkı: (Nemo Tenetur İlkesi),* Adalet, Ankara 2016.
Murat Kayançiçek, *Ceza Hukuku ve Kabahatler Hukukunda Zamanaşımı,* Adalet, Ankara, 2014.
Murat Önok, *Uluslararası Boyutuyla İşkence Suçu*, 2006.
Murat Önok. *Penal Law*, in Introduction to Turkish Law, ed. *Tuğrul Ansay, Don Wallance Jr., Işık Önay,* Seventh Edition, Ch. 10, Kluwer, Deventer 2020.
Murat Volkan Dülger, *Bilişim Suçları*, 8. Baskı, Seçkin Yayınları, 2020.
Mustafa Arslantürk, *Türk Ceza Kanunu Uygulamasında Cinsel Suçlar: Yargılamadan Uygulamalarla, Somut Olaylarla, Pratik Çözümlerle,* 5. Baskı, Seçkin, Ankara 2019.
Mustafa Artuç, Mehmet Tevfik Elmas, *Ceza Yargılamasında Duruşma Yönetimi ve İstinaf,* 2. Baskı, Adalet, Ankara 2017.
Mustafa Avcı, *Osmanlı Ceza Hukuku*, Mimozo, Konya 2014.
Mustafa Ekinci, Sinan Esen, *Hırsızlık, Yağma, Güveni Kötüye Kullanma, Dolandırıcılık, Hileli ve Taksirli İflas, Karkılıksız Yararlanma, Belgelerde Sahtecilik ve Bilişim Alanında Suçlar*, Ankara, Yetkin Yayınları, 2005.
Mustafa Genç, *İmar Hukuku*, Seçkin, Ankara, 2015.
Mustafa Karabulut, *İdari Yaptırımların Hukuki Rejimi*, 2008.
Mustafa Özen, *İdari Ceza Hukuku,* Adalet, Ankara 2013.
Mustafa Özen, *Ceza Muhakemesi Hukuku Dersleri,* 3. Bası, Adalet, Ankara 2019.
Mustafa Özen, *Ceza Hukuku Genel Hükümler Dersleri,* 5. Baskı, Adalet, Ankara 2020.
Mustafa Ruhan Erdem, *Ceza Muhakemesinde Yeni Bir Denetim Muhakamesi Yolu Olarak İstinaf,* Seçkin, Ankara 2010.
Mustafa Ruhan Erdem, Ferda Eser, Pakize Pelin Özşahinli, *6763 Sayılı Kanuna ve Ceza Muhakemesinde Uzlaştırma Yönetmeliğine Göre Güncellenmiş 100 Soruda Uzlaştırma, Uzlaştırmacının El Kitabı,* 2. Baskı, Seçkin, Ankara 2017.
Mustafa Serdar Özbek, Orhan Cüni, Merve Özcan, *Ceza muhakemesi Hukukunda*

Uzlaştırma Eğitim Kitabı, Alternatif Çözümler Daire Başkanlığı Yayını, Ankara 2018.
Mustafa Tören Yücel, *Kriminoloji Suç ve Ceza.* Ankara: Emekli Ofset, 1986.
Muzaffer Yasin Aslan, *Uluslararası Ceza Mahkemesi,* 2. Baskı, Bilge Yayınevi, Ankara 2018.
Necati Meran, *Kişilere Karşı Suçlar; Genişletilmiş ve Gözden Geçirilmiş 2.* Baskı, Ankara, Seçkin, 2008.
Necati Meran, *Sahtecilik: Malvarlığı, Bilişim Suçları ile Ekonomi ve Ticaret Alanında Suçlar*; Genişletilmiş ve Gözden Geçirilmiş 2. Bası, Ankara, Seçkin, 2008.
Necati Meran, *Zimmet-Rüşvet-İrtikap ve Görevi Kötüye Kullanma Suçları, Kamu Görevlisi Kavramı, Kamu İdaresine Karşı İşlenen Diğer Suçlar*, Ankara, Seçkin, 2008.
Necati Meran, *Adli ve Önleme Amaçlı İletişimin Denetlenmesi (Telefon Dinleme, SMS, MMS, e-mail İzleme), Gizli Sorusturmacı, Teknik Takip*, Ankara, Adalet Yayınevi, 2009.
Necati Meran, *Hakaret: İftira, Yargılamayı Etkilemeye Teşebbüs ve Sorusturmanın Gizliliğini İhal Suçları*, Ankara, Seçkin, 2009.
Necati Meran, *İmar Kirliliğine Neden Olma Suçu*, Ankara, 2. Baskı, Adalet Yayınevi, 2013.
Necati Meran, *Kabahatler Kanunu ve Özel Kanunlarda İdari Para Cezaları*, 4. Baskı, Adalet, Ankara 2015.
Necati Meran, *Ceza Yargılamasında İstinaf ve Temyiz,* Adalet, Ankara 2016.
Nejdet Şatır, *Hekimlerin Hukuki ve Cezai Sorumluluğu.* Yetkin, 2. Baskı, Ankara 2018.
Nevzat Toroslu, *Cürumlerin Tasnifi Bakımından Suçun Hukuki Konusu*, Ankara, 1970.
Nevzat Toroslu, *Ceza Hukuku Özel Kısım.* 10. Bası, Savaş, Ankara 2019.
Nevzat Toroslu, *Ceza Hukuku Genel Kısım*, 25. Bası, Ankara, Savaş Yayınevi, 2019.
Neylan Ziyalar, *Çocuk İstismarı ve Çocukla Adli Görüşme,* Seçkin, Ankara 2020.
Nur Centel, *Ceza Muhakemesi Hukukunda Müdafi* İstanbul: Kazancı, 1984.
Nur Centel, *Ceza Muhakemesi Hukukunda Tutuklama ve Yakalama*, Beta, İstanbul 1992.
Nur Centel, Hamide Zafer, Özlem Çakmut, *Kişilere Karşı İşlenen Suçlar*, İstanbul, 4. Baskı, Beta, 2017.
Nur Centel, Hamide Zafer, *Ceza Muhakemesi Hukuku*, 19. Bası, İstanbul, Beta, 2020.
Nur Centel, Hamide Zafer, Özlem Çakmut *Türk Ceza Hukukuna Giriş*, İstanbul, 10. Bası, Beta, 2020.
Nurullah Kantarcı, *Türk Ceza Hukukunda Reşit Olmayanla Cinsel İlişki Suçu,* Adalet, Ankara 2016.
Nurullah Kunter, Feridun Yenisey, Ayşe Nuhoğlu. *Muhakeme Hukuku Dalı Olarak Ceza Muhakemesi Hukuku,* 18. Bası, Beta Yayınevi, İstanbul, 2010.
Nurullah Kunter, *Suçun Kanuni Unsurları Nazariyesi*, İstanbul, İstanbul Hukuk Fakültesi, 1949.
Nurullah Kunter, *Suçun Maddi Unsurları Nazariyesi*, İstanbul, İstanbul Hukuk Fakültesi, 1954.
Oğuz Polat, *Klinik Adli Tıp-Adli Tıp Uygulamaları*, Ankara, Seçkin Yayınları, 2014.

Olgun Değirmenci, *Mukayeseli Hukukta ve Türk Hukukunda Suçtan Kaynaklanan Malvarlığı Değerlerini Aklama Suçu*, Ankara, Turhan, 2007.

Ömer Metehan Aynural, *Soyut Tehlike Bağlamında Trafik Güvenliğini Tehlikeye Sokma Suçu,* İstanbul Arşivi, Onikilavha, İstanbul 2018.

Onur Şahinkaya, *Önleyici Yakalama ve Durdurma,* XII Levha, İstanbul 2020.

Osman Şirin (ed.), *Yargıtay Ceza Genel Kurulu Kararları Kapsamında Yeni Ceza Mevzuatının Yorumu*, 2008.

Öykü Didem Aydın, *Üç Demokraside Düşünce İfade Özgürlüğü*, Ankara, Seçkin Yayınları, 2004.

Özlem Çakmut, *Tıbbi Müdahaleye Rızanın Ceza Hukuku Açısından İncelenmesi*; Legal Yayıncılık, 2003.

Öztekin Tosun, *Suçluların Gözlemi*, İstanbul, İstanbul Üniversitesi, 1958.

Öztekin Tosun, *Suçluların Cezaevinde İyileştirilmesinde Yeni Yöntemler*, İstanbul, 1967.

Öztekin Tosun, *Türk Suç Muhakemesi Hukuku Dersleri, Muhakemenin Yürüyüşü,* Cilt 2, İstanbul, 1976.

Pınar Memiş Kartal, *Türk Ceza Hukukunda Çocukların Cinsel İstismarı,* DER Yayınları, İstanbul 2014.

Ramazan Keklik, *5237 sayılı Türk Ceza Kanunu'nda Etkin Pişmanlık,* Adalet, Ankara 2016.

Recep Gülşen, *Ceza Hukukunda Sorumluluğu Kaldıran Nedenlerden Kaza, Mücbir Sebep, Cebir ve Tehdit*, Ankara, Seçkin, 2007.

Recep Kahraman, Rüşvet Suçu, Seçkin, Ankara 2019.

Remzi Gündüz, *Türk Ceza Kanununda Cinsel Dokunulmazlığa Karşı suçlar: Cinsel Saldırı (TCK 102), Çocukların Cinsel İstismarı (TCK 103), Reşit Olmayanla Cinsel İlişki (TCK 104), Cinsel Taciz (TCK 105),* 2. Baskı, Bilge Yayınevi, Ankara 2017.

Rezzan İtişgen, *Kişinin Kendini Suçlanmaya Zorlanmaması İlkesi (Nomo Tenetur) ve Susma Hakkı.* XII Levha, İstanbul 2013.

Sabih Kanadoğlu, *Kültür ve Tabiat Varlıklarını Koruma Kanunu*, Seçkin Yayınları, Ankara 2003.

Salih Oktar, *Türk Ceza Kanunu'nda Çocuk Düşürtme ve Çocuk Düşürme Suçları*, Seçkin, Ankara 2016.

Salih Özkan, *Ceza Hukukunda Önemsizlik,* Onikilevha, İstanbul 2018.

Sami Onursal, *Kamu Davasına Müdahale*, İstanbul 1968.

Sami Selçuk, *Dolandırıcılığın Kimi Suçlardan Ayrımı*, Ankara, 1993.

Selcen Ataç, *Türk Ceza Hukukunda Kesin Hükmün Önleme Etkisi*. Marmara Üniversitesi Sosyal Bilimler Enstitüsü Kamu Hukuku Doktora Programı, 2010 (Yayımlanmamış doktora tezi).

Selman Dursun, *Sermaye Piyasasında Gerçeğe Aykırılıklardan Doğan Suçlar*. İstanbul 2010.

Serap Keskin, *Ceza Muhakemesi Hukukunda Temyiz Nedeni Olarak Hukuka Aykırılık,* Alfa Basım Yayım Dağıtım, Istanbul 1997.

Serap Keskin Kiziroğlu, *Konut Dokunulmazlığının İhlali Suçu*, Ankara, Adalet Yayınevi, 2010.

Serkan Meraklı, *Ceza Hukukunda Kusur,* Seçkin, 2. Baskı, Ankara, 2020.

Servet Yetim, *Ceza Muhakemesi Hukuku Kapsamında Sosyal Medyadan Elektronik*

Delil Toplama ve Değerlendirme (Facebook örneği), Seçkin, Ankara 2016.
Seydi Kaymaz, *Ceza Muhakemesinde Hukuka Aykırı (Yasak) Deliller*, Ankara, 1997.
Seydi Kaymaz, Hasan Tahsin Gökçan, *Gıda Suçları ve Yeni Gıda Mevzuatı*, Ankara, Seçkin Yayınları, 2002.
Seydi Kaymaz, *Ceza Muhakemesinde Telekomünikasyon Yoluyla Yapılan İletişimin Denetlenmesi. 4.* Bası, Seçkin, Ankara 2015.
Seydi Kaymaz, *Ceza Muhakemesinde İstinaf,* Seçkin, 2. Baskı, Ankara 2020.
Silvia Tellenbach, *Das türkische Strafgesetzbuch* (Translation, Freiburg 1998, 2001, 2008).
Silvia Tellenbach, *Strafbares Verhalten im Vorfeld der Tatvollendung in der Türkei*, in *Nationales Strafrecht in rechtsvergleichender Darstellung, Teilband 3*, ed. Sieber & Cornils, Berlin, 2008.
Silvia Tellenbach, *Subjektive Tatseite in der Türkei*, in *Nationales Strafrecht in rechtsvergleichender Darstellung, Teilband 3*, ed. Sieber & Cornils, Berlin, 2008.
Silvia Tellenbach, *Verjährung in der Türkei,* in Nationales Strafrecht in rechtsvergleichender Darstellung, Teilband 5, ed. Sieber & Cornils (Berlin, 2010).
Silvio Riondato, Rocco Alanga (eds.), *Diritto Penale Della Repubblica di Turchia; Criminal Law of the Republic of Turkey,* Padova University Press, Padova 2012.
Sinan Bayındır, *Türk Ceza Hukukunda Akıl Hastalığı,* On İki Levha, 2. Baskı, İstanbul 2018.
Sinan Sakin, *Türk Ceza Hukuku Genel Hükümler,* Savaş, 7. Baskı, Ankara 2020.
Suat Çalışkan, *Türk Ceza Hukukunda Uyuşturucu veya Uyarıcı Madde Suçları.* Adalet, 2. Baskı, Ankara 2013.
Süheyl Donay, *Güncelleştirilmiş Ceza Yargılaması Hukuku.* Beta, İstanbul 2015.
Süleyman Emre Özdemir, *Ceza Muhakemesinde İtiraz Kanun Yolu,* Adalet Yayınevi, Ankara 2018.
Sulhi Dönmezer, *Criminality in a Small Community of Rapid Urbanization and Industrialization,* in Annales de la Faculté de Droit d'Istanbul XXII, No. 38 (1972–1974).
Sulhi Dönmezer, *Turkey*, in International Handbook of Contemporary Developments in Criminology, ed. E.H. Johnson, Westport, Connecticut: Greenwood Press, 1983.
Sulhi Dönmezer, *Kişilere ve Mala Karşı Cürümler*, 16. Bası, İstanbul, 2001.
Sulhi Dönmezer, Sahir Erman (I). (Yeni basıyı hazırlayanlar: K. Bayraktar, S. Keskin Kiziroğlu, H. Zafer, H. Sınar, R. M. Önok, R. B. Erman) *Nazari ve Tatbiki Ceza Hukuku.* Cilt I, Giriş-Tarihçe-Kaynaklar-TCK'nın Uygulanması 14. Bası, Der Yayınları, İstanbul, 2016.
Sulhi Dönmezer, Sahir Erman (II), (Yeni basıyı hazırlayanlar: K. Bayraktar, S. Keskin Kiziroğlu, H. Zafer, P. Memiş Kartal, H. Sınar, R. B. Erman; F. Eroğlu, R. M. Önok) *Nazari ve Tatbiki Ceza Hukuku, Cilt II, Suçun Unsurları-Teşebbüs-Suçların Birleşmesi-İştirak,* 14. Bası, İstanbul, Der Yayınları, 2019.
Sulhi Dönmezer, Sahir Erman (III). (Yeni basıyı hazırlayanlar: K. Bayraktar, T. Demirbaş, S. Keskin Kiziroğlu, A. Nuhoğlu, H. Zafer, E. Aksoy Retornaz, P. Memiş Kartal, R. M. Önok, H. Toroslu, R. B. Erman) *Nazari ve Tatbiki Ceza Hukuku.* Cilt III, Cezalar-Güvenlik Tedbirleri-İnfaz, 14. Bası, Der Yayınları, Istanbul, 2020.
Sulhi Dönmezer, Sahir Erman (III). (Yeni basıyı hazırlayanlar: K. Bayraktar, F.

Yenisey, D. Tezcan, S. Keskin Kiziroğlu, E. Aksoy Retornaz, P. Memiş Kartal, R. M. Önok, R. B. Erman, Ş. Çakıroğlu) *Nazari ve Tatbiki Ceza Hukuku.* Cilt IV, Uluslararası Ceza Hukuku-Devletlerarası Ceza Hukuku, 14. Bası, Der Yayınları, Istanbul, 2021.
Sulhi Dönmezer, Sahir Erman (Bayraktar, Kiziroğlu, Zafer, Sınar, Önok, Erman), *Nazari ve Tatbiki Ceza Hukuku, Genel Kısım, Cilt I,* 14. Bası, İstanbul: DER Yayınları, 2016, n.406.
Suna Kili, *Turkish Constitutional Developments and Assembly Debates on the Constitutions of 1924 and 1961*, İstanbul: Robert College Research Centre, 1971.
Süreyya Başlı, *5237 Sayılı Türk Ceza Kanunu'nda Hürriyete Karşı işlenen Suçlardan Tehdit ve Cebir Suçu,* Adalet, Ankara 2016.
Tahir Taner, *Ceza Hukuku, Umumi Kısım*, İstanbul, Üçüncü Basım, İstanbul Üniversitesi Hukuk Fakültesi, 1955.
Tahir Taner, *Ceza Muhakemeleri Usulü*, 3. Bası (İstanbul), 1955.
Timur Demirbaş, *İnfaz Hukuku,* Seçkin, Genişletilmiş ve Gözden Geçirilmiş 7. Baskı, Ankara 2020.
Timur Demirbaş, *Türk Ceza Kanununda Özel Tahrik Halleri*, İstanbul, 1985.
Timur Demirbaş, *Sanığın Hazırlık Soruşturmasında İfadesinin Alınması,* İzmir, 1996.
Timur Demirbaş, *Kriminoloji:* Gözden Geçirilmiş 7. Baskı, Ankara, Seçkin, 2020.
Timur Demirbaş, *Ceza Hukuku Genel Hükümler*, 15. Baskı, Seçkin, Ankara 2020.
Tuğrul Katoğlu, *Ceza Hukukunda Hukuka Aykırılık*, Ankara, Seçkin Yayınları, 2003.
Tuğrul Katoğlu, *Ceza Kanunlarının Zaman Yönünden Uygulanması;* Ankara, Seçkin, 2008.
Tuğrul Katoğlu, *Ceza Hukuku ve Kültür Varlıkları,* Seçkin, Ankara 2017.
Turan Tufan Yüce, *Ceza Hukukunun Temel Kavramları*, Ankara, Turhan, 1985.
Türkan Yalçın Sancar, *Çok Failli Suçlar*, 1998.
Türkan Yalçın Sancar, *Müteselsil Suç*, Seçkin Yayınları, 1995.
Türkan Yalçın Sancar, *Alenen Tahkir ve Tezyif Suçları*, Ankara, 2. Baskı, Seçkin Yayınları, 2006.
Türkan Yalçın Sancar, *Türk Ceza Hukukunda Kadın.* Seçkin, 2. Baskı, Ankara 2019.
Uğur Aşkın, *Ceza Muhakemesinde İstinaf Kanun Yolu,* Adalet, Ankara 2018.
Uğur Uruşak, *Ceza Hukukunda Hukuka Uygunluk Sebebi Olarak Bir Hakkın Kullanılması*, İstanbul, Vedat Kitapçılık, 2010.
Ulrich Sieber, (Ed. F. Yenisey, S. Oktar, Z. Başer Doğan), Bilişim Teknolojisi ile Globalleşen Dünyadaki Tehlikelerin Önlenmesi ve Ceza Hukuku, Seçkin, Ankara 2021.
Ümit Kocasakal, *Türk Ceza Kanununda Suçu Bildirmeme Suçları:* TCK 278-279-280, tıpkı bası Vedat, İstanbul 2017.
Vahit Bıçak, Zehrettin Arslan, *Constitutional Law: Turkey*, Holland: Kluwer Law International, 2004.
Vahit Bıçak, E. Grieves, *Türkçe-İngilizce Türk Ceza Kanunu*, Ankara, 2007.
Vahit Bıçak, *Suç Muhakemesi Hukuku.* Seçkin, Ankara 2010.
Vakur Versan, *The Kemalist Reform of Turkish Law and its Impact,* in: *Atatürk and the Modernization of Turkey*, ed. J. M. Landau, Ch. 16, Boulder, CO: Westview, 1984, p.249.

Veli Özer Özbek, *Ceza Hukukunda Suçtan Doğan Mağduriyetin Giderilmesi*, Ankara, Seçkin Yayınvevi, 1999.
Veli Özer Özbek, *Ceza Muhakemesi Hukukunda Koruma Tedbiri Olarak Arama*, Ankara, Seçkin Yayınevi, 1999.
Veli Özer Özbek, *İnfaz Hukuku*, Ankara, 13. Baskı, Seçkin, 2021.
Veli Özer Özbek, *Müstehcenlik Suçu (TCK m. 226)*, Ankara, Seçkin, 2009.
Veli Özer Özbek, TCK *İzmir şerhi, Türk Ceza Kanununun Anlamı, Genel Hükümler (Madde 1–75);* Gözden Geçirilmiş, Genişletilmiş 4. Bası, Ankara, Seçkin, 2010.
Veli Özer Özbek et al., *Türk Ceza Hukuku Genel Hükümler*, Ankara, Seçkin, 11. Baskı, 2020.
Vesile Sonay Evik, *Görevi Kötüye Kullanma Suçları (TCK m.257),* Onikilevha I˙stanbul 2019.
Veysel Gültaş, *5237 Sayılı Türk Ceza Kanununda Suç İşlemek Amacıyla Örgüt Kurma Suçu ve Etkin Pişmanlık (TCK 220-221),* 4. Baskı, Bilge Yayınevi, Ankara 2017.
Veysel Gültaş, *5271 sayılı Ceza Muhakemesi Kanununun Işığı Altında Tutuklama ve Kanun Yolları*, 4. Baskı 2018.
Yener Ünver, *Ceza Hukukunda İzin Verilen Risk*, İstanbul, Beta, 1998.
Yener Ünver, *Ceza Hukukuyla Korunması Amaçlanan Hukuksal Değer*, Ankara, Seçkin Yayınları, 2003.
Yener Ünver, *Çocuklar ve Spor: Ceza*, Ankara, Seçkin Yayınları, 2005.
Yener Ünver, *Adliyeye Karşı Suçlar (TCK. m. 267–298)* 5. Bası, Ankara, Seçkin, 2019.
Yener Ünver, Hakan Hakeri, *Ceza Muhakemesi Hukuku*, 17. Baskı, Adalet, Ankara, 2020.
Yılmaz Yazıcıoğlu, *Bilgisayar Suçları*, 1997.
Yüksel Ersoy, *Çalışma Hürriyetine Karşı Suçlar*, Ankara, 1973.
Yusuf Aksar, *Uluslararası Ceza Mahkemesi ve Uluslararası Ceza Usul Hukuku*, Seçkin Yayınları, 2003.
Yusuf Solmaz Balo, *Çocuk Ceza Hukuku*, 2. Baskı, Seçkin, Ankara, 2015.
Zeki Hafızoğulları, Muharrem Özen, *Türk Ceza Hukuku Genel Hükümler, Gözden Geçirilmiş, İşlenmiş ve Yenilenmiş 12*. Baskı, US-A Yayıncılık, Ankara 2019.
Zeynel Temel Kangal, *Tüzel Kişilerin Cezai Sorumluluğu*, Ankara, Seçkin Yayınları, 2003.
Zeynel Temel Kangal *Kabahatler Hukuku,* 2. Baskı, *On İki Levha,* İstanbul, 2019.
Zeynel Temel Kangal, *Askeri Ceza Hukuku,* 2. Baskı, Seçkin, Ankara 2012.
Ziya Koç, *Ceza Muhakemesinde Katılan.* On İki Levha, İstanbul 2011.

Selected Bibliography

Index

The numbers here refer to paragraph numbers

Index

Index

www.ingramcontent.com/pod-product-compliance
Ingram Content Group UK Ltd.
Pitfield, Milton Keynes, MK11 3LW, UK
UKHW020133290926
15471UKWH00003B/459

9 789403 534428